EDUCATION, GROWTH AND DEVELOPMENT

EDUCATION, GROWTH AND DEVELOPMENT

Edited by

DR. ANIL KUMAR THAKUR

and

DR. MANISH DEV

Published on behalf of
THE INDIAN ECONOMIC ASSOCIATION

DEEP & DEEP PUBLICATIONS PVT. LTD.
F-159, Rajouri Garden, New Delhi-110027

EDUCATION, GROWTH AND DEVELOPMENT

ISBN 978-81-8450-260-2

Typeset by S.S. COMPOSERS
3190, Mohindra Park, Shakur Basti, Delhi-110034.

Printed in India at MAYUR ENTERPRISES
WZ Plot No. 3, Gujjar Market, Tihar Village, New Delhi-110018.

Published by DEEP & DEEP PUBLICATIONS PVT. LTD.
F-159, Rajouri Garden, New Delhi-110027.
Phones: 25435369, 25440916
E-mail: ddpbooks@yahoo.co.in • ddpubs@gmail.com
Showroom:
2/13, Ansari Road, Daryaganj, New Delhi-110002 • Telefax: 23245122

Contents

PART III

EDUCATION IN INDIA: INTER-STATE DISPARITIES

Preface

Education, Growth and Development are so closely interwoven that it is rather difficult to treat one of them as dependent on other two. Education has a crucial role in the growth and development of a region/country. Higher growth certainly enhances the level of education. Economists and thinkers from ancient time to present days have tried their best to establish a correlation between education and growth. In more specific terms, investments in education enhance the level of human capital formation which plays a decisive role in the growth of the economy. Numerous researches on this subject in India and elsewhere, have established that investment in education has resulted into higher growth rate of national income, higher level of standard of living, rise in the income of labourers and farmers, removal of poverty, decline in fertility rate, better health status and in longevity of life.

Indian Economic Association, keeping in view the importance of education for nation-building, declared "Education, Growth and Development" as one of the themes for deliberations during its 91st Annual Conference held at M.S. University, Udaipur (Rajasthan) under the Chairmanship of Prof. G.K. Chadha, during 27th-29th Dec. 2008. Out of several scholarly papers submitted and discussed on this theme during the Conference, 29 papers have been selected and included in this volume.

We are thankful to Indian Economic Association for providing this excellent opportunity. Each one of the contributors of this volume deserves praise for their excellent piece of work. We extend our sincere thanks to each one of them. We also place our thanks and gratitude to Mr. G.S.

Bhatia and his staff at M/s Deep & Deep Publications Pvt. Ltd., New Delhi to bring out this volume with every care and precaution.

ANIL KUMAR THAKUR
MANISH DEV

List of Contributors

A. Sugirtha Rani, Lecturer, Department of Economics, Periyar University, Salem, Tamil Nadu.

Abhishek Kumar, Manager, TATA GIG, Muzaffarpur, Bihar.

Alka Samra, Research Associate, Department of Economics, UCSSH, Mohanlal Sukhadia University, Udaipur.

Anil Kumar Jain, Professor and Formerly Head in the Department of Economics, Banaras Hindu University, Varanasi.

Arvind Awasthi, Reader, Department of Economics, Lucknow University, Lucknow.

Bharat Bhushan, Department of Economics, T.S. College, Hisua, Bihar.

Birendra Kumar Jha, Reader and Head, Department of Economics, DBKN College, Narhan, Samastipur, Bihar.

Bishwa Nath Singh, Professor of Economics, Dean, Faculty of Social Sciences, M.U., Bodh Gaya.

D. Subramanyam, Academic Consultant, Department of Economics, S.V.U. College of Arts, S.V.U., Tirupati.

Deepak Agarwal, Xavier Institute of Management and Entrepreneurship, Bangalore.

E. Nanda Kumar, Ph.D. Research Scholar, Department of Economics, PSG College of Arts and Science, Civil Aerodrome Post, Coimbatore, Tamil Nadu.

G. Savaraiah, Professors, Department of Economics, S.V.U. College of Arts, S.V.U., Tirupati.

Harvinder Kaur, Reader in Economics, Department of Correspondence Courses, Punjabi University, Patiala.

Jandhyala B.G. Tilak, National University of Educational Planning and Administration, New Delhi.

K. Govindarajalu, Professor of Economics, Bharathiar University, Coimbatore, Tamil Nadu.

Kuldip Kaur, Reader, Punjab School of Economics, Guru Nanak Dev University, Amritsar.

M. Devarajulu, Professor, Department of Economics, S.V.U. College of Arts, S.V.U., Tirupati.

Madan Kumar, Department of Economics, R.P.S. College, Patna.

Manish Dev, Research Scholar, Department of Economics, Narain College, Shikohabad, Firozabad (U.P.)

Manmohan Krishna, Professor, Department of Economics, University of Allahabad.

Meera Lal, Senior Consultant, Indian Institute of Economics, Hyderabad, Former Reader in Economics, University of Delhi.

Mukti Patel, Xavier Institute of Management and Entrepreneurship, Bangalore.

Mukul Kumar Singh, Research Scholar, M.U., Bodh Gaya.

N. Jaganathan, Reader in Economics, C.B.M. College, Coimbatore, Tamil Nadu

Neeraj Kumar Singh, Department of Political Science, R.P.S. College, Patna.

Neeraj Kumar, Chhatriya Inter-College, Ara, Bihar.

P.K. Bhargava, Emeritus Fellow of UGC (Economics) and Formerly HOD Economics, Director, I.R.D. Centre and Dean, Faculty of Social Sciences, Banaras Hindu University, Varanasi.

Piyush Kumar, Research Scholar, Patna University, Patna.

R.K. Rana, Professor (Retd.), Department of Economics, Kurukshetra University, Kurukshetra.

R.Y. Mahore, Professor and Head, Department of Economics, RTM Nagpur University, Nagpur, Maharashtra.

Rupinder Kaur, Associate Fellow, National Council of Applied Economic Research, New Delhi.

Sandhya Rani Das, Institute of Economic Studies, Brahmapur, Orissa.

Satyanarayana, H.O.D. of Economics, Kamala Nehru College for Women, Shimoga, Karnataka.

Shalini Tiwari, Research Scholar, Department of Economics, University of Allahabad.

Shambhu Prasad Shah, Head, Department of L.S.W., A.S. College, Deoghar, Jharkhand.

Shweta V., Research Scholar, Ethiraj College for Women, Chennai.

Sindhu T.S., Research Scholar, Ethiraj College for Women, Chennai.

Suparn Kumar, Asstt. Professor, School of Economics, Shri Mata Vaishno Devi University, Katra.

Upendra Prasad Singh, Department of Economics, Guru Gobind Singh College, Patna City.

V. Renuka Devi, Reader and Head, Department of Economics, Ethiraj College for Women, Chennai.

V. Vaithianathan, Lecturer, Department of Economics, Periyar University, Salem, Tamil Nadu.

Varada R. Deshpande, Reader, MES Abasaheb Garware College, Pune.

Vikram Chadha, Professor, Punjab School of Economics, Guru Nanak Dev University, Amritsar, Punjab.

Acronyms

ADB	:	Asian Development Bank
ADFT	:	Augmented Dickey Fuller Test
AYOS	:	Average Years of Schooling
BIMARU	:	Bihar, Madhya Pradesh, Rajasthan and Uttar Pradesh
CMIE	:	Center of Monitoring of Indian Economy
COR	:	Capital-Output Ratio
CTSA	:	Central Tibetan Schools Administration
DESD	:	Decade of Education for Sustainable Development
DPEP	:	District Primary Education Programme
EFA	:	Education for All
EGS & AIE	:	Education Guarantee Scheme and Alternative and Innovative Education
ESD	:	Education for Sustainable Development
GATS	:	General Agreement on Trade in Services
GDP	:	Gross Domestic Product
GED	:	Gross Education Attainment
GHESP	:	Global Higher Education for Sustainability Partnership
GNP	:	Gross National Product
ICOR	:	Incremental Capital-Output Ratio
IT	:	Information Technology
ITES	:	Information Technology Enabled Services
MDGs	:	Millennium Development Goals
NAAC	:	National Accreditation and Assessment Council
NCMP	:	National Common Minimum Programme
NERP	:	New Economic Reform Policies
NLM	:	National Literacy Mission

NPE	:	National Policy on Education
NSDP	:	Net State Domestic Product
NSSO	:	National Sample Survey Organization
OB	:	Operation Blackboard
OECD	:	Organization for Economic Co-operation and Development
OLS	:	Ordinary Least Squares
POA	:	Programme of Action
PPAs	:	Participatory Poverty Assessments
PPP	:	Public-Private-Partnership
S & T	:	Science and Technology
SDP	:	State Domestic Product
SHE	:	Secondary and Higher Education
SSA	:	Sarva Shiksha Abhiyan
TAR	:	Tibetan Autonomous Region
TARBOE	:	Tibetan Autonomous Region Board of Education
TCV	:	Tibetan Children Village
TE	:	Teachers Education
TFP	:	Total Factor Productivity
UGC	:	University Grants Commission
ULSF	:	Association of University Leaders for a Sustainable Future
UNDP	:	United Nations Development Programme
UNESCO	:	United Nations Educational Scientific and Cultural Organization
WSSD	:	World Summit on Sustainable Development
WTO	:	World Trade Organization

Introduction

Education is one of the vital components of human capital. It not only enhances the capabilities of an individual in the form of better efficiency and improved skill, but also contributes in a big way in the nation-building. Higher level of learning along with the longevity of life helps considerably to attain the advantages of 'demographic dividend' with which Indian economy is endowed. Education opens up opportunities leading to both individual and group entitlements. Education is the most crucial input for empowering people, especially the youths, with skills and knowledge and giving them access to productive employment in future. Development of education leads to enhancement in efficiency which results in higher level of earnings and overall quality of life. Education helps people to develop the attitudes, skills and knowledge to make informed decisions for the benefit of themselves and others, now and in the future.

Education has come into its own among economists as crucial to the dissemination of knowledge with the reawakening of the field of economic growth, due largely to the combination of theory with empirical tests, and to a spreading recognisation that the results deal with the question that really matter (McMohan: 1993:3). In the new endogenous growth and augmented Solow Models economists give education and knowledge the crucial role in the growth process. Major recent advances in the field of economic growth at both the theoretical level and in empirical research gave greater importance to human capital and of knowledge externalities in various growth models.

It has been a proven fact that education affects the

development of an individual, a family and the community in both ways—directly and indirectly. Direct effects of education relate to the creation of a skilled labour force that raises the productivity. Indirect effects encourage higher rates of investment in physical capital and stronger export competitiveness with feedback effects on growth and also in the form of generation of additional employment leading to the reduction of poverty. Most of the research on education, growth and development, from classical economist to modern day surrounds these aspects. Hageman and Wolfe (1984) and Wolfe and Zuvekas (1997) have developed conceptual framework for valuing the non-market returns on education. The Education Impact Model by Crouch, Spratt and Cubeddu (1992) deals with interactions among the health, population, and growth sectors. The Chenery *et al.* model (1986) reduced from growth equations that initially contained human capital, eventually omitted it because of the inclusion of other factors with which it is correlated (e.g. the shift of labour from agriculture, the growth of exports, a measure of the level of developments). It builds towards a computable general equilibrium model that stimulates a market economy into which price incentives policies are introduced (Chenery *et al.*, 1986:311). The wheeler model is a long-run socio-economic model that deals with the interaction between education and fertility, population and income per capita in a simultaneously equation contest (1984).

Recent theoretical and empirical researches since about 1988, have given the new dimensions to economic growth and its constituents. Inclusion of Human Capital in the augmented Solow Models have given greater importance to human capital created through education, and the dissemination of new knowledge through education to achieving sustained per capita economic growth. Furthermore, it has now been recognized in more certain terms that a set of government policies including the encouragement of higher rates of human resources development through education is critically important to achieving higher sustainable growth rates.

1990s witnessed two independent developments in economic research related to rate of return to investment in education, some micro-studies in this established that schooling certainly produce monetary return. Macro-growth literature has investigated whether the level of schooling in a cross-section of countries is related to country's subsequent GDP growth rate. Krueger and Lindahl (2001) examined in detail these two aspects of education and its relevance for growth. Mincer model (1974) implies that the change in a country's average level of schooling should be the key determinant of income growth. But studies such as Jess Benhabib and Mark Spiegel (1994) find the change in education is not a determinant of economic growth. Three broad facts about education have emerged from recent empirical researches. Firstly, almost universally education is found to lift people out of poverty. Secondly, when a compression is made between investing in education and other forms of investment, the returns from investing in education are on average lower. Thirdly, the return to education in the sense of the increment in income that accrues to each year of education are much higher for those with higher levels of educations. Households with a higher level of education are less likely to be poor. It is also found in various studies that returns to investment in education rise with the level of education (Appleton *el al.*, 2003).

World Bank policy paper on Primary Education (1990) and subsequent policy papers (1995, 1999) basically argued along the human capital live of thought. According to these papers education is the cornerstone of economic growth and social development, and that primary education lays the foundation for a more productive labour force through promoting literacy and numeracy. Primary education also provides the foundation for secondary and tertiary education. A growing number of studies [Jamison and Lau (1982), Alderman *et al.* (1996), Foster and Rosenzweig (1995) and Murgai *et al.* (2001)] suggests the primary education can enhance the productivity of farmers in developing countries.

Illiteracy is one of the many complex problems faced by developing and under-developed countries. Improvement in literacy is one of main objectives of development in these countries. These countries are part of recent initiatives at global level such as education for all and Education

Millennium Development Goals. The education for all initiatives goes back to the World conference on education for all (1990) in Jomtien, Thailand, where the commitment was made by many international development agencies including the World Bank, to achieve universal primary education for all children by the year 2000. This goal was not achieved, but was reaffirmed at another international conference on education at Dakar, Senegal (April 2000) with a new target date set for the year 2015. These education goals were then included in the set of eight MDGs adopted by a United Nations Conference in September 2000.

Education has been given prime place in the agenda of development in India since the commencement of First Five Year Plan. It got due attention in subsequent plans. The Tenth Plan laid emphasis on Universalization of Elementary Education (UEE) by five parameters:

(i) Universal Access,
(ii) Universal Enrolment,
(iii) Universal Retention,
(iv) Universal Achievement, and
(v) Equity.

Prior to this National Policy on Education, 1986 and National Literacy Mission also give topmost priority to Primary Education keeping in view its role in economic growth and social development. Major schemes for the attainment of universalization of elementary education are Sarva Shiksha Abhiyan (SSA), District Primary Education Programme (DPEP), Mid-day Meal Scheme (MDMS), Teacher Education Scheme and Kasturba Gandhi Balika Vidhyalaya Scheme (KGBVS). The Constitution of India was amended in 2002 to make elementary education a justifiable Fundamental Right. However, 7.1 million children being out of the school and over 50% dropping out at elementary level are matters of serious concern. Moving a step further the Government of India has enacted the Right to Education Act, 2009 under which each and every child in 7-14 age groups will be given free education.

Indian Government is changing and taking a shape of

Knowledge economy. Technological improvements in production and delivery of services require higher level of knowledge and skill. A mere light year of elementary education would be grossly inadequate for young children to acquire necessary skill to complete in the job market. Therefore, a Mission for Secondary and Higher Education is essential to consolidate the gains of SSA and to move forward in establishing a knowledge economy. Twenty papers of this volume deal with the various aspects of educational developments in India and its contribution to economic growth and development.

THEORETICAL PERSPECTIVE OF EDUCATION, GROWTH AND DEVELOPMENT

This First part of this volume contains nine papers focusing on various theories related to education and its relationship with growth and development. Ancient scholars such as Plato, Aristotle, Kautilya, Valmiki, etc. highlighted the importance of education in development. Classical economist discussed the public advantages of education. Neo-classical economists recognized the value of education in development. In more specific terms the Theodore Schultz (1961), Becker (1964), Bowman (1966), Mincer (1974), Arrow (1973), Spence (1973), Stiglitz (1975), Lucas (1988), Romer (1986), Funke and Strulik (2000), Simon Kuznets (1955), Tinbergan (1977), Hanushek (2003), Psacharopoulos (1984), Colcough (1993), etc. have developed theories relating to the contribution of education in the development of an individual, human capital formation and finally the growth of the economy. In India Kothari and Panchmukhi (1985) and Tilak (2006) did commendable job in this field.

Jandhyala B.G. Tilak in his well researched paper—Education, Growth and Development traces the contributions of various thinkers, particularly, Theodore W. Sehulze, Garg Beeker, Jacob Mincer (for their contributions in developing Human Capital Theory), Kenneth J. Arrow, Michel Spence and Joseph Stiglitze (for their contribution in developing signaling and screening theories), Robert Lucas and Paul Romer (for externalities and non-market theory). Tilak concludes that the general presumption on the weak or negligible role of secondary and higher education in development is not valid and that post-primary education plays a significant role in development. Post-primary education leads to economic growth, makes a significant contribution to reduction in absolute as well as relative poverty: it negatively influences infant mortality, is positively related to life expectancy and to overall human development index and even to the gender-based human development index. In his views, the primary education gives the basic three R's and is important and even necessary for development. But, it is wrong to conclude that it is adequate for overall sustainable development. Rarely does it provide skills necessary for employment that can ensure some wages and economic living. Fundamentally, it is secondary and higher education that consolidates the gains received from primary education. It is higher education that can ensure sustainable economic growth, as it is higher education, or specializes human capital that helps individuals and nations to withstands economic shocks, face disequilibria and to be able to restore equilibrium.

Rupinder Kaur is of the view that initial level of literacy and education also play an important role in initiating and sustaining growth. She comes at conclusion, by citing various studies on the quality of education—mainly primary education, that the current education system is reinforcing rather than reducing existing inequalities in India. Poorly functioning government schools catering to the poor children on the one hand and select few getting quality educations is costly in private schools on the other is creating a situation which may defeat the agenda of 'inclusive growth'.

Shalini Tiwari and Manmohan Krishna emphasized in their paper that education had emerged as an important factor in economic growth. An approach to education from its investment aspect is based on an understanding that the general development of human abilities, which is essential to the economic growth in the future, depends upon both quantitative and qualitative developments in education. Empirical evidence from cross-country analysis shows that exact nature of the causal link between the education and economic growth remains undetermined. At the same time they are of the firm view that rapid introduction and development of new techniques and development of new techniques and technologies, will certainly require higher investment in education which will ultimately boost future rates of economic growth.

Arvind Awasthi in his paper Human Capital and Growth Theories: A Case of Augmented Solow Model in the context of Major States of India examined the contribution of education in the growth of per capita income. With the help of a regression model, Awasthi categorically emphasis that if average years of schooling in five major state namely—Uttar Pradesh, Madhya Pradesh, Bihar, Rajasthan and Orissa is not raised significantly in the near future through sustained efforts of the government then inequalities in economic growth between two categories of major states (BIMARU + Orissa on one hand and remaining major states on the other hand) will rise considerably.

The paper 'Education and Economic Growth: Some Leading Aspects' by **Bishwa Nath Singh and Mukul Kumar Singh**, speaks in clear terms that the expenditure on education in India has seldom been approached as an investment in human resources rather it has been treated as social expenditure. Authors are of the view that investment in education is basically productive as it enhance the scientific creativity, skill and other qualitative factors of labour force which contribute to the growth of economy. Paper emphasis the need of modernization and up-gradation of infrastructural facilities, quality improvement in technical and management education and the strategy for raising non-budgetary resources.

R.Y. Mahore treats education and development as two sides of the same coin in his paper "Education and Development". He argues that education should lead to development and development should create the motivation for more education and provides tools for it. Mahore discussed the role of education, especially the higher education on development. He is of the view that growth is insignificantly related to male schooling at the primary level. However, primary education is a prerequisite for secondary education and thus, affects growth of the economy. Education of women at the primary level stimulates economic growth indirectly by including a lower fertility rate. He emphasise the need for quality education as it has a stronger relationship to growth than the duration of schooling.

Satyanarayana in his paper "Quality in Education is the Key towards Development: Issues and Challenges" discussed the quality aspect of Education. Increase in absolute number of institutions and students there, certainly a parameter to judge the growth of the education system. The Paper suggests some key for enhancement of Quality in Education. Quality and excellence should be an agenda for the further development of education.

Abhishek Kumar and Upendra Prasad Singh discussed in detail the inequalities in education in their paper "Education and Inequality: The Theoretical Framework" discussed by Willian Tyler. According to one such model, biological inheritance of ability is the engine of inequality since family; school and work simply reinforce genetic endowments. Another model considers social and family background as the prime determinants of educational inequalities rather than inherited ability. Conservatively, it is said that the children of privileged class are better endowed intellectually go to better schools and dominate the elite institutions of learning. Against these and some other light arguments, liberal model in generated views that academic credentials are awarded on merit in a system of fair competition. Authors are of the firm view that individual's performance in educational and occupational field are neither determined by family and social background nor by biological inheritance, but by individuals own efforts. Even than they think that education has a role in economic development but it cannot be equalizer to bridge the gulf between rich and poor. Education maintains *status quo* and perpetuates the interest of dominant social class. For the authors education cannot be stimulates to inclusive growth. Theoretically it might be seems true, but empirically it has been found that education changed the lives of many people from socially disadvantaged groups, especially in developing countries as India.

Neeraj Kumar Singh, Madan Kumar and Piyush Kumar emphasise in their paper "Higher Education: New Challenges and Emerging Roles for Human and Social Development", that benefit of college education must be weighed against the full costs of obtaining that education. Costs associated with earnings foregone while in college, and in case of universities and colleges run by Government, the public expenditure incurred by the state. The return on investment in education calculated using full cost is a more useful guide for public policy than one calculated using only the costs incurred by the student. Authors correctly say that India's elite educational institutions stand like isolated ivory towers amidst encircling poverty, illiteracy and backwardness. Rural India is completely neglected in health, education, nutrition and other elements of human capital. In this scenario, they suggest that policies that eliminate barriers (informational, ability or financial) and results in tangible increases in the number of degree-holders are interventions that should be pursued.

EDUCATIONAL AND ECONOMIC DEVELOPMENT OF INDIA

This part of the present volume contains thirteen papers covering various aspects of education and their role in the economic development of India. India, endowed with second largest workforce in the world, has the largest number of illiterate in the world. Highly educated and skilled techno rates have proved their worth in most of the countries of the world. But, at the same time the whole system of Indian education is still not in a position to provide quality education at affordable cost to all eligible children at primary level and youth at secondary and higher level education. Access, equity and excellence in education still seem a distant dream. Contributors in this section utilized their skill and efforts to provide.

Vikram Chadha in his paper acknowledges had come to occupy the centre stage in the economic growth of nations. In his view knowledge and information are replacing capital and energy as the primary wealth creating assets. There is rising trend in the total stock of India's educated and Science and Technology human resource, yet there are a number of lacunae mainly on the front of quality of human capital which has serious inadequacies for the employability potential and growth steering capabilities of those who acquire a degree or diploma. Chadha seems in a compromising position when he suggest that now the government must shed to quantity aspect of education in India, and instead focus a refurbishing the quality of its human resources, firstly by expending more and more on higher and technical education and secondly, on monitoring and overseeing the introduction of modern course content and instructions of the state-of-the-art education with the requirements of the contemporary competitive world.

'New Growth Theories' emphasize the importance of education in the creation of knowledge and in the growth of living standards overtime. Knowledge and skill of workforce in an economy affect the growth and development. **Kuldip Kaur** has tries in her paper 'Education, Growth and Wages in India: An Interrelationship' to establish a relationship between education and growth through a simple regression analysis by using state-wise data on net attendance ratio, total enrolment ratio and per capita net state domestic product. Findings of Kaur's study suggest that better educated workers are likely to reap more financial benefits than the uneducated ones as these workers generate more value additions. Finally, she observes that benefits of higher education for individuals can be reaped through better employment prospects, higher wages and greater ability to save and invest.

N. Jaganathan in his paper 'Education and Economic Development in India' made a comprehensive analysis of trends in public expenditure on various levels of education, development of infrastructure in educational sector (particularly number of schools and teachers) and attainment of education in terms of enrolment ratio. His studies spread for 24 years—from 1981-82 to 2004-05 and is sub-divided into periods—(i) 1981-82 to 1990-91, and (ii) 1991-92 to 2004-05. The demarcation line being the commencement of economic reforms. His observations are simple, but of greater importance for policy planning. The paper revels that public expenditure on education increased by more than three times during 1981-82 to 2004-05, but compound growth rate of public-expenditure declined during post-economic reform period. The decline was sharper in university education expenditure. So far as the development of Education infra-structure is concerned, number of primary schools and secondary schools per lakh population declined, so is the case with the number of teachers per ten thousand students. The results of causality analysis by Jaganathan suggest that educational attainment increases the labour productivity and thereby contributed to economic development. It is another thing that correlation between educational attainment and economic development is complex.

It has been accepted at the top echelon of power that growth of the Indian economy is not inclusive. The advantages of higher growth could not percolate downward, as a result inequalities of income and wealth have increased many fold, especially during the last two decades. **Meera Lal** raised this issue in her paper 'Inclusive Education for Inclusive Growth'. She questioned, with the help of findings of ASER Report, 2006, the claims of government that 99 per cent boys and 82 per cent girls aged 6-10 years are enrolled in schools. The paper highlights deplorable conditions of primary schools in India. The issue of medium of instruction is equally significant, especially for tribals because their mother tongue often quite distinct from the prominent languages in the state or regional languages. Lal has elaborately suggested an action-plan to make the education more and more inclusive.

P.K. Bhargava in his paper 'Indian Education System: The Turmoil Continues' highlighted the shortcomings of the entire education system of the country. According to Bhargava there is a paradoxical situation in the country and in education sector higher level of expenditure in education has resulted into increase in number of institutions on the one hand and, on the other, the existing facilities are not utilized properly. Bhargava is rather septical about the proper functioning of the regulatory bodies of higher education. At times these regulatory bodies at cross-purposes.

Globalization has opened Vistas for Indian higher education system. **Anil Kumar Jain** took up this issue in his paper 'Liberalization, Globalization and Higher Education:

The Current Indian Scenario'. In the light of increase in demand of qualified and skilled professionals in India and abroad, Indian Universities require an overhauling for which Jain has suggested some measures which if adopted, will certainly make the system world class.

Gender discrimination in India as common as in any other field of social-economic-political erena. **Sandhya Rani Das** raised this issue in her paper 'Education and Economic Development: A Gender Perspective'. Gender gap in literacy rate is prevalent in all the states. It is lowest in Kerala (6.5 percentage point). According to her there is positive correlation between income and literacy. Total literacy influences income to the extent of 21.62 per cent. Influence of female literacy income is higher (23.07 per cent) than the male literacy (17.15 per cent).

Dalits—Scheduled Castes and Scheduled Tribes—have been a deprived class in Indian Society from the time immemorial special provisions in the contribution and in various programmes of development, for the upliftment of deprived class have changed the equations but with limited success. Reservation of seats for SCs and STs in educational institutions has opened the door for these classes to attain education on priority basis and uplift themselves from the clutches of social-economic-political discrimination. The paper 'Impact of Reservation on Education and Employment Development of Scheduled Castes in India: Some Issues' by **G. Savaraiah, M. Devarajulu and D. Subramanyam** deals this issue in relation to policy implications of reservation for education and employment. According to contributors, although the outcome of reservation in education and employment is positive, yet, its impact is rather weak. The backlog of vacancies for SCs/STs in central government departments and in public undertakings has been increasing since 1995. Share of SCs/STs in the faculty of Universities is only 1.4 per cent for professors and 8.02 per cent for others which confirms the premise that higher position in educational institutions are still out of the reach of dalits.

Varada R. Deshpande's paper 'Education—A Key to Economic Development' highlights that lack of investment in human capital is responsible for the slow growth of underdeveloped countries. Education, a key component of human capital formation, can transform the entire process of development through the development of skill of workforce.

Paper 'Implications of Expansion in Higher Education on the Labour Market' by **V. Vaithianathan and A. Sugirtha Rani** deals with the changes in labour market as a result of expansion in the higher education. The Study, based on Tamil Nadu, gives some insight into the problems of unemployment among educated youth. Expansion of higher education is a necessity to attain higher level of growth, but at the same time concerted efforts are also required to provide employment to those who have got higher level of education and skill. India has sufficient number of engineers and scientists and has advantages over China in moving towards an information-based advanced service economy.

Mukti Patel and Deepak Agarwal are hopeful in their paper 'India and the Knowledge Economy: India, China and 21st Century' that India is in a position to reap tremendous economic gains by developing policies and strategies that focus on making more effective use of knowledge to increase the overall productivity of the economy and the welfare of the mass. India has a critical mass of skilled, English speaking knowledge worker, especially in the sciences. This educated and skilled workforce can be helpful to obtain higher level of 'demographic dividend' which India has. The authors say that India possesses a large pool of highly educated and vocationally trained workfore which has proved its worth. Worldwide, but it is only a small fraction of total population. Sustained efforts are required to enlarge the base of technology enable workforce.

Birendra Kumar Jha and Shambhu Prasad Shah in their paper 'Higher Education: A Critical Factor for Human Development in India in the Era of Globalization' treats education as a basic ingredient of human capital base in this age of knowledge economy. Higher education, essentially, upgrades the individual's capacity to produce more on the one hand, while on the other it enables a nation to achieve higher rates of growth. The authors points out that the disturbing feature of Indian higher education system has been the proliferation of universities and colleges, especially for general education, which do not prepare for a career while a majority terminate at the bachelor's degree level, majority of degree holders Indian youths are unemployable because they often lack basic practical knowledge to work in real life situations. Authors are of the view that globalization, driven by market forces, has let to the emergence of higher education is a matter of concern for many right-minded people because it has eroded the quality aspect. Investment in education, by private investors is solely guided by the profit maximization instinct which compromises with the quality and excellence.

Bharat Bhushan and Neeraj Kumar argues in their paper 'Access to Higher Education Weaker Section and Equity' that increasing costs of higher education, especially technical education have made it out of the reach of scheduled castes and scheduled tribes. Although, the government has extended a helping hand, to the students of weaker sections of the society in the form of scholarship and bank loans on easy terms, yet other costs related to education still make the choice difficult for the people.

EDUCATION IN INDIA: INTER-STATE DISPARITIES

Level of Education in India is not evenly distribution. Inter-State disparities in growth and development are also visible in education. There is a weak correlation between the level of education and economic development. According to economic development index Gujarat, Haryana, Himachal Pradesh, Jammu and Kashmir, Kerala, Maharashtra, Punjab and Tamil Nadu are categorized as developed states, while Assam, Bihar, Madhya Pradesh, Orissa and Uttar Pradesh are poorly developed states. Andhra Pradesh, Karnataka and West Bengal can be categorized as moderately developed. Surprisingly education development of Haryana and Punjab is low yet their economic development is high. Kerala has almost cent per cent literacy rate and also tops in human development index, is a moderately developed state. Gross enrolment ratio is a better measurement of educational development in a state. Uttar Pradesh with 54.91 per cent enrolment ratio in Classes I-VIII, followed by Bihar (61.35 per cent) is poorly placed, while the state like Gujarat (13.26 per cent) and Maharashtra (101.05 per cent) have higher GER in the category. Inter-state disparities in education are more wide in higher education. GER in higher education at aggregate level was 10.08 per cent in 2000. It was more than national average in states like Kerala (18.08%), Goa (17.56%), Himachal Pradesh (15.22%) and Maharashtra (14.15%). GER in Bihar was only 6.16% and West Bengal has only 6.30% GER. Orissa (8.21%), Uttar Pradesh (9.59%), Rajasthan (8.85%), Karnataka (7.96%), Haryana (9.99%), Assam (9.40%) and Andhra Pradesh lesser GER in higher education than national average. Seven papers in this section have presented the trends in the development of education in various states of India.

R.K. Rana and Suparn Kumar have examined the effect of literacy rate on the growth and development of Indian states by taking per capita state domestic product as a proxy measure for the growth and development of a state. They conclude that corresponding to one unit increase in literacy rate there is an increase of Rs. 446.40 in per capita income of a state. They suggests that the states who are still backward must concentrate in enhancing their literacy level. Inter-regional disparities in income distribution urbanization, agriculture, education, industrial production and the state of infrastructure has been the common phenomenon during the plans. In fact, these disparities have increased in the post-reforms era.

Alka Samra in her paper 'The Role of Education in Economic Development—An Inter-state Analysis', identified regional disparities in education and development. For the better understanding of inter-relationship between the two she developed the Education Development Index with the help of adult literacy rate, enrolment ratio, number of primary schools per thousands population, percentage of habitations having educational amenities and teacher-pupil ratio. Simultaneously she also developed by using per capita gross domestic product at constant price, per capita consumption-expenditure for 30 days, percentage of people above poverty line and employment rate. Correlation coefficient between education development index and economic development index is 0.167 which shows a weak relationship, but bivariate analysis confirms the higher level of disparities among various states in relation to education as well as development.

Manish Dev in his paper 'Higher Education and Growth of the Indian Economy: The Emerging Scenario in Relation to Inter-State Disparities' discussed in detail inter-state disparities in higher education in relation to access, quality and excellence. Undoubtedly, highly educated and trained manpower from India has proved its worth in whole of the world. Higher level of growth of the economy will require a large army of skilled workforce for which higher education system has to be revamped Inter-state disparities in income and its growth pattern also reflect in attainment of education. This disparity is more significant in literacy rate in general and Gross Enrolment Ratio in Higher Education is highly skewed in India with wide variations in Gross Enrolment Ratio which ranges from 2.42 per cent in Arunachal Pradesh to 18.08 per cent in Kerala. Variations in GER also prevalent on the basis of gender, Occupation, Caste, religion and income. Indian higher education system also suffers from the quality as more than half of the young graduates who acquire a degree from the universities are unemployable because of lack of practical knowledge and skill required for a job.

K. Govindarajalu empirically has proved in his paper 'Distribution of Benefits of Government Expenditure on Education—An Empirical Analysis of Coimbatore District in Tamil Nadu' that the lower levels of education are pro-poor and higher levels of education pro-rich. In more specific terms higher income groups prefer private institutions as far as lower levels of education is concerned. The government assistance provided in the form of fee concession, books, bus fare concession, uniform, scholarship and mid-day meal scheme have positive influence on the enrolment of students. Another significant aspect of this study is that the specific expenditure on higher education has benefited higher income groups of the society.

In another micro-study in Tamil Nadu **E. Nanda Kumar** observed that income was the important determinant for investment in education. Higher the income more the investment on education. However, gender discrimination is a common phenomenon, so far as the expenditure on education is concerned. Educational expenditure on male child is more than on female child.

V. Renuka Devi, Shweta V. and Sindhu T.S. highlighted the problems of Tibetan people regarding attainment of higher standard of learning, in their paper 'Tibetans Higher Education: A Socio-economic Outlook'. Though there are a number of Tibetan schools, collegiate education seems a far dream for most of the Tibetan students who pass out from intermediate education. The paper based on a small study in Chennai, raised some issues related to the problems faced by Tibetan students eager to take up higher education.

In another paper **Harvinder Kaur** analysed level of education and employment in Punjab. Composition of workfore in Punjab has changed significantly. Sectoral shift towards non-agriculture sector require more educated and skilled workers. Punjab a developed state holds 16th rank amongst all the States/UTs so far as the literacy rate is concerned. Author observes that more than 90 per cent workforce is employed in unorganized sector. Employment in organised sector is declining continuously since 2004, as a result the magnitude of employment continues to be a cause of serious concern. New employment opportunities in the unorganized sector are not able to keep pace with the growth in the labour force.

References

Alderman. H., J. Behrman, D. Ross and R. Sabot (1996), "The Returns to Endogenous Human Capital in Pakistan's Rural Wage Labour Market". *Oxford Bulletin of Economics and Statistics*, 58(1): 29-35.

Appleton, Simon; Geetan Kingdom; John Knight, Mans Soderborn and Francis Teal (2003); Does investing education reduce poverty? Evidence from Ghana, Uganda and South Africa, Development Research Reporting Service.

Benhabib, Jess and Mark M. Spiegel (1984): The Role of Human Capital in Economic Development: Evidence from Cross-country Data, *Journal of Monetry Economics*, 34.2, pp. 143-74.

Boiddiere, M (2004): Rationale for public Investments in Primary Education in Developing Countries: Background paper for the evaluation of

World Bank's support to primary education operations, Evaluations Division, World Bank, Washington DC.

Chenery, H.B., Robinson, S. Srquin, M. (1986): Industrialisation and Growth: A Comparative Study, World Bank, Washington.

Crouch, L.A., Spratt, J.E and Cubeddu, L.M. (1992): Examining Social and Economic impacts of educational investment and participation in developing eucational impacts model (EIM) approach, Basic Research and Implements in Developing Education system project.

GOI (1986): National Policy on Education, 1986, Ministry of HRD, New Delhi.

GOI (1988): National Literacy Mission, Ministry of HRD, New Delhi.

GOI (2008): Eleventh Five Year Plan (2007-12), Planning Commission, Vol. III.

Haveman, Robert and Barbara Wolfe (1984); Accounting for the Social and Non-Market Benefits of Education, The Paper is part of Research supported by a grant from US Department of Health and Human Service.

Haveman, Robert and Barbara Wolfe (1984); Schooling and Economic Well-being: The Role of Non-market effects, *Journal of Human Resources*, (19(3):377-407.

Jamison, Dean; and Lawrence Lan (1982); "Farmer Education and Farm Efficency", Oxford University Press, World Bank.

Krueger, Alan B. and Mikael Lindahl (2001); Education for Growth : Why And For Whom, *Journal of Economic Literature*, Vol. 39, pp 1101-36.

McMohan, Walter (1999): Education and Development : Measuring the social benefits, Oxford University Press, Oxford.

Mincer, Jacob (1974): Schooling, Earnings and Experience, Columbia University Press, New York.

Psacharopolous, George and Harry Patrinos (2002), "Returns to Investment in Education: A further update". World Bank Policy Research Working paper 2881.

Rosenbeig Mark (1995); "Why are they Returns to Schooling", *American Economic Review and Proceedings*, 85(2): 153-58.

UNESCO (1990): World Declaration on Education for All, Jomtien, Thailand.

UNESCO (2003): Education for All, Global Monitoring Report.

UNESCO (2003): "The Dakar Framework for Action Education for All: Meeting our Collective Responsibilities", World Education Forum. Dakar, Senegal.

Wheelar, D. (1984): Female Education, Family Planning, Income and Population: A long-run econometric simulation model, Nova, pp. 84-171.

Wolfe, Barbara and Zuvekas, Samual (1997); Non-Marketing outcomes of schooling, *International Journal of Educational Research*, Vol. 27, pp. 491-501.

World Bank (2002); World Development Indicators, World Bank Data Group.

PART I

THEORETICAL PERSPECTIVE OF EDUCATION, GROWTH AND DEVELOPMENT

Education, Growth and Development

JANDHYALA B.G. TILAK

I. INTRODUCTION

Ancient scholars in many countries highlighted the importance of widespread education in development. Education, Plato believed, is indispensable to the economic health of a good society, for education, he said, makes citizens 'reasonable men'. Education was regarded important on its own. Since education has high value in the society, Plato argued that a considerable part of a community's wealth must be invested in education. The positive contribution of education was emphasised by many philosophers and thinkers over centuries. A major contribution to the discussion on the contribution of education to development was made by several social thinkers and philosophers for several centuries. The role of education in economic development, in reducing poverty and inequality, as a possible contributor to greater social and economic equality and as an enhancer of development was widely recognised from the days of Adam Smith. Even prior to Adam Smith, we find significant references in the literature to the equity role of education, besides the economic role in the creation of wealth of nations (see Vaizey, 1962; Blaug, 1975). It was William Petty who first advocated equitable distribution of education. Nehenia Green and James Stewart of the Mercantilist period also advocated mass education so as to increase agricultural productivity in particular and society's progress in general. Palmerstone favoured spread of literacy for various social and political purposes. The 18th and 19th Century school reformers in the US like Horace Mann, Henry Barnard, James Carter, Robert Dale Owen and George Evans favoured educational opportunities to be extended to poorer groups of population. Horace Mann, a typical example of these reformers, viewed the school as an effective instrument to achieve justice and equality of opportunity and to remove poverty. As early as in 1896, the role of education in reducing poverty was clearly recognised in Russia: "An increase of labour productivity is the only means to erase poverty in Russia and the best policy to achieve it is through the spread of education and knowledge" (Kahan, 1963, pp. 400-1). Among economists, Adam Smith made extensive references to education, including generation of public benefits by education of all levels, university education included, and hence the role of the 'publik' in providing it. He was followed by a long and honourable tradition of classical and neo-classical economists. By the end of the 19th century the thesis was clear: education makes significant contribution to development. John Stuart Mill, who followed Adam Smith, recognised the social benefits more clearly and more explicitly than Smith and others. In the early 20th century, Marshall emphasised that "the most valuable of all capital is that invested in human beings" and that "knowledge is our most powerful engine of production; it enables us to subdue Nature and force her to satisfy our wants..." (Marshall, 1920, pp. 138-39).

While there is a long tradition of economists who recognised the value of education in development, the importance of education in the well-being of the nations is more clearly recognised since the heralding of the human capital theory by Theodore Schultz (1961). Schultz has convincingly demonstrated that education is an investment leading to human capital formation that contributes to economic growth. According to the human capital theory, education transforms raw human beings into productive 'human capital' by imparting knowledge and inculcating skills required by both the traditional sector and the modern sector of the economy, and makes individuals more productive members of the society, not only in the market place but also in the households and also in the whole society. The core of the human capital theory lies in the thesis that education increases productivity of the population in general and of labour force in particular, leading to increase in individual earnings and thereby contributing to economic growth and reduction in poverty.

The process of education influencing growth and income distribution is as follows: education creates a more skilled labour force, which produces a shift from low-paid, unskilled and below-poverty employment levels, to better-paid, skilled and above-poverty levels of employment. This shift produces higher labour incomes, a reduction in skill differentials, and an increase in the share of wages in total output. The increase in the number of more educated and skilled people increases the ratio of such people and decreases the ratio of less educated people in the total labour force. However, in the labour market over-supply of highly educated people results, given no change in demand, in lowering their wages and increase in wages of those with less education, thus contributing to overall reduction in income differences in the labour market (see Ahluwalia, 1976, p. 322). Thus, expansion of education influences not only the wages of those who receive better education, but also of those who do not have education or have less education. Education also compensates for adverse socio-economic background and opens up better socio-economic opportunities for weaker sections of the society leading to faster mobility and to higher wages. In short, education reduces poverty and improves income distribution at the same time.

The human capital theory propounded by Schultz laid a strong foundation for treating education as an investment in human beings and for treating it as an important source of economic growth. It is now widely accepted that investment in human capital is one of the important factors of economic growth and development and the research that followed further highlighted the number of ways in which education influences socio-economic well-being of the individuals and the society. First and directly, at individual level, it increases one's human capital; increases one's productivity in the labour market, and increases his/her earnings. Second, there are consumption effects of education. Educated people make more informed choices in their consumption patterns. Third, education reduces search time in labour markets for employment. Fourth, at societal level, there is found to be a positive correlation between education and health of the people. Fifth, there is an inverse relationship between average level of education and fertility rates, meaning that education reduces growth of population, which in developing countries is generally regarded as a positive aspect. Sixth, there is a direct relationship between education level of children and their parents' education. Seventh, education has an inverse effect on crime, a direct positive effect on social cohesion and technology development. Lastly, education produces several other positive externalities simple, and dynamic—social, economic, political and cultural, some of which can even be inter-generational.

The theoretical developments on the examination of the contribution of education to economic growth are very important. The neo-classical growth theory (Solow, 1956, 1957) did not recognise education as a major input for production and hence education was not included in growth models. Economic growth in the long-run was explained by assuming an exogenous technological development; initially it focused much on physical capital accumulation. Schultz's human capital theory has indeed created a "human investment revolution in economic thought" (Bowman, 1966). The contributions of Schultz (1961), Becker (1964) and Mincer (1974) have formalised the treatment of education as an investment and as a factor in growth theory. The seminal contributions of Arrow (1973), Spence (1973) and Stiglitz (1975) raised questions on the human capital theory and the possibility of treating education as a signal to the employer in stead of having any economic value on its own, a thesis which remained as a hypothesis, and which did not last (Blaug, 1985). Schultz and Denison's growth accounting equations were again considered to be valid. According to the endogenous growth theories (Lucas, 1988; Romer, 1986, 1990a,b), stock of human capital affects the growth rates of the economy: education facilitates technological development; higher levels of human capital lead to more innovations and higher efficiency or total factor productivity, which causes higher growth rates of aggregate income. The level of human capital is co-integrated with the growth rate of the aggregate income. The production function now is a two-step simultaneous process, in which resources are used to produce education, and education enters the production process in a way that allows increasing to returns to scale. These endogenous growth theories (e.g., Mankiw, 1995; Mankiw *et al.*, 1999) use two sector growth models and consider manufacturing firms as producing goods and (research) universities as producing knowledge, which in is used in both sectors. The research on endogenous growth theories was enriched by consideration of externalities (Webbink, 2000). The endogenous growth models show that the steady-state growth rate of output per worker depends positively on the level of available stock of human capital or endowment of skilled labour. Hence, an increase in the average educational attainment of the labour force will lead to a permanent increase in the long-term growth rate of per capita income. When a country reaches an advanced stage of development, the role of human capital on economic growth moves from direct impact on labour productivity to an indirect impact through increase in capability of labour force as a whole to manage innovation and technical progress (Funke and Strulik, 2000). As Chen and Lee (2008) stated, in the subsequent R&D based growth models, growth rate of per capita income depends only on parameters that are usually taken as exogenous, such as the growth rate of population, and no longer depends on the level of R&D resources or the stock of human capital. In such models, the levels of human capital and other R&D resources affect only the long-run level of per capita income, but not the growth rate.

Thus, as Psacharopoulos (2004) summed up, the major landmarks in theoretical contributions, beginning with Schultz's pioneering contributions, are as follows:

TABLE I

Landmark Theoretical Contributions on Education and Economic Growth

Period	*Theory*	*Exponents*
1960s	Human capital theory	Theodore W. Schultz, Gary Becker, Jacob Mincer
1970s	Signaling and Screening	Kenneth J. Arrow, Michael Spence, Joseph Stiglitz
1980s	Endogenous growth theory	Robert Lucas, Paul Romer
1990s+	Externalities, non-market	R. Venikker

Source: Psacharopoulos, 2004, p. 342.

2. EMPIRICAL RESEARCH: ROBUST AND POPULAR FINDINGS

Following Schutlz (1961); there has been a phenomenal growth in research in Economics of Education, including in India (see Kothari and Panchamukhi, 1985; Tilak, 2006b for surveys), that concentrated on estimating the contribution of education to growth and development. Studies include those on rates of return to education, production function methodologies applied to national income, agricultural productivity, poverty, income distribution, etc. In recent years, empirical research on endogenous growth models has become popular, that emphasised that the level of education attainment itself is based on initial level of education.

The nexus between education and development is so all pervasive, that it is difficult to systematically describe, decompose and quantify the effect of education on each specific aspect of development. Secondly, the relationship between education and development is not uni-directional. Education contributes to development, and development of the economy contributes to further development of education. It is not exactly possible to assert which is the cause and which is the effect. Both are causes and both are effects. This bi-directional relationship is very important in understanding the role of education in development. However, I concentrate here on findings on the contribution of education to development. Based on an extensive review of literature (Tilak, 1989a, 1994, 2006a,b; Psacharopoulos and Woodhall, 1985), covering a wide variety of empirical studies—national, sub-national and international level studies, case studies based on field level data and observations, one can list a few robust findings on the contribution of education to growth and development.

1. Education-Earnings

Economics of Education is abundant with studies that firmly established the existence of positive correlation between education and earnings. Individual wage earnings systematically increase significantly by increasing levels of education. Earnings rise with increase in education levels, not rarely but almost universally and quite steeply and systematically, in case of the general population and also of sub-groups of the population—males, females, rural, urban, socially backward sections, etc. (Psacharopoulos and Tilak, 1992). Higher levels of schooling are consistently associated with higher earnings. Studies using Mincerian earnings function have also shown that the relationship to be quite consistent. It is not mere correlation. Education has been found to have a strong casual effect on individual wages, the effect being higher in case of regular workers, compared to causal workers and the effect increases systematically by increasing levels of education, the effect being the highest in case of those who have higher education. As Blaug (1972) noted, the universality of this relationship is well recognised beyond doubt.

2. Rates of Return

Conventionally the contribution of education to economic development is analysed in terms of education-earnings relationships and more conveniently in the form of rates of return. Rates of return are a summary statistic of the relationship between lifetime earnings and the costs of education. Beginning with Strumilin (1926), the first attempt on cost benefits analysis in education and Becker (1960) the first more systematic attempt after the beginning of the human investment revolution, we have a large number of studies on rates of return to education in various countries. Based on international comparative studies on this aspect (e.g., Psacharopoulos and Patrinos, 2004), it has been concluded that the economic returns to education are reasonably high; they are comparable to rates of return to investment in physical capital. Investment in education may be equally if not more conducive to economic growth as investment in physical capital. On average, the rate of return to education in many countries has been around ten percent. Further, in many countries they are found to be increasing (Bourguingnon and Rogers, 2008).

3. Agricultural Productivity

A large body of empirical evidence on the contribution of education to agricultural productivity is available that shows that increase in educational levels of workers enhances labour productivity significantly. Physical effects of education on agricultural productivity of workers include: (a) innovative effects such as ability to decode new information, know what, why, where and how; ability to estimate costs and benefits of alternatives, and ability to establish quicker access to newly available economically useful information; (b) allocative effects such as ability to choose optimum combinations of crops and agricultural practices in least number of trials, and ability to choose optimum time for marketing, transportation, etc.; (c) worker effects such as ability to perform agricultural operations more efficiently in the economic sense; and (d) externalities (see Welch, 1970; also Schultz, 1975). Abundant research on the relationship between education and agricultural productivity (Jamison and Lau, 1982; Lockheed *et al.*, 1980; Tilak, 1994) shows that education significantly influences productivity directly and indirectly by influencing the selection of methods of production, use of modern inputs like fertilizers, seeds and machines, selection of crops,, etc.

4. Education and Economic Growth

Not only rate of return studies, but also studies that used production functions—starting from residual to endogenous growth functions, have highlighted the vital role of education in improving the productivity of the labour force and/or total factor productivity. A good proportion of rate of economic growth is estimated to be attributable to investment in education in many countries. The effect of education on growth is direct, as well as indirect. When a country reaches an advanced stage of development, the role of human capital on economic growth moves from direct impact on labour productivity to an indirect impact through increase in capability of labour force as a whole to manage innovation and technical progress. Further, as knowledge economy expands, the role of human capital may outstrip physical capital and labour in determining aggregate growth rate (Romer, 1998).

5. Education and Poverty

Voluminous research in the last 2-3 decades (e.g., Fields, 1980a, 1980b) clearly shows that education and poverty are inversely related: the incidence of poverty is the largest among the illiterate households, and the higher the level of education of the population, the lower would be the proportion of poor people in the total population, as education imparts knowledge and skills that are associated with higher wages. In addition to this direct effect of education, the effect of education on poverty could be indirect through its fulfillment of other basic needs like better utilisation of health facilities, shelter, water and sanitation. Fulfillment of education and other basic needs reinforce each other (Noor 1980; Tilak, 1989b). In fact, education is recognised as an important basic need fulfillment of which helps in the fulfillment of others that results in amelioration of poverty. Further, among the various anti-poverty measures, it has been found tht education is a very powerful, statistically significant factor that breaks the poverty cycle, and takes people above the poverty line. In fact, the relationship between education and poverty is bi-directional: education reduces poverty and reduction in poverty helps in improving educational levels of the population; this bi-directional relationship is found to hold good both at micro/household and macro-levels. It is increasingly noted, education might serve as a better measure to break this education-poverty cyclical trap.

6. Education and Income Distribution

Simon Kuznets (1955) predicted that income distribution in capitalist countries would become more equal as the labour force becomes more educated. Schultz (1963, p. 65) had showed more clearly in case of US, "these changes in human capital are a basic factor reducing the inequality in the personal distribution of income. Analyzing the problem in his numerous works, both from a positive point of view (Tinbergen, 1977) and a normative point of view Tinbergen (1970 and 1980) concluded that human capital is one of the most important determinants of income inequality. Many empirical studies in the later period have shown that education is one of the most important variables influencing positively the income distribution.

7. Women's Education and Development

Substantial research has shown very clearly that education of women matters a lot. It significantly contributes towards demographic improvement by reducing fertility, and improving the use of better methods of population control, by influencing the age of marriage, desired family size, etc., improvement in infant mortality, child nutrition, health of the members of the family, improvement in participation of children in education and in their levels of educational achievement through improving pre-school abilities of children, and improvement in the economic status of the family with increase in the labor force participation of women, thereby in the household earnings, etc. The effects of women's education on women's behaviour on decisions relating to fertility, family welfare and health, etc., are very significant (Noor, 1980; Cochrane, 1988) which in turn enhance the productivity of the people and yield higher wages. In fact, a large amount of research has concluded that women's education has a higher effect than the education of men on several dimensions of development, which are not only related to women, but also related to the total population.

8. Education, Social and Political Development

It has also been observed historically that education helps to broaden the base of understanding among people, and thereby helps to strengthen the democratic process, which in turn could pave the way to the promotion of sustainable development, through a better understanding of the intimate relationships between environment, ecology and sustainable development. By strengthening democratic forces, education would help in promoting sustainable human development, making rapid social progress, including abolition or containment of the elite's discretionary power (see Cohen, 1998, p. 15). As Sen (2001) notes, education enhances individuals' choices in life. It is an instrument of economic expansion; it influences balance of power in the society: lower classes can acquire higher ability and more articulation to influence social decisions, thus contributing to more participatory democracy. Changes in power distribution will have positive effects on social relationships. The contribution of education is significant not only in the improvement of basic needs like health and nutrition, and in demographic development, but also thereby in strengthening democracy and political stability.

9. Threshold Level of Education and Development

All types and nature of education do not necessarily lead to economic growth. Education has to be not only widely spread, but also qualitatively rich. It is important to note that there is a threshold level of education development for education to have an effect on growth. The coefficients of education in wage regressions in India (Vasudeva-Dutta, 2004) show that there is a significant jump in the coefficient between secondary and higher education, suggesting that secondary education may be a threshold level for education to influence the earnings. Literature on education and agricultural productivity also makes it clear that there exists a threshold level of education for its impact to be significant and while this level varies for different regions marginally and for different purposes, mostly it is secondary level of education of about ten years of schooling. The threshold level of education is relevant not only for farm efficiency, but also for other activities like utilisation of credit facilities, adoption of family planning methods, etc. The multiplier effects of a modernizing environment on agricultural productivity gains are more likely to be available only where education is widely spread (Lockheed *et al.*, 1980). As the economy develops and technological advancement takes place, this threshold level goes up.

Secondly, there is a threshold level in terms of quality of education as well. It is increasingly found that mere expansion of education which does not have good quality may not produce significant effects on growth. Very poor quality education may not lead to development at all. As many (e.g., Behrman and Birdsall, 1983; Fuller, 1990; Fuller *et al.* 1986; Hanushek, 2003) have shown, returns to investment in quality of education are much higher than returns to investment in quantitative expansion of education. Recently based on extensive cross national data, Hanushek and Woessmann (2008) have found that cognitive skills of the population, rather than mere school attainment, are powerfully related to individual earnings, to the distribution of income and to economic growth. This also helps in reducing gap between rich and the poor countries.

10. Technology, Education and Development

The effect of education on growth differs due to other factors like technology. In case of agriculture, the level and type of farming and the overall general and technological environment are also seen to be resulting in varying effect of education on agricultural productivity. As Schultz (1964) demonstrated, education would be more effective in a changing, modernizing agricultural environment where fertilizers and new technologies are becoming available, than in a traditional one. Impact of education on agricultural productivity in high technology and better environmental conditions like Japan, will be different from the impact of education on agricultural productivity in low technology and poorer environmental conditions like in Nepal and Pakistan. In fact, because of differences in level of technology development, certain growth models are not found to be relevant. For instance, Leeuwen and Foldvari (2008) showed that Lucas model—accumulation of human capital affects economic growth, is relevant for developing countries like India; and Romer's model explains the growth of experience of developed counties like Japan, which are near the technological frontier and where human capital is employed to expand the technological frontier.

To sum up, extensive empirical research during the last four decades has established that education makes a significant positive contribution to development directly as a factor of production, or indirectly through innovations and technological development and through several externalities (Outlon, 1997). It has been found to improve productivity of labour force, enhance individual earnings, raise national income, increase economic growth, raise agricultural productivity, reduce poverty, improve income distribution, etc. It also reduces infant mortality, improves life expectancy, reduces fertility and thereby it reduces growth in population, etc. Whether the impact is measured in monetary terms or in non-monetary terms, the positive contribution of education to development is quite significant in many countries. The contribution of education to development is widely recognised. Some have described the modern development in economies such as those in Asia, as 'human resource led development' (Behrman, 1990).

While education contributes to development in general, the relationship is not automatic, and not necessarily linear. It depends upon a large set of factors. Both the nature and quantum of effect of education varies from country to country, depending upon the level of development of the education system, the level of socio-economic development, and the level of technological development. In some cases, education may not necessarily lead to higher growth. This is also partly due to errors in measurement of educational attainment (Pritchett, 2001, Wolf, 2002).

An important aspect relating to the research studies is worth noting. Though education is rightly regarded as an important factor of economic growth and development, within education, focus has been relatively more on primary education. Several studies have analysed the contribution of literacy and primary education to improvement in poverty, agricultural productivity, health and nutrition, growth in population, human development indicators like infant mortality, life expectancy, etc. Very few studies have examined the role of secondary and higher education in case of these aspects; and firmly concluded that literacy and primary education have significant effects on poverty reduction. Studies on rates of return, though estimated returns to all levels of education, by showing that primary education yields higher returns than secondary and higher education, justified concentration of attention of policy researchers and planners on primary education and its effects on development (Psacharopoulos, 1984; Colcough, 1993). In other words, secondary and higher education received only secondary attention. As a result, the role of primary education in poverty reduction and development is often highlighted and the role of secondary and higher education is ignored. All this neglect in research, but for a few important studies in recent years (discussed in the following section), led many researchers to conclude that secondary and more importantly higher education is not important for development in developing countries. Consequently, the attention of the policy-makers in developing countries and of the international development organisations got narrowly concentrated on primary education only, as reflected in the global statements on Education For All, or the United Nations' Millennium Development Goals.

3. EMPIRICAL RESEARCH: ROBUST BUT LESS POPULAR FINDINGS

Higher Education and Development

But there does exist some important research, some of which is, however, more recent, that analysed the relationship between post primary education and development, and did find significant impact of secondary and higher education on growth (e.g., Barro, 1991; Barro and

Salai-i-Martin, 1995; Lucas, 1988; Mankiw *et al.*, 1992; Barro and Lee, 1993a,b; Benhabib and Spiegel 1994; Petrakis and Stamatakis, 2002; Romer, 1986). For instance, the panel analysis of real per capita GDP growth rates in about 100 countries over three periods, 1965-75, 1975-85 and 1985-90 by Barro (1991) showed that secondary and tertiary levels of education attainment of male adult population have significant effects on growth, and more over the growth is not significantly related to primary education. An increase in male secondary schooling by one standard deviation is estimated to raise the growth by 1.1 percentage points annually and higher education by 0.5 percentage points. According to Barro and Lee (1994), countries where the labour force had one year of secondary level or more experienced a higher annual growth rate of about 1.34 points more. This is robust even with the introduction of additional variables like political stability, openness of the economy and black market. Benhabib and Spiegel (1994) have found that secondary education helps in innovating technology and in sustaining growth. Self and Grabowski (2004) found significant impact of secondary education on economic growth and the relationship is causal and statistically significant when secondary education is measured in terms of enrolments or in the form of stock of human capital. Jorgenson (2000) estimated that a considerable part of the growth during the 1990s was attributable to research innovations at universities and larger proportion of higher educated workforce. While primary education serves as a threshold level of human capital development for economic growth (Azariadis and Drazen, 1990), it is secondary and higher education including investment in science and technology that accelerates and sustains high economic growth (see McMahon, 1999).

Even in case of India, there are a few important studies on this subject. Using recent data Mathur and Mamgain (2004) found significantly increasing effects of education on economic development (NSDP per capita) by increasing levels of education. It is important to note that the regression coefficients for not only illiteracy but also for just literacy are negative and highest effects are found of higher education, followed by higher secondary and secondary education.

Very few major empirical estimates are available on the quantitative effect of specialised human capital (Schultz, 1988) on economic development. In a relatively recent growth accounting exercise, Mathur (1987) estimated the contribution of 'technological change' to economic growth in India to be quite significant. Such research is relatively abundant particularly referring to agricultural productivity in India (see Tilak, 1994). Malathy and Duraisamy (1993) estimated rates of return (using Mincerian earnings function) to scientific and technical education in India. The average rates of return based on 1981 census survey data, are high and vary between 17.4 per cent (Under-Graduate Diploma) and 70.8 per cent (Ph.D. Degree). Though few studies are available on the effect of research and development on other aspects of national development, its contribution is well noted.

Estimates based on production functions on a cross section data on India (Tilak, 2007), similar cross-section studies on 49 countries in Asia (Tilak, 2003a), and larger number of countries (Tilak, 2006a) indicate a strong effect of higher education on development. Higher education—measured in terms of the gross enrolment ratios or in terms of higher education attainment, i.e., proportion of population with higher education—is found to have a positive effect on the level of economic development; and if time lag is allowed in the production functions, the effect is found to be higher.

Higher education is also positively related to several human development indicators, in addition to economic development. Higher education is found to be very significantly related to the human development index and also to the gender development index. The higher the level of higher education in a society, whether in stock or flow forms, the higher can be the level of human development, through its influence on two main components of human development index, viz., the life expectancy, and GDP per capita. It is not only life expectancy that is significantly related to higher education, but also infant mortality, another measure of health is significantly related to higher education. Poverty is also found to be inversely related to the level of higher education in these analyses. The relationship between poverty and gross enrolment ratio in higher education is negative and is statistically significant. An analysis of logarithmic trend values of enrolment ratio in higher education on poverty on data on 77 developing countries indicates as the enrolment ratio crosses 40 per cent, poverty ratio tends to reach nearly zero levels! In general, one can argue that while basic education may take people out of poverty, this can be sustained well by secondary and higher education, which help in upward mobility and offer better economic opportunities.

The level of achievement in technology critically depends upon the level of higher education in a given economy. After all, it is higher education and research that help in developing new technology; it is higher education and research that contributes to innovations and in their diffusion. So one can expect a very strong effect of higher education on the development of technology in any society. In fact, the level of achievement in technology may be a close indicator of economic growth itself. Most countries with high enrolment ratios in higher education became 'leaders' in technology, with high levels of achievement in technology. The converse is also true: a large number of countries with low enrolment ratios (say less than ten per cent) are 'marginalized' in the area of technology. Those with medium level of enrolment ratios, nearly 20 per cent, like Singapore and Hong Kong are indeed 'potential leaders' in technology. A few countries like Philippines and Thailand with medium and high levels of enrolment ratios are classified by the UNDP (2001) as 'dynamic leaders'. The rest who did not expand their higher education systems well, are indeed 'marginalized.' We find not even a single country with a low enrolment ratio (less than ten per cent) in higher education to have achieved high or medium level of achievement in the technology achievement index. The simple coefficient of correlation between enrolment ratio in higher education and technology achievement index on the Asian countries is as high as 0.8 and that between technology and higher education attainment is 0.65 (Tilak, 2003).

Thus the available, though meagre, research evidence shows that higher education has a very significant role in the development of the societies—in terms of economic development, human development, gender-based development, improvement in health, life expectancy, and reduction in fertility, infant mortality and poverty. Hence, the general presumption that higher education is not necessary for economic growth and development, particularly in developing countries and on the other hand, and that it is literacy and primary education that is important, is not a correct presumption. But these findings are not yet as popular as the rate of return estimates and other findings described earlier that emphasised the role of primary education *vis-à-vis* other levels of education. As a result, attention continues to be focused on primary education and at best on lower secondary education.

SUMMARY AND CONCLUDING OBSERVATIONS

The contribution of basic education to development is widely recognised. Ever since 1985 when the World Bank set poverty reduction as an important agenda of the Bank, and highlighted the role of primary education there in, the attention of the policy-makers, planners and development thinkers has shifted very systematically in favour of primary education. Substantial policy research has established the strong linkages between primary education and development —growth and poverty reduction, reduction in infant mortality, reduction in fertility, improvement in life expectancy and so on. Research also covered literacy and non-formal education. Very rarely the linkages between post-primary education and development have been analysed. The extensive empirical research, a substantial part of which originated from the World Bank, that established that returns to primary education are high and higher than returns to secondary and higher education, had also led many to conclude that it is only primary education and literacy that matter for development—economic, social and even human development, and secondary and higher education does not matter. The conclusion also led many to recommend that developing countries better concentrate on primary education and deliberately ignore secondary and more specially higher education. It was also felt by many that primary education cannot be provided to all children, unless the growth in post primary education is capped. Accordingly, many developing countries have not paid much attention to secondary and higher education in their national educational policy and planning exercises. The subsequent developments, including the World Bank policy papers, the structural adjustment policies that were to be adopted by most of the developing counties, and the Jomtien (and later the Dakar) conferences on Education For All (EFA), the Millennium Development Goals (MDGs) all have contributed to strengthening these trends. The problem of resource scarcity added further to the neglect of higher education. Though the World Bank (1980, p. 49) has clearly stated that "renewed emphasis on the importance of primary education, its high returns relative to secondary and higher education, should not start the pendulum swinging too far in the other direction," it did happen over the years and the World Bank's policy research is found to be mainly responsible for the same. As Bloom *et al.* (2005) summed up, the World Bank's lack of emphasis on tertiary education has resulted in the absence of higher education in the poverty reduction strategies in all but a few African countries.

However, a careful review of recent research leads us to conclude that the general presumption on the weak or negligible role of secondary and higher education in development is not valid and that post-primary education plays a significant role in development. Post-primary education leads to economic growth, makes a significant contribution to reduction in absolute as well as relative poverty; it negatively influences infant mortality, is positively related to life expectancy and to the overall human development index and even to the gender-based human development index.

After all, while primary education gives the basic three r's and is important and even necessary for development, it is not adequate for overall sustainable development. Rarely does it provide skills necessary for employment—self-employment or otherwise that can ensure some wages and economic living. More over, most of the literacy and primary education programmes are also found to be not imparting literacy that is sustainable, so that children do not relapse into illiteracy. Secondly, primary and even elementary education rarely serves as a terminal level of education. Thirdly, even if primary education imparts some valuable attributes, in terms of attitudes and skills and if primary education is able to take the people from below the poverty line to above the poverty line, it is possible that this could be *just above* the poverty line, but not much above; and more importantly the danger of their falling below poverty line at any time could be high. On the other hand, it is secondary and higher education that consolidates the gains received from primary education, as it is secondary and higher education that provides skills that could be useful in the labour market; it is secondary and higher education that can keep the people above poverty line without such a danger of falling back into poverty trap—educational poverty or income poverty; and in fact, it is secondary and higher education that can take people to much above poverty line, by increasing the social, occupational and economic levels of the households. Further, it is higher education that can ensure sustainable economic growth, as it is higher education, or the specialised human capital that helps individuals and nations to withstand economic shocks, face disequilibria and to be able to restore equilibrium (Schultz, 1975, 1990). Lastly, this is secondary and higher education that forms a 'human capability' and 'human freedom' that Sen (1999) champions, a freedom that helps in attaining other 'freedoms'. It is higher education that can ensure the basic human right of the people to live like human beings with dignity, as the Supreme Court of India (1992) observed.

References

Ahluwalia, Montek S. (1976), Inequality, Poverty and Development, *Journal of Development Economics,* 3: 307-42.

Arrow, Kenneth J. (1973), Higher Education as a Filter, *Journal of Public Economics,* 2(3) July: 193-216.

Azariadis, C., and A. Drazen (1990), Threshold Externalities in Economic Development, *Quarterly Journal of Economics,* 105 (May): 501-26.

Barro, Robert (1991), Economic Growth in a Cross-Section of Countries, *Quarterly Journal of Economics,* 106(2): 404-44.

Barro, R.J. (1997), *Determinants of Economic Growth: A Cross-Country Study*. Cambridge, MA: MIT Press.

Barro, R.J. (1999), Human Capital and Growth in Cross-Country Regressions, *Swedish Economic Policy Review*, 6(2): 237-77.

Barro, R.J. (2001), Human Capital and Growth, *American Economic Review*, 91 (Papers and Proceedings): 12-17.

Barro, R.J. and Jong-Wha Lee (1993a), International Comparisons of Educational Attainment, *Journal of Monetary Economics*, 32(3) (December): 363-94.

Barro, R.J., and J.W. Lee (1993b), Losers and Winners in Economic Growth, *Proceedings of the World Bank Annual Conference on Development Economics, 1993*: 267-97.

Barro, R.J. and J.W. Lee (1994), Sources of Economic Growth, *Carnegie-Rochester Conference Series on Public Policy*, 40: 1-46.

Baro, R.J., and X. Salai-i-Martin (1995), *Economic Growth*. New York: McGraw-Hill.

Becker, Gary S. (1960), Underinvestment in College Education, *American Economic Review*, 50(2) (May) (Papers and Proceedings): 346-54.

Becker, G.S. (1964), *Human Capital*. New York: National Bureau of Economic Research.

Behrman, Jere R. (1990), *Human Resource Led Development? Review of Issues and Evidence*. New Delhi: ILO-ARTEP.

Behrman, Jere R., and Nancy Birdsall (1983), The Quality of Schooling: Quantity Alone is Misleading, *American Economic Review*, 73(5): 928-46.

Benhabib, J. and M.M. Spiegel (1994), Role of Human Capital in Economic Development: Evidence for Aggregate Cross-Country Data, *Journal of Monetary Economics*, 34: 134-74.

Blaug, M. (1972), Correlation between Education and Earnings, *Higher Education*, 1(1): 53-76.

Blaug, Mark (1975), The Economics of Education in English Classical, Policy Economy: A Re-examination, in *Essays on Adam Smith* (eds. A.S.. Skinner and T. Wilson), Oxford: Clarendon Press, pp. 568-99.

Blaug, M. (1985), Where are We Now in Economics of Education? *Economics of Education Review*, 4(1): 17-28.

Bloom, David E. and Henry Rosovsky. 2006. Higher Education and in Developing Countries, in *International Handbook of Higher Education* (eds. James J.F. Forest and Philip G. Altbach), Dordrecht: Springer, pp. 443-59.

Bloom, D.E., D. Canning, and K. Chan (2006), Higher Education and Poverty in Sub-Saharan Africa, *International Higher Education*, No. 45 (Fall).

Bourguingnon, Francois and F. Halsey Rogers (2008), Global Returns to Higher Education: Trends, Drivers, and Policy Responses, in Justin Yifu Lin and Boris Pleskovic, eds., *Higher Education and Development*. [Annual World Bank Conference on Development Economics, Regional 2008] Washington DC: World Bank, pp. 25-40.

Bowman, M.J. (1966), The Human Investment Revolution in Economic Thought, *Sociology of Education,* 39(2) (Spring): 111-37.

Chen and Lee (2008), Knowledge and Endogenous Growth, *Asian Economic Review.*

Cochrané, S., O' Hara, D. and Leslie, J. (1980), The Effects of Education on Health. World Bank Staff Working Paper No. 405. World Bank, Washington D.C.

Cochrane, S.H. (1988), *The Effects of Education, Health and Social Security on Fertility in Developing Countries.* WPS 93. Washington D.C.: World Bank.

Cohen, Daniel (1998), *The Wealth of the World and the Poverty of Nations.* Cambridge, MA: MIT Press.

Colclough, Christopher (1983), The Impact of Primary Schooling on Economic Development : A Review of the Evidence, *World Development,* 3: 167-85.

DeMeulemeester, Jean-Luc and Denis Rochat (1995), A Causality Analysis of the Link Between Higher Education and Economic Development, *Economics of Education Review,* 14(4): 251-361.

Fields, Gary S. (1980a), *Poverty, Inequality and Development.* Cambridge, Cambridge University Press.

Fields, G.S. (1980b), Education and Income Distribution in Developing Countries: A Review of the Literature. In: *Education and Income* (ed. T. King), Staff working paper No. 402. Washington DC.: World Bank, pp. 231-315.

Fuller, Bruce (1990), What Investments Raise Achievement in the Third World, in David W. Chapman and Carol A. Carrier (eds.) *Improving Educational Quality: A Global Perspective.* Portsmouth, NH, USA: Greenwood Press.

Fuller, Bruce; John H.Y. Edwards; and Kathleen Gorman (1986), When Does Education Boost Economic Growth? School Expansion and School Quality in Mexico, *Sociology of Education,* 59(3) (July): 167-81.

Funke, M. and H Strulik (2000), On endogenous growth with physical capital, human capital and product variety, *European Economic Review,* 44: 491-515.

Gemmell, N. (1995), Endogenous Growth, the Solow Model and Human Capital, *Economics of Planning,* 28: 163-83.

Gemmell, N. (1996), Evaluating the Impacts of Human Capital Stocks and Accumulation on Economic Growth: Some New Evidence, *Oxford Bulletin of Economics and Statistics,* 58: 9-28.

Gemmell, Norman (1997) Externalities to Higher Education: A Review of the New Growth Literature. Report 8. The National Committee of Inquiry into Higher Education. [http://www.leeds.ac.uk/educol/niche/r8_]

Hanushek, Eric A., ed. (2003), *Economics of Schooling and School Quality.* Cheltenham, UK: Edward Elgar.

Hanushek, Eric A., and Lundger Woessmann (2008), The Role of Cognitive Skills in Economic Development, *Journal of Economic Literature,* 46(3) (September): 607-68.

Jamison, Dean and Lawrence Lau, 1982, *Farmer Education and Farm Efficiency*, Johns Hopkins Press, Baltimore.

Kahan, A. (1963), Some Russian Economics on Returns to Schooling and Experience, in M.J. Bowman *et al.*, eds., *Readings in Economics of Education*. Paris: UNESCO, pp. 399-410.

Kothari, V.N., and P.R. Panchamukhi (1980), Economics of Education: A Trend Report, in D.T. Lakdawala, ed., *A Survey of Research in Economics*, Vol. VI, New Delhi: Allied, pp. 169-238.

Kuznets, Simon (1955), Economic Growth and Income Inequality, *American Economic Review*, 45(1) (March): 1-28.

Leeuwen, Bas van and Peter Foldvari 2008 Human Capital and Economic Growth in Asia 1890-2000: A Time-Series Analysis, *Asian Economic Journal*, 22(3) (September): 225-40.

Lockheed, M., Dean Jamison, and Lau (1980), Farmer Education and Farm Efficiency: A Survey, *Economic Development and Cultural Change*, 29(1): 37-76.

Lucas, Robert E. Jr. (1988), On the Mechanics of Economic Development, *Journal of Monetary Economics*, 22(1): 3-42.

Malathy, D., and P. Duraisamy (1993), Returns to Scientific and Technical Education in India, *Margin*, 25(4) (July-September): 396-406.

Mankiw, N.G. (1995), The Growth of Nations, *Brookings Papers on Economic Activity*, 1: 275-326.

Mankiw, N.G., D Romer, and D.R. Weil (1992), A Contribution to the Empirics of Economic Growth, *Quarterly Journal of Economics*, 107(2): 407-37.

Marshall, A. (1920), *Principles of Economics*, London: Macmillan, 1947 [Eighth Edition.

Mathur, Ashok (1987), Why Growth Rates Differ within India: An Alternative Approach, *Journal of Development Studies*, 23(2) (January): 167-99.

Mathur, Ashok and Rajendra P. Mamgain (2004), Human Capital Stocks, Their Level of Utilization and Economic Development in India, *Indian Journal of Labour Economics*, 47(4): 655-75.

McMahon, W.W. (1999), *Education and Development: Measuring Social Benefits*. New York: Oxford.

Mincer, J. (1974), *Schooling, Experience and Earnings*. New York: National Bureau of Economic Research.

Noor, A. (1980), Education and Basic Needs. Staff Working Paper No. 450. Washington D.C.

Oulton, N. (1997), Total Factor Productivity Growth and the Role of Externalities, *National Institute of Economic Review*, 162: 99-111.

Petrakis, P.E. and D. Stamatakis (2002), Growth and Educational Levels: A Comparative Analysis, *Economics of Education Review*, 21(5): 513-21.

Pritchett, Lan (2001), Where Has All the Education Gone? *World Bank Economic Review*, 15(3): 367-91.

Psacharopoulos, George (1984), Contribution of Education to Economic Growth: International Comparisons, in *International Productivity*

Comparisons and the Causes of the Slowdown, ed. J. Kendrick. Ballinger for the American Enterprise Institute, pp. 335-60.

Psacharopoulos, G. (2004), Economics of Education: From Theory to Practice, *Brussels Economic Review*, 47(3-4) (Winter): 341-57.

Psacaharopoulos, G. and Harry Patrinos (2004), Returns to Investment in Education: A Further Update, *Education Economics.* 12(2): 111-34.

Psacharopoulos, G., and Maureen Woodhall (1985), *Education for Development*. New York: Oxford for the World Bank.

Psacharopoulos, G., and J.B.G. Tilak (1992), Education and Wage Earnings, in *The Encyclopedia of Educational Research* (Editor-in-Chief: M.C. Alkin), New York: Macmillan/American Educational Research Association, pp. 419-23.

Romer, Paul M. (1986), Increasing Returns and Long-Run Growth, *Journal of Political Economy*, 94(5): 1002-36.

Romer, P.M. (1990a), Endogenous Technological Change, *Journal of Political Economy*, 89(5): S71-S102.

Romer, P.M. (1990b), Human Capital and Growth: Theory and Evidence, *Carnegie-Rochester Series on Public Policy*, 32: 251-86.

Schultz, T. Paul (1993), Investments in Schooling and Health of Women and men: Quantities and Return, *Journal of Human Resources*, 28(4): 694-734.

Schultz, Theodore W. (1961), Investment in Human Capital, *American Economic Review*, 51(1) March: 1-15.

Schultz, T.W. (1963), *Economic Value of Education*. New York: Columbia University Press.

Schultz, T.W. (1964), *Transforming Traditional Agriculture*. New Haven: Yale University Press.

Schultz, T.W. (1975), The value of ability to deal with disequilibria, *Journal of Economic Literature*, 13(3) September: 827-46.

Schultz, Theodore W. (1988), On Investing in Specialized Human Capital to Attain Increasing Returns. In: *The State of Development Economics: Progress and Perspectives* (eds. Gustav Ranis and T. Paul Schultz). Oxford: Basil Blackwell, pp. 339-52.

Schultz, Theodore W. (1990), *Restoring Economic Equilibrium*. Cambridge: Basil Blackwell.

Self, Sharmistha and Richard Grabowski (2004), Does Education at all Levels Cause Growth: India, A Case Study, *Economics of Education Review*, 23: 47-55

Sen, Amartya (1999), *Development as Freedom*. Oxford: Clarendon.

Solow, R.M. (1956), A Contribution to the Theory of Economic Growth, *Quarterly Journal of Economics*, 70: 65-94.

Solow, R.M. (1957), Technical Change and Aggregate Production Function, *Review of Economics and Statistics*, 39: 312-20.

Spence, A.M. (1973), Job-market signaling, *Quarterly Journal of Economics*, 87(3), (August): 355-74.

Stiglitz, J.E. (1975), The theory of 'screening' education and the distribution of income. *American Economic Review*, 65 (June): 283-300.

Strumilin, S.G. (1925), The Economic Significance of National Education, reprinted in E.A.G. Robinson and J. Vaizey, eds., *The Economics of Education*. London: Macmillan, 1966, pp. 276-323.

Supreme Court of India (1992), Judgement on *Miss Mohini Jain versus State of Karnataka and Ors.* New Delhi (30 July 1992). [Reproduced in *Journal of Higher Education,* 16(1) (Autumn 1992): 73-86.]

Tilak, J.B.G. (1989a), *Education and its Relation to Economic Growth, Poverty and Income Distribution: Past Evidence and Further Analysis*. Discussion Paper No. 46. Washington D.C.: World Bank, February 1989

Tilak, J.B.G. (1989b), Education and Basic Needs, in: *Human Resource Development for Rural Development*. (eds. M.K. Rao and P.P. Sharma) Bombay: Himalaya, pp. 47-67.

Tilak, J.B.G. (1994), *Education for Development in Asia*. New Delhi: Sage Publications.

Tilak, J.B.G. (2003), Higher Education and Development, in the *Handbook on Educational Research in the Asia Pacific Region* (eds. J.P. Kleeves and Ryo Watanabe) Dordrecht: Kluwer Academic Publishers, pp. 809-26.

Tilak, J.B.G. (2006a), *Role of Post-Basic Education in Alleviation of Poverty and Development.* PBET Working Paper No. 7. Edinburgh: University of Edinburgh, Centre of African Studies.

Tilak, J.B.G. (2006b), Economics of Human Capital in India, *Indian Economic Journal* (89th IEA Annual Conference Volume): 3-20.

Tilak, J.B.G. (2007), Post-Elementary Education, Poverty and Development in India. *International Journal of Educational Development,* 27(4) (July): 435-45

Tinbergen, Jan (1970), A Positive and A Normative Theory and Income Distribution, *Review of Income and Wealth,* 16(2) (June): 221-34.

Tinbergen, J. (1977), Income Distribution: Second Thoughts, *DeEconomist,* 125(3): 315-39.

Tinbergen, J. (1980), Two Approaches to Quantify the Concept of Equitable Income Distribution, *Kyklos,* 33(1): 3-15.

UNDP (2001), *Human Development Report.* New York: Oxford University Press.

Vaizey, John (1962), *Economics of Education*. London: Faber and Faber.

Vasudeva-Dutta, Puja (2004), The Structure of Wages in India, 1983-1999, Discussion Paper 102, Sussex: University of Sussex, Dept. of Economics.

Webbink, Dinand (2000), Social Returns to Education: A Survey of Recent Literature on Human Capital Externalities. http://www.cpb.nl/nl/cpbreport/2000_1/s3_4.pdf

Welch, F. (1970), Education in production, *Journal of Political Economy,* 78(1) January-February: 32-59.

Wolf, Alison (2002), *What is Education for? Myths about Education and Economic Growth*. London: Penguin.

Wolfe, B., and S. Zuvekas (1997), Non-market Outcomes of Schooling, *International Journal of Educational Research,* 27(6): 491-502.

Wolff, E.N. and M. Gittleman (1993), The Role of Education in Productivity Convergence: Does Higher Education Matter? in A. Szirmai, B. van Ark and D. Pilats (eds.) *Explaining Economic Growth*. Amsterdam: North-Holland.

World Bank (1980), *Education Sector Policy Paper*. Washington DC.

2

Education and Development: Quality and Equity Concerns

Rupinder Kaur

BACKGROUND

The issue of development came into prominence when large number of countries in Asia and Africa attained political freedom, after World War-II. Initially the development, both in theory and policy, was equated to achieving sustained growth in per capita GNP. During 1950s and 1960s many developing countries realized their growth targets but quality of life of majority of people did not improve much. There was a growing disillusionment with growth, which was not benefiting all sections of society. As a result, in 1970s issues of poverty and inequality came into focus. During the last two decades, an alternative view is propagated by UNDP, which measure, progress in terms of human development. In measuring human development, average achievement in education (knowledge) of a particular country is taken as one of the three basic dimensions of human development; the other two being healthy life and decent standard of living measured in terms of per capita GDP in purchasing power parity terms.

In fact, education is both on input as well as an indicator of development. Sen (1999) defines development in terms of the expansion of the real freedoms that the citizens enjoy to pursue their objectives and the expansion of human capability is recognised as the central feature of the process of development. In this context education plays an important role in improving the quality of life through expanding human capabilities. Birdsall *et. al.* (2005) also argue that access to basic education is an end in itself, a human right, and a vital part of individuals' capacity to lead lives they value. Moreover, they recognise it as an important instrument with which people can improve their lives in many other ways. Education enhances the capacity of the people to participate in the political process and thus come together for other social and political rights and to demand accountability from their governments.

However, access to education and other resources is not uniform across different social groups and gender. Women face number of constraints which put them in a disadvantageous position. These constraints include disproportionate burden of reproductive work, restrictions on mobility, lower say in decision-making, oppressive social norms and other cultural and ideological constraints. Children from poor and socially disadvantaged families also suffer from resource crunch and quite often discrimination in schools. These constraints reduce opportunities available to them to improve their knowledge and skills, increase productivity, and hence affect their ability to successfully compete with relatively better placed sections in different income earning activities.

RETURNS TO EDUCATION

The role of human capital in increasing productivity has been realized by the economists since long. T.W. Schultz appreciated the importance of investment in human capital to transform the low productivity traditional agriculture into modern agriculture. He argued that to produce an abundance of farm products required that the farmer has access to and knowledge to use what science knows about soils, plants, animals, and machines. The knowledge that makes the transformation possible is a form of capital and it entails investment; rapid and sustained growth in agriculture rests heavily on particular investments in farm people helping them acquire new skills and new knowledge. Jamison and Lau (1982) also observed that earning of farmers are higher in settings in which education helps them take advantage of new seed and other technologies. Education also plays an important role in enhancing earnings of small business owners and other self-employed workers (Schultz, 1993, 2001).

Based on a survey of large number of studies Psacharopoulos (1991: 8-15) concludes that compared with developed countries, returns to education are much higher in developing countries because of scarcity of human capital and barriers to allocation of funds for human capital investment. A typical pattern discovered by Psacharopoulos in these studies is that returns decline with increase in the level of education. Thus, returns are higher to primary education relative to secondary and latter are higher than returns to university education. Another pattern which emerges from the review is that investment in the education of females yields higher rate of return than that in male education. This is despite the fact that male earnings are generally more than females. In fact, it is because the opportunity cost of women's labour is lower and a major component of the cost of education is income forgone during the study period. The patterns of rate of return established in this review are upheld in latter study also (Psacharopoulos, 1994).

Another review-based study (Birdsall et. al., 2005: 23-30) brings out somewhat different results. The authors observe that wage returns to education vary by level and differ across economies. In most developing economies the private wage returns to higher education are very high relative to private returns to primary and secondary education. In growing economies this often reflects the fact that the demand for educated workers exceeds the supply, especially for university graduates, because educational opportunities are still limited. It also reflects the fact that those who achieve higher levels of education probably benefited at lower levels from higher quality schooling, which enabled and encouraged them to continue and which ensured that they have more of the human capital that makes them more productive. In fact, returns to education are not confined to higher wages and incomes. Mothers with primary education have better access to the information they need to help keep their children healthy. Education, particularly girls' education, has social returns to society at large as well, since society captures some of the benefits of improved health, lower fertility, and the at-home education that educated mothers transfer to their children.

However, benefits of education are conditioned by the political, social, and economic context. Schools and education systems in themselves do not necessarily guarantee faster economic growth. Rapid increases in average education in Latin America, and much of Africa has not spurred growth in the past three decades. Pritchett (2001) argues that where the relationship between "more" education and faster growth has failed to materialize, one or more of the following factors may be responsible. First of all, if education systems are weak, more spending and higher enrolment may not translate into learning and concomitant increases in the human capital stock. Secondly, problems in other policy spheres (macroeconomic instability, civil unrest, market distortions) may prevent gains in education from being translated into economic growth. Thirdly, the effect of education on growth will be minimal if technological progress or some other key complementary factor, such as adequate infrastructure or contract enforcement, is missing. Fourth, as long as the stock of human capital remains below some threshold, marginal increases in education for a few people may be ineffective in producing growth.

Initial level of literacy and education also play an important role in initiating and sustaining growth. East Asia's experience over the past five decades also suggests the role other factors play in ensuring that education contributes to growth. Educational systems were relatively good, market and other distortions were limited, technology was adapted, and investment in infrastructure and other complementary inputs was high. In this context, education contributed to high and relatively equitable growth (Birdsall, Ross, and Sabot 1995).

INDIAN EXPERIENCE

Compared with East Asian countries India lagged much behind in literacy and education. The development of basic education was significantly more advanced in all those East Asian countries with successful growth-mediated progress at the time of their economic breakthrough compared with India—not just at that time but even today. Adult literacy rates (age 15+) for South Korea, Hong Kong and Thailand in 1960 were around 70 compared with 28 for India. Even in 1990 these rates were over 90 in these East Asian countries but less than 50 for India. China is also much ahead of India; in 1990 and 1999, China's literacy rate was 28 and 27 per cent higher respectively than that of India (Dreze and Sen, 2002: 73-77).

Young population of India is considered as an important asset when ageing is becoming a major problem in developed nations. Over half of India's population is of below 25 years age and it forms around one-fourth of worlds young population. However, numbers alone are not important, quality of human resources is also importance. In today's world uneducated and malnourished workers find little place in productive employment. India, despite having edge in young population, lags behind other countries, including some developing nations, as far as education and health levels of the people are concerned.

It is argued (Chadha, 2004) that for ensuring competitive levels of productivity in various sectors, particularly in the context of fast changing technologies, products and market strategies, India will have to improve its human capital levels. A poor human capital base of a vast segment of India's labour market, most markedly for its rural areas, is indeed the basic problem of the economy. Chadha emphasises the fact that the sectors which are big from the point of view of employment—agriculture being the main example—are also the ones that suffer a fairly sizable handicap of low quality of workforce. This is so when new agriculture is highly technology intensive and numerous soil related and environmental issues have to be resolved at the farm household level. The study estimates that even by 2009-10 there will be large number of illiterate job-seekers and between 15 to 25 per cent persons in urban and rural areas in 5-9 and 10-14 age groups will not be attending school.

Education is also an important tool for reducing inequalities and poverty. Broadly shared education ensures that growth itself will be broadly shared. Education that reaches the poor, women, and marginalized ethnic groups brings private benefits to them as well as benefits to society as a whole by reducing inequality, diminishing discrimination, and creating more cohesion in the long-run. It is contended (Birdsall *et. al.*, 2005: 25) that educating the poor is particularly important for triggering broader social change. Education has a special quality: the human capital acquired through formal education cannot be expropriated. In that respect it is different from land or financial assets. Education that reaches the poor can contribute to a more equal society, in which power is more broadly shared, and which in turn leads to a more equitable pattern of growth.

In India, elementary education has been declared as a fundamental human right. With the launching of *Sarva Shiksha Abhiyaan (SSA)* in 2000, it is envisaged that all children, in the relevant age group, will complete five years of primary schooling by 2007 and eight years of schooling by 2010. All gender and social gaps at primary stage will be bridged by 2007 and elementary level by 2010. Universal retention is to be achieved by 2010.

Substantial gains have been made in literacy and education levels in India during the last fifty years. From around 16% in 1950, literacy rate increased to over 65% in 2001. Progress in enrolment in primary and upper primary schools since 1990 is also noteworthy. Total enrolment at primary stage increased from 97.4 million in 1990 to 122.3 million in 2002-03 (GOI, 2004). At the upper primary level, the increase in enrolment during this period was from 34 million in 1990 to 46.95 million in 2002-03.

However, we have to be cautious about the fact that at primary level, where students are generally not failed till fourth standard and fee in Government and aided schools is very meagre, artificially high enrolment levels are maintained by the teachers. A study (Dreze and Gazdar, 1997) based on the functioning of primary schools in rural Uttar Pradesh revealed that in order to avoid being transferred, teachers ensure that enrolment does not fall below the official norm. Teachers, if necessary by paying fees out of their own pockets, in the names of children who have actually dropped out (or have never been enrolled in the first place), are able to maintain inflated registers and to reduce the chances of being transferred.

A variety of efficiency-related indicators are used to check the retaining capacity of the education system. Dropout rate is one of these indicators. A very high school dropout rate is a matter of concern. However, over a period of time the dropout rate in primary and upper primary classes has been decreasing, though slowly (GOI, 2007). For classes I to VIII, the dropout rate was 51 per cent during 2004-05. This means more than half of the students do not complete 8 years of schooling. A very large number of these dropouts belong to the poorer sections of the society. Thus, India is unlikely to achieve the target that 'all children, in the relevant age group, complete five years of primary schooling by 2007 and eight years of schooling by 2010'.

The National Policy on Education (NPE) emphasizes the need to address the quality concerns in school education on priority basis. Improvement in provision of infrastructure and human resource is another important concern. However, quality of learning is quite poor in our schools. A study by Pritchett and Pande (2006) based on data from four states viz. Karnataka, Rajasthan, Kerala and West Bengal, brings out that the quality of learning is both low and highly variable. Using the mathematics examination for illustration, they found that between 50 to 80 per cent children did not have adequate basic primary schooling competencies. Interestingly, highest proportion of students getting less than 50% scores is in Kerala; the state having high literacy and enrolment rates. In West Bengal, where proportion of not reaching Grade V is high but of those scoring less than 50% is low; overall around half of the students achieve adequate competency levels in basic primary schooling. Along with dropout rate, this is a subject of serious concern for the government and civil society.

As stated earlier, progress in literacy and education and improvement in the quality of learning depends upon a number of factors, which include socio-economic status of the family, accessibility to school, infrastructural facilities, teacher competency and the teaching-learning process. Above all, motivation and accountability of the teachers are the most important factors influencing both quality and quantity of education. Teacher absenteeism is a serious issue in most states in India.

Some researchers have highlighted the lack of infrastructural facilities, prevalence of teacher absenteeism and other problems faced by the elementary education in some states of India. Dreze and Gazdar (1997) investigated the functioning of primary schools in rural Uttar Pradesh. The study discovers that the existence and accessibility of schools does not seem to be the main cause of persistent educational backwardness in this region. However, there are other serious problems. Most of the sample schools had dilapidated buildings, without much furniture. The most commonly used part of the school building was the *verandah*, where children of all grades were often huddled together. None of the sample schools had a female teacher. In fact, the absence of female teachers may act as a serious constraint in the expansion of girls' education. Dreze and Gazdar (1997: 69) argue that parents often have greater confidence in sending their daughters to school if the school has some female teachers. The presence of female teachers is also important in so far as schooling is as much a socialization experience as a process of formal learning.

The pathetic physical condition of the sample schools is in sharp contrast with the claims made by the government of India in connection with the expansion of schooling infrastructure under Operation Blackboard (OB). Minimum infrastructural facilities to be provided under the 'Operation Blackboard' scheme, initiated in 1987-88, include '(i) a building comprising at least two reasonably large all-weather rooms with *verandah* and separate toilets for boys and girls,

(ii) at least two teachers in every primary school, as far as possible one of them a woman, and (iii) essential teaching-learning equipment including blackboards, maps, charts, toys and equipment for work experience'. Department of Education claimed that by the end of 1993-94 OB had been implemented in 99.9 per cent of the country's primary schools (Dreze and Gazdar, 1997: 65).

The existence of infrastructural deficiencies has also been pointed out by the Public Report on Basic Education in India (Probe Team, 1999). The Probe Report is based on the survey of schools from 234 randomly selected villages of Bihar, MP, Rajasthan, UP and HP, along with a sample of 1376 households from these villages. The Report observes that the main issue, as far as school availability is concerned, is the absence of an upper primary school in 71% of the surveyed villages. This is a serious problem because parents are often reluctant to send their daughters to school outside the villages. Moreover, quite a significant proportion of schools do not fulfil the norms established under OB launched in 1987-88. For instance, only 58% schools in the sample villages had at least two *pacca* classrooms, and 12 per cent had a single teacher. Only a small number of schools had a library (23%), maps and charts (41%), or any usable teaching kit (33%). Nearly three-fifths of the sample primary schools were without a functional water supply, 89 per cent lacking a functioning toilet and none had separate toilet for boys and girls. Report remarks that only one-fourth of sample primary schools attain a more liberal benchmark (than the benchmark set by OB), with the following components: (1) at least two all weather rooms, (2) at least two teachers, and (3) at least some teaching aids.

Teacher absenteeism is an endemic problem prevalent in almost all the states in India. Dreze and Gazdar (1997: 62-67), during their enquiries conducted through unannounced visits to 15 schools in four districts of UP (Moradabad, Rae Bareli, Pratapgarh, and Banda), found that two-thirds of the teachers in the sample schools were absent, for one reason or other, at the time of unannounced visits of the survey team. In some cases, particularly when the school had only one teacher, the absence of teacher implied that the school remained closed for the day. Another aspect of the problem of teacher absenteeism observed by Dreze and Gazdar is that most teachers come late and leave early. The team rarely found a school to be open on time in the morning or after 12.30 (lunch break) in the afternoon. Further, the study found that teachers actually performed very little teaching even when they were present. A similar conclusion is also reached by the Public Report on Basic Education in India (Probe Team, 1999: 44-49).

Another important study (Kremer *et al.* 2005) is based on nationally representative data on teacher absence from unannounced visits to Indian primary schools. The study covered 20 Indian states, representing 98 per cent of the population, or roughly one billion people. Three unannounced visits were made to each of 3700 schools. The survey focused on government-run primary schools, but it also covered rural private schools and private-aided schools located in villages where government schools were surveyed. Main conclusions of this study are worth reporting.

The study found that 25 per cent of teachers were absent from school, and only about half were teaching, during unannounced visits. Absence rates varied from 15 per cent in Maharashtra to 42% in Jharkhand, with higher rates concentrated in the poorer states. The authors also observe that higher pay is not associated with lower absence. In fact, they found that older teachers, more educated teachers, and head teachers are all paid more but are also more frequently absent; contract teachers are paid much less than regular teachers but have similar absence rates; and although relative teacher salaries are higher in poorer states, absence rates are also higher. Teacher absence is more correlated with daily incentives to attend work: teachers are less likely to be absent at schools that have been inspected recently, that have better infrastructure, and that are closer to a paved road. The study finds little evidence that attempting to strengthen local community ties will reduce absence. Teachers from the local area have similar absence rates as teachers from outside the community. Locally controlled non-formal schools have higher absence rates than schools run by the state government. The existence of a PTA is not correlated with lower absence. Private-school teachers are only slightly less likely to be absent than public-school teachers in general, but are 8 percentage points less likely to be absent than public-school teachers in the same village.

Summarising the findings of eleven case studies based on data from different states of India, Vaidyanathan and Nair (2001) conclude that there are indeed many dedicated teachers who are doing wonders with the meagre resources available, and there are examples of teacher-initiated educational campaigns. However, the fact remains that in practically all the villages, complaints of absenteeism of teachers, irregular classes and indifferent teaching were widespread. The governmental machinery of supervision and inspection is practically defunct. The communities most directly affected have no effective mechanism to redress their grievances under the existing arrangements.

Government schools cater essentially to poor children and poor parents and communities do not have a voice in the running of these schools and thus cannot persuade teachers to do their job honestly. In fact 'social distance' between teachers and children in government schools is wide and social attitude and community prejudices play an important role in determining the ability and willingness of teachers to empathise with children (Ramachandran, 2005). Systemic issues like corruption in appointments, transfers, special assignments, etc. have also vitiated the teaching environment. Ramachandran argues that in such a situation building networks with patrons and supporters is more important than doing duty honestly.

Another issue afflicting some schools is discrimination against students from under-privileged groups. Probe Team (1999) highlighted this problem of unequal treatment of different sections of the population. The Report observed that discrimination against under-privileged groups is endemic, in several forms. In some schools children of different social backgrounds often receive unequal treatment. In few schools dalit children had to sit separately from other children. And in some instances children of some castes sat on benches while others sat on the floor. Far more widespread than these cases of blatant discrimination, however, are subtle forms of unequal treatment in the classroom. This can take various forms, such as telling dalit children that they are 'stupid', making them feel inferior, using them for menial chores, and giving them liberal physical punishment.

Dreze and Gazdar (1997: 85) also observe different forms of discrimination against children of disadvantaged castes. Some examples of these are: (1) discrimination against schedule-caste settlements in the location of schools, (2) teachers refusing to touch schedule-caste children, (3) children from particular castes being special targets of verbal abuse and physical punishment by the teachers, and (4) low-caste children being frequently beaten by higher caste classmates.

Asian Development Bank (ADB) carried out a study (ADB, 2007) over a period of 5 years (2001-05) interacting with poor using the method of participatory poverty assessments (PPAs) and encompassed 842 locations in 72 districts spread over seven states in India. It covered over twenty thousand poor persons and brought to light some interesting facts. Among other concerns of the poor, the study attempted to understand the issues relating to performance of various institutions on wide range of criteria. The study observes that in state-run schools, free books and lunch are distributed in many locations. Despite this the poor weigh the cost of education, including forgone child earnings, against their perception of benefits that they think they can get from the education. One important reason for the poor not sending their children to school is that they do not find education useful. Though there is a feeling that education may help in earning money, they do not see any evidence around them. Secondly, there is a shortage of infrastructure and of teachers that acts as a barrier to pursuing sustained education. In many cases, teachers "manage children" rather than teach them. Moreover, children of poor families are treated badly by teachers, with the result that they dropout gradually. In some cases children from certain social groups are asked to sit away or are asked to do manual work, which again encourages them to dropout.

What emerges from the above is that the current education system is reinforcing rather than reducing existing inequalities in India. The children of the rich study in well functioning private unaided schools and acquire more and better education than the children of the poor. Number of schemes have been introduced to reduce social and gender gaps, but as discussed above, on the ground level such schemes are making little impact. In the absence of a concerted policy, effective monitoring, and accountability in the education system, increasing access of the poor to good education, which almost always means making societies more inclusive and egalitarian, may not happen. Poorly functioning government schools catering to the poor children on the one hand and select few getting quality education in costly private schools on the other is creating a situation which may defeat the agenda of 'inclusive growth' laid down by the Eleventh Five Year Plan. The way the education system works is creating a vicious cycle thus locking out generations of the poor. To change it requires political will, institutional reform, and additional investments in education.

References

Birdsall, N., D. Ross and R. Sabot (1995), "Inequality and Growth Reconsidered: Lessons from East Asia." *World Bank Economic Review*, 9(3): 477–508.

Birdsall, N., Ruth Levine and Amina Ibrahim (2005), Towards Universal Primary Education: Investments, Incentives and Institutions, UN Millennium Project, Earthscan, London.

Chadha, G.K. (2004), "Human Capital Base of The Indian Labour Market: Identifying Worry Spots", *The Indian Journal of Labour Economics*, Vol. 47, No. 1.

Dreze, Jean and Amartya Sen (2002), India: Development and Participation, OUP, New Delhi.

Dreze, Jean and Haris Gazdar (1997), "Uttar Pradesh: The Burden of Inertia" in Jean Dreze, Jean and Amartya Sen (eds.) Indian Development: Selected Regional Perspectives, OUP, Delhi.

Government of India (2004), Education for All: India, Marches Ahead, Dept. of Elementary Education and Literacy, MHRD.

Government of India (2007), Selected Educational Statistics: 2004-5, MHRD, New Delhi.

Jamison, D.T., and L.J. Lau (1982), Farmer Education and Farm Efficiency. Baltimore, Md.: Johns Hopkins University Press.

Kremer, Michael, Nazmul Chaudhury, F. Halsey Rogers, Karthik Muralidharan and Jeffrey Hammer (2005), "Teacher Absence in

India: A Snapshot", *Journal of the European Economic Association*, April/May, 2005, Vol. 3, No. 2-3, pp. 658-667.

Pritchett, L. (2001). "Where Has All the Education Gone?", *World Bank Economic Review*, 15(3): 367-91.

Psacharopoulos, George (1991), The Economic Impact of Education: Lessons for Policy-makers, San Francisco: ICS Press.

Psacharopoulos, George (1994), "Returns to Investment in Education: A Global Update", *World Development*, Vol. 22(9), Sep.

Probe Team (1999), Public Report on Basic Education in India, OUP, Delhi.

Ramachandran, Vimala (2005), "Why School Teachers are Demotivated and Disheartened", *Economic and Political Weekly*, Vol. XL, No. 21.

Schultz, T.P. (1993). "Returns to Women's Schooling." In Elizabeth King and M. Anne Hill, eds., Women's Education in Developing Countries: Barriers, Benefits, and Policy. Baltimore, Md.: Johns Hopkins University Press.

Schultz, T.P. (2001), "Why Governments Should Invest More to Educate Girls", Discussion Paper 836. Yale University, Economic Growth Center, New Haven, Conn.

Schultz, T.W. (1964) Transforming Traditional Agriculture, Lyall Book Depot, Ludhiana.

Sen, A. (1999), Development as Freedom, Oxford University Press, Oxford.

Vaidyanathan, A. and P.R. Gopinathan Nair (2001), Elementary Education in Rural India: A Grassroots View, Sage, New Delhi.

3

Higher Education, Research and Development: Determinants of Growth

Shalini Tiwari and Manmohan Krishna

A competitive economy can only be based on a well-educated population as well as a dynamic Research and Development sector. The two components of knowledge, the human beings ("human capital") and the technology have become central to economic growth. In the age of globalisation, the knowledge, economy discourse has become a way to characterize the new relationships between the state, society and economy and rendered higher education increasingly important for the international competitiveness of the nation-states through central tasks of generation, application and dissemination of knowledge and training of high skilled labour force.

In this paper the authors have analyzed the role of higher education, research and development to economic growth. In addition, the authors have made an overview of empirical studies, providing us with the evidence from cross-country analysis whether higher education, research and development promotes economic growth at macroeconomic level. This paper emphasizes the importance of higher education, which assigns the highest priority to stimulating and supporting education and research.

Education is one of the determinants of endogenous growth theory and makes way of on inclusive growth of an economy. Expenditure on higher education in any country provides mainly three types of benefits—

- Stable growth rate of an economy
- Technological upgradation
- Stability

Those countries of the world that spend more on higher education on Research and Development (R&D) and provide better technical education and are better placed to make innovations and claim patents for that has ensured more, rapid growth rate compared to others. This positive sign also provides the higher value of Gini-Coefficient through which the ultimate objective of inclusive growth (high growth rate) can be achieved. Therefore, we can say that to achieve the objective of inclusive growth we have to adopt the endogenous growth model.

In endogenous growth model, skill, research, education and health are internalized; out of these four, education stands alone in this paper, only emphasis is given to higher technical education which leads skill (COR) and research (ICOR) for future, which is essential for overall growth of an economy.

Endogenous growth theory demonstrated that policy measures could have an impact on the long-run growth of an economy. For example, subsidies on research and development or education increase the growth rate in some endogenous growth models by increasing the incentive to innovative.

Knowledge is an important input into the economy's production—both its production of goods and services and its production of new knowledge. Compared to others form of capital, however, it is less natural to assume that knowledge exhibits the property of diminishing returns. If we accept the view that knowledge is a type of capital, then this endogenous growth model with its assumption of constant returns to capital becomes a more plausible description of long-run economic growth.

Mankiw (1999) explains the endogenous growth model by way of two-sector model; according to him, "the economy has two sectors, which we can call manufacturing firms and research universities. Firms produce goods and services, which are used for consumption and investment in physical capital. Universities produce a factor of production called 'Knowledge' which is then freely used in both sectors. The economy is described by the production function for firms, the production function for universities and the capital accumulation equation:

$Y= F (K, \{1-\Sigma\} EL)$ [Production in manufacturing firms]

$\Delta E = g(\Sigma)E$ [Production function of research in universities]

$\Delta K = sY-\delta K$ [Capital accumulation]

where Σ is the fraction of the labour force in universities, $1-\Sigma$ is the fraction of the labour force in manufacturing and g is a function that shows how the growth in knowledge depends on the fraction of the labour force in universities. The rest of the notation is standard.

As usual, the production function for the manufacturing firms is assumed to have constant return to scale: if we double both the amount of physical capital (K) and the number of effective workers in manufacturing ($\{1-\Sigma\}$ EL), we double the output of goods and services (Y).

Education has always been regarded as a vital factor in achieving the general aims of society. What is more recent is the emergence of a concept of education as an important factor in economic growth. An approach to education from its investment aspect is based on an understanding that the general development of human abilities, which is essential to the economic growth in the future, depends upon both quantitative and qualitative developments in education. This study aims at analyzing education as an investment in the development of education in connection with the economic growth.

Higher education influences economic well-being in

three ways:

- First, the direct expenditures by the institutions, their employees and their students impact the local economy. This spending multiplies through the local economy until the monies are used to purchase goods and services from outside the local area.
- Second, higher education provides financial and non-financial benefits to the individual who pursues an advanced education and to society in general.
- Third, institutions of higher education are increasingly focused on knowledge creation. Thus, universities are sources of key research and development innovations that simultaneously can be beneficial to society and conducive to economic growth.

Our academic institutions are publicly funded institutions entrusted with two main tasks: to carry out research and to educate part of the next generation at a higher level. In this context, the qualitative aspect of the expansion of higher education has been concerned with the strategic options that have ranged from the priority given to broadening access to undergraduate studies, with an implicit endogenous growth model based on the importance of human capital accumulation, to priority given to research activities, with an implicit endogenous growth model based on the importance of human capital accumulation, to priority given to research activities, with an implicit exogenous growth model based on the importance of technical innovation as a driving force behind future economic growth. Although education policy-makers when allocating funds always have to choose between those options, in fact, a combination of both is important if higher growth is to be achieved. Besides, at a micro-level it is particularly difficult to distinguish and separate the respective contribution to economic development of the technological infrastructure and know-how and of human capital, understood as the quantitative and qualitative characteristics of the workforce measured by using the average educational level of the population (OECD, 1998).

Analyzing the contribution of higher education to economic well being we will discuss benefits provided to individuals by acquiring a university degree, as well as try to describe benefits, that society in general experiences because of better educated individuals.

Chinese higher education has been transformed since 1997. To accomplish this transformation China shifted to cost sharing. The financing of higher education in China changed drastically since 1990. From a system that was paid for mainly by direct government contributions (83% of funding) and the revenues from industries affiliated with universities (about 10% of total funding) to a system in which almost 30 per cent of funding in 2002 came from tution and only 50 per cent of funding from direct government contributions.

There are significant social and economic differences between developed and developing countries. The differences in the scientific and technological infrastructure and in the popularization of science and technology in the two groups of countries are the most important causes of differential social and economical levels. An essential prerequisite to a country's technological progress is early recognition of necessity of a good educational system. This was one of the key factors that contributed to Japan's economic success. The role of Technion, the Hebrew University of Jerusalem and the Weizmann Institute in Israel's rapid development cannot be underestimated.

As Abdus Salam, the Nobel Laureate in physics in 1979, observes: "in the final analysis it is basically mastery and utilization of modern R & D that distinguishes the South from the North". Some developing countries have made important contributions to the development of research, science and technology in the past and some even served as the cradle of human civilization. But the flowering of research, science and technology that began in Europe in the 17th century was used to advantage by only a relatively small group of nations. This situation created not only a difference in material aspects of culture, but also a difference in the social climate of the two groups of countries. The practical use of science through technology created the climate for ever increasing emphasis on the pursuit of science and education in developed countries, where funding scientific enterprises is widely accepted as a vital and long-term investment. For example, federal funding alone provided for non-defence basic and applied research in the States, was $7.9 billion in 1985 and more than half of this kind of support is given to the universities. Contributions of industry to national expenditures on research and development are about twice this amount.

Today, in developed countries basic and applied scientific research is an essential investment in the long-term welfare. In the universities, they assign highest priority to stimulating and nurturing scientific and technical talent, and to the concomitant training of students. What is emerging from this priority is the close association of education and economical growth. Stimulating and supporting scientific education in universities can basically help accelerate the rate of growth and rate of productivity. The critical size of human resources and infrastructure, and the amount of investments in these areas, illustrates how research, science and technology are neglected in developing countries. Industry and Universities in Turkey face shortages of researchers—10 for every 100,000 of population compared with 280 in US, 240 in Japan, 150 in Germany, 140 in the UK. In 1984, in Turkey non-defence research expenditures were 0.20 per cent of GNP, while in the US they were 2.74 per cent, 2.65 per cent in Japan, and 2.54 per cent in Germany. Thus, developing countries have principal shortcomings in their funding and supporting scientific infrastructure.

In short, the social and economic growth of the developed countries is dependent on an essential emphasis on education, science, and technology. The basic problems of developing countries are the weak educational and scientific infrastructure, and a lack of appreciation of the importance of science as an essential ingredient of economical and social development.

In developing countries economic growth can mainly be enhanced by a Research and Development (R & D).

However, they can play their role in development only when the integrity of the whole enterprise-research institutions, universities, publications, research priorities on emphasis and the education of creative researcher, as well as those active in research is preserved. Thus, the simplest strategy in developing countries is first of all, to increase the percentage of GNP that is to be devoted to universities and research institutions.

Developing countries should understand the fact that perceiving investment in research as a time-consuming, wasteful and costly activity will bring further limitations on their economic growth.

Here we try to see some region specific position on higher education expenditure and their growth position. Table 1 shows the percentage of enrolment ratio in higher education for selected regions under the study and find that, developed regions like Northern America and Europe had large number of students in higher education as compared to those regions who were less developed, e.g. Latin America, Asia and Africa. On the other side, the expenditure on higher education is higher in developing countries as compared to developed countries, which is clear from Table 2, but the table also shows that the trend of this expenditure in developing countries is more unstable as compared to developed countries. This is a policy issue, which was not decided timely in developing countries and if it was then not effectively and timely implemented, so the outside lag is the main problem facing the developing countries.

Table 3 shows that the growth rate of developing countries was always ahead of developed countries. The increasing trend of higher education enrolment led to higher growth rates in developing regions. The correlation value between enrolment ratio and growth rate (GDP) for Africa (0.976) and Latin America (1.000), which is significant at 5 per cent, shows this very effectively. Hence we conclude that the higher education expenditure and larger number of students in higher education is necessary for better performance of any developing country, and this leads to research and development procedures through which innovations can be possible and they become empowered.

TABLE 1

Higher Education Enrolment Ratio (%)

Region	*1950*	*1960*	*1970*	*1980*	*1990*	*2000*	*2005*
Africa	0.8	0.7	1.5	3.5	4.3	10.3	12.8
Asia	1.5	2.6	3.5	5.6	7.3	16.2	18.6
Latin America	1.6	3	6.3	13.5	16.9	20.3	28.7
Europe	2.2	10.3	17.3	22.1	25.2	40.9	44.2
Northern America	7.2	28.9	45.4	54.3	63.8	68.1	70.2

TABLE 2

The Share of Higher Education in Public Recurrent Expenditure (1970-2005)

(in percentage)

Year	*Africa*	*Asia*	*Latin America*	*Europe*	*Developing Countries*	*Developed Countries*
1970	16	14.2	18.7	12.4	16.1	16.1
1980	16.4	13.1	18.9	12.5	15.8	15.5
1990	158.7	12.2	16.5	11.5	14.5	14.1
2000	16.4	12.7	15.3	12.2	14.7	13.7
2005	18.1	14.2	16.8	13.2	15.1	14.8

TABLE 3

GDP Growth Rates in Percentage (1990-2007) for Selected Regions

Year	*World*	*North America*	*Latin America*	*Europe*	*Africa*	*Developed Countries*	*Developing Countries*
1990	2.683466	1.639975	0.479464	2.307115	2.570911	2.689526	3.441978
1995	2.752781	2.303234	1.395377	2.566137	3.71894	2.216275	5.198794
2000	4.413100	4.322875	3.729045	4.311465	4.766152	3.98711	5.622037
2005	3.653982	3.597486	4.509182	1.776177	4.945368	2.707056	6.308724
2006	3.923165	3.639322	4.551377	2.431612	5.792158	3.03565	6.345507
2007	3.589114	3.262212	4.229294	2.183564	5.542369	2.649371	6.086528

The objective of inclusive growth can only be possible if developing countries focused on higher education as possible for them. For this purpose international agencies have to come forward and help them.

BENEFITS OF HIGHER EDUCATION

Monetary Benefits

In micro-economic terms human capital theory relies on the implicit understanding that through education the individual acquires competence and skills whose essential characteristic is the ability to be transferable and negotiable on the job market and which also have a transactional value and a direct bearing on individuals' average income throughout his live. The average earning of individuals are closely related to their educational attainment. In particular, those with a bachelor's degree earn substantially more than even those with some college education. Relative to those with a bachelor's degree, a post-graduate degree provides nearly as large a boost in earnings. The higher salaries that educated entrants are able to command on the job market represent both the interest on the capital they have invested in education and the fact that they have become more productive by having invested, regardless of the type of education they have received. However, rapid changes in employment conditions, the future macroeconomic environment, technical innovation and skills obsolescence are amongst the variables that throw into question the full validity of the human capital model applied to the individual.

To compare the return on investment offered by a university education with other investments, it is useful to compute the "internal rate of return". This is the discount rate that equalizes the present value of benefits and costs. The concept of internal rate of return is equivalent to what financial economists refer to as the 'yield to maturity' on a financial asset. Returns calculated in this way can be compared across all kinds of loans or bond purchases, regardless of the time pattern of interest and principal payments. Based on a cost-benefit analysis over a person's working life, the expected net return from an individual's payment of tution and fees and foregone income while obtaining a bachelor's degree, in most studies is estimated to be between 10 and 13 per cent. Such estimates suggests, that financial returns from higher education compare favorably with real returns on most financial assets and this kind of investment is as good as or better than most investments a family could make for its children. A reverse corollary of this understanding might be, that when employers are prepared to hire less qualified people, rates of participation in formal education decrease accordingly as the possibility of earning an immediate salary increases the opportunity cost of staying longer in formal education.

The differential in earning based on educational attainment has increased over time. Analysis confirms that the incomes of university graduates, especially those with advanced degrees, have been rising faster than the income of those with no university education. This rising differential constitutes the principal evidence for the emerging "Knowledge economy".

Non-Monetary Benefits

In addition to higher earning opportunities, individuals with higher education also experience some non-monetary benefits. University education makes individuals more entrepreneurial and adaptable through increased flexibility in the face of change and difficulties, so besides increased income it also provides a good protection against unemployment; Internationai statistics presented in the work of Howe (1994) reveals a clear relationship between the education level and the employment prospect. The highest employment rate is observed among persons with tertiary education, followed by persons with secondary education. The highest unemployment rate is recorded for persons with basic education or less. Wang (2003), in an extensive study of the impact of universities on surrounding cities, finds that proximity to institutions of higher learning even induce greater rates of job growth.

Education provides a variety of benefits to students including enhanced social skills, greater awareness of human achievement, and an appreciation for cultural diversity. Increasing education is associated with better working conditions, lower disability rates, longer job tenure, more on the job training opportunities, and more promotion opportunities. The value of these non-monetary benefits adds to the economic return to education.

Social Benefits

Human capital theory proponents cite two types of the benefits to society from investments in higher education: monetary and non-monetary. Societal monetary benefits of a workforce with greater educational attainment and skill can be traced to the enhanced worker productivity associated with greater educational attainment. These productivity gains translate into higher output and incomes for the economy.

Romer (1998) provides an explanation of substitution effects. As the knowledge economy increases in importance, the role of human capital may outstrip physical capital and labour in determining aggregates growth rates across countries. Using this argument, the acquisition of knowledge capital creates "endogenous" growth—growth that feeds on itself—and economic returns that accelerate. This argument is widely discussed among economists as one of the most important ways in which bigger accumulation of highly educated workforce and higher education institutions impact regions economy through innovation driven endogenous growth. University boosters often cite links between scientific breakthroughs from university research and subsequent product development by high-tech firms. Jorgensen (2000) estimates that a considerable portion of the late 1990s growth was directly attributable to roles played by research innovation at institutions of higher education and the greater absorptive capacity of a labour force with greater proportions of college graduates. However, some economists find such benefits fleeting, because products are usually developed elsewhere. Even though investments in research at a number of institutions may increase the inventive activity of Research and Development (R & D) laboratories located within the same metropolitan region, any resulting new products or processes will frequently be developed in other locations, where labour force is cheaper.

One more source of monetary social benefits that has to be mentioned is that to the extent that university graduates earn and spend more than those without a degree, the government collects more tax revenue from university graduates, which represents a social good. The taxes paid by university graduates repay the public cost of their education several times over.

In addition to monetary benefits, a long list of non-monetary societal benefits from enhanced educational attainment in regions with greater shares of educated workers, especially highly educated workers have been documented. Wolf and Haveman (2002) have suggested the following list of non-monetary societal benefits:

- Educational attainment levels positively affect non-wage labour market remuneration, such as fringe benefits, and the quality of working conditions.
- Consumer choices are more rational and efficient.
- Job searches are more extensive among the more highly educated, resulting in, a better match between the individual and the company, which enhances efficiency.
- Savings rate is higher among the more highly educated.
- Research and development activities are more common and numerous in regions with higher educational attainment.
- Education is inversely related to reliance on public assistance. Investing in education reduces the necessity to invest in other public income transfer programs. Twenty-four per cent of individuals without a high school diploma have at some time participated in a public assistance programme, compared with 4.6 per cent of those with a bachelor's degree (Lee, 2003).
- Less criminal behavior and lower incarceration rates occur among the more highly educated.
- Charity contribution increase with educational attainment.

- Social cohesion is higher among the more highly educated, as reflected in higher voting rates. Informed and involved voters are the foundation of a democratic society, and education helps develop skills for a democracy. Milton Friedman, a conservative economist, believed that public support for the laissez-faire approach to economic market mechanisms could be achieved by increasing knowledge; more educated individuals are less influenced by populist rhetoric and make more rational, informed decisions in voting behavior.
- Perhaps most important are the integrational effects that accrue to investments in higher education. The educational attainment and cognitive development of children are positively affected by the educational attainment of parents (first generation effects). The quantitative importance of these effects is very difficult to estimate precisely since costs to society incurred today to create opportunities for individuals to acquire university degrees must be compared to benefits realizable two, three or four generations in the future.

The health of individuals, their spouses, and their children are positively related to educational attainment. Desired family size is more commonly attained among those with higher educational attainment.

As difficult as the social monetary benefits are to quantify, the implicit value of non-monetary benefits are even less conducive to measurement. However, the non-monetary contributions that more educated individuals bring to society, coupled with the reduction in social costs that they incur over their lifetimes, suggests that the non-monetary benefits represents considerable return on social investments made to support higher education. From what is said above, we can conclude that we all benefit from the monetary and non-monetary public effects of higher education and lack of university-educated individuals could represents a huge cost to our society.

Now, when authors have highlighted the benefits of university education, it is just the right time to make an overview of empirical studies, providing us with the evidence from cross-country analyses whether higher education promotes economic growth at macroeconomic level or not. Although this may appear to be obvious as there is the common belief of the importance of universities as an engine of growth, deeper examination has proved to be an uneasy task for economists. Given that human capital is individually productive, existing models of economic growth predict that education should enhance growth (e.g., Barro and Sala-I-Martin, 2004). The growth accounting literature devotes enormous effort to confirming this reduction using aggregates data, but so far, most studies only find weak and elusive connections between education and economic growth. Using the Solow (1956) growth model, Mankiw, Romer and Weil (1992) argue that a large part of cross-country differences in steady state income is explained by a certain measure of human capital. Using growth accounting techniques, King and Smith (1998) estimated that only 1.9 per cent of annual economic growth rates from 1940 to 1980 were non-education-related. Pencavel (1991) estimates that from 1913 to 1950 only 1.3 per cent of total growth was directly attributable to higher education, but higher education accounted for 14.6 per cent of the growth from 1973 to 1984.

Economic growth may have taken place because of rising education in certain countries such as Germany, Britain or France, but until a clear methodology can demonstrate that historical events have persistently followed the logic that states that education precedes any economic development, it is equally plausible to suggest that nations which have experienced fast economic growth and increased wealth have consequently been able to invest more in education. Empirical evidence from cross-country studies allows us to draw an inference that the exact nature of the causal link between the two—education and economic growth—remains undetermined. With the rapid introduction and development of new techniques and technologies, it is reasonable to think that more investment in education in industrialized countries will help boost future rates of economic growth. However, whether this will generate for individuals and society returns on the scale of the two-digit figures that are currently being advanced to justify expansion remains to be seen. In purely economic terms, this may turn out to be speculative bubble.

Reference

Barro, R. and Lee, J.H., Sources of Economic Growth, Carnegic Rochester Conference Series on Public Policy, No. 40, 1994.

Benhabib, J. and Spiegel M., The Role of Human Capital in Economic Development: Evidence from Aggregate Cross-country Data, *Journal of Monetary Economics*, No. 34, 1994.

Mankiw, N.G., Romer, D. and Weil, D.N., A Contribution to the Empirics of Economic Growth, *Quarterly Journal of Economics*, No. 107, 1992.

Pencavel, J., Higher Education Productivity and Earning: A Review, *Journal of Economic Education*, Vol. 22, No. 4, 1991.

Romer, P.M., Human capital and growth: Theory and evidence, NBER Working Papers No. 3173, 1989.

Human Capital and Growth Theories: A Case of Augmented Solow Model in the Context of Major States of India

ARVIND AWASTHI

I. INTRODUCTION

Economists have long recognised education or human capital as an important source of economic growth. As early as in 1957, Robert Solow clearly showed that of all the three sources of economic growth viz. stock of capital, amount of labour, and the residual, it was the residual which contributed most in the growth of per capita income. Solow called the residual as technical progress and mentioned specifically that, "improvements in the education of labour force" is one of the residual factors, which contributed to the growth of per capita income. Subsequently, efforts were made to empirically estimate the contribution of education in economic growth. In one of the important studies Edward Denison (1985) found that education contributed around 30 per cent in the growth of output per worker in the non-residential business sector of the U.S. economy during 1929 to 1982.

The significant contribution of education in economic growth shifted focus on the issue whether education should continue to be a part of residual in economic growth or should it be assigned a key role in theory of economic growth. An important development in this direction was the works of Romer (1986) and Lucas (1988) since both of them cited non-applicability of Solow's model in exhibiting cross-country convergence of per capita income which is regarded as a natural inference of Solow's theory (1956) of economic growth. Moreover, Romer (1987) observed that the value of the share of capital as estimated through 'growth regression approach' was comparatively high than its value usually considered by economists for 'growth accounting' purposes, which enabled him to suggest about the positive externalities playing role in enhancing the impact of physical capital on output per worker. Therefore, in order to put right the extent of impact of physical capital on output per worker both Romer (1986) and Lucas (1988) assigned an important role to education or human capital in the growth theory. According to them if capital is considered in a broader sense to include both physical and human then instead of diminishing return to a factor there are constant returns to a capital. They, therefore, suggested models of the type Y = AK, where Y is output, K is capital (both physical and human) and A is constant. It also follows from their approach that if all factors are considered then there are increasing returns to scale.

Thus the introduction of human capital as an explicit variable (rather than being a part of residual) enabled both Romer and Lucas to effectively substantiate the empirical finding about the lack of unconditional convergence in per capita income among different countries of the world. However, the share of capital (both physical and human) which they theoretically considered as unity did not match with its estimated value which lies between 0.4 to 0.6. This led Mankiw, Romer and Weil (1992) to the amend Solow model (1956) by assuming diminishing returns to a factor and by considering human capital as a separate independent variable in the production function of the type given by :

$$Y(t) = K(t)^{a} H(t)^{b} \{A(t) L(t)\}^{1-a-b}$$

where, Y, K, H, L and A are output, physical capital, human capital, amount of labour and technical change respectively.

Mankiw, Romer and Weil (1992) by explicitly considering the human capital as an independent variable were able to show that the share of each factor contributes about one-third to economic growth and variations in these variables across countries should be controlled for conditional convergence hypothesis to become valid.

Their empirical finding clearly reflect a consistency in the estimate regarding share of physical capital as considered in the 'growth accounting' approach and as measured by the 'growth regression' approach. However, an important point to note is that their estimate regarding share of capital was based on a proxy variable for human capital rather than investment in human capital as outlined in their theoretical model. The use of proxy variable is correct if economies are in their steady state but if economies are out-of-steady-state then use of proxy variable should be avoided because in such cases it may not deliver the desired results.

It is true that investment in education is difficult to measure accurately but there are indirect ways of estimating it. One such way which we have used in the paper and which has been employed usually in empirical estimation is that if 'u' is the time spent in working then '1-u' is the time spent in acquiring skills, which a person could utilize in generating additional return in the future. Thus the additional returns as a percentage of total could be used to represent fraction of investment to education for acquiring skills. Using this method Bosworth and Collins (2008) estimated for India that the contribution of education in output per worker is about 12 per cent for the period 1978 to 2004. Thus contribution of education in output per worker is quite moderate in the Indian context which seems to be on account of substantial variation of investment in education among different Indian States. This possibility assumes significance in the light of the fact that there are reasonable differences in average years of schooling among major states of India. (Refer Table 1).

TABLE I

Average Years of Schooling (AYOS) of Total Workforce (Rural + Urban) in Major States of India

(in Years)

States	*1993-94*	*2004-05*
Andhra Pradesh	6.13	7.54
Gujarat	8.19	8.93
Haryana	8.90	9.70
Karnataka	7.53	8.45
Kerala	11.30	11.77
Maharashtra	7.98	9.50
Punjab	9.66	10.00
Tamil Nadu	8.08	9.40
W. Bengal	9.39	10.10
Bihar	2.02	2.68
M.P.	2.44	3.29
U.P.	2.39	3.06
Rajasthan	2.24	3.38
Orissa	2.24	3.08

Source: Derived from Reports on Employment-Unemployment in India for Years 1993-94 and 2004-05, MOSPI, NSSO, Government of India.

Our observation therefore, suggests that rate of investment in education could be an important variable for explaining differences in output per worker across major states of India and therefore, variation in it should be controlled for allowing states to exhibit conditional convergence. This is indeed relevant because there is hardly any study in the recent past which favours convergence hypothesis in the Indian context. Most of the studies (Rao, Shand and Kalirajan, 1999, Dasgupta *et. al.*, 2000, Kurian, 2000, Jeffery D. Sachs, 2001) attempted to test unconditional convergence in output per worker across Indian states but did not find any tendency of convergence. It is therefore an opportune time to look into the aspect that if education is assigned a key role in economic growth by considering it as one of the separate independent variables as suggested in the augmented Solow model which predicts conditional convergence then does it empirically hold good in the Indian context or not?

II. OBJECTIVE, SCOPE AND METHODOLOGY

As is evident from our preceding discussion that the inclusion of human capital in growth models has resulted in two distinct categories of economic growth theories—one which does not favour the 'convergence hypothesis' and the other supports the convergence phenomenon but of a modified form which is dubbed by economists as 'conditional convergence'. Since the focus of the paper is to assess the role of human capital in growth models we have therefore considered the 'Augmented Solow Model' and accordingly the main objective of the paper is to examine 'whether major states of India exhibit conditional convergence in output per worker or not'. Moreover, if the phenomenon of conditional convergence is found to be correct then 'speed of convergence' is also estimated and the impact of human capital in causing change in output per worker across states is also examined.

The scope of the paper is confined to 14 major states of India, viz. Andhra Pradesh, Bihar, Gujarat, Haryana, Karnataka, Kerala, Maharashtra, Madhya Pradesh, Orissa, Punjab, Rajasthan, Tamil Nadu, Uttar Pradesh and West Bengal. It is in place to mention that Jharkhand is included in Bihar, Chhattisgarh in Madhya Pradesh and Uttaranchal in Uttar Pradesh. The period of study is from 1993-94 to 2004-05 for which consistent data is available for different variables considered in the paper. The period 1993-94 to 2004-05 is no doubt short and is also regarded as a transitional phase because the process of liberalisation and globalization picked up during this period, therefore, different state economies are considered out-of-steady-state. Accordingly the regression equation as outlined in the augmented Solow model is estimated with investment in human capital as one of the explicit independent variable as against a proxy variable used in the augmented Solow model. The type of regression equation estimated is as follows :

$$\ln Y_t - l_n Y_0 = (1-e^{-\lambda t})\frac{\alpha}{1-\alpha-\beta}\ln_{Sk} + (1-e^{-\lambda t})\frac{\beta}{1-\alpha-\beta}\ln_{Sh} - (1-e^{-\lambda t})\frac{\alpha+\beta}{1-\alpha-\beta}$$

$$\ln(n+g+\delta) - (1-e^{-\lambda t})\ln Y_0$$

where, l_n stands for natural log while Y_t and Y_0 refers to output per worker in the final year 2004-05 and initial year 1993-94 respectively. Further $s_{K,}$ s_h represent fraction of income invested in physical and human capital while n, g and d are respectively population growth rate, labour augmenting technical change that grows exogenously and depreciation rate. Both g and d are assumed to remain constant for different states, which could be an important limitation of the analysis. Moreover, a, b are respectively output elasticity with respect to physical and human capital while l indicates the speed of convergence.

It is in place to mention that investment in education is determined indirectly by assuming a constant annual return of 7 per cent for each additional year of schooling for each state, i.e. if a year time is not spend in working, instead is used for acquiring skills than 7 per cent return is sacrificed which is considered as investment rate in education. Therefore, if 'S' represents average years of schooling (i.e. time spend in acquiring skills) then investment in education a variable representing human capital (H) is given by :

$$H = (1.07)^S$$

In this paper we have considered average annual change in investment rate in education during the period 1993-94 to 2004-05. It may also be mentioned that 7 per cent constant rate of return is not arbitrary but is used by many other economists (Bosworth and Collins, 2004) for countries like India and China. Normally estimates for return on each additional year of schooling across world varies between 7 per cent to 12 per cent (Bosworth and Collins, 2004).

Another adjustment that we have made in this paper is regarding investment in physical capital because of lack of updated state-wise data for this variable. For investment in physical capital we have used the state-wise data pertaining to credit-deposit ratio in utilization terms. Therefore, investment rate regarding physical capital during the period 1993-94 to 2004-05 is the average annual change in state-wise credit-deposit ratio which is a fairly good indicator representing private investment since it is the most important component of physical capital for most of the states of India during the phase of liberalization (1993-94 to 2004-05) which we have considered in the analysis.

III. ANALYSIS

The inclusion of human capital in the Solow's theory of economic growth could only be justified if conditional convergence could empirically be demonstrated for major states of India. In order to examine conditional convergence across 14 major states of India we have estimated the regression equation whose details are given in Table 2.

It is evident from the table that the coefficient associated with output per worker for the initial year of study, i.e. 1993-94 has a positive sign indicating absence of conditional convergence across 14 major states of India. However, the value of this coefficient is not only statistically insignificant but is also too low necessitating a thorough scrutiny of the inter-relationship of different variables considered in the analysis for each of the 14 major states of India. If the relationship among variables for a state or two do not exhibit consistency then such state or states must be dropped from the analysis and regression equation for the remaining states must be re-estimated so that 'convergence hypothesis' could be accepted or rejected on a more firm basis.

Our scrutiny of the relationship among different variables for each state has revealed definite inconsistency between economic and social variables for the state of Kerala. This is considered as one of the best state in terms of human development index especially education (refer Table 1) but in

TABLE 2

Test for Conditional Convergence Across Major States of India

CONSTANT Term and Explanatory Variables	*Dependant variable: Log Difference GSDP/Worker 1993-94 and 2004-05*				
	Values of the Constant term and Coefficients Associated with explanatory variables				
	All 14 major states	*13 major States (Kerala excluded)*		*12 major States excluding Kerala and West Benga*	
		with human capital	*without human capital*	*without human capital*	*without human capital*
Constant	1.0542	1.5019	-1.20	1.8761	-1.06
	(1.05)	(1.24)	(-0.97)	(2.19)	(-0.89)
ln (Year 1993-94)	0.0109	-0.0029	0.06	-0.0057	0.07
	(0.14)	(-0.03)	(0.56)	(-0.098)	(0.60)
ln (n+g+d)	-0.1442	-0.0916	-0.27	-0.0324	-0.23
	(-1.59)	(-0.77)	(-1.79)	(-0.38)	(-1.56)
ln (I/GSDP)	0.0370	0.0366	0.014	0.0431*	0.02
	(1.82)	(1.75)	(0.51)	(2.92)	(0.67)
ln (H)	0.2364*	0.2590*	–	0.2788*	–
	(3.26)	(3.20)		(4.89)	
R^2 (%)	69.28	69.24	29.82	83.99	29.29
(Adjusted) R^2 (%)	55.63	53.86	6.42	74.84	2.77
F-Ratio	5.07	4.50	1.27	9.18	1.10
1 (%) not applicable	0.03	not applicable	0.052	not applicable	

Note: Figures in parentheses indicate t-values.

terms of economic growth it lags behind many other states. This peculiar paradox is often termed as Kerala model of development by experts. The paradox reflected in the Kerala model of development is on account of the fact that for a long time government accorded high priority to a strong social welfare system by undertaking development responsibility through public investment rather than encouraging private investment. As a consequence economic growth suffered adversely and unemployment rate remained high. Thus high unemployment rate coupled with high literacy rate in the state induced people to migrate to other states and especially to other countries for lucrative job opportunities. Thus state of Kerala does not fit well in our scheme of analysis as we have considered change in gross state domestic product per worker (excluding remittances) on one hand and investment in human capital on the other hand as one of the explanatory variable. Therefore, Kerala is dropped from the initial list of 14 states and regression equation is again estimated for the 13 major states of India.

The details of the estimated regression equation are given in Table 2. It is now evident that the coefficient associated with the output per worker for the initial year 1993-94 has a negative sign, which is a pre-requisite for the convergence hypothesis to hold good. It is also evident from the estimated equation that the coefficient associated with investment in human capital is the only coefficient which is statistically significant. This clearly reflects that during the period 1993-94 to 2004-05 differences in output per worker across states can be effectively explained by variations in the variable representing human capital. Therefore, if we drop human capital from the regression equation then conditional convergence among 13 major Indian states ceases to exist (refer Table 2). Even if we drop West Bengal on the ground it is quite similar to Kerala and consider only 12 states, conditional convergence across states is only possible when human capital is considered otherwise if we ignore it phenomenon of conditional convergence vanishes (refer Table 2).

Therefore, those states which have a lower investment rate in human capital will also have a lower level of output per worker as compared to other states where investment in human capital is high. Since investment in human capital depends on time devoted in acquiring skills or to say on average years of schooling, therefore as a matter of policy implication if average years of schooling in five states namely: Uttar Pradesh, Madhya Pradesh, Bihar, Rajasthan and Orissa is not raised significantly in the near future through sustained efforts of the government then inequalities in economic growth between two categories of major states (U.P., M.P., Bihar, Rajasthan, Orissa on one hand and remaining major states on the other hand) will rise considerably. Imposition of Secondary and Higher Education (SHE) cess is a novel beginning but a substantial part of it must be spent in the aforementioned five states so as to bring average years of schooling in these states at least at par with other states of the country.

Another important finding of our analysis is based on the value of l, which indicates the speed of convergence. The value of l for 13 major states is 0.03 per cent, i.e. economies of 13 different states are converging to their steady state at a rate of 0.03 per cent per annum. This is certainly low as compared to the speed of convergence for economies of countries with similar cultures and policies where the value of l is about 2 per cent per annum. One possible reason for it is that the time period which we have considered is small because of paucity of consistent and systematic data and the other is that certain states accorded high priority to a strong social welfare system by undertaking development responsibility through public investment rather than encouraging private investment. This was true for the state of Kerala and is also correct for the state of West Bengal. If we drop West Bengal too from our analysis then speed of convergence improves to 0.05 per cent per annum (refer Table 2). Moreover, the coefficient associated with physical capital which in our case in fact symbolises private investment also becomes statistically significant (refer Table 2). This reflects some degree of complementarity between private investment and average years of schooling in enhancing speed of convergence and effectively explain the fact that as economies move towards their steady state those states, which have higher private investment and higher human capital, will have output per worker far above the other states lagging in both. But those having better average years of schooling could improve their output per worker by encouraging private investment. Thus as a matter of policy implication states with good human capital index must encourage private investment too for enhancing economic growth while states lagging in both should concentrate on improving average years of schooling through sustained efforts of government on the one hand and encouraging private investment on the other.

It may further be suggested that the observed complementarity between private investment and average years of schooling could be a panacea for the state of Kerala to harmonise the relationship between economic growth and human capital index. A cursorily look on these two variables for the state of Kerala immediately reveal absence of any significant relationship between the two, which is valid only as long as private investment is not pushed in the state. Lack of sufficient private investment in Kerala coupled with the best index of human capital among Indian states has induced brain drain to other countries of the world, thus depriving the state of the benefits of its skilled manpower. Therefore, efforts should be to employ its skilled manpower by encouraging private investment and promoting economic growth rather than allowing the workers to go abroad and make the state rich by way of remittances. Considering the boom prevailing in the Information Technology (Information Technology) and Information Technology enabled services (ITES), Kerala can emulate the path of Karnataka, which has accelerated its economic growth through exports of software services and which at present contributes about 90 per cent of share in the India's net of exports of various non-factor services on the invisible account. West Bengal too having a fairly good level of human capital index in terms of average years of schooling could follow the Karnataka's way for improving its economic growth.

IV. CONCLUSIONS AND POLICY IMPLICATIONS

The following conclusions and policy implications have emerged from our analysis :

(a) An important inference of our analysis is that difference in human capital must be controlled across states for conditional convergence to hold true, since human capital is the only significant variable which explains differences in output per worker across Indian states. Thus states whose workers have devoted less time in acquiring skills their output per worker is significantly lower than output per worker of other states whose workers have devoted more time in acquiring skills. In the states namely—Uttar Pradesh, Madhya Pradesh, Bihar, Rajasthan and Orissa average years of schooling of workers is about 2.72 years while in the remaining states it is about 8.70 years during the period 1993-94 to 2004-05. Thus as a matter of policy implication if average years of schooling in Uttar Pradesh, Madhya Pradesh, Bihar, Rajasthan and Orissa is not raised significantly in the near future through sustained and sincere efforts of the government then inequalities in economic growth between the two categories of states (U.P., M.P., Bihar, Rajasthan and Orissa on one hand and remaining states on the other) will rise considerably. Imposition of secondary and higher education (SHE) cess is a novel beginning but a substantial part of it must be spent in the aforementioned five states so as to bring average years of schooling in these states at least at par with other states of the country.

(b) Another important inference of our analysis is that the speed of convergence (1) is 0.03 per cent which is quite low as compared to its value of 2 per cent normally estimated for economies of countries with similar cultures and policies. One possible reason is that the time-period which we have considered is small because of paucity of consistent and systematic data for a longer period and the other is that certain states have a good track record of human capital in terms of average years of schooling but in these states government accorded high priority to strong social welfare system by undertaking development responsibility through public investment rather than recognizing the complementarity between high average years of schooling and high private investment. Therefore, as a matter of policy implication for states like Kerala and West Bengal, has good human capital index is to encourage private investment for enhancing economic growth while states lagging in both should concentrate in improving average years of schooling, through sustained efforts of government on one hand and encouraging private investment on the other.

(c) Considering the complementarity between human capital index and private investment, the state of Kerala especially, with best in terms of human capital index in the country could improve its economic growth by attracting private investment in the field of information technology and information technology enabled services since both these areas have rich growth potential in regions where skilled manpower is available. Our suggestion is based on the experience of Karnataka which has enhanced its economic growth through the export of software services and which at present contribute about 90 per cent of share in the India's net of exports of various non-factor services in the invisible account of balance of payments. Another state namely, West Bengal which have a fairly good level of human capital index in terms of average years of schooling could also follow the Karnataka's way for improving its economic growth.

References

Bosworth, Barry and Susan M. Collins, 'The Empirics of Growth: An Update', Brookings Papers on Economic Activity, No. 2, 2004.

——, 'Accounting for Growth: Comparing China and India', *Journal of Economic Perspectives*, Vol. 22, No. 1, Winter 2008.

Dasgupta, D. *et. al.*, 'Growth and Inter-State Disparities in India', *EPW*, Vol. XXXV, No. 27, July 1, 2000.

Denison, Edward, 'Trends in American Economic Growth', 1929-82, Washington D.C., The Brookings Institution, 1985.

Employment and Unemployment in India, 1993-94, NSS 50th Round and 2004-05, NSS 61st Round, MOSPI, New Delhi.

Kurian, N.J., 'Widening Regional Disparities in India—Some Indicators', *EPW*, Vol. XXXV, No. 7, Feb. 12-18, 2000.

Lucas, Robert E., 'On the Mechanics of Economic Development', *Journal of Monetary Economics*, 22:1, June 1988.

Mankiw, G.N., Romer David and David N. Weil, 'A Contribution to Empirics of Economic Growth', 107, May 1992.

Pack Howard, 'Endogenous Growth Theory: Intellectual Appeal and Empirical Shortcomings', *Journal of Economic Perspectives,* Vol. 8, No. 1, Winter 1994.

Rao, M.G., R.T. Shand and K.P. Kalirajan, 'Convergence of Incomes Across Indian States—A Divergent View', *EPW,* Vol. XXXIV, No. 13, March 27, 1999.

Report on Trend and Progress of Banking in India, 2003-04, R.B.I., Mumbai.

Romer, Paul. M, 'Increasing Returns and Long-run Growth', *Journal of Political Economy,* October 1986, 94:5.

——, 'Crazy Explanations for Productivity Slowdown', NBER Macroeconomics Annual, Cambridge MIT Press 1987.

——, 'The Origins of Endogenous Growth', *Journal of Economic Perspectives,* Vol. 8, No. 1, Winter 1994.

Solow, Robert M., 'A Contribution to the Theory of Economic Growth', *Quarterly Journal of Economics,* LXX (1956).

——, Technical Change and the Aggregate Production Function', *The Review of Economics and Statistics,* Vol. 39, Aug 1957.

Sachs Jeffrey D., N. Bajpai, A. Ramiah, 'Understanding Regional Economic Growth in India', Asian Economic Panel Meeting, October 22-26, 2001, New Delhi.

State-wise Gross State Domestic Product, 1993-94 to 2004-05, MOSPI, C.S.O., New Delhi.

Statistical Statements Relating to Banks in India, Different Issues, RBI, Mumbai.

Education and Economic Growth: Some Leading Aspects

Bishwa Nath Singh and Mukul Kumar Singh

Education, the means to translate 'Demographic Dividend' into 'Developmental Dividend' is the most important and vital element for prosperity of a nation and its sustainable growth and development in future. Education in general and higher education in particular, which ensures availability of manpower of right quantity and quality for all activities including health and education has to be the equalizer in an otherwise efficiency driven market economy (Reddy, K.C. 2006). Its externalities including the dynamic externalities of higher education are indeed immense and they have profound positive effects on economic growth (Tilak, 2005). Hence, this paper tries to analyse some vital links between education and economic growth.

IDEAS BEHIND EDUCATION AND ECONOMIC GROWTH

The concept of education as 'engine of economic growth' is based on the new theory of economics that scientific creativity, skill and other qualitative factors of the labour force or the manpower will contribute to the economic development no less than reproducible physical capital and labourforce. These factors, which had been paid little attention in the past are now called 'human abilities' and the expenditure on the creation and promotion of human abilities is an investment for future. E.J. Hawkins has very aptly remarked, "production functions are in reality imposed by the laws of humanity and not of physics." Marshall (1938) emphasised the importance of education as a national investment and in his views, the most valuable of all capital is the 'investment in human beings.' Sen's capability notion has also much to do with health, education and nutrition. Investment in these areas that raises human capability, yields a return, as Paul Streeten (1981) argues, no less than the return from physical capital. Here, it is worth-mentioning that not only the studies in west has ascertained the role of education in economic development, but it has been established by the economic miracles in Asea too, visible not only in the rapid growth of Japan or China but also in the development of East Asean Tigers, namely South Korea, Taiwan, Hong Kong and Singapore as well as some newely emerging East-Asean economies such as Malayasia, Thailand, Indonesia, Vietnam and Philippines, who have proved that how an useful role can be played by education and skill formation even though most of these countries have paucity of natural resources. So far as the case of Indian economy is concerned, the modern brilliant thinking transcends, beyond revolutions (green revolution or white revolution or mechnical revolution) and looks aspirantly at 'Knowledge Society'. Since it is powered by 'innovative capacity' (Kalam, APJ, 2006).

Therefore, an approach to investment in education must be based on an understanding that the general development of human abilities which is essential to the economic development in future, depends upon both quantitative and qualitative development in education.

APPROACHES TO INVESTMENT IN EDUCATION

The socio-economic thinkers have viewed investment in

education from different angles. Some of them have realised it as social investment whereas others as economic one and they have emphasized their priorities accordingly. However, in modern era, the economic consideration has become more predominant with the view that education affects efficiency and productivity of the entire system and progress or prosperity of a nation is basically the result of human efforts. The builders of economies are elites of various kinds who organise and lead the march towards progress. The effectiveness of the elites as prime movers depends not only on their own development but on the capabilities of those whom they lead as. Thus in a sense, the real wealth of a country and its potential economic development stem from the power to develop and effectively utilize the innate capacities of people. The economists like Solow, Schultz, Denison and Todaro have calculated the benefits of investment in education either in terms of input-output analysis or the relationships between expenditures on education and income or physical capital formation. According to Todaro education contributes to economic growth in the developed and developing economies in the following ways:

(i) It helps in creating a more productive labour force and endowing it with increased knowledge and skills
(ii) It helps in providing wide spread employment and income-earning opportunities for teachers, school and construction workers, text book and paper printers, school uniform manufacturers, etc.
(iii) It helps in creating a class of educated leaders to fill vacancies left by departing expatriates or otherwise vacant positions in government services, public corporations, private businesses, and
(iv) It helps in providing basic skills and encourages modern attitudes in the diverse segments of the population (Todaro, Michael, P., 2003).

In order to calculate the benefits of education, economists have developed some approaches to investment in education also such as, (i) the simple correlation approach, (ii) the direct returns to education approach, (iii) the residual approach, and (iv) the relationships between expenditure on education and income or physical capital formation approach, etc.

The simple correlation approach or inter-country correlations of school enrolment ratios and gross national product approach consists of correlating some overall index of educational acivity with some index of the level of economic activity. The economists likes vennilson, Edding and Elvin have done major work in this field and have come to the conclusion that the poor economies are compelled to have less investment on education and consequently lower level of gainful employment and output. In their own words, ... a country with a low Gross National product percapita cannot afford to have most of its young people between 15 to 19 in full time education and thus withheld from gainful employment. On the other hand, a highly industrialised country with a high 'Gross National Product' per capita can hardly afford to break-off education as current consumption and the margin of income available to satisfy this demand is large....."

Generally speaking, the income level as expressed by GNP percapita seeems to set a lower limit of educational effort. But above that level, there is a wide margin for choice, whether it be determined by private consumer preferences or by political decision to invest heavily in education in order to accelerate economic development.

The another approach, i.e., the direct returns to education approach, an obvious and simple way of studying the economic consequences of education is by contrasting the life time earnings of people who have had 'more' education with the life time earnings of the people who have had less education. The criteria for this type of calculation is based either on the personal profit orientation or the national productivity orientation.

The personal profit orientation consists in looking at differences in the net earnings of people with varying amounts of education as evidences of the amount of personal financial gain that can be associated with the attainment of a given level of education; whereas the 'national productivity orientation' consists in looking at education-related earnings differentials as partial evidence of the effects of education on the production or output of the country, and is based on the premise that in a market economy, differences in earnings reflect differences in productivity depending upon the quality of the manpower. This orientation is relevent to the question of whether society as a whole investing the right share of its resources in education or not?

There are several difficulties with these measures on returns from education, growing out of explicit or implicit assumptions, and earnings at different educational or age levels are not solely the result of formal education, but reflect on-the-job training, experience, differences in natural ability, family income, social status and other factors.

However, despite the debate between qualificaiton and limitations of these estimates, the results obtained from several developed countries like U.S. and other do offer rather consistent support for the nation that education, on the average, has paid significant financial as well as non-financial reward and therefore, this approach also leads to the conclusion that expenditure on education and especially the quality education must be regarded as a good investment for future.

As regards the residual approach, in general terms, it consists of taking the total increase in economic output in a country over a given period of time, identifying as much of the total increase as possible with measurable inputs (capital and labour being the two measurable inputs usually chosen) and then saying that the residual is attributable to the unspecified inputs such as education and advances in knowledge, which are usually regarded as the most important of the unspecified inputs.

In the actual implementation of the residual approach a number of alternative techniques can be adopted. First, it is possible to proceed by calculating an input series for the labour input (based for instance, on hours worked), a separates constant price, input series for the capital input and then combining these two input series into an overall arithmatic index of inputs (using the relative shares of labour and capital in the total GNP as weight). Next, the rate of increase in this aggregate input series is compared with the rate of increase in aggregate output series (also expresses in constant prices) and by simply substracting it is possible to obtain a measure of the contribution of the third factor.

Robert M. Solow concentrated on determining this increase in Gross National Product due to increased use of capital with the remainder 'attributable to technical change'. Under the assumptions of a linear homogenous production function and a neutral technical change which does not affect substitution between capital and labour, Solow thus computed a 'residual' equal to 87.5 per cent of increase in output per man hour in the united states between 1901 to 1949 (Solow, Robert M.) and despite several difficulties in this method of calculation it still holds good for studies regarding the impact of educaton and skill formation on the level of output and skill formation on the level of output and economic development.

The last but not the least approach in the series is the relationship between expenditure on education and income or physical capital formation. Theodore W. Schultz has analysed this relationship in the U.S. for 1900k to 1956 and has shown that "the resources allocated to educaiton rose about three and a half times (i) relative to consumer income in dollar, and (ii) relative to gross formation of capital in dollars ....." (Schultz, T.W).

In other words, the 'income elasticity' of the demand for education was about 3.5 over the period and alternatively, education was considered as 3.5 times more attractive than investment in physical capital. Schultz has also tried to measure the total stock of 'educational capital' at different points in time (Schultz, T.W.). By adding together the possible earned income forgone by those enrolled in schools, colleges and universities (that is the 'opportunity cost' of education) and the expenditure for formal education of all types (with allowance for depreciation) he calculated a figure for the total annual investment in education in U.S. by decades from 1900 to 1956. The total stock of 'educational capital' in the labour force of U.S. rose from $ 63 billion in 1900 to $ 180 billion in 1930 and $ 353 billion in 1957 at 1956 constant prices. It is also significant that the ratio of stock of 'educational capital' to the stock of reproducible non-human wealth (physical capital) rose from 22 per cent in 1900 to 42 per cent in 1957.

Thus it appears that a large nubmer of econonists have realised expenditure on education as economic investment since it promotes economic development though some others contend that it is a social investment and it should be determined residually. However, Charles A. Myers and Fredrick Harbison point out that "it is virtually impossible to calculate the rate of financial return on an educational project in the same manner as on a dam or factory because of difficulty of ascertaining how much is really consumption and how much represents investment". (Myers and Harbison)

But it must be realised that economic development of a country does not merely consist in building dams and factories and so forth. The progress or development is basically the result of human efforts. It takes human agents to exploit natural resources, to build dams and factories, to mobilise capital and to carry on business. The builders of economies as mentioned above are elits of various kinds who organise and lead the march towards progress. The effectiveness of the elites as prime movers depends not only on their own development but on the knowledge, skills and capabilities of those whom they lead as well and therefore, a sizeable proportion of investment must be directed towards development of education—both quantitatively and qualitatively.

However, in most of the countries including India, financial support to education, though greater than even before has failed to keep pace with the increased social demands upon education. It is perhaps, not unfair to say that political leaders and the general public almost everywhere are somewhat 'schizophrenic' on the subject of education. They have high praise for the virtue of education, they rely heavily upon it to help the new generation solve great problems to which the old generation has found no solutions; but when it comes to spending more money for education, their deeds fail to match their words, (Phillip, 1960) and even today, they, especially in the developing countries, spend a very little proportions of their Gross National Product (GNP) on education and thus, education, the catalyst of 'modernising society' 'the key to the abundance of modern economy' (Schultz, 1968), which prepares the 'bed rock' for development of human capability, has not acquired is real share in the total investment of such economies. Hence, illiteracy and inadequate education at the higher level still retards growth as it constrains skill formation.

EDUCATION IN INDIA : OUTLAY AND ACHIEVEMENTS

In India, the expenditure on education has seldom been approached as an investment in human resources rather it has been treated as social expenditure. No doubt, the social gains of education of elementary and secondary levels are more important, but at the level of higher and technical educations, the economic gains predominate.

The governments in India, both at the centre and state levels, have been playing an important role in the quantitative and qualitative expansion of education and the share of invesement in education in total outlay has always been increasing during the Five year plans. To quote Economic Survey of the Government of India, 2002-03; "Education is a critical input of investment in human capital. Plan expenditure on education has also increased rapidly since the First Five Year Plan. A high priority has been recorded to this sector in the Tenth Five Year Plan with on allocation of Rs. 43,825 crores as against Rs. 24,908.38 crores made available in the Ninth Plan, representing an increase of 76 per cent" (*Economic Survey*, 2002-03). However, the total expenditure has been around Rs. 0.54 lakh crores (at 2006-07 prices) during the Tenth Five Year Plan. The Eleventh Five Year Plan has proposed a massive increase in expenditure on education amounting to Rs. 2.37 lakh crores (at 2006-07 prices) as against Rs. 0.54 lakh crores during the Tenth Five Year Plan. The share of education in total plan outlay will correspondingly increase from 7.7 per cent to 19.4 per cent. Around 50 per cent of Eleventh Plan outlay is for elementory education and literacy, 20 per cent for secondary education and 30 per cent for higher education including technical education (Planning Commission, 2007-12, Vol. II, p. 37).

Though it is a fact that expenditure on education in India has not seriously been considered as an investment in human resources and consequently, the share of expenditure on education as percentage of Gross Domestic Product (GDP) is still around 3.8 per cent (during 2002-05) as against the goal of 6 per cent of GDP for expenditure on education which is much lower in comparison to several other countries of the world. Among 124 countries of world in 2006, India ranked as low as ninety seventh in terms of the proportion of the public expenditure on education to GDP (UNDP, 2006). During the first three decades of planning, the proportion of public expenditure on education to GDP in India had almost stagnated but since mid-1980s it started to increase and now there has been some significant improvement but that too in the field of elementary education and as a mattu of fact, expenditure on education is quite inadequate. However, due to incrasing expenditure on education during subsequent Five Year Plans, educational facilities have been expanded at all levels in India and as a result, not only the literacy rate has risen but the percentage of children availing school education has also incrased over the years. At persent, the country has abundent facilities for higher and technical as well as vocational education which is playing an important role in economic, scientific and technical and self-reliant growth of the economy by producing quality manpower. The enrolment of students in institutions of higher education was 75 million in 2002 which rose to 140 million in 2007. If we take an overall view of educational achievements in absolute terms, they are quite impressive, but when we make the relative analysis, they appear still to be meagre and inadequate.

So for as the literacy ratio is concerned, the national average increased to 65.38 per cent in 2001 as against only 16.67 per cent in 1951. In isolation this may look quite impressive, but the fact remains that even after more than 50 years of planned development in the country, 35 per cent of the population remained illiterate in 2001. In twelve states, literacy rates are lower than the national literacy rate and in Bihar it is only 47.53 per cent and the rate of female literacy is much lower at (33.57% as against the national average of 52.1 per cent (census of India, 2001). In comparison to several

Asian countries also India's attainments in terms of literacy are rather disappointing. According to World Develpment Report, 2008, adult male illiteracy rate was 39 per cent in India in 2000-05, as against 9 per cent in China, 9 per cent in 'Sri Lanka, 7 per cent in Philippines and 3 per cent in Argentina. In all these countries female illiteracy rates are also substantially lower than that in India'. Most development economists now believe that the poor performance of India on the literacy front has affected its overall development performance.

The government has launched several schemes, the Sarva Shiksha Abhiyan being the most important among them, for universalistion of education at the elementary level, the Gross Enrolment Ratio (GER) has gone up at 107.8 per cent at the primary level (I-V) and 69.9. per cent at upper primary level (VI-VII), but a major problem at this level of education is the high dropout ratio and the low rate of girls participations. Hence, for the realisation of the goal of universalisation of elementary education, the National Policy on Education has also Stressed on retention, participation and achievement rather than more enrolment. Enrolment is a necessary but not a sufficient condition for achieving this goal.

At the secondary and senior secondary levels, the gross enrolment ratio is only 39.91 per cent during 2000-05, where as the dropout ratio is as high as 62 per cent (Planning Commission, Eleventh Five Year Plan). This shows that the spread of secondary eduction in India is also quite limited. In recent years, in order to make secondary education more meaningful for remunerative work without necessarily having to go in for higher education, a schemed of vocationalisation of secondary education was started in the seventh plan. For giving a new thrust to vocationalisation of secondary education, a centrally sponsored scheme was launched in Feb. 1998. Other important scehmes include the schemes for empmovement in science education, the open school system, encouragements to the deprived sections like children with rural background, girls and SCs/STs and revision of the curricula in order to make it more Job-oriented. In 2004-05, there were 152,045 secondary and senior secondary schools in India.

The higher education system at present also suffers from several weaknesses, such as proliferation of substandard institutions, deterioration of academic standards, outdated curriculum, failure to maintain academic calendar and lack of adequate support for research. Moreover, there are wide disparities between rural and urbn areas as well as male and female enrolment ratios. Apart from these problems higher education is highly subsidised which has put unnecessary financial burden on the government.

Further, technical education including management education is one of the most effective ways to create skilled manpower required for developmental purposes. During the last five decades there has been a spectacular expansion of technical education in the country. In the year 2005-06 there were 1969 recognised technical education institutions at the first degree level and more than 2475 post-graduate institutions recognised by All India Council for Technical Education. There were seven IITs providing top quality personnel of world level as well as a large number of ITs, RITs, engineering colleges, research institutes, six Indian Institutes of Management as well as other institutes offering the MBA, MCA, Information Technology and other such courses. The Indian Institutes of Mangaement with their high quality products are assisting private and public enterprises in meeting their needs for managerial manpower through Post-graduate programmes. In addition, 990 approved Mangement Institutes inpart MBA courses in both general and functional areas of management.

But in the area of technical education at present, various imbalances and distortions exist. Over the years, quantitative expension of technical education has lowered the standards and now there is a structural imbalance in skill requirement of the business sector and the traditional curriculum followed by the engineering and management institutions. The infrastrural facilities available in most of these institutions are inadequate and yet there has been enormous increase in public expenditure on technical education.

Therefore, there is a need of modernisation and upgradation of infrastructural facilities, quality improvement in technical and management education and the strategy for raising non-budgetary resources.

Besides, the Indian educational system suffers from several other problems like the unplanned growth of higher education, poor quality of education in several institutions and high percentage of failure and dropouts, the tendency of highly qualified persons to go abroad for earning a lot and make contributions to the development of other countries, a large number of educated unemployed and under employed people who represent the wastage of resources, as well as the disparities in the standards and awareness of rural and urban, male and famale education. Inadequacy of teachers, lack of infrastructural facilities and teaching aids, dull teaching method, over crowded class rooms and poor pupil achievements, etc. are the other problems which all result in discouragement effect (Dreze and Sen, 2006).

THE WAY-OUT : HOW TO IMPROVE THE EDUCATIONAL SYSTEM

If education has to raise the quality of human resources and make desirable contribution for economic development of the country, following changes are to be made in the educational system of the economy

First of all, some restrictions must be imposed on the quality of university education and admission to post-graduate courses should be allowed only for those who satisfy its norms and requirements. The substandard and unproductive research work, which involve public expenditure, should not be allowed as it involves a colossal waste of resorces for making research both meningful and productive, emphasis should be on quality and not on quantity.

Secondly, education should be made job-oriented. In other words, emphasis should be on vocational education rather than on general education.

Thirdly, technical education should be planned properly. Since it involves heavy cost, the government must ensure jobs to all the technical hands. Further, if a person getting technical education at the state's expense wants to go abroad, the government must claim the money which it has spent on his education.

Fourthly, instead of opening new institutions of higher education, the government must try to raise the standards of education in the existing ones.

Fifthly, education in science is costly and, therefore, its expansion should be planned carefully. There is no need of producing science graduates if they can get only the clerical jobs. For these jobs commerce and arts graduates will not be less competent while the cost of their education is comparatively much lower.

In rural areas, emphasis should be on agriculture and vocational education. General education has been found less useful in these areas. For instance, the persons with higher education do not find themselves fit for agricultural activities and they migrate to cities in search of employment opportunities.

Further, at the primary and secondary levels, the government must investigate the reasons behind the large number of dropouts and should make attempts to solve this problem. It has to make the efforts to overcome the discouragement effects as mentioned by Dreze and Sen (2006). Overcoming this effect depends crucially on improving the accessibility affordability and equality of schooling in India. According to Dreze and Sen, much can be done without delay in this field by the steps like opening more schools, improving the infrastructure, appointing more teachers, simplifying the curriculum, organising enrolment drives, providing free text books and mid day meals of reasonable quality, etc. However the primary challenge wourld be to improve the teachnig standards in the classroooms (Dreze and Sen, 2006).

References

Dreze, Jean and Sen, Amartya (2006), India: Development and Participation, New Delhi, p. 158.

Government of India: Census Report (2001), Series 1.

Government of India: *Economics Survey*, 2002-03 and 2007-08.

Kalam, APJ (2006), 'Knowledge Economy Vision: Innovation is the Key', *Yojana*, Feburary.

Marshall, Alfred (1938), Principles of Economic, Mcmillan.

Myers, Charles A. and Harbison, Fredrick (1997), Education Manpower and Economic Growth, New Delhi, p. 25.

Phillip, H. Coombs (1960), 'Educational Planning in the Light of Economic Requirements: Forecasting Manpower Needs for the Age of Science, Office for Scientific and Technical Personnel, OECD, September.

Planning Commission, Government of India: Eleventh Five Year Plan, 2007-12 (Delhi-2008), Vol. II, pp. 12-13, 37.

Reddy K.C. (2006), Presidential Address to the Indian Economic Association, p. 1.

Schultz, T.W. (1960), 'Capital Formation by Education', *Journal of Political Economics*, Vol. 67, No. 6, December, pp. 571-83.

Schultz, T.W. (1961), 'Education and Economic Growth' in Henry, Nelson B. (ed.) the Sixtieth Yearbook of the National Society for the Study of Education, Part-2 Social Forces Influencing American Education, University of Chicago Press, p. 60.

Schultz, T.W. (1977), Investment in Human Capital. The Role of Education and Research, New York, p. 36.

Solow, Robert, M. (1957), 'Technical Change and the Aggregate Production Function', *Review of Economicand Statistics*, Vol. 34, No. 3, August, pp. 312-30.

Streeten, Paul (1981), First Things First : Meeting Basic Human Needs in the Developing Countries, Oxford Univ. Press, New York.

Tilak (2006), quoted by Reddy, K.C. in Presidential Address to IEA, p. 1.

Todaro, Michael P. and Smith Stephen C. (2003), Economic Development, Pearson Education, Asia, Eighth Edition, p. 385.

UNDP (2006), Human Development Report, 2006, Delhi, Table 11, pp. 319-22.

6

Education and Development

R.Y. MAHORE

Education and development are not two different things but merely two sides of the coin. It is observed that education should lead to development and development should create the motivation for more education as well as provide tools for it. Education influences and in turn is influenced by access to other needs—adequate nutrition, safe drinking water, health services and shelter. It prepares and trains skilled workers at all levels to manage capital, technology, services and administration in every sector of the economy. Education can help the society to overcome its ills and problems. It has to be made application-*cum*-life-oriented and has to be taken to the door-steps of the villagers without delay. It should deal with the variety of aspects. One deals with in life so as to enrich it and to make it useful for oneself and for the service of mankind. Such type of education is necessary for development. In this sense it is something wider than mere schooling.

Gandhiji's concept of education stands for the balanced and harmonious development of all the aspects of human personality. One of the first attempts to measure the contribution of education to growth was made by Denison. He argued that about 23 per cent of the increase in the United States national income was due to the increased education of the labour force. Education affects economic development both directly and indirectly. There is a positive correlation between the level of education and the level of earnings. The findings of the socio-economic surveys in the cities of Bombay, Hyderabad and Delhi all unanimously indicate that earning rise with every successive level of education.

When the importance of education is stressed in relation to the development of the underdeveloped countries, the Japanese experience is often referred to as an interesting lesson. The policy statement of Meiji's Government was that, "the efforts should be made so that there will be no uneducated homes in the village and no uneducated persons in the homes." The programme priorities of the Meiji's Government were armament, education and legislation. According to Koichi Emi the enormous educational investment was by no means a mistake.

T.W. Schultz has given three ratios in relation to education and growth—

1. Education-labour ratio to show the amount of human effort going into education relative to the total labour force.
2. Education-income ratio which relates the resources entering into education to consumer income.
3. Education-income ratio to show the relation between the resources entering into education and the resources going into reproducible physical capital.

Since the late 1980s, much of the attention of macroeconomists has focused on long-term issues, notably the effects of government policies on the long-term rate of economic growth. This emphasis reflects the recognition that the difference between prosperity and poverty for a country depends on how fast it grows over the long-term. The macro-economic policies are important for growth; other aspects of "policy" broadly interpreted to encompass all government activities that matter for economic performance are even more significant. The human capital includes education, health, and per capita income, the main focus of the present study is on education. The analysis stresses the distinction between the quantities of education measured by years of attainment at various levels and the quality gauged by scores on internationally comparable examinations.

The recognition that the determinants of long-term economic growth were the central macroeconomic problem was fortunately accompanied in the late 1980s by important advances in the theory of economic growth. This period featured the development of "endogenous-growth" models, in which the long-term rate of growth was determined within the model. A key feature of these models is a theory of technological progress, viewed as a process whereby purposeful research and application lead over time. The new and better products and methods of production to the adoption of superior technologies are developed in other countries or sectors. One major contributor in this area is Romer (1990).

EFFECTS OF EDUCATION

Governments typically have strong direct involvement in the financing and provision of schooling at various levels. Hence, public policies in these areas have major effects on a country's accumulation of human capital. One measure of this schooling capital is the average years of attainment, as constructed by Barro and Lee (1993, 1996). These data are classified by sex and age (for persons aged 15 and over and 25 and over) and by levels of education (no school, partial and complete primary, partial and complete secondary, and partial and complete higher). These data have been refined and updated in Barro and Lee (2000).

Male primary schooling is insignificant for growth. The female primary schooling is positively related with growth and, thus, is significant. The particular importance of schooling at the secondary and higher levels (for males) supports the idea that education affects growth by facilitating the absorption of new technologies which are likely to be complementary with labor educated to these higher levels. Primary schooling is, however, critical as a prerequisite for secondary education.

Another role for primary schooling involves the well-known negative effect of female primary education on fertility rates. However, the female primary attainment variable would not be credited with this growth effect, because the fertility variable is already held constant in the growth panels. If fertility is not held constant, then the estimated coefficient on female primary schooling becomes significantly positive. Hence this result suggests that female primary education promotes growth indirectly by encouraging lower fertility.

The years of schooling (for males at the secondary and higher levels) are insignificantly related to the investment ratio. Hence, the linkage between human capital and growth does not involve an expansion in the intensity of physical capital. This result is inconsistent with some of the theoretical effects mentioned before involving the ratio of human to physical capital.

HIGHER EDUCATION AND ECONOMIC GROWTH

The future of higher education and its relationship to economic growth were the focus of a one-day conference at the Chicago Fed on November 2, 2005. Co-sponsored by the bank, the Committee on Institutional Cooperation, and the Midwestern Higher Education Compact, the event brought together over 100 academic, business, and government leaders. The perception of higher education as an important public good has eroded. Higher education is viewed by some as a private good with the benefits accruing to the student in the form of higher future wages and quality of life. In opening remarks, Chicago Fed President and CEO Michael Moskow noted that while the relationship between education, productivity, and economic growth has never been clearer, financial support for higher education has waned while costs have continued to rise. While private universities have been able to raise tuition and draw on endowments to maintain fiscal health, public universities have faced difficult times as states have reduced financial support and often limited their ability to offset cuts with large tuition increases.

Moskow suggested several strategies for restoring the higher education social compact. First, universities must be more transparent in their operations. Part of this transparency includes more tightly defining the mission of the university in meeting the multiple goals of education, research and public outreach. Moskow recommended that institutions make explicit how money is spent and what resources are available to ensure that tuition is not a barrier to attendance for talented students regardless of income. Finally, Moskow urged higher education to address graduation rates that currently hover around 50 per cent.

Next, Michael McPherson, president of the Spencer Foundation, discussed measures of the affordability of higher education for private individuals and the public. McPherson argued that the real question here is how public resources should be allocated between rich and poor students and among different types of institutions to achieve an optimal distribution for society. Is it more efficient to invest in our most talented students and our best institutions, or can more gains be made for the economy by increasing resources to community colleges and Non-traditional student populations?

McPherson cited a study that found the family income and parental education are still major predictors of academic success. Students from the top income quartile receive a combined SAT score of 1200 or better by a ratio of six to one over students from the lowest income quartile. A similar ratio holds for students with at least one parent who graduated from college *versus* students without a parent who graduated from college.

Offering a perspective from the front lines, B. Joseph White, president of the University of Illinois, characterized the three campuses of the University as the most valuable assets that the state possesses to ensure that globalisation benefits rather than harms Illinois residents. However, the university's financial constraints represent a significant obstacle. Currently, the university provides an education per student that has a price tag of $25,000; however, it charges the students only $8,000 to $10,000 each. The clear message from the state government is that the university must develop other funding sources to supplement state support. These options include increasing revenue from tuition, having faculty find external sources of funding to support their research, and raising more private donations and endowments. Finally, leadership is needed to push cost reductions and increase productivity.

HIGHER EDUCATION FINANCE

Professor and former provost Paul Courant of the University of Michigan and Professor Richard Vedder of Ohio University and the American Enterprise Institute offered perspectives on what drives higher education costs. Courant began by asking:

- How is a university like, and not like, a business?
- Why does tuition fee keeps rising faster than the cost of living?
- How happy or unhappy should we be about the answers to the first and second questions, or in other words, how close are universities to producing educated citizens and research efficiently?

Silberman cited three drivers of Strayer's success. First, there is open enrolment. Strayer graduates large numbers of minorities and admits students regardless of high school record, as long as they have graduated. Second, the program promotes academic rigor. Strayer is regionally accredited and offers BAs, MBAs, and technical degrees. Third, high student achievement is required. It is inferred that between 5 per cent and 10 per cent of Strayer's student population fail in each quarter.

Duderstadt argued that the region needs to develop a strategic plan such as the Michigan Roadmap, to harness these economic forces. Michigan's economy is facing significant challenges. Its largest city, Detroit, is among the poorest in the nation, and one of its major industries, domestic autos, is suffering staggering losses. One-quarter of the state's adult population lacks a high school diploma and only one-third of its high school graduates are ready for college. Yet, the state has a system of higher education that is regarded as among the finest in the nation, although it too is beginning to suffer from a withdrawal of state support

CHALLENGES IDENTIFIED BY HIGHER EDUCATION LEADERS

Lou Anna Simon, president, Michigan State University; Paul Courant, professor and former provost, University of Michigan; and Richard Saller, provost, University of Chicago, shared their views on the challenges facing their own and many other institutions. Simon noted that the universities' core mission of providing access to cutting edge knowledge and democratizing information is unchanged. But higher education must have public trust that it provides access in an inclusive fashion, and it must make the benefits of basic, applied, and commercial research readily apparent. In its 57th meeting in December 2002, the United Nations General Assembly proclaimed the UN Decade of Education for Sustainable Development, 2005-14, (DESD) 'emphasising that education is an indispensable element for achieving sustainable development'. It also designated UNESCO as the lead agency to promote and implement the decade.

The vision of Education for Sustainable Development (ESD) is a world where everyone has the opportunity to benefit from quality education and learn the values, behaviour and lifestyles required for a sustainable future and for positive societal transformation. ESD is for everyone, at all stages of life and in all possible learning contexts. ESD employs a partnership approach that engages multiple sectors and stakeholders—including media agencies and the private sector—and utilizes all forms and methods of public awareness raising, education and training to promote a broad understanding of sustainable development.

ESD equally addresses all three pillars of sustainable development—society, environment and economy—with culture as an essential additional and underlying dimension.

By embracing these elements in a holistic and integrated manner, ESD enables all individuals to fully develop the knowledge, perspectives, values and skills necessary to take part in decisions to improve the quality of life both locally and globally on terms which are most relevant to their daily lives.

EDUCATION FOR SUSTAINABLE DEVELOPMENT

The concept of sustainable development touches upon all aspects of the social and institutional fabric. In this sense sustainable development provides a way of articulating the overall social project and aim of development. Since the Earth Summit in 1992 in Rio de Janeiro, there has been increasing recognition of the critical role of education in promoting sustainable consumption and production patterns in order to change attitudes and behavior of people as individuals, including as producers and consumers, and as citizens. If other related international education initiatives look at education as a fundamental human right and focus on providing educational opportunities to everyone and reducing illiteracy, ESD focuses on the underlying principles and values conveyed through the content and purpose of education. Chapter 36 of Agenda 21 specifically discusses re-orienting education towards sustainable development, and encompasses all streams of education, both formal and non-formal, basic education and all the key issues related to educating for sustainable human development.

Chapter 36 of Agenda 21, adopted at the 1992 Earth Summit in Rio, is devoted to 'Promoting Education, Public Awareness and Training'. It identifies four major thrusts of Education for Sustainable Development:

PROMOTION AND IMPROVEMENT OF BASIC EDUCATION

- Reorienting Existing Education at all Levels to Address Sustainable Development,
- Developing Public Understanding and Awareness of Sustainability, and
- Training.

MAIN CHALLENGES OF EDUCATION FOR SUSTAINABLE FUTURE

In spite of multiple efforts to strengthen ESD, many challenges remain. In particular, there is a need:

- to integrate sustainable science and education;
- to strengthen co-ordination and collaboration between different levels of education for Sustainable Development; and
- to mitigate information and knowledge gaps between different parts of the world.

MAJOR INTERNATIONAL EFFORTS UNDERTAKEN IN THE AREA OF ESD

Since the Earth Summit, sustainable development has been high on the political agenda. During the World Conference on Higher Education in 1998, a thematic debate was organised (by the UNU at the request of UNESCO) on "sustainable (human) development," which brought fourteen different organisations together. This was the first major step towards uniting educators as a major stakeholder group.

The following year the first discussions were held to form the Global Higher Education for Sustainability Partnership. In 2000 the Agreement was signed and during the World Summit on Sustainable Development (WSSD) in Johannesburg in 2002, the International Association of Universities (IAU), the Association of University Leaders for a Sustainable Future (ULSF), Copernicus Campus, and UNESCO launched the Global Higher Education for Sustainability Partnership (GHESP) as a Type II Partnership to promote education for sustainable development in particular among higher education institutions. The Japanese as well as Swedish Governments chose education for sustainable development as the focus of their contributions.

During the World Summit on Sustainable Development in 2002, the UNU-IAS took the lead in bringing together the Ubuntu Declaration Group for the signature of the Ubuntu Declaration in an effort to integrate science, technology and ESD.

India has one of the largest higher education systems in the world

The objectives of higher education in a changing World have been mentioned by the first Prime Minister of India. Addressing the graduates of the Allahabad University in 1947, Jawaharlal Nehru said:

> "A university stands for humanism, for tolerance, for reason, for the adventure of ideas and for the search for truth. It stands for the onward march of the human race toward higher objectives. Universities are places of ideals and idealism. If the universities discharge their duties adequately, then, it is well with the nation and the people."

This statement effectively initiated the formulation of the essential purpose of university education in independent India

The first major step taken by the Ministry of Education after independence (1947) in higher education was to appoint a Commission on university education under the Chairmanship of Dr. S. Radhakrishnan to report on Indian university education. In its report, the Commission said: "Democracy depends for its very life on a high standard of general, vocational and professional education. Dissemination of learning, incessant search for new knowledge, unceasing effort to plumb the meaning of life, provision for professional education to satisfy the occupational needs of our society are the vital tasks of higher education."

The past is our foundation, the present our material, the future our aim and summit. Each must have its due and natural place in a national system of education.

Prabha Panth focuses on the scope, methods of dissemination and the target of Education for Sustainable Development (ESD). It is argued that ESD should not be mere information sharing, but should be aimed at educating those who can fabricate a sustainable future. Since environmental crises are being increasingly felt in every field and sector, it is necessary to concentrate on imparting ESD to those who can bring about environmental improvements immediately. The role of ESD in the short and the long-run is examined with a view to identifying and targeting the group that can best bring about Sustainable Development (SD). It is said that Environmental Education (EE) can be envisaged as formal and informal education, the latter is more relevant to ESD. It also discusses the various difficulties that may be encountered in the course of reaching out to the target audience.

According to Fein, "Education for Sustainable Development has come to be seen as a process of learning how to make decisions that consider the long-term future of the economy, ecology and social well-being of all communities. "Capacity building for such future-oriented thinking is a key task of education" (Fien, J. 2003) ESD denotes a shift from mere theoretical discussions of environmental problems, to pragmatic solutions that can lead to SD. For this, the task of achieving SD has to be shared by all sections of society—not just the Ministry of Environment, or international environmental bodies. No single unit can take on the tremendous responsibility of achieving SD by itself, for it requires the concerted and urgent efforts of many agents, and a sea change in the type of development (Rao, 2001).

Indian Higher Education in the Global Context Panjab Singh said that today the key concerns of Indian Higher Education are low General Enrolment Ratio (GER) at 11 per cent compared to world average of 23.2 per cent, low public spending on per student in India at US$ 400 compared to the average developing country spend about US$ 1000. China spends about US$ 2500 and developed countries like US spend US$ 10,000.

Globally, the traditional Universities are in a transition phase and should be gradually getting prepared for transformation. With the Internet and technological advances in Information Technology, the educational needs are changing. Students, faculty, administration, every component of the education system will have to change to face these new requirements. The financial aspects and markets of the education system as a whole will determine the levels of all the attributes including but not limited to: excellence, equity, commitment, autonomy, accountability and most important— its relevance to the societal and national development. The Government of India has formally accepted importance and role of higher education for nation building. How much and how long the governments should continue supporting higher education is a key question. World Development Report 1998 observes that the capacity to adopt and disseminate rapid technological advances is dependent on better public support for tertiary education

Recent initiative of the Ministry of HRD in setting-up more Central Universities, Indian Institutes of Science, Education and Research (IISERs), NITs Central Institutes of Technologies, IITs, IIMs and access to education through open and distance learning are a few positive initiatives.

Quality of Education Many researchers argue that the quality of education is more important than the quantity, measured, for example, by years of attainment. Barro and Lee (1998) discuss the available cross-country aggregate measures of the quality of education. Hanushek and Kimko (2000) find that scores on international examinations indicators of the quality of schooling capital matter more than years of attainment for subsequent economic growth.

With respect to education, growth is positively related to the starting level of average years of school attainment of adult males at the secondary and higher levels. Since workers with this educational background would be complementary with new technologies, the results suggest an important role for the diffusion of technology in the development process. Growth is insignificantly related to years of school attainment of females at the secondary and higher levels. This result suggests that highly educated women are not well utilized in the labor markets of many countries. Growth is insignificantly related to male schooling at the primary level. However, this level of schooling is a prerequisite for secondary schooling and would, therefore, affect growth through this channel. Education of women at the primary level stimulates economic growth indirectly by inducing a lower fertility rate.

Data on students' scores on internationally comparable examinations in science, mathematics, and reading were used to measure the quality of schooling. Scores on science tests have a particularly strong positive relation with economic growth. Given the quality of education, as represented by the test scores, the quantity of schooling measured by average years of attainment of adult males at the secondary and higher levels is still positively related to subsequent growth. However, the effect of school quality is quantitatively much more important.

The results from a broad panel of countries were compared with findings for rich and poor countries considered separately. (The results for OECD countries were similar to those for the larger group of rich countries.) Some differences that emerge for the determination of economic growth are a higher convergence rate in rich countries, larger effects from international openness and terms-of-trade changes in poor countries, and more negative effects from government consumption in poor countries. Despite these differences and issues about data quality in poor countries, the conclusion is that the broad sample of countries should be used, even if one's interest is limited to rich countries. The reason is that the observed variations in policy and other variables among rich countries are too limited to make accurate inferences.

In defining what "quality education" means in the context of education for sustainability, UNESCO calls for the "reorientation of education systems, policies and practices in order to empower everyone, young and old, to make decisions and act in culturally appropriate and locally relevant ways to solve the problems which threaten the prospect."

Thus, quality education is a prerequisite for education for sustainable development. Achieving sustainable development requires:

- Recognition of the challenge
- Collective responsibility and constructive partnership
- Acting with determination
- The indivisibility of human dignity

Education provides the skills for:

- Learning to know
- Learning to live together
- Learning to do
- Learning to be

Education not only provides scientific and technical skills, it also provides the motivation, justification, and social support for pursuing and applying them. The international community now strongly believes that we need to foster through education the values, behaviour and lifestyles required for a sustainable future.

Finland is an excellent example of how these factors operate together to support sustained, equitable growth. In the early 1990s there was a significant recession throughout the Finnish economy with an average annual GDP growth rate of -3.68 per cent from 1990 to 1996. This set off a series of government policy decisions that helped create a fundamental structural transformation of the country's economy from that of a raw materials-based manufacturing economy to one that concentrated on high-tech products, particularly in the area of telecommunications. This resulted in a dramatic turn around with a per capita annual GDP growth rate of 4.39 per cent from 1994 to 2007 and, along with Singapore.

Finland became one of the most competitive economies in the world. During this period, unemployment was cut in half, the balance of trade moved from a large deficit to a significant surplus, and the value of Helsinki's stock market rose well over 200 per cent. Most notably, this economic growth was accomplished without creating great disparities in income and it generated revenue to sustain a variety of social programs and services, such as universal health care and free education through the university level. What were the policy decisions that supported this dramatic turn around? Early in the 1990's, the Government of Finland created a vision for a Finnish Information Society.

In implementing this vision, they made investments in technological infrastructure, education, and research and development, emphasizing the creation and sharing of new knowledge. Public research and development investments grew rapidly during this period, funded by revenue from the privatization of uncompetitive state-owned enterprises, and these investments were structured to encourage cross-sector, private public collaborations in research and innovation. Private research and development investments grew at an even faster pace and Finland became a world leader in the support of research and development. The government encouraged entrepreneurial activity and the development of small and medium enterprises (SMEs) by supporting incubators for start-ups and by promoting capital investments and knowledge sharing between SMEs and large businesses. Knowledge sharing within and between organizations and companies in turn encouraged innovation and competition in product development and production. The result was broad-based growth with one of the world's lowest differentials between high and low income wage earners.

Singapore, on the other hand, has had one of the world's highest income differentials. Economists noted that Singapore's early economic strategy created silos of capital deepening, narrowly concentrated within transnational corporations, and its growth was not broad-based. Ultimately, Singapore, too, picked up on the technological innovation productivity factor. In the late 1990s, the country's economic development plan shifted toward a knowledge-based economy and broader-based economic participation. In conjunction with this shift, the Education Ministry instituted a number of reforms to improve the quality of their education system and support students' development of critical thinking, creativity, and enterprise. The plan also strengthened the connections between school, home, and community, as part of a larger social development plan that encouraged a more active participation of citizens in community life and economic innovation.

EDUCATION AND ITS CONTRIBUTION TO ECONOMIC GROWTH

Quality education has a high social value in both

Singapore and Finland, as evidenced by the fact that their students consistently score among the highest of all students in the world on international assessments. Education also has a high economic value. This is supported by the results of both international micro and macro-economic studies. Micro-economic studies focus on the benefit of educational investments to individuals while macroeconomic studies focus on returns to the economy more generally. Micro-economic data from 42 countries found that an average rate of return for an additional year of schooling was a 9.7 per cent increase in personal income. A cross-country macroeconomic study found that there was an additional .44 per cent growth in a country's per capita GDP for each additional average year of attained schooling, a return on investment of 7 per cent to 10 per cent. Other studies have found returns that go as high as 12 per cent. The quality of education had an even stronger relationship to growth than did the duration of school participation; the amount learned was more important than the number of years of schooling. Higher test scores of one standard deviation equated to 1 per cent growth in per capita GDP.

However, the limitation of both microeconomic and macroeconomic studies is that they treat the educational system as a black box. They do not describe how curriculum, teaching, assessment, teacher quality, or the use of ICT can actually influence what it is that students know and are able to do as a result of their educational experience or how these education factors contribute to economic growth and social development. Yet the details of these connections are very important to educational policy-makers who are charged with trying to prepare citizens to participate in the knowledge economy and information society and create a workforce that is globally competitive. What kind of education reform will contribute to sustained and equitable economic growth? How can teachers and schools better prepare students to meet the challenges of the future? What are the skills students will need to succeed in the 21st century global economy and information society?

A number of academic and business groups have commented on these questions. In order to be more productive and to contribute to society, students will need to understand what they learn deeply enough to use it to solve the complex problems they will encounter in the real world. They will also need to be able to use technology, manage information, communicate effectively, think critically, work well in teams, and produce new intellectual and creative works that have value to others. Perhaps most importantly, they will need the skills to continuously learn and create new knowledge throughout their lives. These are the skills that students will need in the 21st century.

This is mainly education through development work-giving paid services to the community and using this as a means of education that imparts hands-on training in all skills relevant to rural areas. The RDES exists in both a formal mode (8-10th standards in schools) as well as in a non-formal mode as a one year course targeted at school dropouts (post 8th standard). The formal course is recognised by the Maharashtra State Board of Secondary and Higher Secondary Education. There are about 20 schools implementing this in different parts of the state. The course for post 8th standard dropouts helps the students learn in real life situations in the areas of Home-Health, Agriculture-Animal Husbandry, Engineering and Energy-Environment. Necessary theoretical briefing is also included. Students also earn by taking jobs on contract. The course is fully residential and awards a diploma from the National Institute of Open Schooling, (MHRD, Delhi).

References

Naik, J.P. (1979), "Education Elsewhere and Here: A Key to Prosperity," Bhartiya Vidya Bhavan, Bombay, p. 5.

Joshi, R.N. (1979), *Ibid.*, pp. 15-16.

Mangal, S.K. (1984), "The Ground Work of Education," Arya Book Depot, New Delhi, p. 54.

Lakdawala, D.T. (1975), "Works, Wages and Well-being in an Indian Metropolist," University of Bombay, quoted in Goel, S.C., Education and Economic Growth, The Macmillan, Delhi, p. 7.

Indian Institute of Education (1975), "A Socio-Economic Survey, Hyderabad," quoted in Goel, S.C. *op. cit.*, p. 7.

Rao, V.K.R.V. and Desai, P.B. (1975), "Delhi Survey," 1965, quoted in Goel S.C. *op. cit.*, p. 7 .

Kochi Emi (1971), "Economic Development and Educational Investment in the Meiji Era," Bowman M.J. *et al.* (ed)., "Readings in Economics of Education," UNESCO," pp. 94-100.

Schultz, T.W. (1971), "Economics and Economic Growth," Bowman, M.J. *et al.* (eds.) *op. cit*, p. 277.

Barro, Robert J. and Jong-Wha Lee (1993), "International Comparisons of Educational Attainment", *Journal of Monetary Economics*, 32(3): 363-94.

Barro, Robert J. and Jong-Wha Lee (1996), "International Measures of Schooling Years and Schooling Quality", *American Economic Review*, 86(2), pp. 218-23.

Barro, Robert J. and Jong-Wha Lee (2000), "International Data on Educational Attainment: Updates and Implications" unpublished, Harvard University, in Oxford Economic Papers.

Mattoon, Richard H. (2006), "Higher Education and Economic Growth," The Federal Reserve Bank of Chicago, pp. 1-4.

World Bank (2001), "What is Sustainable Development", Deb Web.

UNESCO, 'Bangkok Website and United Nations University: Institute of Advanced Studies', Website.

Kartikeya, V. Sarabhai (2005), 'Education for Sustainable Future', International Conference, Ahmedabad, India, January, 18-20.

Kozma Robert (2005), 'ICT, Education Reform, and Economic Growth', San Francisco, California.

Mahore, R.Y. (1984), 'Economics of Primary Education: A Case Study of Nagpur District', unpublished Ph.D. Thesis, Nagpur University, Nagpur.

Quality in Education is the Key towards Development: Issues and Challenges

SATYANARAYANA

Education is an instrument for social transformation and Economic as well as human resource development. It is an important component of human development index of any Nation. Education has the inherent capacity to act as a powerful tool to face the challenges arising out of globalisation. It is the need of the hour to strengthen educational system and its processes to build potential human resources in order to meet the ever growing challenges and rapid changes taking place in the knowledge society. In the overall educational framework acquisition of marketable skills and competence for employability have come to assume a critical role in the technologically changing world. In the present era of globalisation and newer technologies it is clear that any human being can be successful only if he has the requisite competency. Quality in education is a mix of knowledge and skill. So manpower which we produce should not be ill-equipped instead should be well equipped, to meet the needs of the community service and industries.

According to Gnanam and Stella, "Transnational factors are speedily entering into the educational delivery with growing number of countries entering into the GATS of W.T.O". This process is gathering momentum making the present regulatory frameworks of higher education in India inadequate and ineffective.

At the same time global efforts are being made to evolve same new international code of practice international regulatory frameworks of higher education for transnational provisions, regional co-operation and mutual recognition agreements among quality assurance agencies all over the world. On the global level France, UK, New Zealand, Netherlands, etc., are engaged in the renewal of assessment and accreditation process to keep pace with the even changing scenario of higher education on the global level. We have to consider our efforts for the quality assurance in the institutions of higher education in India in such a global context.

The most relevant question at present is, is the Administration of Higher Education in India well geared up to face the challenges of the global competition? The internal challenges before us in the context are of two-fold nature, one is administrative-oriented and another is financial-oriented.

Quality is linked with teamwork and quality culture. It paves the way for work culture. Though NAAC is encouraging work culture in higher education. Indian human element pushes the people back to "Staff room culture". Some times people spend their time and energy not in extending co-operation in this endeavour, but in inventing and presenting 'cleverly' various excuses for their non-participation. It is very difficult to manage the total volume of work assigned to a college or institution. It is due to controlling agencies within the framework. Multiplicity of control is the major obstacle in the improvement of quality in higher education. The sooner we realise it, the better. First of all the head of the institution should have quality culture. He should have necessary ability and skill. His attitude should become model to others. He should act as a leader not a follower. The role of government and university is also important. The rules and policies framed should be 'quality education-oriented' on the other hand the role of parents, teachers and NGO's is also equally important. They should have awareness about quality and excellence. Though the attitude of the students is like raw material, we have to convert it into qualitative finished product. It is possible to change the attitude of students through motivation. It needs the commitment among teachers and staff. Because, skilled cultural well trained, well nourished, enlightened well protected human personnel pave the may for development of the economy. Expansion of human capabilities and personality development are important. The stake-holders should acquire necessary knowledge and skill in this regard.

The new challenge before our society is to make every individual productive and competitive. The quality and competence are the new Icons which open up the window to the world of excellence. So every educational institution should become a center of excellence. Quality can be linked to performance needing to scaling of newer and higher standards. It is linked with quality assessment and quality management. A commitment to quality and the mission to enhance excellence in education should aim it:

- To provide man-making education.
- To help in Self-development, mutual development, organisational development and eventually societal development.
- To Initiate total quality education.
- To make education relevant and useful.
- To build analytical minds with scientific temperament to develop problem-solving capabilities.
- To inculcate total commitment and ability to work in groups.

Public sector and Private sector, both are important, as for as quality is concerned. When private entrepreneurs set-up higher education facilities, in addition to the criticality of equity and access, there is also the worrisome dimension of wide variation in quality. On the other hand, there are a few institutions that provide top quality faculty and excellent infrastructure, targeting high caliber output. On the other hand, there are numerous educational enterprises that pay scant attention to quality and are only interested in maximising net revenues. Thus there is a strong case for effective and creative, but not choking and destructive regulation that will go a long way in achieving the quantitative expansion without jeopardising quality.

The two concerns that should guide higher education polity and regulation are equity and quality. On the first, let me borrow a quote from an article by Amandapalla's and Sarah Turner of the university of Virginia published in the *National Tax Journal* of June 2006 in which they refer to Lawrence summers description of "Manifest inadequacy of higher education's current contribution to equality of opportunity in America."

The implication is that the state has to continue to play a dominant role in higher education in developing countries like India as argued succinctly by Tilak in an article published in September 2005 in *EPW* and by Courant, Mc Pherson and Research in their paper in the *National Tax Journal* of June 2006.

"Improving access to all and ensuring access to weaker sections, inducting governance systems that assure transparency and accountability, continued state funding and raising the budgetary allocation for higher education, increase in grants and scholarships for students, building and sustaining quality and finally the regulation of the higher educational institutions in general and those in the private sector in particulars are some of the pressing issues that need to be urgently addressed".

Apart from being a facilitator and a social welfare agent, Government in developing countries is expected to be a proactive institution to build social infrastructure in order to move towards the goal of equitable and sustainable. In the emerging knowledge economy, building a strong human capital base to complement the natural resource endowments and available physical capital and to exploit the human resource potential is regarded critical in India at this stage of an expanding economy. Tertiary education is now considered critical from the stand point of achieving overall economic and social development. Recent research suggests that the increase in the number of skilled workers may have in fact boosted the value of further education and made it more important for growth. Indeed, building a workforce with higher order skills in an important part of improving the climate for investment, acquiring a competitive edge and generally maintaining an engine of growth. The situation of young people today presents the world with an unprecedented opportunity to accelerate growth and reduce poverty. Because labour is the main asset of the poor, making it more productive is the best way to reduce poverty. This requires enhancing the opportunity to earn money and developing the human capital to take advantage of those opportunities. Quite appropriately the Eleventh Plan approach paper aims at 15 per cent enrolment towards the end of the Eleventh Plan.

On the basis of my study, I have arrived at some conclusions to main quality and excellence in higher education—

- Identifying specific objective and strategic plan to attain their vision and mission.
- Introducing more range of options, career-oriented and computerised courses keeping in mind the latest trends and societal needs.
- Digital Library and internet facilities to the students is the need of the hour.
- Introducing new and modern teaching aids and new age of communication techniques for the use of students and teachers.
- It is necessary to establish national and international linkage for teaching and research.
- Faculty development programmes are necessary to empower the teachers.
- Development of soft skills among students is the need of the hour.
- Self-assessment mechanism helps for continuous improvement of institutions.

- Introducing the choice-based credit system.
- Infrastructure should be need-based.
- Upgradation of syllabus keeping with global standards.
- Value education is also the need of the hour.
- The leaner should be trained to develop self-awareness and self-esteem along with self-discipline.
- Total quality management in the institution is the need of the hour.

CONCLUSION

Sustainable economic development is depending upon proper nexus between economic growth and human development. Human development is depending to a great extent on quality and excellence in education. Quality Assurance in higher education under globalisation will have a meaning when all the concerned servants and masters alike, will answer affirmatively one question mentioned by Prof. Nigavekar. The question is, "Do I love and respect myself for what I am or what I have?" Our pursuit need to be to demonstrate that we are capable of responding to the needs of the day and to shape the destiny of our economy.

References

Beord, Ruth and Hartley, James (1984), Teaching and Learning in Higher Education, London Harper and Row Publications.

Mehta, G.S. (1990), Education, Employment and Earnings, Deep & Deep Publications, New Delhi.

Sen, Amartya (1999), "Beyond the Crisis"; Development Strategies in Asia, Capital Publishing Company, India, pp. 12-24.

World Bank (2003), World Development Indicators, Oxford University Press, New Yark.

University News, 41(10) March 10-16 2003.

Sen, Amartya (2006), Indentity and Violence: The Illusion of Destiny.

Tilak, JGB (2005), "Higher Education in Trishanku: Hanging Between State and Market", *Economic and Political Weekly*, September 10.

World Bank (2007), World Development Report—Development for Next Generation.

Govenment of India, *Economic Survey*, 2005-06.

Shastree, Nalin K. (2004), 'Privatizing Higher Education: Global Challenges and National responses" *University News,* Feburary.

Jandhayala, B.G. Tilak (2004), "Public Subsidies to Education in India", *Economic and Political Weekly,* January.

Thomas, Joseph (2004), "Privatisation and Commercialisation: The New Paradigm in Higher Education", *University News,* February.

8

Education and Inequality: The Theoretical Framework

Abhishek Kumar and Upendra Prasad Singh

Education aims at providing a person an ability and taste for pursuits which are worthwhile in themselves. This aim is achieved by introducing a student to a form of rational knowledge or a discipline such as natural sciences, mathematics, literature, economics or history and by initiating him into rational procedures such as inventing, developing and testing hypotheses; critically assessing arguments and making and testing hypotheses and thereby achieving a progressive mastery over a rational discipline and a gradual command over the rational procedures. A student learns to care for the intrinsic quality of experiences and activities apart from intrumental value they may possess in making the life of the individual and the community more easy and comfortable, (Shah, 1978; 7). Therefore we see that education is of immense importance for the overall development of a person. But opportunities for the access to education and therefore such development is not equally available to all.

There are various factors that help or hinder a person

to acquire education. A child brought up in an educated family acquires a strong motivation for education. The upper status of the family in the society facilitates helpful contacts with teachers and co-learners which are powerful aid to education. Children coming from lower strata will be denied these and similar advantages (Rege, 1978: 119). William Tyler in his book, 'the Sociology of Educational Inequality' observes that there can be five different kinds of educational inequality-inequality due to achievement, inequality due to education background, due to aptitude or ability and inequality of school environment (Tyler, 1962: 10)

The first one, that is inequality in terms of achievement refers to the fact that some children can read better than others of their age and are more likely to stay on at school and go on the University. This educational inequality is in terms of achievement. The second type of inequality is due to educational background. This means that some children come from families that give them certain advantages such as encyclopedias, visit to art galleries and museums and help with their homework. This refers to inequality in educational background. Third and the more unusual meaning an educational inequality, view of Tyler is that some children are able to need at higher love than others of the same age because they were born that way. This inequality is that of aptitude or ability, that is potential for learning.

The fourth type of educational inequality is about the advantages that come from different experiences and stimulation that the several provides. Because of the better or more educational facilitates and climate of school; the children will learn faster, stay on longer and pick up credentials that will increase his lifetime earnings. It is school environment inequality.

Tyler also mentioned about five models through which educational inequality can be understood the first model is the mertocratic model proposed by Richard Herrnstain (1971). According to this model rich and intellectually competent parents pass on all their children a similar head start. In such a model, biological inheritance of ability is the engine of inequality since family, school and work simply reinforce genetic endowments.

The 'radical' or 'class conflict' model of educational inequality propose a different set of relationships in which social and family background rather than inherited ability is the driving force. Family background is a more determinant of educational success that is ability. Children from the poorer backgrounds never have, in words of Newson Report (1963) 'an equal opportunity for acquiring intelligence'. They are often labled as in educable and the expectation is that they will leave early (as edited in H.M.S.O., 1967, paras 53-56)

The third model of educational inequality is the conservative model which believe that a system that restricts opportunity is not early inevitable but indesirable. It is in nature of things, . that the children of privileged class are better endowed intellectually go to better schools and dominate the elite institutions of learning. Adhorents of both conservative and the radical models agree that intelligence is not a natural talent but rather something conferred by society. All natural qualities have a social origin.

The evolutionary liberal model is similar to merit to create model but proposes a weak connection between intelligence and family background they refuse the claim that there is a restricted pool of ability which explains the different class rates of achievement and success.

The fifth approach is of compensating liberal which resembles class conflict model but proposes that school environment and credentials can significantly improve the life chances of working class children. Education is seem to offer a ladder of opportunity, however restricted, to the children of working and lower classes. Education give, everyone an equal opportunity for developing mental, physical, emotional and spiritual talents to the full. Educational system is viewed as a means for compensating for the deprived environment of the (Tyler, *ibid*: 13).

The liberal model in general views that academic credentials are awarded on merit in a system of fair competition. In the same way, jobs are awarded on merits and there is a strong relationship between educational qualifications and occupational status school provides equality of opportunity for all members of society regardless of their position in the stratification system, a more open society and therefore a higher rate of social mobility will result.

Besides these five models, many thinkers have expressed their own different views. For example, Emile Durkhaim (1922: 67) maintained that there were as many different kinds of education as there were social milieus in any given society. In ancient Romes the education of the plebian was very different from that of the patrician. In India Brahmin Kshatriyas had quite separating education to Shudras. Karna had to suffer a lot to get Brahmin education. Douglas, Flaud, A.H. Halsey, F.M. Martis, J. Barron Mays all agrees on the effect of environmental factors upon children. Herbert H. Hyman in an article entitled, the value system of different classes was the entitled, the value system of different classes was the first to point out that class and ethnic stratification are directly related to educational attainment, values system of the lower classes creates a 'self-imposed' barrier to an improved position. Members of the working class place a lower value on education as a means to personal advancement. They emphasize stability, security and immediate economic benefits while evaluating jobs and tend to reject the risks and investments involved. The motivation to achieve whether in school or in job, will generally be lower for the members of the working class (Hyman, 1967: 8). According to J.W.B. Douglas (1964: 75) inequalities is increased by self-fertilizing nature of education. In the Crowther report, it was indicated that the chances of the children of professions and managerial parents continuing their education to 17 or beyond were 25 times more than the son of unskilled workers (Crowther Report, 1959: 118). Similarly, Robbins Reports, 1963: 50, registered that 15 per cent boys from non-manual classes entered university degree courses as against 3 per cent from manual classes.

Newsom and powden Reports (1967, pp. 53-54 and 320) has observed that potential ability among the children of the lower classes have been masked by the inadequate power of speech. Linguistic adequacy is closely linked with home and social background. According to Bernstin the middle class child is brought up in an ethos of formal language or in 'elaborate code' while working class child is limited to use of 'restricted codes' (1961: 55). Formal education is conducted in terms of an elaborate code and restricted code, by its very nature, reduces the chances of working class pupils to successfully acquire some of the skills demanded by the educational system. From this view point, equality of opportunity can become a reality by compensating for the deprivations and deficiencies of low incomes groups. Professor Rahim Pedly in his discussion of 'A New Society' states that the first need is a culturally rich environment of the neighborhood, the home and the school within which children can both learn and grow. (Pedley, 1963: 31)

French Socioligist Raymond Boudon in his work education, opportunity and social inequality argues that inequality of education opportunity is produced by 'two component process'. The first component, he refers to as the 'primary effects of stratification'. It involves sub-cultural differences between social classes which are produced by the stratification system. The secondary effects of stratification are more important. These stem simply from a person's actual position in the class structure. He maintains that even if there were no sub-cultural differences between classes, the very fact that people start at different positions in the class system will produce inequality of educational opportunity. He calls it positional theory. Moreover, there are greater pressures on the upper middle class boy to select a higher level educational course, if only to maintain his present social position (Bouden: 75)

Pierre Bourdieu, Michael F.S. Young, D. Lawton, Jane Torrey form another group of thinkers who argue that dominant groups in society have the power to define what counts as knowledge in the educational system. And if classroom knowledge is based largely upon the knowledge of dominant groups then schooling will automatically favour the children of powerful and discriminate against those from lower social strata. Bourdieu (1973:3) argues that the major role of the educational system is 'cultural reproduction'. This means reproduction of the culture of dominant class and to establish if as the basis of knowledge in the educational system. The dominant culture is the 'Cultural Capital' to be translated into wealth and power. The class differences in educational attainment is largely because of this uneven distribution of cultural capital children from dominant classes internalise most of the skills and knowledge during their pre-school years and therefore have a higher rate of success than working class students. He further says that educational system plays the role of the elimination. It eliminates members of working class from higher level of education, either by examination failure or by self-elimination. Thus, it filters in students of dominant class and filters out students of working class. In this way education is concerned with reproduction of established order.

F.D. Young (1971) also concludes that powers and privilege remain within the same social groups on account of inequalitarion character of education system. Tyler also observes that there is a lightening word between education and occupation. A.H. Halsey is also supportive of the view that social backgroung has an increasing effect on educational attainment and at the same time bond between education and occupation. Thus Halsey concludes that 'education is increasingly the mediator of the transmission of status between generations' (Halsey, 1961). It is only through educational system that privilege is passed on from father to son. Therefore, this view of Halsey is opposed to meritocratic model and views education as a mechanism for the maintenance of privilege rather then as a means of role allocation.

To conclude, education may push up the rate of economic development but it cannot be equalizer to bridge the gulf between rich and poor on the contrary education helps in maintaining *status quo* and perpetuates the interest of dominant social class. It cannot be a stimulus to inclusive growth.

References

Bounden, R. (1974): Educaiton, Opportunity and Social Inequality, New York, John, Wiley and Sons.

Bourdieu, P. and Passeraan, J. (1997): Reproduction in Education, Society and Culture, London, Sage.

Bernstein B, (1961) Social Class and Linguistic Development in Halsey (Edited).

Crowther Report (HMSO, 1959), Ministry of Education, Part one.

Durkhim, E.: Education and Sociology, Paris: Allam.

Douglas, J.W.B. (1967): The Home and the School Mac Gribbon and Kee.

Halsey, A.M. and Floud, J. (1961): Education, Economy and Society, New York: Free Press.

Herrnstein, R. (1973). IQ in the Meritocarcy, London, Alber Lane.

Hyman, H.H.: The Value System of Different Classes in Bundix and Lipset

Iylor, William: The Sociology of Educational Inequality.

Malsey, A.H.: Education: Culture, Economy, Society, Oxford University Press.

Newsom and Plowdum Report (MMSO) Children and the Primary Schools.

Plowden Report (HMSO, 1967) Children and Primary Schools, Paras, 53-54.

Pedley R. (1963): The Comprehensive School. Penguin Books.

Rege, M.P. (1978): Education and Social Justice: Conceptual Framework in A.B. Shah (eds.), The Social Context of Educations.

Robbins Report (HMSO, 1963), Committee on Higher Education, Higher Education, Take 21.

Shah A.B. (1978): The Social Context of Education Essays in Honour of Prof. J.P. Naik, Delhi, Allied Publishers.

Higher Education: New Challenges and Emerging Roles for Human and Social Development

NEERAJ KUMAR SINGH, MADAN KUMAR AND PIYUSH KUMAR

INTRODUCTION

Education builds character, contribute to efficient human development, improvement of human capital needs higher investments on social sector, which lead to higher growth of a Nation.

Our Puranas and Ithihasas have laid great stress on education and health and have shown characters that contributed to the growth of the Nation. Lord Rama is a great example for reputed character and immense health, which made Him contribute a great deal for the rule of Rama Rajya—a perfect democracy linked to efficient development of the State. Even today His rule and His State Ayodhya is a model being pursued through with the help of modern science and technology. Education has a positive role in human development.

Mahatma Gandhiji very clearly and correctly wrote that

education is the strong base for building a strong India. He emphasised "basic education" to all so that people can live a happy life living only in villages, avoiding migration to cities. Moreover, he advised government to educate women who are the main pillars of society. Swami Vivekananda wanted strong man (woman also included) with strong mind and strong health, so that India could become a strong and wealthy Nation in the entire world. He, in particular, wanted to promote women's education in the entire Nation. In a sense he advocated universalisation of education and health in India so that strong Nation can be built with the efficient human resources. The core components of human development are: education and health.

Education provides a variety of benefits to students including enhanced social skills, greater awareness of human achievement, and an appreciation for cultural diversity. But education is increasingly viewed as an economic investment. Education provides a student with skills that are valued by employers and increases lifetime earnings capacity. In this chapter the statistical evidence on the effect of educational attainment on earnings is examined to determine the economic rate of return realised when an individual invests in a college education. Particular emphasis is placed on the value an individual receives from completing a bachelor's degree.

In calculating the return on a college education, this chapter considers as benefits only the incremental earnings realised by the individual who earns the college degree. Spillover the return to education presented in this chapter is referred to as the "private return to education." Benefits that accrue to other parties are potentially significant, but they are not considered until the next chapter of the report. Following the conventional language used by economists, when all benefits are considered, including spillovers received by other individuals, the calculated returns referred to as the "social return to education."

To determine the economic value of a college education, benefits must be weighed against the full costs of obtaining that education. These costs include the tuition payments made by the college attendee, the opportunity costs associated with earnings foregone while in college, and in the case of a public university the appropriations of state and local governments. The return on investment calculated using full costs is a more useful guide for public policy than one calculated using only the costs incurred by the student. College may represent a good personal investment for an individual if that education is highly subsidized by the government. But College is shown to represent a wise use of society's resources when the value of the enhanced skills the individual receives, as measured by increased earnings capacity, exceeds the full resource costs of providing that education.

Higher education in India is gradually entering into crisis situation, facing many problems and inadequacies. Though its spread is quite rapid, its steep decline in quality is equally rapid, what with scarcity of financial resources, proper infrastructure, adequate qualified staff, etc. Though government is advised to allot nearly one percent of G.D.P for higher education, government has settled at 0.8% in 2005-06, which may further decline for want of sufficient resources. Whereas foreign countries are enhancing their allocation on higher education, research and development, India has not taken a leaf out of their experience.

The enrolment of persons in higher education is only 10% of population; whereas it is higher at 20-25% in developed countries. Hence both in enrolment and promoting efficiency and quality, India is at a low level. Even China, Malaysia, Philippines are in a better position compared to India, not to speak of Western Developed countries.

Entire education system in our country is in a mismatch. While around forty percent of population is virtually illiterate, the top-level limited education centers of education are beyond the reach of common men. Most of our high level education centers and universities are ill-equipped and inefficient. Hence the products of those institutions are not sufficiently capable for technical employment.

India's elite scientific and educational institutions maintain quite high standard. In some universities the quality of education is very high and at par with the rest of the world. Since salary of professionals in India is very low in comparison to the industrial world, professional services in India enjoy a very favorable international competitiveness. Right now this is utilized mainly in information technology, biotechnology, health care, banking, finance and in few other services. But there is a great deal of scope to expand it in almost all other services where we have already attained a fair degree of professional expertise. India can also be a center of research and development due to high quality educational base in many fields of science and technology.

One of the major lacunas of India's development strategy is that while it thrives on highly skilled services, it had all throughout neglected mass education and health services. India's elite educational institutions stand like isolated ivory towers amidst encircling poverty, illiteracy and backwardness. Rural India is completely neglected in health, education, nutrition and other elements of human capital. The number of universities and colleges are also very small. For one billion plus population 400 odd universities and odd colleges are too few 16000. According to the latest count, only 8% of youth manage to get admitted in colleges and universities. Most children dropout of school for a variety of reasons ranging from poverty to parents unwillingness to get their children educated due to socio-cultural inhibitions. Girls are particularly deprived of education. But even if the parents are willing to educate their children, the shortage of schools and colleges hinders education. According to the Indian Planning Commission half the villages do not have a primary school.

- In India the average workers, especially in the Informal sector, whether in agriculture, manufacturing, or in services, is poorly educated. They also suffer from poor health. Their average labour productivity is therefore low, and in spite of low wage, the real cost of labour is quite high.

In India however, a small proportion of manpower is highly educated. The technically qualified manpower has now become the engine of growth in India not only in services but also in manufacturing sectors. Services now have fastest GDP growth. Within services sector, services utilizing professionally qualified manpower, such as finance, banking, software, media, entertainment, etc. are recording fastest growth, ranging between 20% to even 50% growth per annum. In these sectors there is as yet no sign of diminishing returns. Manufacturing growth on an average has been lower than services. Again within manufacturing sector, large-scale industries using more technical labours are having faster growth than small and medium industries employing more unskilled labours. Agriculture using least skilled workers is having the slowest growth among all sectors.

THE RELATIONSHIP BETWEEN EARNINGS AND EDUCATIONAL ATTAINMENT

The economic value of educational attainment is apparent from cross-tabulations of national data on individual earnings and educational attainment—

- Is the question of access to higher education still the principal problem? What general implications, within and outside of higher education, result in certain careers being mainly chosen by one or the other gender?
- What role can/must higher education or its institutions play to lead the transformation towards a more egalitarian, inclusive and equal society with respect to gender?
- Once the problem of access is faced, what is the following step that higher education could take in order to build a more egalitarian, inclusive and equal society with respect to gender issues?

Artistic disciplines and practices, as well as knowledge and experimentation areas, which draw on or inspire creativity deliberately, tend to have little influence on the debates about the improvement or the future of higher education. In view of the new and complex challenges which higher education institutions (HEIs) are facing, however, spaces for reflection, creation and action through the arts can be especially fruitful, provocative and innovative.

HIGHER EDUCATION FOR INTERCULTURAL DIALOGUE AND MULTICULTURALISM

The dynamics caused by migration, transnationalism and the process of globalisation all contribute to the coexistence between different societies and cultures being probably the major challenge faced by humanity in the XXI century. The construction of a plural society, where different cultural conceptions and world visions have to fit, is indispensable in a globalised world. The processes and mechanisms to understand dialogue and live are the basis to create a multicultural society—

- How can higher education contribute to these processes?
- In what way is higher education prepared—or can prepare itself—to train its graduates, so that they are capable to act within multicultural social and work contexts, which cease to be exceptional and become normal?
- What do HEIs need to undertake to adapt themselves to the new multicultural reality?
- How can migrations affect HEIs?
- How can HEIs be active agents to preserve and foster cultural diversity?

HIGHER EDUCATION FOR SUSTAINABLE DEVELOPMENT

The UN considers the period 2005-14 as the Decade of Education for Sustainable Development. Since the 1993 Kyoto Declaration on Sustainable Development of the International Association of Universities (IAU) identifying the central role of higher education for transition towards a sustainable human development, the international debate has been intensified. However, the concepts and national educational programmes about how to incorporate sustainability in higher education focus on different issues.

In this sense, the transition towards sustainability can be seen as a transforming process of social learning, in which the role of academia is not one of integration of sustainable development, but is one of innovation and systematic change in our institutions, allowing increased social learning. This evidence of the fact that the real challenge is not only about including sustainability into the internal activities of HEIs. It is even more necessary to integrate them into the steps society is taking towards sustainable development, even transforming them into one of its main motors.

Thus, the need for Education for Sustainable Development is a major challenge today for HEIs. It implies deep changes, so as to overcome the disciplinary division or to allow transformative learning to take place. Dealing with complexity, structural changes, teaching organisation and pedagogy and the role of research, are the main themes for the implementation of sustainable development in HEIs.

This thematic line emphasises some of the following questions:

- How should educational reforms be, to accompany this process?
- How to define and reorient the competences for global sustainable change?
- How can the university articulate global networks with local actors?

HIGHER EDUCATION AND CITIZENSHIP, PARTICIPATION AND DEMOCRACY

Participatory processes have been identified as one of the most powerful engines to provoke real transformations in contemporary society and in HEIs. They help these institutions and those with whom they engage, face the growing demands and challenges of an increasingly globalize world.

In the context of globalization and great media simplifications, an active and responsible citizenship is particularly required. It should be aware of the ethical implications and the vast consequences of its professional activity, as well as aware and committed to the values and fundamentals of respect, tolerance and democracy. Thus, in many places of the world, HEIs have played and can play a very important role as beacons of freethinking and democracy. Maybe another world is possible, in which individuals are valued as productive and trained citizens and as potential agents for *good change*.

These three factors (citizenship, participation and democracy) draw vectors of change in society and in HEIs. In this thematic line we look for contributions, which examine any of these factors. The contribution may focus on processes and experiences taking place inside HEIs, or relate to relationships between HEIs and/or towards society, or a combination of these. Some key questions could be:

- What roles have HEIs to play in order to specify and put into practice democratic values?
- How can HEIs move towards participatory approaches in education, research, planning and decision-making processes from a bottom-up perspective?
- In the context of globalisation, is it necessary that higher education plays a major role with respect to citizenship?
- How can processes be implemented successfully, so that they respond to poverty and social injustice?

HIGHER EDUCATION'S ROLE

Higher education has historically included economic development as part of its core mission. The colleges and universities serving the region have allocated fiscal, physical, and human resources and created entrepreneurship systems within the institutions to advance economic development. Senior administrators provide strong, visible leadership designed to—

- create a quality workforce by growing, training, and attracting the finest talent,
- support current business and industry,
- improve learning and teaching from pre-school through graduate school,

- take strong and visible roles in regional initiatives,
- disseminate research and promote technology transfer,
- enhance the technology infrastructure,
- promote livable communities, and
- employ a diverse workforce.

A Quality Workforce: Growing, Training, and Attracting the Finest

Higher education will be a dominant, if not decisive, factor in preparing workers with the robust skills needed to adapt to changing job requirements. The transition from manufacturing to the Technology-based new economy dramatically raised the skill level needed to get a job. Higher education prepares a quality workforce by offering instructional programs, matching instruction to the needs of business and industry, and helping individuals learn throughout their lives.

Support to Cure Business and Industry

Current business and industry receives support through the customized services offered by higher education. As technology and the economic climate change, higher education can be a valuable resource to businesses in these ways:

- identifying employee skills gaps and providing customized training,
- conducting organizational assessments and providing management development,
- providing technical assistance, industrial liaison programs, and support centers,
- assisting in the identification of new markets for products,
- offering specialized help for small-to-medium sized businesses for planning, resource acquisition, and marketing, e.g., entrepreneurship training and assistance,
- providing customized research and data,

- procuring grants which support current business and industry,
- providing conference and meeting facilities Examples of Alliance member support for current business and industry include:
- Members of the Alliance provide customized training and services to businesses.

Strong and Visible Roles in Regional Initiatives

Efforts to enhance economic growth are shifting from tax-based incentives to attract businesses to strategies that develop industry clusters designed to increase regional competitiveness and wealth. The success of the industry clusters depends on the region's science and technology capacity, ability to develop global markets; availability of lifelong learning and training for employers and employees; and collaborative relationships among research, capital, business, and public policy. Higher education, with its networks and linkages throughout the region and state, is uniquely positioned to convene the necessary representatives from the diverse government, business, education, social, and civic groups and to serve as the third-party, neutral catalyst to create the collaborations needed to develop industry clusters.

Enhance the Technology Infrastructure

Higher education can be a technology driver and instrumental in raising the economic development of the region by doing the following:

- designing cutting-edge technologies, which result in new products, businesses, and jobs,
- supplying advanced technology for use by the region,
- providing technology instruction to create a skilled workforce,
- addressing the digital divide for targeted areas and populations, and
- creating e-learning and innovative delivery to expand access to education.

Livable Communities

Livable communities are viewed as great places to live and work. Higher education institutions provide instruction and training, but they also provide arts, entertainment, sports, and recreation programs that attract and retain a quality workforce. Professional-quality events are available to the public free or at reasonable costs.

Higher Education as Employer

The role of higher education as a major employer of a diverse pool of workers cannot be ignored. As a basic, revenue-generating industry, higher education directly, and through related multipliers, impacts the economy of the region.

EXECUTIVE SUMMARY: THE VALUE OF HIGHER EDUCATION

Higher education provides considerable value to individuals, the economies where educated individuals work and live, and society in general.

Private Returns

- Individual earnings are strongly related to educational attainment. People who have more than those with only a high school diploma; and those with a graduate education earn more than those with only an undergraduate education.

Average annual earnings of individuals with a bachelor's degree are more than 75 percent higher than the earnings of high school graduates. These additional earnings sum to over $1 completed high school earn more than those who have not; people with a bachelor's degree earn associated with having a bachelor's degree *versus* a high school diploma has risen from 38 percent in the 1980-84 period to 94 percent in 2000-03.

- The benefits to an individual from a university

education vary with the quality of the institution attended. Those who graduate from an elite university earn substantially more than those who graduate from a lower-quality institution.

- To properly assess the economic value of a college education, the benefits realized in terms of higher future earnings must be discounted to adjust for the time value of money. The discounted earnings must then be weighed against the full costs of acquiring a college education including not only the tuition paid by the student, but the earnings foregone while the student is in college and the appropriations of state and local governments. When these calculations are made, the benefits of a college education are seen to be more than three times as large as the costs.
- If the value of a college education is expressed on the same basis as the return on a financial investment, the net return is on the order of 12 percent per year, over and above inflation. This compares favorably with annual returns on stocks that historically have averaged 7 percent.
- Despite the very high return on investment for the time and money spent on attaining a college degree, only one-quarter of the U.S. adult population has at least a bachelor's degree.
- The academic ability of the individual—which is shaped throughout his/her life by a variety of family and environmental factors—and the values and goals of the individual—which are strongly influenced by the education of his/her parents—are important determinants of educational attainment.

Societal Benefit

Social benefits of a workforce with greater educational attainment and skills can be traced to the enhanced worker productivity associated with greater educational attainment. These productivity gains translate into higher output and incomes for the economy.

Overview

Higher education provides considerable value to individuals, to the economies where educated individuals live and work, and society in general. Economies that have experienced substantial investment in either private or public institutions of higher learning have realized Considerable growth and prosperity. Higher education influences economic well-being in three ways. First, the direct expenditures by the institutions, their employees, and their students impact the local economy. This spending multiplies through the local economy until the monies are used to purchase goods and services from outside the local area. Such economic impacts have been estimated at many institutions of higher education.

Public Policy Issues

A primary conclusion of this report is that college education yields high rewards that accrue to individuals and to the communities where they ultimately find employment. Policies that eliminate barriers (informational, ability, or financial) and result in tangible increases in the number of degree-holders are interventions that should be pursued. Considerable effort has already been undertaken to alleviate financial barriers and these efforts have brought results.

Effective policies aimed at increasing both enrolment and degree completion rates simultaneously could be equally rewarding. The barriers pose significant challenges and debate over the efficacy and cost of alternative policy options will occur, but in the end the potential rewards are very high. Empirical estimates capturing the magnitude of these rewards are detailed in this report—including significant monetary returns as well as a long list of non-monetary returns that continue to yield benefits over generations.

References

Philippe Aghion and Steven, N., Deulauf Handbook of Economic Growth, Vol. 1B, North Holland, 2005.

Philip Arestis (2006), John McCombie or Roger Vickerman (ed.), Growth and Economic Development, Essays in Honour of A.P. Thirwall, Edward Elgar.

B.B. Bhattacharya and S. Kar (2007), Macroeconomics Reforms, Growth and Stability, Oxford University Press, Delhi

—— (2004), "Macroeconomic Projections" in R.K. Sinha (ed.), India 2025, Centre for Policy Research, New Delhi, 2004.

World Bank, World Development Report (2007), Oxford University Press.

Yun Peng Chu and Hal Hill (ed.) (2006), The East Asian High-Tech Drive, Edward Elgar.

PART II

EDUCATION AND ECONOMIC DEVELOPMENT OF INDIA

10

Nature, Composition and Extent of the Stock of India's Educated Manpower: Problems and Implications for Growth and Employment

VIKRAM CHADHA

Since the seminal work of Schumpeter (1961) on the sources of growth, and more recently of Rivera-Batiz and Romer (1991), 'knowledge' has come to occupy the centre stage in the economic growth of nations. Just as neo-classical economics premised the accumulation of physical capital and labour as the main sources of economic growth; now, in the contemporary world, knowledge and information are replacing capital and energy as the primary wealth creating assets. The New Growth Theory attaches a premium on knowledge accumulation as the sole driver of economic growth.

Modern developed societies have become information-based knowledge economies, where knowledge accumulation has taken place through a long history of discoveries, inventions, learning and improvements in the past. New ideas, methods, skills and know-how, which are intangible assets of a knowledge economy, have not only contributed to the physical capital accumulation and accelerated the growth of these societies, but such immaterial investments in knowledge building through education and R&D, has further accentuated knowledge accumulation at a still accelerated pace. So, knowledge manifested in new ideas, skills, methods, R&D and learning-by-doing, has become invisible and subtle sources of socio-economic growth of societies.

Growth of knowledge hinges on the nature and extent of human capital of a nation. Human capital, reflecting the nature and depth of education, skill; innovativeness, creativity and capabilities of the people of a country, determine, the pace of growth of knowledge. Thus to accelerate the pace of growth of knowledge, human capital and hence the speed of economic and technological growth of nations, large investments in education, research, training and skill formation are needed.

The most facile method to form human capital and hence knowledge accumulation, is to invest in education and training of a country's human resource. Soskice (1993) and Bowles and Gintis (1976) assert that education is the principal enabler in a knowledge economy to exacerbate economic growth and development. Higher levels of investment in education and learning helps in forming both the basic and cognitive skills, which help the countries to adapt and innovate technology faster (Harbinson and Myers, 1965; Benhabib and Spiegel, 1994; Barro, 2001; Psacharopoulos, 1988).

It is in the above context that the present paper aims at carrying out a cross-section analysis of the stock of India's educated manpower with reference to the faculty enrolments, discipline and areas of specialization, levels of study and the gender configuration, etc. It also endeavours to decipher the implications of such human capital formation for its employment and the country's economic growth.

GROWTH OF EDUCATION AND STOCK OF EDUCATED MANPOWER IN INDIA

Since independence the Indian economic development hinged on the strategy to achieve economic and technological self-reliance. It was evidently visualised that economic self-reliance would be unattainable unless it is based on domestically groomed manpower and skills. A strong emphasis was laid on an accelerated rate of human capital formation by perceptibly investing in education, research and training. The whole edifice of social and economic development needed to be raised on the institutions of learning and research. Thus a wide network of universities, engineering colleges and institutes of technology including medical and other technical and research institutes was forged, which eventually created in India the largest reservoir of technically trained and skilled manpower in the world.

PLAN EXPENDITURE ON EDUCATION

A glimpse of India's efforts in building its knowledge base can be had from Table 1, which depicts India's Plan expenditure on education and research. It highlights that the Plan expenditure on education escalated from barely Rs. 588.7 crore during Third Five Year Plan, to Rs. 101364.2 crore during Tenth Five Year Plan. During the XIth Plan, about 20 per cent of the total Plan outlay is contemplated to be spent on education, which is indeed a phenomenal increase in the expenditure on education and marks a spectacular deviation from the past trends when it never exceeded 6.6 per cent of the total Plan outlay. In the Budget of 2008-09 alone, Rs. 34400 crore have been allocated for the education sector (Tilak, 2008).

STOCK OF S&T PERSONNEL

As a result of the concerted efforts of the Government in the domain of higher education, India can boast of a significant stock of scientific and technical (S&T) personnel who have perceptibly contributed towards India's economic

TABLE I

Plan Outlay for Education and Research Sectors

(Rs. crore)

Plan/ Sector	*IIIrd Plan (1961-66)*	*IVth Plan (1969-74)*	*Vth Plan (1974-79)*	*VIth Plan (1980-85)*	*VIIth Plan (1985-90)*	*VIIIth Plan (1992-97)*	*IXth Plan (1997-2002)*	*Xth Plan (2002-07)*	*XIth Plan (2007-11)*
Education	588.7	774.3	1710.3	2523.7	7685.5	19599.7	49838.5	101364.2	287000
	(6.9)	(4.9)	(4.3)	(2.6)	(3.5)	(4.5)	(6.12)	(6.6)	(20.00)
Scientific Research	71.6	130.8	–	865.2	3023.9	9041.7	18458.0	30424.0	87933
	(0.8)	(0.8)		(0.9)	(1.4)	(2.1)	(2.1)	(2.0)	(2.4)

Note: (i) Figures in parentheses are % of total Plan outlay
(ii) 'a' includes combined outlay on education and scientific research

Source: (i) Government of India (Various Issues), *Economic Survey*, New Delhi: Ministry of Finance, Economic Division.
(ii) Tilak, J.B.G. (2008), "Education in 2008-09 Union Budget", *Economic and Political Weekly*, Vol. XLIII, No. 20, pp. 49-56

TABLE 2

Estimated Stock of S&T Personnel

(Fig. in '000)

Category/ Year	*1991*	*1996*	*1998*	*1999*	*2000*	*2001*	*Annual Growth Rate*
Engineering Degree Holders	519.6 (10.82)	753.3 (11.94)	859.1 (12.30)	913.7 (12.45)	969.5 (12.43)	1024.4 (12.67)	10.71
Engineering Diploma Holders	859.3 (17.89)	1173.1 (18.60)	1312.3 (18.79)	1379.5 (18.80)	1546.0 (19.82)	1531.7 (18.94)	10.59
Medical Graduates	310.3 (6.46)	358.4 (5.68)	380.4 (5.45)	391.7 (5.34)	403.4 (5.17)	415.9 (5.14)	10.30
Agricultural Graduates	168.4 (3.51)	202.3 (3.21)	216.5 (3.10)	223.8 (3.05)	231.2 (2,96)	238.6 (2,95)	10.35
Veterinary Graduates	34.4 (0.72)	40.2 (0.64)	42.7 (0.61)	44.0 (0.60)	45.3 (0.58)	46.7 (0.58)	10.30
Science Graduates	2430.3 (50.59)	3154.8 (50.01)	3479.3 (49.81)	3655.4 (49.81)	3837.7 (49.20)	4024.9 (49.77)	10.52
Science Post-Graduates	482.0 (10.03)	626.1 (9.93)	695.5 (9.96)	730.6 (9.96)	767.1 (9.83)	805.0 (9.95	10.52
Total	4804.3 (100)	6308.2 (100)	6985.8 (100)	7338.7 (100)	7800.2 (100)	8087.2 (100)	10.53

Note: Figures in parentheses are % of total.
Source: Government of India (2006), Research and Development Statistics, New Delhi: Ministry of S&T, DST.

growth. Table 2 presents an overview of India's estimated stock of scientifically and technically trained manpower. It highlights that the total S&T manpower in India grew at over 10 per cent per annum during 1991 to 2001. The table reveals that about 50 per cent of the S&T personnel are merely science graduates. Who have mainly basic knowledge of sciences. Thus the table reflects an abysmal dearth of S&T personnel with critical skills, since veterinary, medical, engineering and agricultural graduates form less than 10 per cent of the total S&T manpower during this period. A visible shortage of agricultural, medical and engineering experts with critical skills, as depicted in this table, in a rapidly growing economy in the contemporary globalised milieu, does not augur well for the country.

ENROLMENT IN HIGHER EDUCATION

Faculty-wise enrolment of pupils in higher education is depicted in Table 3. The table reveals that during 1985-2004, the ratio of science/technology *vs.* non-science disciplines has hovered around 30:70. Among the S&T disciplines, student enrolment in pure science subjects dominates with around 20 per cent of the total. This again betrays the relative neglect of cutting edge areas of science and technology that includes engineering and technology (only 5-7 per cent of total enrolment), and medical; veterinary and agricultural sciences with less than 3 per cent of the aggregate enrolments. This pattern of students' enrolments in our universities and technical institutions does not forebode well for accelerating the pace of India's development. Similarly, very small fraction of the students' enrolment in the field of Education (about 2% of the total) shows a trend towards a serious paucity of trained and skilled teachers (to which a reference was widely made recently by the Pay Revision Committee of the UGC).

FEMALE ENROLMENT IN HIGHER EDUCATION

The proportion of women enrolment in higher education is presented in Table 4. The table presents a promising picture of equality of gender participation in the

TABLE 3

Faculty-wise Enrolment in Higher Education (1985-2004)

(Fig. in '000)

Area of Study	*1985-86*	*1995-96*	*1996-97*	*1997-98*	*1998-99*	*1999-00*	*2001-02*	*2002-03*	*2003-04*
1	*2*	*3*	*4*	*5*	*6*	*7*	*8*	*9*	*10*
Science and Technology Disciplines (A)									
Sciences	700.99	1288.51	1341.51	1423.04	1510.28	1537.67	1739.15	1884.32	2035.06
	(19.4)	(19.6)	(19.6)	(19.6)	(19.6)	(19.1)	(19.4)	(19.8)	(20.4)
Engineering and Technology	176.54	322.13	335.29	355.76	377.57	402.53	618.56	713.76	716.65
	(4.9)	(4.9)	(4.9)	(4.9)	(4.9)	(5.0)	(6.9)	(7.5)	(7.2)
Medicine	123.06	223.52	232.65	246.85	261.99	281.77	277.91	314.05	313.49
	(3.4)	(3.4)	(3.4)	(3.4)	(3.4)	(3.5)	(3.1)	(3.3)	(3.2)
Agricultural Sciences	41.90	72.31	75.27	79.87	84.76	88.56	89.65	57.10	58.70
	(1.2)	(1.1)	(1.1)	(1.1)	(1.1)	(1.1)	(1.0)	(0.6)	(0.6)
Veterinary Sciences	9.49	19.72	20.53	21.78	23.12	24.15	17.92	19.03	14.86
	(0.3)	(0.3)	(0.3)	(0.3)	(0.3)	(0.3)	(0.2)	(0.2)	(0.2)
Total (A)	1051.98	1926.18	2004.88	2127.30	2257.72	2334.68	2743.19	2989.27	3138.76
	(29.2)	(29.3)	(29.3)	(29.3)	(29.3)	(29.0)	(30.6)	(31.4)	(31.5)

(Contd.)

TABLE 3 (Contd.)

1	2	3	4	5	6	7	8	9	10
Other Disciplines (B)									
Arts	1466.30	2655.90	2764.41	2933.21	3113.03	3268.55	4132.72	4292.07	4490.72
	(40.7)	(40.4)	(40.4)	(40.4)	(40.4)	(40.6)	(46.1)	(45.1)	(45.1)
Commerce	782.07	1439.71	1498.53	1590.03	1687.51	1763.08	1604.68	1713.02	1790.64
	(21.7)	(21.9)	(21.9)	(21.9)	(21.9)	(21.9)	(17.9)	(18.0)	(19.0)
Law	196.11	348.42	362.66	384.80	408.39	418.63	286.87	304.5	303.63
	(5.4)	(5.3)	(5.3)	(5.3)	(5.3)	(5.2)	(3.2)	(3.2)	(3.1)
Education	82.64	151.20	157.38	166.99	177.23	185.16	116.54	133.24	146.04
	(2.3)	(2.3)	(2.3)	(2.3)	(2.3)	(2.3)	(1.3)	(1.4)	(1.5)
Others	25.95	52.59	54.74	58.08	61.64	80.51	80.68	85.65	83.72
	(0.7)	(0.8)	(0.8)	(0.8)	(0.8)	(1.0)	(0.9)	(0.9)	(0.8)
Total (B)	2553.05	4647.82	4837.72	5133.12	5447.80	5715.93	6221.49	6528.51	6814.75
	(70.8)	(70.7)	(70.7)	(70.7)	(70.7)	(71.0)	(69.4)	(68.6)	(68.5)
Total (A+B)	3605.03	6574.01	6842.60	7260.42	7705.52	8050.61	8964.68	9516.77	9953.51
	(100)	(100)	(100)	(100)	(100)	(100)	(100)	(100)	(100)

Note: Figures in parentheses are % of total.
Source: Same as Table 2, p. 86.

TABLE 4

Faculty-wise Enrolment of Women in Higher Education (1974-2004)

(Fig. in '000)

Year	Science and Technology Disciplines					Other Disciplines					
	Science	Engeering	Medicine	Agriculture	Vet. Science	Arts	Commerce	Law	Education	Others	Total
	(1)	(2)	(3)	(4)	(5)	(6)	(7)	(8)	(9)	(10)	(1 to 10)
1974-75	106.2	1.3	21.0	0.3	0.1	363.0	22.1	5.9	29.0	4.1	553.0
	(22.9)	(1.5)	(19.7)	(0.9)	(1.2)	(34.0)	(5.6)	(4.4)	(37.6)	(32.6)	(23.4)
1979-80	140.1	4.4	24.4	1.1	0.2	397.9	68.0	11.0	34.5	7.4	689.0
	(27.5)	(3.7)	(21.8)	(2.8)	(2.7)	(37.0)	(13.2)	(6.2)	(47.3)	(38.8)	(26.0)
1985-86	215.7	12.2	37.5	2.3	0.6	576.3	156.7	17.6	38.6	9.0	1067.5
	(30.8)	(6.9)	(30.5)	(5.5)	(6.3)	(39.3)	(20.0)	(9.0)	(46.7)	(34.7)	(29.6)
1991-92	302.0	18.3	51.1	3.6	0.9	824.9	212.0	24.9	58.1	15.1	1512.2
	(33.5)	(8.1)	(32.6)	(7.5)	(8.6)	(44.2)	(21.0)	(10.0)	(54.8)	(39.7)	(32.8)
1992-93	318.6	19.2	53.8	3.8	1.0	867.5	222.0	26.2	61.1	15.9	1590.3
	(33.8)	(8.2)	(32.9)	(7.6)	(8.7)	(44.6)	(21.2)	(10.3)	(55.3)	(40.0)	(33.1)
1993-94	334.4	20.0	–	–	–	905.1	235.3	30.0	65.1	74.1	1664.1
	(29.3)	(7.1)				(38.5)	(18.4	(9.7)	(48.7)	(23.2)	(28.6)
1994-95	415.0	24.9	–	–	–	1123.2	292.0	37.3	80.8	91.9	2065.0
	(34.6)	(8.3)				(45.4)	(21.8)	(11.5)	(57.5)	(27.3)	(33.8)

(Contd.)

TABLE 4 (Contd.)

	(1)	(2)	(3)	(4)	(5)	(6)	(7)	(8)	(9)	(10)	(1 to 10)
1995-96	440.4	26.4	–	–	–	1191.8	309.8	39.6	85.7	97.6	2191.3
	(34.2)	(8.2)				(44.9)	(21.5)	(11.4)	(56.7)	(27.4)	(33.3)
1996-97	462.9	27.6	–	–	–	1252.7	325.7	41.7	90.1	102.5	2303.2
	(34.5)	(8.2)				(45.3)	(21.7)	(11.4)	(57.3)	(27.1)	(33.7)
1997-98	469.6	51.3	80.7	14.7	2.4	1330.5	332.6	48.9	83.2	31.8	2445.7
	(33.0)	(14.4)	(32.7)	(18.4)	(11.0)	(45.4)	(20.9)	(12.7)	(49.8)	(54.7)	(33.7)
1998-99	494.2	54.1	84.9	15.4	2.6	1400.3	350.1	51.5	87.5	33.5	2574.0
	(34.1)	(14.4)	(33.7)	(18.9)	(11.7)	(46.7)	(21.5)	(13.1)	(51.3)	(56.5)	(36.3)
1999-00	520.9	63.1	90.5	15.5	2.7	1489.5	381.4	54.8	87.6	35.6	2741.6
	(33.9)	(15.7)	(32.1)	(17.5)	(11.2)	(45.6)	(21.6)	(13.1)	(47.3)	(44.2)	(34.1)
2001-02	699.4	131.8	123.0	9.1	3.2	1820.1	582.0	56.9	59.4	29.5	3514.4
	(40.2)	(21.3)	(44.3)	(10.2)	(17.8)	(44.0)	(36.3)	(19.8)	(51.0)	(36.6)	(39.2)
2002-03	736.9	154.0	134.4	9.3	3.0	1889.8	608.9	61.9	67.1	30.6	3695.9
	(39.1)	(21.6)	(42.8)	(16.3)	(15.8)	(44.0)	(35.5)	(20.3)	(50.4)	(35.7)	(38.8)
2003-04	809.0	165.3	145.3	9.9	3.0	2041.8	657.7	62.5	76.0	31.6	4002.1
	(39.8)	(23.1)	(46.3)	(16.9)	(20.2)	(45.5)	(36.7)	(20.6)	(52.0)	(37.7)	(40.2)

Note: Figures in parentheses are enrolment of women as % of overall aggregate enrolment.
Source: Same as Table 2, p. 87.

process of learning across various fields of study. During the period of analysis from 1974 to 2004, the proportion of women enrolment increased from a little over 23 per cent to about 40 per cent. The ratio of women enrolment in fundamental science disciplines jacked up from 23 per cent in 1974-75, to about 40 per cent in 2003-04. Likewise, female enrolment in medical discipline has ostensibly increased from about 20 per cent to over 46 per cent. Even for other S&T areas, including engineering and technology, the female enrolment increased perceptibly, from over one per cent in 1974, to over 23 per cent in 2004; and in veterinary sciences, to over 20 per cent, and in agricultural sciences to 17 per cent.

Similarly, for other non-science disciplines, female enrolment, e.g. in commerce faculty has consistently expanded from over five per cent to over 36 per cent during this period. In Law, female enrolment shot up from 4.4 per cent of the total, to over 20 per cent, and in the Education discipline, from over 37 per cent to 52 per cent, after touching the highest proportion of about 57 per cent during 1994-97.

The overall inference that can be drawn from Table 4 is that, with rising awareness and liberalization and modernization of the social values and mores in the Indian society, women are taking up all the modern and futuristic areas of education and learning, which had hitherto been treated as the male bastion. Thus the table clearly highlights the progressive rationalization and modernization of a so far regressive society.

OUT-TURN OF S&T PERSONNEL FROM INDIAN UNIVERSITIES

Table 5 presents the analysis of the various classifications of the S&T personnel graduating from the Indian Universities during the period 1954-95. Among the total scientific personnel coming out of universities, 55-63 per cent were only science graduates, acquainted with merely fundamental science disciplines. On the other side, the S&T personnel, who can be termed as highly specialised with

TABLE 5

Turn Out of Scientific and Technical Personnel from Universities in India (1955-95)

(Numbers)

Degree/Year	*1955*	*1960*	*1970*	*1975*	*1985*	*1986*	*1987*	*1988*	*1989*	*1995*	*Annual Growth Rate*
B.Sc. (Sc.)	14427	22706	83654	95395	120006	122579	129940	129981	134366	139257	10.58
	(58.43)	(55.02)	(59.16)	(63.44)	(59.25)	(59.03)	(57.91)	(57.43)	(57.93)	(59.06)	
M.Sc. (Sc.)	2911	5382	16742	17557	19377	20300	23669	24301	24591	23807	10.54
	(11.79)	(13.04)	(11.84)	(11.68)	(9.57)	(9.78)	(10.55)	(10.79)	(10.60)	(10.10)	
Ph.D. (Sc.)	164	361	1212	1484	2838	2814	3038	3038	3044	3155	10.76
	(0.66)	(0.87)	(0.86)	(0.99)	(1.40)	(1.36)	(1.35)	(1.35)	(1.31)	(1.34)	
B.E./B.Sc. (Engg.)	3207	6031	19204	15316	22998	25272	28345	27894	28927	32250	10.59
	(12.99)	(14.62)	(13.58)	(10.18)	(11.35)	(12.17)	(12.63)	(12.38)	(12.47)	(13.68)	
M.E./M.Tech. (Engg.)	147	764	1733	2068	3228	3806	4465	4306	4560	3667	10.91
	(0.60)	(1.85)	(1.23)	(1.40)	(1.59)	(1.83)	(1.99)	(1.91)	(1.97)	(1.56)	
Ph.D. (Engg.)	19	38	247	445	559	603	675	573	560	546	10.87
	(0.08)	(0.09)	(0.17)	(0.30)	(0.28)	(0.29)	(0.30)	(0.25)	(0.24)	(0.23)	
MBBS	2582	3387	9562	10144	16370	16105	17538	18038	17968	19613	10.52
	(10.46)	(8.21)	(6.76)	(6.75)	(8.08)	(7.76)	(7.82)	(8.01)	(7.75)	(8.32)	
MD/MS	110	397	1266	2204	5017	5319	5228	5802	5945	4634	10.98
	(0.45)	(0.96)	(0.90)	(1.47)	(2.48)	(2.56)	(2.33)	(2.58)	(2.56)	(1.97)	

B.Sc. (Agri.)	910	1700	5909	3966	8257	7414	7810	7757	8301	5752	10.62
	(3.69)	(4.12)	(4.18)	(2.64)	(4.08)	(3.57)	(3.48)	(3.44)	(3.58)	(2.44)	
M.Sc. (Agri.)	208	488	1670	1511	3119	2767	2827	2752	2876	2284	10.62
	(0.84)	(1.18)	(1.18)	(1.00)	(1.54)	(1.33)	(1.26)	(1.22)	(1.24)	(0.97)	
Ph.D. (Agri.)	4	11	217	289	782	684	832	832	792	827	11.42
	(0.02)	(0.03)	(0.15)	(0.19)	(0.39)	(0.33)	(0.37)	(0.37)	(0.34)	(0.35)	
Total	24689	41265	141406	150379	202551	207663	224367	225274	231930	235792	10.58
	(100)	(100)	(100)	(100)	(100)	(100)	(100)	(100)	(100)	(100)	

Note: Figures in the parentheses are % of total.
Source: Same as Table 2, p. 89.

doctoral level knowledge, formed just one per cent or less of the total scientific personnel coming out of universities during the study period. This indicates a grim shortage of highly skilled workforce in applied areas of S&T including medical, agricultural sciences, engineering and technology disciplines.

Table 6 presents further disaggregated information on the highly skilled and qualified scientific personnel with doctoral level training. The table portrays that whereas both in the basic sciences and Arts and Humanities streams, the proportion of doctoral degree holders was in the range of 30-40 per cent of the aggregate during 1985-2003, but this highly skilled manpower in the applied scientific areas including engineering, medicine, and agricultural science disciplines have been too few. This presents a dismal picture of the economy which requires highly skilled and specialised workforce to accelerate the pace of development consistent with the contemporary globalised and competitive market environment. Again taking Tables 5 and 6 together one can infer that there is a disconcerting shortfall of doctoral level S&T personnel who would be needed to further train and educate the next generation of students. Of the over 16 thousand teachers required in our educational institutions, with doctoral level qualification, less than 13 thousand would be available; less said about the quality of teachers available, which may have gloomy forebodings for our educational and other productive sectors.

IMPLICATIONS FOR GROWTH AND EMPLOYMENT

The above analysis of India's stock of educated manpower throws up the following implications for employment and growth:

(i) Although the outlay allocation for education during the Eleventh Five Year Plan has been hiked by 5 times, and is 20 per cent of the total Plan outlay as compared with the earlier 7.7 per cent during the Tenth Five Year Plan, yet as a proportion of GDP, education development

TABLE 6

Doctorate Degrees Awarded Faculty-wise (1985-2003)

(Numbers)

Faculty/Year	1985	1990	1993	1994	1995	1996	1997	1998	1999	2000	2001	2003
1	2	3	4	5	6	7	8	9	10	11	12	13
Science and Technology Disciplines (A)												
Science	2922	2950	3386	3467	3861	3498	3894	3836	3885	3727	3955	4497
	(39.28)	(35.19)	(37.33)	(34.94)	(37.39)	(33.61)	(35.19)	(35.03)	(34.39)	(32.29)	(33.03)	(32.75)
Engg./Tech.	509	629	323	329	374	298	744	696	723	778	734	779
	(6.84)	(7.50)	(3.56)	(3.32)	(3.62)	(2.86)	(6.72)	(6.36)	(6.40)	(6.74)	(6.13)	(5.67)
Medicine	70	140	116	145	135	133	200	190	228	221	219	243
	(0.94)	(1.67)	(1.28)	(1.46)	(1.31)	(1.28)	(1.81)	(1.74)	(2.02)	(1.91)	(1.83)	(1.77)
Agriculture	576	715	611	769	780	968	849	785	787	889	838	1042
	(7.74)	(8.53)	(6.74)	(7.75)	(7.55)	(9.30)	(7.67)	(7.17)	(6.97)	(7.70)	(7.00)	(7.59)
Veterinary Sciences	102	145	112	114	138	152	122	101	146	110	110	153
	(1.37)	(1.73)	(1.23)	(1.15)	(1.34)	(1.46)	(1.10)	(0.92)	(1.29)	(0.95)	(0.92)	(1.11)
Total (A)	4179	4579	4548	4824	5288	5049	5809	5608	5769	5725	5856	6714
	(56.18)	(54.62)	(50.14)	(48.61)	(51.81)	(48.51)	(52.49)	(51.21)	(51.07)	(49.59)	(48.91)	(48.69)

(Contd.)

TABLE 6 (*Contd.*)

1	*2*	*3*	*4*	*5*	*6*	*7*	*8*	*9*	*10*	*11*	*12*	*13*
Other Disciplines (B)												
Arts	2754	3210	3621	4039	3957	4245	4058	4189	4280	4398	4524	5034
	(37.03)	(38.29)	(39.92)	(40.70)	(38.32)	(40.79)	(36.67)	(38.25)	(37.89)	(38.10)	(37.78)	(36.66)
Commerce	185	290	453	515	612	502	541	541	571	621	728	857
	(2.49)	(3.46)	(4.99)	(5.19)	(5.93)	(4.82)	(4.89)	(4.94)	(5.05)	(5.38)	(6.08)	(6.24)
Education	239	188	247	308	295	295	342	310	364	399	420	554
	(3.21)	(2.24)	(2.72)	(3.10)	(2.86)	(2.83)	(3.09)	(2.83)	(3.22)	(3.46)	(3.51)	(4.03)
Law	25	51	72	73	75	65	67	75	74	105	110	138
	(0,34)	(0.61)	(0.79)	(0.74)	(0.73)	(0.62)	(0.61)	(0.68)	(0.66)	(0.91)	(0.92)	(1.00)
Others	56	65	129	164	170	252	249	228	238	296	336	436
	(0.75)	(0.78)	(1.42)	(1.65)	(1.65)	(2.42)	(2.25)	(2.08)	(2.11)	(2.56)	(2.81)	(3.17)
Total (B)	3259	3804	4522	5099	5109	5359	5257	5343	5527	5819	6118	7019
	(43.82)	(45.38)	(49.86)	(51.39)	(49.47)	(51.49)	(47.51)	(48.79)	(48.93)	(50.41)	(51.09)	(51.11)
Total (A+B)	7438	8383	9070	9923	10327	10408	11066	10951	11296	11544	11974	13733
	(100)	(100)	(100)	(100)	(100)	(100)	(100)	(100)	(100)	(100)	(100)	(100)

Note: Figures in the parentheses are % of grand total

Source: Same as Table 2, p. 91.

expenditure has remained less than 3 per cent in 2007-08, whereas the growth sustaining investment in education should be at least 6 per cent of GDP

(ii) Because the largest proportion of the educated manpower, ranging between 50-60 per cent, remain stuck at the under graduate level, both in the science and non-science disciplines—mainly trained in basic sciences, they remain largely unemployable, and represent the largest chunk of the educated unemployed.

(iii) There is absolute dearth of specialists with critical skills in the science and technology and related fields of study. For instance, the graduates in the medical and vetrenary sciences form the smallest fraction of India's S&T manpower. Engineering degree holders are in short supply. The IT and related sectors are expected to throw up about 8 million new jobs in the near future, but engineering degree holders in India constitute just 12.67 per cent of the stock of S&T manpower available. Every year the Indian universities and engineering and technology institutes are turning out only about 3 lakh engineering graduates. That is why due to the pressure of demand high salaries are being paid to the available engineering specialists.

(iv) Female participation in all the disciplines is rising-both in the S&T related areas of study, as well as the non-S&T fields. This is both the cause and effect of the economic and social emancipation of the hitherto deliberately restrained section of the Indian society. This fact gets credence from the conceivable transformation in the structural pattern of employment since the economic reforms during early 1990s. Female work participation rates and the rate of enrolment in diverse fields of study have been visibly climbing up since the liberalization of the economy. This indicates a rapidly transforming society.

(v) The rising stock of scientifically groomed and technically trained manpower notwithstanding, the quality of technical talent of our manpower has come in for some criticism since it has been found wanting to match the requirements of the contemporary competitive world. In the absence of a certain level of uniformity and standardization of the course content of the various S&T institutions and universities; lack of quality monitoring mechanisms; improvisations and tinkering with education policy; dwindling expenditure on higher and technical education (which is around barely 10 per cent of the total educational budgetary expenditure), the quality of particularly engineering and technical human resource has been found to be below par. The American and European MNCs outsourcing jobs recklessly earlier to the Indian job markets, offering unbelievably high pay packets, and also the deluging MNCs coming in the Indian markets particularly in the IT and Telecommunication sectors, have now started looking askance at the capabilities and talent of the Indian engineering specialists, and have started cutting jobs and pay packets; they new prefer to train the new incumbents in their own in-house training centers before finally inducting them in their business.

CONCLUSION

The foregoing analysis and discussion does show a rising trend in the total stock of India's educated and S&T human resource, yet there are a number of lacunae mainly from the point of view of the quality of the human capital which have serious inadequacies for their employment potential and growth steering capabilities. With over 60 years on, since independence, now the Government must shed the quantity aspect of education in India, and instead focus on refurbishing the quality of its human resource, firstly by expending more and more on higher and technical education;

and secondly, and more importantly, on monitoring and overseeing the introduction of modern course content and instructions of the state-of-the-art education consistent with the requirements of the contemporary competitive world.

References

Barro, R.J. (2001), "Human Capital and Growth", *AEA Papers and Proceedings*, Vol. 91, No. 2, pp. 12-17.

Benhabib, J. and M.M. Spiegel (1994), "The Role of Human Capital in Economic Development: Evidence from Aggregate Cross-Country Data", *Journal of Monetary Economics*, Vol. 34, No. 2, pp. 143-74.

Bowles, S. and H. Gintis (1976), *Schooling in Capitalist America: Education Reforms and Contradiction of Economic Life*, New York: Basic Books.

Harbison, F. and C. Myers (eds.) [1965], Manpower and Education, New York: McGraw Hill, p. xi

Psacharopoulos, G. (1988), "Education and Development: A Review", *Research Observer*, Vol. 3, No. 1, pp. 99-115.

Rivera-Batiz, L.A. and P. Romer (1991), "Economic Integration and Endogenous Growth", *Quarterly Journal of Economics*, Vol. 106, pp. 531-56.

Schumpeter, J. (1961), *Theory of Economic Development*, New York: OUP.

Tilak, J.B.G. (2008), "Education in 2008-09 Union Budget", *Economic and Political Weekly*, Vol. XLIII, No. 20, pp. 49-56.

11

Education, Growth and Wages in India: An Interrelationship

KULDIP KAUR

INTRODUCTION

Investment in people plays a key role and appears attractive relative to alternative assets because it is seen as both an essential growth factor and key level of social cohesion policy. There is a broad consensus in the academic literature that human capital is a determinant of productivity and other economic outcomes, both at the individual and at the aggregate level and that its role is particularly crucial in today's knowledge driven economy. It plays a key role in fostering technological change and diffusion of technology.

Human capital is a broad and multifaceted concept encompassing different types of investment in people. Health and education are certainly an important aspect of such investment, particularly in developing countries like India. Here deficiency in these respects may severely limit the population's ability to engage in productive activities, as human capital represents the skills, knowledge, ability to labour and good health that together enable people to pursue different sustenance strategies to achieve their livelihood objectives. The practical knowledge acquired skills and learned abilities of an individual that makes him or her to earn income in exchange for labour, is commonly termed as human capital. The key aspect of human capital is related to the knowledge and skills embodied in people and accumulated through schooling, training and experience that are useful in the production of goods, services and further knowledge.

The available evidence suggests that the importance of education as an input has grown over time as production processes have become increasingly knowledge intensive. Workers with greater problem-solving and communication abilities not only perform better than their less skilled counterparts at any task that requires more than routine application of physical labour but also learn faster. Hence skilled workers can be expected to be more productive than unskilled ones for any given production and should be able to operate more sophisticated technologies that place greater demand on their capacities.

The hypothesis that human capital is a key determinant of productivity, has received considerable attention in the literature. At micro-level, labour economists have long been concerned with labour market outcomes. However building on this work, macroeconomists have been using growth accounting techniques to analyze the contribution of education to aggregate economic growth since the 1960's. Research in the second area has received a new impetus in recent years, with the development of a new generation of theoretical models that attribute to the accumulation of knowledge and skills, a central role in the process of economic development and with the construction of broad cross-country data sets that can be used in empirical analysis of determinants of economic growth.

While traditional neo-classical models focused almost exclusively on the accumulation of physical capital, more recent contributions have attributed increased importance to the accumulation of human capital and productive knowledge and the interaction between the two. Hence 'new growth theory' emphasizes the importance of education in the creation of new knowledge and in the growth of living standards over time (Riddell, 2001). The need for appropriate human capital development and accumulation is a prerequisite for modern economic growth in both developed and developing economies.

The relevance of human capital accumulation to the process of economic development stems from its potential beneficial impact on macroeconomic productivity and on the long-run distribution of incomes, once some basic conditions are met. The 1960's and early 1970's were marked, in the western world mostly by an enthusiasm for the issue of education and its presumed positive impact on economic growth. The pioneer in the field, Schultz (1960) talks about, "the moral issue of treating education as in investment in man" and he suggests to treat its consequences as a form of capital. This enthusiasm for education led to various attempts at measuring both capital and the rate of returns on investment in education such that the expenditure on education becomes an investment rather than consumption.

To measure costs and benefits of education, Schultz (1960) formulated the following hypothesis: "Some important increases, in national income are a consequence of additions to the stock of this form of capital". The formulation of this 'kind of capital' is probably responsible for the 'unexplained' increases in the national income. After this the issue of education and its impact on the long-term economic growth started to dominate social science discourse. This line of thinking for example was explored by Dension (1967). The dominant hypothesis was that, education affects positively the economic growth since it increases the level of cognitive skills possessed by the labour force and consequently its marginal productivity.

Eventually, the debate among the economists shifted during the 1980's to the impact of technology combined with knowledge and skills, on economic growth. This was partly as a response to the criticism voiced by the development economists. It became obvious that technical change could not be seen independently from human interaction, therefore from human capital. Technology could not be seen separately from the human inputs who create them or who utilize them.

Using a historical approach, Easterlin (1981), pointed out the reason why economic growth has spread so slowly among the developing nations of the world? This is because of limited geographical diffusion of technology. This limitation is in turn linked to both the quantity and quality of educational system. In various empirical studies, increasing attention has been paid to the role of education in explaining any country's economic growth. According to Wang and Yao (2003) using national data from 1978 to 1999, human capital stock, measured by average years of schooling, contributed 11 per cent of GDP growth in China in the reform period. Based on provincial data from 1978 to 1989, using higher education enrolement as an indicator of human capital accumulation. Chen and Feng (2000) found that education had a positive and significant effect on economic growth. Chen and Fleisher (1996) found a statistically insignificant relationship between human capital investment and economic growth at the provincial level when their measure of human capital was in terms of secondary schooling; however, in a later study (Fleisher and Chen, 1997) when their measure of human capital was university level education, they found a positive relationship between human capital and growth in total factor productivity in China.

This way, the conventional wisdom on the role of education in economic growth is being revised in terms of both theory and new evidence. Tertiary education or higher education is now considered critical from the standpoint of achieving overall economic and social development. Thus rising premium on higher education reflects the growing demand for skills driven in large part by the spread of new technologies. Recent research suggests that the increase in the number of skilled workers may have in fact boosted the value of further education and made it more important for growth. Indeed in many countries building a work force with higher order skills is an important part of improving the climate for investment, acquiring a competitive edge and generally maintaining an engine of growth (World Development Report, 2007).

Lee (2006) in his paper has tried to shed light on the educational attainment as a factor effecting the speed of transition movement of labour force from agricultural sector to non-agricultural sector. Barro (1998) analysed the determinants of economic growth and investment in a panel of around one hundred countries over the period 1960 to 1995. With respect to eduction he found that growth is positively related to the starting level of average years of schooling attainment of adult males at the secondary and higher levels. He analyzed that growth is insignificantly related to years of school attainment of females at the secondary and higher level suggesting that highly educated women are not well utilized in the labour markets of many countries. He found that growth is insignificantly related to male schooling at the primary level and education of women at the primary level stimulates economic growth indirectly by inducting a lower fertility rate. Abril (2003) highlights that although women have almost reached the same level of education as men and in some countries have even surpassed them, they continue to participate less in the labour market and earn less than men.

While studying the education-growth relationship, following major conclusions can be drawn from the various studies undertaken on this issue: (i) educational attainment indicators are highly correlated with the wealth levels of countries, in particular, mass primary education has positive impact on growth, (ii) different levels of education have different impacts on growth depending upon the stage of economic development reached by various countries and also on the quality of education, (iii) higher education boosts economic growth through helping countries to gain ground on more technologically advanced societies as graduates are likely to be more aware of and better able to use new technologies, (iv) economic returns to investment in education for women are significantly lower than the men because of low participation rates, (v) returns to education in urban areas are likely to be higher than rural areas because of poor rural school quality, (vi) educated workers are likely to reap more benefits than uneducated one's because of better employment prospects. It is in this context that the present study aims at studying the impact of different levels of education on the economic growth of various states of India with the following specific objectives in mind;

1. To study the relationship between Net State Domestic Products (NSDP) of major states of India and levels of education in three major sectors (Primary, Secondary and Tertiary) of these states.
2. To study the impact of education levels on the wages in major industry groups over a period of time (i.e. for 1990-2000).
3. To analyze the relationship between male and female education at various levels of education and per capita NSDP.
4. To study the relationship between rural and urban education at various levels and per capita NSDP.
5. To draw some policy implications and conclusions from the study.

The study is divided into three main sections including the present one. Second part discusses the database and methodology. Third one highlights major findings of the study and draws some conclusions and policy implications

II. DATABASE AND METHODOLOGY

As per the first objective of study it was proposed to study the relationship between share of three sectors, i.e. primary, secondary and tertiary in Net State Domestic Product of the respective states (as an indicator of economic growth) and levels of education, i.e. illiterate, primary, middle school and secondary level and above (as an indicator of human capital). This was to study the relationship between economic growth and human capital formation in 17 major states of India and at all India level for the year 1999-2000. Following the usual convention, secondary or higher secondary level of schooling and other higher qualifications have been taken as the dividing line between educated and uneducated workers. For analytical convenience those with primary and/or middle level schooling are categorized as semi-educated workers. Going by this classification, illiterate workers are synonymous with low-quality workers (proxy for low level of human capital) semi educated workers represent medium quality workers and educated workers, as defined above are proxies for high quality workers (Chadha, 2004). However, the main source of data regarding different education levels of workers (principal status) in major states and major industry groups is the household level data on CD-ROM for the year 1999-2000, supplied by NSSO, New Delhi. Data regarding the wages of the workers for the year 1999-2000 has been collected from various reports of Centre of Monitoring Indian Economy (CMIE). CSO compiled data on NSDP has been used to get sectoral composition of NSDP for seventeen major states of India for the year 1999-2000 at constant prices (1993-94=00).

For the last two objectives, data for 26 major states of India for net attendance ratios and total enrolment as per cent of their total population for the years 1995-96 and 2000-01, for rural and urban males, rural and urban females for different education levels have been compiled from Manpower Profile published by Institute of Applied Manpower Research, New Delhi; Per capita net state domestic product at constant prices has been used as an indicator of economic growth. Four to five years of lagged regression equations have been fitted to analyze the impact of education on per capita net state domestic product, as children enrolled in a particular year will not enter the labour force immediately, but after completing certain years of schooling.

To compute the impact of education on economic growth, simple regression analysis has been used. These equations are expressed as follows:

AGRICULTURE SECTOR

1. $NSDP_{AS} = f\ (PPW)$
2. $NSDP_{AS} = f\ (PMW)$
3. $NSDP_{AS} = f\ (PSW)$

SECONDARY SECTOR

1. $NSDP_{SS} = f\ (PPW)$
2. $NSDP_{SS} = f\ (PMW)$
3. $NSDP_{SS} = f\ (PSW)$

TERTIARY SECTOR

1. $NSDP_{TS}$ = f (PPW)
2. $NSDP_{TS}$ = f (PMW)
3. $NSDP_{TS}$ = f (PSW)

$NSDP_{AS}$ = Per cent Share of Respective State's Agricultural Sector in its Net State Domestic Product in 1999-2000.

$NSDP_{SS}$ = Per cent Share of Respective State's Secondary Sector in its Net State Domestic Product in 1999-2000.

$NSDP_{TS}$ = Per cent Share of Respective State's Tertiary Sector in its Net State Domestic Product in 1999-2000.

PPW = Per cent of workers (Principal Status) having Primary Level of Education.

PMW = Per cent of workers (Principal Status) having Middle Level of Education.

PSW = Per cent of workers (Principal Status) having Secondary and above level of Education.

To explain the impact of human capital formation on wages of the workers in major industry groups of India, the equations fitted are as follows:

1. $W_{99\text{-}00}$ = f ($PPW_{99\text{-}00}$)
2. $W_{99\text{-}00}$ = f ($PMW_{99\text{-}00}$)
3. $W_{99\text{-}00}$ = f ($PSW_{99\text{-}00}$)

where,

$W_{99\text{-}00}$ = Wages of the workers in respective industry group in the year 1999-00.

$PPW_{99\text{-}00}$ = Percentage of the workers in the respective industry group having primary level of education 1999-00.

$PMW_{99\text{-}00}$ = Percentage of the workers in the respective industry group having middle level of education 1999-00.

$PSW_{99\text{-}00}$ = Percentage of the workers in the respective industry group having secondary and above level of education 1999-00.

To analyze the impact of net attendance ratio of males, females in rural and urban areas, on per capita net state domestic product following lagged equations have been fitted

1. $PC\ NSDP_{99\text{-}00} = f\ (UM\ NAR_{95\text{-}96})$
2. $PC\ NSDP_{99\text{-}00} = f\ (UF\ NAR_{95\text{-}96})$
3. $PC\ NSDP_{99\text{-}00} = f\ (RM\ NAR_{95\text{-}96})$
4. $PC\ NSDP_{99\text{-}00} = f\ (RF\ NAR_{95\text{-}96})$
5. $PC\ NSDP_{2004\text{-}05} = f\ (TMER_{2000\text{-}01})$
6. $PC\ NSDP_{2004\text{-}05} = f\ (TFER_{2000\text{-}01})$

where,

1. PCNSDP = Per capita Net State Domestic Product for respective years.
2. UM NAR = Urban Male Net Attendance Ratio as per cent of total population in respective years.
3. UF NAR = Urban Female Net Attendance Ratio as per cent of total population in respective years
4. RM NAR = Rural Male Net Attendance Ratio as per cent of total population.
5. RF NAR = Rural Female Net Attendance Ratio as per cent of total population.
6. TMER = Total Male Enrolment as per cent of population
7. TFER = Total Female Enrolment as per cent of population

III. RESULTS AND DISCUSSION

To capture the essence of the human capital accumulation process, empirical growth models have concentrated on the three main levels or stages of education—primary, secondary and tertiary. Production relevant skills are assumed to be embodied to a greater extent in those individuals who have acquired greater quantity and quality of education, with a 'skills hierarchy' rising from the primary to tertiary levels (Gemmell, 1996). In plain terms the quality of workforce definitely influences the economic growth. Table 1 shows the results of the regression explaining the relationship between NSDP and education level of the workers.

TABLE I

Net State Domestic Product (Sector-wise) and Education Nexus (1999-00)

Equation No.			*Equation*				R^2
			Primary Sector				
1.	$NSDP_{AS}$	=	33.10	+	0.215	PPW	0.34
			(4.98)*		(9.21)*		
2.	$NSDP_{AS}$	=	29.31	+	0.016	PMW	0.22
			(5.68)*		(7.59)*		
3.	$NSDP_{AS}$	=	24.49	+	0.302	PSW	0.34
			(6.06)*		(9.13)*		
			Secondary Sector				
4.	$NSDP_{SS}$	=	28.08	+	0.23	PPW	0.17
			(5.57)*		(5.89)*		
5.	$NSDP_{SS}$	=	28.80	+	0.37	PMW	0.27
			(7.43)*		(7.82)*		
6.	$NSDP_{SS}$	=	24.29	+	0.21	PSW	0.43
			(5.75)*		(11.18)*		
			Tertiary Sector				
7.	$NSDP_{TS}$	=	47.76	+	0.25	PPW	0.15
			(15.15)*		(1.58)*		
8.	$NSDP_{TS}$	=	36.68	+	0.30	PMW	0.26
			(4.76)*		(5.85)*		
9.	$NSDP_{TS}$	=	29.53	+	0.76	PSW	0.46
			(7.22)*		(3.42)*		

Note: Figures in the brackets are respective t-values
* Significant at 1 per cent level

It is clear from the above table that a connection between human capital accumulation and NSDP does exist because in the present case almost in all the cases positive and significant relationship has been detected between NSDP and level of education of the workers in primary, secondary and tertiary sectors as well. In case of agricultural sector 34 per cent of the variations in the share of this sector in NSDP were explained by the percentage of workers having secondary level or higher education. In secondary sector this figure was 43 per cent and in service sector it being the 46 per cent. This means highly educated and skilled workers contribute maximum in the tertiary sector followed by secondary and primary sector. Workers with primary level of education contributed maximum in the agricultural sector as compared to secondary and tertiary sectors. The respective figures for R^2 are 34 per cent in agricultural sector, 17 per cent in secondary and 15 per cent in tertiary sector. This means that workers with low education contribute more in agricultural sector, because they are in the habit of putting in more physical efforts rather than mental efforts. However, all the regression coefficients except one (in case of tertiary sector's share in NSDP and percentage of workers having only primary education) are positive and significant at one per cent level of significance. Highest value of regression coefficient among all the nine equations was 0.76 in case of tertiary sector. This suggests that one per cent increase in workers having secondary or above level of education leads to 0.76 per cent increase in tertiary sector's share in NSDP. The minimum value of regression coefficient is 0.016 in case of agriculture sector. This coefficient suggests that one per cent increase in workers with middle level of education leads to only 0.016 per cent increase in NSDP in the agricultural sector.

Table 2 shows that it is not only the human capital and NSDP that are positively and significantly related to each other, rather the wages and human capital formation in the industrial sector are also positively and significantly related to each other. In case the percentage of workers have secondary or higher level of education in the major industry groups of India then 55 per cent of the total variations in their wages are explained by this variable. Fifty-three per cent of the total variations in worker's wages are explained by the workers having middle level of education. Regression

TABLE 2

Wages and Education Nexus (1999-00)

Equation No.		*Equation*			R^2
1. $W_{99\text{-}00}$	=	644.84 +	0.23	PPW	0.30
		(1.44)	(5.69)*		
2. $W_{99\text{-}00}$	=	1030.93 +	0.23	PMW	0.53
		(1.62)	(8.89)*		
3. $W_{99\text{-}00}$	=	1619.71 +	0.06	PSW	0.55
		(1.64)	(7.82)*		

Note: Figures in the brackets are respective t-values
* Significant at 1 per cent level

coefficient (i.e. 0.23) in this case suggests that one per cent increase in percentage of workers having middle level of education leads to 0.23 per cent increase in their wages. Again in this case all the three regression coefficients are positive and significant at one per cent level of significance, suggesting the strong and positive relationship between the two variables in the major industry groups of India.

Tables 3 to 6 show how per capita net state domestic product is affected by primary, middle, secondary, senior secondary education levels of males and females in rural and urban areas of various states of India. Net attendance ratio and total enrolement as per cent of total population has been used as indicators of education. The point which catches attention in both the tables 3 and 4 is the fact that all the regression coefficients are positive, though majority of them are insignificant. Urban female's education at senior secondary level only is positively and significantly associated with per capita NSDP. Correlation coefficient also in this case is 0.53 and 0.43 respectively. The next high correlation coefficient is in case of both rural and urban males at secondary level of education.

From Tables 4 and 5 again it can be observed that regression coefficients are negative though insignificant in case of total enrolement of males and females both at the primary and middle levels of education. The culprit may be high dropout rates at primary and middle levels of education

TABLE 3

Urban Net Attendance Ratio as Per cent of Total Population in 1995-96 and Per Capita Net State Domestic Product (1993-94=00) in 2000-01 Nexus

S. No.	*Level of Education*		*Constant*	*Regression Coefficient*	*Correlation Coefficient*	R^2
1.	Primary	Males	10272.83	98.61	0.15	0.02
	(I-V Class)		(8.15)	(0.71)		
		Females	10491.36	43.78	0.08	0.01
			(8.43)	(0.40)		
2.	Middle	Males	9922.93	284.97	0.23	0.05
	(VI-VIII Class)		(7.74)	(1.14)		
		Females	10369.24	108.33	0.12	0.02
			(8.40)	(0.62)		
3.	Secondary	Males	9941.36	352.93	0.27	0.07
	(IX-X Class)		(8.24)	(1.36)	91.01	0.14
		Females	10424.00	(8.84)	(0.67)	0.02
4.	Senior Secondary	Males	10296.93	313.79	0.19	0.03
	(XI-XII Class)		(8.74)	(0.92)		
		Females	9053.78	1509.90	0.53	0.28
			(8.31)	(2.99)*		

Note: Figures in the brackets are respective t-values
* Significant at 5 per cent level

since here the independent variable is total enrolment ratio rather than net attendance ratio. It is everywhere that in case of secondary and senior secondary levels of education the regression coefficients are positive and significant. Since the regression fitted is with the lag of 5 years, it is certain that after five years of completing their secondary and senior secondary level of education both male and female enter labour force and start contributing at micro and micro-level. However, there is no evidence to support the argument that returns to education in case of females and rural areas are less as compared to males and urban areas.

So the hypothesis that knowledge and skills embodied in human directly raise productivity in all the sectors and increase the economy's ability to grow and adopt new technologies stands tested by the study. The new agriculture

TABLE 4

Rural Net Attendance Ratio as Per cent of Total Population in 1995-96 and Per Capita Net State Domestic Product (1993-94=00) in 2000-01 Nexus

S. No.	*Level of Education*		*Constant*	*Regression Coefficient*	*Correlation Coefficient*	R^2
1.	Primary (I-V Class)	Males	10168.25 (8.23)	135.05 (0.93)	0.19	0.04
		Females	10348.79 (8.41)	80.82 (0.66)	0.14	0.02
2.	Middle (VI-VIII Class)	Males	9985.15 (8.01)	320.95 (1.16)	0.33	0.11
		Females	9611.19 (7.84)	527.57 (1.71)	0.23	0.06
3.	Secondary (IX-X Class)	Males	9499.05 (8.06)	1363.03 (2.03)	0.39	0.15
		Females	10180.65 (8.57)	455.18 (1.07)	0.22	0.05
4.	Senior Secondary (XI-XII Class)	Males	9707.93 (7.71)	2571.27 (1.58)	0.31	0.10
		Females	9452.72 (8.26)	4425.47 (2.86)*	0.43	0.18

Note: Figures in the brackets are respective t-values
*Significant at 5 per cent level

is likely to become bio-tech concentrated. Environmental degradation and its sustainability, safety of the workers, farm production and management and problems of land and soil, etc. are the problems that need skilled and educated farm workers to solve them. For the agricultural products catering to export market, competitiveness in terms of quantity and quality is a must. Ignorance of the marketing system and pattern is also not acceptable in agricultural sector today. Obviously well educated agricultural workers are the need of the hour.

Similarly the growth and the performance of the industrial sector also depends not only on the quantity but also on the quality of the workers. In today's liberalized regime where new products with new designs and higher

TABLE 5

Total Enrolment as Per cent of Total Population in 2000-01 and Per Capita Net State Domestic Product (1993-94=00) in 2004-05 Nexus

S. No.	Level of Education		Constant	Regression Coefficient	Correlation Coefficient	R^2
1.	Primary (I-V Class)	Males	25047.05 (8.51)	- 954.20 (- 0.65)	- 0.14	0.02
		Females	25056.46 (8.38)	- 825.57 (-0.62)	- 0.13	0.02
2.	Middle (VI-VIII Class)	Males	33375.45 (3.64)	- 805.78 (- 1.05)	- 0.22	0.05
		Females	30143.06 (2.39)	- 544.66 (- 0.49)	- 0.10	0.01
3.	Secondary (IX-X Class)	Males	11328.70 (1.06)	2521.57 (1.23)	0.26	0.07
		Females	- 3024.72 (- 0.36)	6157.29 (3.34)*	0.59	0.35
4.	Senior Secondary (XI-XII Class)	Males	- 2673.67 (0.26)	7102.02 (2.68) *	0.50	0.25
		Females	4013.08 (0.70)	6908.67 (3.74)*	0.64	0.40

Note: Figures in the brackets are respective t-values
* Significant at 5 per cent level

performance capabilities are pouring in, unskilled labour cannot cope with this phenomenon. Moreover, from consumer's point of view, more and high standards are being set. Particularly in food processing, hygiene and health safety standards are required. Similarly in agro-processing especially relating to export market designing, quality, finishing, colour combination, etc. are the main requirements. In today's high-tech industrial world, scientific approach and standardisation are also required.

India's highly growing tertiary sector cannot also bear the burden of unskilled and uneducated labour force. Hotel and restaurant activities, transport, communication, storage, banking, insurance, real estate, personal services, etc. require

TABLE 6

Total Enrolment as Per cent of Total Population in 2000-01 and Per Capita Net State Domestic Product (1993-94=00) in 2004-05 Nexus

S. No.	Level of Education	Constant	Regression Coefficient	Correlation Coefficient	R^2
1.	Primary (I-V Class)	25103.63 (8.32)	-853.94 (- 0.64)	-0.14	0.02
2.	Middle (VI-VIII Class)	45680.53 (3.36)	-1870.56 (- 1.61)	-0.33	0.11
3.	Secondary (IX-X Class)	12199.61 (1.25)	2569.09 (1.27)	0.27	0.07
4.	Senior Secondary (XI-XII Class)	-3372.21 (-0.45)	8140.67 (3.83) *	0.64	0.41

Note: Figures in the brackets are respective t-values
* Significant at 5 per cent level

highly educated workers. Basic computer understanding for accounting, product development and designing, market exploration, information gathering, etc. is required in this sector too. This is an area that can absorb many of the upcoming educated job-seekers.

Also it is clear from the study that educated workers are likely to reap more financial benefits than the uneducated ones as these workers generate more value additions. Theoretical models of human capital and growth suggest that some of the benefits of a more educated labour force will typically 'leak-out' and generate macroeconomic benefits that cannot be appropriated in the form of higher earnings by those who undertake the relevant investment. These leakages are often called externalities and they provide an important rationale for education subsidies and for other policies aimed at increasing human capital investment above its 'free market' value.

On the whole, the evidence from the study is consistent with the view that measures aimed at increasing the quantity and quality of the stock of human capital should be an important part of any growth promoting policy package. Implementation of human capital policies is important for those regions or states that are lagging in productivity in NSDP, as a balanced education system promotes not only economic development but also productivity. The benefits of higher education for individuals can be reaped through better employment prospects, higher salaries and greater ability to save and invest.

References

Abril, M.E.R. (2003), "Challenges and Opportunities for Gender Equality in Latin America and Caribbean", World Bank, 1998

Barro, R.J. (2001), "Human Capital and Growth", *American Economic Review*, Vol. 91, No. 2, pp. 12-17.

Centre for Monitoring Indian Economy,Various Reports.

Chadha, G.K. (2004), "Human Capital Base of the Indian Labour Market—Identifying Worry Spots", *The Indian Journal of Labour Economics*, Vol. 47, No. 1, Jan-March, pp. 02-38.

Chen, Band Y, Feng (2000), "Determinants of Economic Growth in China : Private Enterprise, Education and Openness", *China Economic Review*, Vol. 11, pp. 1-15.

Chen, J and B.M. Fleisher (1996), "Regional Income Inequality and Economic Growth in China", *Journal of Comparative Economics*, Vol. 22, pp. 141-164.

Denison, E.F.(1967), "Why Growth Rates Differ: Post War Experience in Nine Western Countries", Brooking Institutions, Washington, D.C.

Easterline, R.A. (1981), "Why isn't the Whole World Developed"?, *Journal of Economic History*, Vol. 41, No.1, pp. 1-19.

Fleisher, B.M. and Chen, J (1997), "The Coast, Non-coast Income Gap, Productivity and Regional Economic Policy in India", *Journal of Comparative Economics*, Vol. 25, No. 2, pp. 220-236.

Gemmell, Norman (1996), "Evaluating the Impacts of Human Capital Stocks and Accumulation on Economic Growth: Some New Evidence", *Oxford Bulletin of Economics and Statistics, Special Issue on Human Capital in Economic Development*, Vol. 58, No.1, Feb.

Government of India (2001), Employment and Unemployment in India, 1999-00, NSS 55th Round (July 1999- June 2000), NSS Report No. 458, NSSO, May.

Government of India (2003), National Accounts Statistics 2002, Central Statistical Organisation.

Institute of Applied Manpower Research, 'Manpower Profile—India Year Book 2003', Concept Publishing Company, New Delhi.

Lucas, R.E. (1988), "Mechanisms of Economics Growth", *Journal of Monetary Economics*, Vol. 22, pp. 03-42.

Lee, S (2006), "The Role of Education in Economic Growth through the Sectoral Reallocation of Labour", Society for Economic Dynamics, Meeting Papers No. 814.

Nelson, R.R. and E.S. Phelps (1966), "Investment in Humans-Technological Diffusion and Economic Growth", *The American Economic Review*, Vol. 2, No. 56, pp. 69-75.

Riddle, Craig W. (2001), "Education and Skills—An Assessment of Recent Canadian Experience", Forthcoming in the State of Economics in Canada, Festshrift in honour of David Slater, Discussion Paper No. 1-26, Nov.

Schultz, T. Paul (2002), "Why Governments Should Invest More to Educate Girls", *World Development*, Vol. 30, No. 2, pp. 207-25.

Schultz, Theodore, W. (1960), "Capital Formation by Education", *Journal of Political Economy*, Vol. 68, No. 6, Dec., pp. 571-83.

Wang, Y and Y, Yao (2003), "Soruces of China's Economic Growth, 1952-1999: Incorporating Human Capital Accumulation", *China Economic Review*, Vol. 14, pp. 32-52.

12

Education and Economic Development in India

N. JAGANATHAN

Economic development is a process whereby the real per capita income of a country increases over a long period of time. The increase in the quality of human beings by way of education, healthcare, nutrition, etc. helps to increase the physical output. Therefore, human resource development along with physical capital formation plays a useful role in economic development. The human resources can be developed by providing formal education from elementary to the higher level, technical and professional, on the job training, adult education programmes, and correspondence or distance education.

Although mass education is an essential input, the quality and level of literacy also matter substantially in development. All concerned with education know that the human resources of a nation can be developed by making investments in education on a scale commensurate with the nature and dimension of the task. The provision of educational expenditure is important under the state activities for economic development.

Throughout the history of independent India, the Indian government has strived to work for educational development and thereby to increase productivity and economic development. A lot has been achieved in the past five decades. Hence, an attempt is made in this study to anlayse the educational development and the relationship between educational development and economic development.

OBJECTIVES

The specific objectives of the study are given below:

1. to study the size, composition, and growth of educational expenditure;
2. to study the growth of educational infrastructure facilities and attainments; and
3. to study the interrelationship between educational development and economic development.

Sources of Data

The secondary data were collected for Gross Domestic Product at factor cost, population, wholesale price index, educational expenditure and its components, educational institutions, teachers in schools, enrolment by levels of education, and literacy by age and sex from Indian Public Finance Statistics, Indian Economic Survey, Socio-Economic Indicators—India, Women and Men in India, Manpower Profile—India Year Book, and Educational Statistics at a Glance.

Period of the Study

The data regarding educational expenditure and its components, educational infrastructures and attainments and economic development were collected for 24 years, i.e., from 1981-82 to 2004-05. The total period was divided into two sub-periods, viz., 1981-82 to 1990-91 and 1991-92 to 2004-05 in order to make a comparative analysis between pre and post-New Economic Reform Policy periods.

Tools of Analyses

The secondary data were collected and the analytical tools such as the percentage analysis, Chow test, growth analysis, test for difference between means, elasticity of educational expenditures, ADF test and Granger's causality test were used. Before calculating percentage values, the expenditure in current year value was converted into constant year value taking 1993-94 price as the base year.

Scope and Limitation of the Study

This kind of study will unfold the involvement of central and state governments for the allocation of educational expenditures, exhibit the growth of educational infrastructure facilities and the attainments in them, and the relationship between educational development and economic development.

There is a need for rising trend in educational expenditure by the governments and private sector. But the data for private sector educational expenditures are not available. Therefore, the study has to be limited to educational expenditure by the governments.

EMPIRICAL ANALYSIS

Growth of Educational Expenditure

Expenditure on education improves the knowledge and skill of the people. Hence, as attempt is made to anlayse the size, composition and growth of educational expenditure in this section. The major educational components are elementary, secondary and university education as shown in Table 1. The size of expenditure on elementary, secondary and university education was Rs. 4598 crores, Rs. 3431 crores and Rs. 1853 crores respectively in 1981-82, which increased to Rs. 11727 crores, Rs. 8314 crores and Rs. 3697 crores in 1990-91 and Rs. 256.85 crores, Rs. 186.23 crores and Rs. 5426 crores in 2004-05. It shows that the expenditure on education increased in both the periods. This uptrend was confirmed by larger mean values in period II than in period I for all the components of educational expenditure. The 't' test values for the difference between means of period I and period II was

TABLE I

Educational Expenditure

(Rs. 100 crores)

Years	*Elementary*	*Secondary*	*Adults*	*Technical*	*University*	*Others*	*Total*
			Period I				
1981-82	45.98	34.31	1.06	05.66	18.53	4.57	110.11
1982-83	55.37	38.96	1.32	06.57	20.11	4.90	127.24
1983-84	58.51	41.38	1.77	06.57	20.97	5.59	134.78
1984-85	60.10	43.23	1.13	07.41	22.85	6.62	141.34
1985-86	74.98	51.16	2.71	10.38	26.65	5.59	171.46
1986-87	79.95	55.78	3.00	10.82	29.69	6.54	185.78
1987-88	91.89	61.96	3.08	12.43	30.02	5.45	204.83
1988-89	99.82	72.70	4.09	12.28	36.33	6.09	231.32
1989-90	114.54	79.67	4.13	12.58	39.58	6.71	257.21
1990-91	117.27	83.14	4.92	13.12	36.97	6.17	261.59
Mean	79.84	56.23	2.72	9.78	28.17	5.82	182.57
C.V.	31.69	31.21	50.60	29.88	26.99	12.54	030.07
C.G.R.	11.21*	10.82*	19.29*	10.74*	09.27*	3.02#	10.59*
			Period II				
1991-92	113.65	82.45	3.61	12.47	34.66	5.75	252.59
1992-93	114.74	81.86	3.52	12.79	34.60	7.08	254.59
1993-94	120.82	83.58	4.39	13.49	33.82	11.56	267.65
1994-95	124.17	86.34	4.50	13.70	33.62	9.66	271.99
1995-96	133.70	94.43	5.02	14.61	34.88	6.54	289.18
1996-97	149.79	105.23	5.73	16.04	35.99	6.49	319.26
1997-98	161.57	111.85	6.50	18.51	38.74	6.97	344.14
1998-99	191.05	133.70	8.27	20.72	42.68	7.38	403.80
1999-00	225.31	159.16	10.30	23.74	45.81	7.70	472.02
2000-01	214.22	150.81	10.04	22.77	42.14	6.00	445.97
2001-02	221.65	163.52	10.55	24.15	46.15	6.85	472.87
2002-03	235.45	169.45	10.82	26.45	49.23	7.26	498.66
2003-04	242.36	178.45	11.05	27.15	51.24	9.45	519.70
2004-05	256.85	186.23	11.45	30.12	54.26	10.25	549.16
Mean	178.95	127.65	7.55	19.77	41.27	7.78	382.97
C.V.	29.66	30.92	40.77	30.47	17.21	22.44	28.38
C.G.R.	07.44*	07.70*	10.92*	07.59*	03.92*	00.94@	07.03*
t(m)	-05.45*	-05.33*	-04.62*	-04.83*	-04.23*	-03.33*	-05.34*

Note: C.G.R.- Compound growth rate.
C.V. - Coefficient of variation.
* - Statistically significant at one per cent level.
# - Statistically significant at five per cent level.
@ - Statistically not significant at five per cent level.
t(m) - 't' test values for the difference between means of two periods.

TABLE 2

Chow Test for Educational Expenditure

Sl. No.	Details	S_5 Value	S_4 Value	F Value
1.	Elementary	1815.37	3116.10	17.17*
2.	Secondary	1045.24	1967.33	18.82*
3.	Adult	8.12	17.59	21.66*
4.	Technical	22.43	60.68	27.05*
5.	University	90.73	166.96	18.40*
6.	Others	41.40	1.93	0.47@
	Total	7309.19	13589.46	18.59*

Note: $S_1 = RSS_T$ $S_2 = RSS_1$ $S_3 = RSS_2$
$S_4 = (S_1 + S_2)$ $S_5 = (S_1 - S_4)$.
RSS – Residual sum of squares
* - Statistically significant at one per cent level.
$ - Statistically significant at five per cent level.
@ - Statistically not significant at five per cent level.

statistically significant at one per cent level. The C.V. value for most of the components was comparatively less in period II than in period I, showing relatively less instability during the post-economic reform period.

The compound growth rate was less for all the components in period II than in period I. It was again due to the reason that the base for the estimation of growth rate was larger in period II than in period I. Hence, one could observe that there was an increasing trend in the educational expenditure during post-economic reform period in order to serve the increasing educational needs of the people.

Therefore, the general inference was that governments had allocated more funds for educational improvement during the post-economic reform period. There was more stable uptrend in educational expenditure, even though the growth rate was comparatively smaller in period II. Thus, it could be inferred that the uptrend in expenditure on education of governments during post-economic reform period had welfare implication.

The estimated 'F' values of the different components of educational expenditures of combined, union and state governments for the Chow test are given in Table 2. It shows that all the estimated 'F' values are statistically significant. It indicates that there was a structural change or structural instability between period I and period II in the different components of educational expenditure for all the governments.

ELASTICITY OF EDUCATIONAL EXPENDITURE

In order to estimate the elasticity of the components of educational expenditure, a log-linear function (In Y_t = $á_0$ + $á_1$, In X_t + u_t) was used, with the assumptions of the Classical linear regression model. The dependent and independent variables are different components of educational expenditure (Y_t) and GDP (X_t).

The elasticity of educational expenditures with respect to GDP is presented in Table 3. The elasticity of total educational expenditure and its components was less in period II than in period I. Thus, the elasticity of educational expenditure with respect to GDP was relatively less for education during the post economic reform period.

EDUCATIONAL INFRTASTRUCTURE AND ATTAINMENT

For an overall development of the economy, development of education is important. Hence, the effect of educational expenditure in terms of educational infrastructure development and educational attainment is discussed in this section. Number of schools per lakh population and teachers in schools per 10,000 students were taken as the educational infrastructure development. Enrolment by level of education and male and female literacy was taken as the educational attainment.

The number of primary and secondary schools per lakh population was an indicator of educational infrastructure development and therefore the details are given in Table 4. As seen in Table 4, the number of primary schools per lakh population declined by six schools in period I and by eight

TABLE 3

Elasticities with Respect to GDP (%)

Sl. No	*Details*	*Period I*	*Period II*
1.	Elementary Education	1.91	1.33
2.	Secondary Education	1.87	1.30
3.	Adult Education	3.18	2.06
4.	Technical Education	1.80	1.26
5.	University Education	1.61	0.52
	Total	1.82	1.20

Note: All the values of the elasticity values are statistically significant at one per cent level.
I – Period I (1981-82 to 1990-91).
II – Period II (1991-92 to 2004-05).

schools in period II. The fall was higher in period II. But the number of secondary schools per lakh population increased by 0.37 in period I and by eight schools in period II.

The mean value was significantly lesser for secondary schools and larger for primary schools in period II. The compound growth rate was negative for primary schools and positive for secondary schools, but the negative growth rate was relatively lesser in period II. The C.V. was relatively smaller for primary schools and larger for secondary schools in period II compared to period I.

Therefore, the number of primary schools declined at a lesser rate and secondary schools per lakh population was at a higher rate during the post-economic reform period. The inference is that the number of primary schools had increased slower than the population and that was inconsistent with the goals of universal education and 100 per cent enrolment. Addition in investment by the governments and encouragement of private investment in primary schools should be the policy. It would call for further increase in secondary schools also to discourage drop-out at that level.

Number of teachers in primary and secondary schools

TABLE 4

Number of Schools Per Lakh Population

Years	*Primary Schools*	*Secondary Schools*
	Period I	
1981-82	72.80	17.68
1982-83	71.15	17.42
1983-84	70.42	17.48
1984-85	70.32	17.57
1985-86	70.05	17.86
1986-87	68.84	17.90
1987-88	68.40	18.09
1988-89	67.41	17.98
1989-90	66.68	17.90
1990-91	66.86	18.05
Mean	69.29	17.79
C.V.	02.88	01.35
C.G.R.	-00.93*	00.37*
	Period II	
1991-92	66.21	18.22
1992-93	65.51	18.18
1993-94	63.95	18.25
1994-95	64.48	18.55
1995-96	63.95	18.77
1996-97	63.81	19.06
1997-98	64.23	19.29
1998-99	63.76	19.35
1999-00	64.11	19.78
2000-01	62.68	20.24
2001-02	61.56	21.26
2002-03	60.25	23.15
2003-04	59.46	25.56
2004-05	58.21	26.48
Mean	65.62	19.34
C.V.	05.82	12.67
C.G.R.	-00.80@	01.36*
t(m)	03.06*	-2.35*

Note: C.G.R. - Compound growth rate.
C.V. - Coefficient of variation.
* - Significant at one per cent level.
** - Significant at five per cent level.
t(m) - 't' test values for difference between means of two periods.

TABLE 5

Teachers in Schools per 10,000 Students

Years	*Primary Schools*	*Secondary Schools*
	Period I	
1981-82	189.73	438.92
1982-83	179.05	381.32
1963-84	174.92	355.58
1984-85	173.44	354.60
1985-86	171.17	354.58
1986-87	172.33	363.21
1987-88	170.44	352.48
1988-89	170.36	347.14
1989-90	169.43	339.05
1990-91	166.02	315.59
Mean	173.69	360.25
C.V.	03.81	08.97
C.G.R	-01.06*	-02.34*
	Period II	
1991-92	162.93	303.09
1992-93	165.76	318.18
1993-94	167.32	331.09
1994-95	160.61	317.58
1995-96	161.90	317.87
1996-97	162.20	314.96
1997-98	165.28	313.16
1998-99	171.69	317.12
1999-00	168.93	308.31
2000-01	166.61	309.81
2001-02	169.45	311.26
2002-03	172.23	312.45
2003-04	174.23	314.23
2004-05	177.45	316.75
Mean	167.61	314.70
C.V.	02.99	02.03
C.G.R.	00.57*	-0.09@
t(m)	02.56*	05.18*

Note: C.G.R. - Compound growth rate.
C.V. - Coefficient of variation.
* - Significant at one per cent level.
** - Significant at five per cent level.
t(m) - 't' test values for difference between means of two periods.

per 10,000 students was taken as another indicator of educational infrastructure. It is shown in Table 5. It could be seen that the number of teachers per 10,000 students in primary schools declined in period I from 190 teachers in 1981-82 to 166 teachers in 1990-91. But in period II, the number of primary school teachers increased from 163 to 177, i.e., by 15. It increased relatively more in period II than in period I. In the secondary schools also number of teachers per 10,000 students declined from 439 in 1981-82 to 316 in 1990-91, i.e., by 123 teachers per 10,000 students. In period II, there was a marginal increase by 14 teachers per lakh population.

The mean value for teachers in primary and secondary schools was significantly lesser in period II. The negative growth rate of teachers in primary schools in period I became positive in period II. The negative growth of teachers in secondary schools in period I became less negative in period II. The C.V. value was for primarily relatively smaller in period II than in period I. The results revealed the need to employ more teachers in the years to come, if the spread on education had to be sustained, in its present expansion stage, in India.

Enrolment of students is a measure of immediate attainment in education. The enrolment of males and females at different levels of education is presented in Table 6. The enrolment of students in primary, secondary and high/higher secondary schools was 76.16 million, 21.94 million and 12.55 million respectively in 1981-82. It increased to 97.4 million, 34 million and 19.1 million in 1990-91 and 122.31 million, 47.26 million and 34 million in 2004-05. It showed that there was a steady increase in the total enrolment in schools. The mean values were significantly larger with relatively lesser C.V. value in period II. It was relatively larger for primary schools in period II. But the growth rate was lesser for the enrolment in primary and secondary schools in period II. It was higher for high/higher secondary schools in period II. Thus, the enrolment in schools showed an uptrend with larger mean values and smaller C.V. and CGR value during the post-reform period.

TABLE 6

Enrolment by Levels of Education

(Million)

Years	*Primary*			*Secondary*			*High/Higher*		
	M	*F*	*T*	*M*	*F*	*T*	*M*	*F*	*T*
				Period I					
1981-82	46.77	29.39	76.16	14.67	7.28	21.94	8.93	3.61	12.55
1982-83	48.66	30.87	79.53	15.63	7.51	23.13	9.81	3.94	13.75
1983-84	50.31	32.24	82.55	16.59	8.59	25.17	10.22	4.26	14.48
1984-85	51.96	33.72	85.68	17.14	9.03	26.17	10.84	4.63	15.47
1985-86	52.20	35.20	87.40	17.70	9.60	27.30	11.50	5.00	16.50
1986-87	51.73	35.43	87.16	17.80	9.65	27.45	11.47	5.17	16.65
1987-88	53.62	36.91	90.53	18.81	10.43	29.25	10.87	4.95	15.82
1988-89	53.85	37.36	91.22	19.22	10.71	29.93	10.98	5.27	16.25
1989-90	54.33	38.05	92.37	19.77	11.10	30.88	11.72	5.64	17.36
1990-91	57.00	40.40	97.40	21.50	12.50	34.00	12.80	6.30	19.10
Mean	52.04	34.96	87.00	17.88	09.64	27.52	10.91	04.88	15.79
C.V.	05.65	09.80	07.29	11.33	16.82	13.26	09.90	16.45	11.82
C.G.R.	01.82*	03.29*	02.41*	03.77*	05.70*	04.44*	02.98*	05.49*	03.74*

				Period II					
1991-92	58.60	42.30	100.9	22.00	13.60	35.60	13.50	06.90	20.40
1992-93	57.90	41.70	99.60	21.20	12.90	34.10	13.60	06.90	20.50
1993-94	55.10	41.90	97.00	20.60	13.50	34.10	13.20	07.50	20.70
1994-95	60.00	45.10	105.10	22.10	14.30	36.40	14.20	07.90	22.10
1995-96	60.90	46.20	107.10	22.70	14.80	37.50	14.60	08.30	22.90
1996-97	61.40	46.80	108.20	22.90	15.20	38.10	16.30	08.70	25.00
1997-98	62.30	48.00	110.30	23.60	15.90	39.50	16.10	09.30	25.40
998-99	62.70	48.20	110.90	24.00	16.30	40.30	17.30	10.50	27.80
1999-00	64.10	49.50	113.60	25.10	17.00	42.10	17.20	11.00	28.20
2000-01	64.00	49.80	113.80	25.30	17.50	42.80	16.90	10.70	27.60
2001-02	65.12	50.23	115.35	25.85	17.84	43.69	17.26	11.02	28.28
2002-03	66.45	51.42	117.87	26.12	18.25	44.37	18.56	11.85	30.41
2003-04	67.85	52.32	120.17	27.56	18.63	46.19	19.85	12.05	31.90
2004-05	69.42	52.89	122.31	28.14	19.12	47.26	20.74	13.26	34.00
Mean	62.56	47.60	110.16	24.08	16.06	40.14	16.38	9.71	26.09
C.V.	06.35	07.93	06.98	09.68	12.81	10.88	14.42	21.15	16.81
C.G.R.	01.46*	01.90*	01.65*	02.26*	03.11*	02.59*	03.38*	05.22*	04.05*
t(m)f	-07.08*	-08.20*	-07.80*	-06.77*	-08.20*	-07.40*	-06.80*	-07.05*	-06.95*

Note: C.G.R. – *Compound growth rate.*

C.V. – Coefficient of variation,

* – Significant at one per cent level.

t(m) – 't' test values for difference between means of two periods.

The analysis of enrolment of male and female students in primary, secondary and higher secondary also showed similar results as seen in the total enrolment of students. Thus, the enrolment in schools showed a significant increase with larger mean and relatively lesser C.V. and CGR for period II as compared to period I, the inference being that during post-economic reform period the enrolment significantly increased in schools, especially in high/higher secondary schools.

The literacy rate is an important indicator of educational attainment. The details are given in Table 7. The total literacy rate increased in period I by 6.02 per cent and in period II by 16.78 per cent. Male and female literacy rates also increased by 9.34 per cent and 4.51 per cent in period I and 15.94 per cent and 17.98 per cent in period II. It indicated that the increase literacy was less for females than that for males in period I, but it was reversed largely in period II. Thus, the literacy rate, especially for females increased largely during the post-economic reform period.

EDUCATIONAL ATTAINMENT AND ECONOMIC DEVELOPMENT

Given the other resources, the economic development of a country mostly depends on the development of human resources through education and training and health. Therefore, the relationship between educational attainment and economic development was studied for their strength and the direction of causality. That is, the impact of educational attainment (proxied by the proportion of the population allocated to higher education institutions, i.e., number of students enrolled per capita in general education, engineering education, and medical education) of the level on growth rate of GDP per capita at constant (1993-94) prices was studied.

In order to test causality between education attainment and economic development, two different sets of variables foı education were used. Firstly, the causality link between the number of students per institution enrolled in higher education (education attainment in general education-GEN,

TABLE 7

Male and Female Literacy Rates

(%)

Years	*M*	*F*	*T*	*F/M Ratio*
Period I				
1981-82	54.50	29.75	43.56	54.59
1982-83	55.63	30.25	43.85	54.38
1983-84	56.35	30.65	44.10	54.39
1984-85	56.93	21.41	44.75	37.61
1985-86	58.08	31.65	45.02	54.49
1986-87	59.24	31.90	45.94	53.85
1987-88	60.39	32.34	46.85	53.55
1988-89	61.54	32.98	47.76	53.59
1989-90	62.69	33.62	48.67	53.63
1990-91	63.84	34.26	49.58	53.67
Period II				
1991-92	64.00	39.00	52.00	60.94
1992-93	68.00	43.00	56.00	63.24
1993-94	69.00	44.00	57.00	63.77
1994-95	69.00	46.00	58.00	66.67
1995-96	70.00	47.00	59.00	67.14
1996-97	71.60	50.00	60.85	69.83
1997-98	72.50	52.30	61.25	72.14
1998-99	73.45	53.45	62.45	72.77
1999-00	74.15	53.94	63.65	72.74
2000-01	75.85	54.16	65.38	71.40
2001-02	77.67	55.25	66.12	71.13
2002-03	78.52	55.96	66.95	71.27
2003-04	79.75	56.25	67.56	70.53
2004-05	79.94	56.98	68.78	71.28

engineering education—ENG, and medical education—MED) and GDP per capita at (1993-94) constant prices. The focus here is on the relationship between the intensity of the efforts made by a society concerning educational attainment and their level on economic development. Secondly, the link between the rates of growth of these variables (GRGEN, GRENG, and GRMED) and GDP per capita was attempted.

TABLE 8

Results of Bi-Variate Granger's Causality Test

Equations	Dependent Variable	Causal Variable	'F' Statistic for Causality Test
1.	GDP	GED	F(2,15) = 57.26*
	GED	GDP	F(2,15) = 4.15@
2.	GDP	EED	F(2,15) = 38.11*
	EED	GDP	F(2,15) = 9.48*
3.	GDP	MED	F(2,15) = 61.33*
	MED	GDP	F(2,15) = 34.77*
4.	GRGDP	GRGED	F(1,17) = 12.04*
	GRGED	GRGDP	F(1,17) = 4.32@
5.	GRGDP	GREED	F(1,17) = 83.69*
	GREED	GRGDP	F(1,17) = 54.58*
6.	GRGDP	GRMED	F(1,17) = 11.21*
	GRMED	GRGDP	F(1,17) = 33.72*

Note: Lag length for the variables of actual data and growth rate (GR) were two and one respectively for independent variables.
* - Significant at one per cent level.
$ - Significant at five per cent level.
@ - Not significant at five per cent level.

The focus here is to examine the causality between increase in education attainment and economic growth. The data used for this purpose was for a period of 24 years, from 1981-82 to 2004-05.

The Augmented Dickey Fuller (ADF) test was carried out for the actual data and growth rates (in percentage values). The results showed that there is stationarity both in the actual data and growth rates. Hence, the test for causality between educational attainment and economic development was carried out directly within the Classical framework of Granger (1969) for actual data and growth rates.

The results obtained from the Granger's causality test are given in Table 8. The results also confirmed the presence of causality link between education attainment and economic development. The causality link was one directional between GED and GDP both in actual data and growth rates. It means that economic development contributed to general education but the reverse was not so. There was bi-directional causal relationship between engineering education and economic development and medical education and economic development, both in actual data and growth rates. It confirmed the presence of causality link from engineering and medical education to economic development, and from economic development to engineering and medical education. It suggested the presence of a long-run stable linear relationship between education attainment and economic development. Even for GED to GDP, there was a long-run linear relationship but that relationship was not significant as found in actual data and growth rates.

The results of causality analysis suggested that educational attainment increased the labour productivity and thereby contributed to economic development, even though the link between educational attainment and economic development was complex. Intuitively, one would come to the conclusion from empirical results that, educational attainment through expansion of general education, engineering education and medical education, and educational attainment contributed to economic growth during the period of the study.

SUMMARY OF FINDINGS

The issues pertaining to educational development are receiving increasing attention from academicians as well as policy-makers. Hence, an attempt was made in this study to analyse the relationship between educational development and economic development in India. The inferences derived from the data analysis are summarized in this section.

- The expenditure on education revealed a steady increase but at lower rate during post-economic reform period. There was structural change between the two periods in the different components of educational expenditure.
- The elasticity for the different components of educational expenditure with respect to GDP declined for all governments in period 2.

- Number of primary schools and secondary schools per lakh population also increased but primary schools had not increased consistently with the increase in size of population, as a reflection of priority in education policy.
- Number of teachers per 10000 students showed a steady increase in primary schools but at lesser rate in secondary schools. It was because the governments had accorded priority to increase the number of teachers in primary schools, with the goal of enrolling all eligible students at that level.
- The enrolment of males and females in primary, secondary and high/higher secondary schools showed an uptrend, especially in high/higher secondary schools during the post-economic reform period.
- The male and female literacy had increased in both periods but at a higher rate in period II, showing that the new economic reform policy increased the literacy rate, especially for females during post-economic reform period.
- The Granger's causality test proved that there was a stable and precise relationship between educational attainment and economic development in India during the period of the study, viz., 1981-82 to 2004-05. This might be attributed to increase in labour productivity by educational attainments.

This study analysed the growth of educational expenditure of the governments. This expenditure was analysed for its impact on infrastructural development and attainment and thereby economic development ultimately. There was bi-directional causality between educational development and economic development. The comparative study of pre and post-reform periods showed that the NERP had a positive impact on educational development as well as on economic development. The results showed that educational development and economic development are complementary to each other.

As educational development and economic

development are interacting and impacting on each other, the economic growth has become a necessary condition for educational development and gender parity in development. The emphasis on attaining eight per cent to ten per cent annual growth in real GDP (economic growth) is a right policy and efforts to achieve the target have to be intensified.

References

Barrera, Albina (1990), "The Role of Maternal Schooling and Its Interaction with Public Health Programs in Child Health Production", *Journal of Development Economics*, Vol. 32, No. 1.

Ghosh, Arun (1992), "Education for All—The Financing Problem", *Economic and Political Weekly*, April 4.

Chaubey, P.K. and Chaubey, Geeta (1998, "Gender Equity Sensitive Literacy Rates: An Alternative Approach", *Anvesak*, Vol. 28, No. (1).

Gosal, (1964), "Inequalities in the Levels of Literacy: A Regional Analysis", Occasional Paper (4): *NIEPA*, New Delhi.

Hussain, M.A. (1981), "Continuing Education and Its Role in Human Resource Development in India", *Journal of Higher Education*, Vol. 7, No. 1.

Pulparampil, John (1999), "Educational HRD", New Frontier in Education, 24(4).

Bhatty, Kiran (1998), "Educational Deprivation in India—A Survey of Field Investigations", *Economic and Political Weekly*, Vol. 23, No. 28.

Karlekar, Malavika (2000), "Girl's Access to Schooling: An Assessment", The Gender Gap in Basic Education (ed) Rakha Wazir, (New Delhi: Sage Publications).

Mehrotra, Santosh (2006), The Economics of Elementary Education in India: The Challenge of Public Provisioning and Household Costs, (New Delhi: Sage Publication).

Nambissan, Seetha B. (1996), "Equity in Education? Schooling of Dalit Children in India", *Economic and Political Weekly*, Vol. 31, Nos. 16 and 17.

Haldar, Sisir Kumar (1969), "Public Expenditure on Education—The Search for Criteria", *Yojana*, July 27.

13

Inclusive Education for Inclusive Growth

Meera Lal

INTRODUCTION

"There is in our time no well educated literate population that is poor; there is no illiterate population that is other than poor."

—*John Kenneth Galbraith*

In recent years sustained and high levels of economic growth provide a unique opportunity and momentum for faster social sector development. Investing in education plays a key role in meeting the World Bank's social development objectives, which support inclusive growth, social cohesion, and accountability in development. Professor Amartya Sen recently emphasised education as an important parameter for any inclusive growth in an economy. The policies have to focus on inclusive rather than divisive growth strategies. Japan's Fundamental Code of Education of 1872 had resulted in total literacy by 1910 and by 1913. Japan was publishing books twice as much as U.S.

The recent Education for All (EFA) Global Monitoring report 2008, released by UNESCO marks the midway in the ambitious movement to expand learning opportunity to every child by 2015. The UNESCO defined six EFA goals:

1. Expanding and improving comprehensive childhood care and education, especially for the most vulnerable and disadvantaged children;
2. Ensuring that by 2015 all children, particularly girls, children in difficult circumstances and those belonging to ethnic minorities, have access to free and compulsory primary education of good quality;
3. Ensuring that the learning needs of all young people and adults are met to equitable access to appropriate learning and life skills programme;
4. Eliminating gender disparities in primary and secondary education by 2005 and achieving gender equality in education by 20015; and
5. Improving all aspects of quality of education and ensuring excellence so that recognised and measurable learning outcomes are achieved, especially in literacy, numeracy and in essential life skills.

RIGHT TO EDUCATION IN INDIA

In India the right to free and compulsory education was retained in Article 45 of Part IV of the Constitution that incorporates The Directive Principles of the State Policy, thus making a distinction from the Fundamental Rights. The most relevant interpretation of Article 21 from education point of view was the Supreme Court's Unnikrishnan Judgement (1993). The Court ruled that Article 45 of the Directive Principles of State Policy must be read in harmonious conjunction with Article 21 since right to life and personal liberty loses its meaning if a child is deprived of elementary education (*Unnikrishnan* v. *State of Andhra Pradesh,* 1993, Supreme Court of India, 217).

However, though this Article 21A has provided

renewed opportunity to reduce the increasing inequality in education at the elementary level and achieve the goals of justice—social, economic and political, it has yet to acquire the stature of other fundamental rights. The recent report of the CABE (Central Advisory Board of Education) Committee (2005) advocated Free and Compulsory Education Bill.

Recently, the 93rd Constitution Amendment Bill making education a fundamental right for children between six and 14 has secured the Parliament's nod. With the law backing the Centre's Sarva Shiksha Abhiyan, Human Resource Minister, believed that all out-of-school children would now be able to attend school.

THE EXISTING SCENARIO IN EDUCATION

Education is universally recognised as a central component of human capital. The role of education as a contributor to economic growth and its impact on population control, life expectancy, infant mortality, improving nutritional status and strengthening civil institutions is well recognised. Moreover, the social rates of return on investments in all levels of education much exceed the long-term opportunity cost of capital. In normal course educated parents would send their children to schools. But where parents are not educated they may send their children to schools if there are enough incentives to attract and retain the children in schools. However, it has been seen that as the child grows, the opportunity cost of sending the child to schools increases and incentives become less important. It has also been observed that socio-economic factors often come in the way of educating girls beyond a certain class. On the supply side the reasons observed for children not being in school extend from non-availability of schools, poor quality of education, including irregular opening of schools, poor learning environment, etc.

Plan expenditure on education has increased rapidly since the First Five Year Plan. A high priority was accorded to this sector in the Ninth Five Year Plan, with an allocation of Rs. 24,908 crore against an expenditure of Rs. 8,522 crore in the Eighth Plan, representing a three-fold increase in funds available to this sector. The 11th Plan proposes 19.9 per cent share for education. Roughly Rs. 2.85 lakh crore is proposed to be set aside for Elementary, Adult, Secondary and Higher Education. Top Planning Commission sources have said that in terms of percentage, this is almost 2.7 times the allocation in the last plan.

Whereas the rising enrolment in elementary schools is a source of satisfaction, there is concern about the percentage of students actually attending school and those dropping out of the education system altogether. Though dropout rates at the elementary education stage have declined over the years, they are still relatively high especially in the case of girl students for whom the rates are 42 per cent and 58 per cent at the Primary and Upper Primary stages respectively. Within the education sector, elementary education has been given the highest priority in terms of sub-sectoral allocations. Several schemes have been launched by the Central government to meet the needs of the educationally disadvantaged and for strengthening the social infrastructure for education viz. Operation Blackboard (OB), District Primary Education Programme (DPEP), Education Guarantee Scheme and Alternative and Innovative Education (EGS&AIE), Mahila Samakhya, Teacher Education (TE), Mid-day Meals Scheme, Lok Jumbish, Shiksha Karmi Project (SKP), Janashala, etc. In 2001-02 significant steps have been taken towards achievement of the goals of UEE through a time bound integrated approach, in partnership with the States through launching of the Sarva Shiksha Abhiyan (SSA). The planning in SSA has been decentralized and highest priority is accorded to community ownership and monitoring. This programme will subsume all existing programmes including externally aided programmes in due course within its overall framework with district as the unit of programme implementation.

India is one of the least literate societies in the world. The Census of India 2001 revealed that despite a host of schemes and programmes only 65.38 per cent of Indian people are literate (75.85% men and 54.16% women). Literacy rates in the States of Bihar, Rajasthan, Uttar Pradesh and Andhra Pradesh were below 37 per cent according to 2001

TABLE I

Principal Component Loading and Coefficient of Variation for Educational Variables

S. No.	Variables	Mean	Factor Loading	Coefficient of variation
1.	Adult literacy rate	63.88	.42807	17.78%
2.	Percentage of Enrolment in 6-14 age group	94.25	.70845	15.68%
3.	Primary schools per thousand population	1.179	.70636	51.06%
4.	Percentage of habitations having educational amenities	79.39	-.37845	17.94%
5.	Teacher-pupil ratio	34.42	-.73938	37.19%
	Variation explained		37.4%	

Source: Computed.

census. For SC/ST students the figures are even below 24 per cent.

The recent Annual Status of Education Report (ASER, 2005) prepared by Pratham to assess the learning levels of children across schools reveals a rather dismal picture, which is the inability of class III to read a story of class II level. This is more glaring when it comes to subjects like Mathematics where a class V student is unable to solve problems of class III level. There are also considerable rural-urban differentials in the Gross Primary School Enrolment Ratio (GPER) particularly among girls. According to Selected Education Statistics, 2006, 99 per cent boys and 82 per cent girls aged 6-10 years are enrolled in schools. However, it is also a fallacy that a staggering number of children, close to 38.41 per cent of boys and 51.88 per cent of girls in the age group of 6-14 years are not attending school at all. This has also been more or less confirmed in the ASER 2005-6 Report by Pratham India Educational Initiatives. Disaggregated data on-out-of school children who have never enrolled in schools reveal a disproportionate presence of special groups like working children, residents of far-flung habitations, SCs/STs. Within all these categories, the percentage of girls is very high. A large proportion of the child labourers belong to the scheduled caste/scheduled tribe community working in unorganised sector. Many of them again are girls which are the neglected and deprived lot. These children are often referred to as "no-where children" neither on account of the fact that that they show up neither in labour statistics nor at schools.

The ASER Report 2006 shook the world in its path-breaking survey. The findings of the report are striking and important for any future policy formulation:

- In rural India, of 100 children in the age group 7-16, 71.3 per cent go to government schools, while only 18.5 per cent go to private schools.
- In recent years preference for private schools has increased on account of three reasons—firstly, government schools have low-quality teaching, secondly, government schools are non-English medium and lastly, Dalits and Muslims are often not welcome at government schools in rural areas on account of pre-dominance of the upper castes.
- Free government schools which are mostly well-funded are rejected in favour of small private schools mostly missionary.
- Nearly 30 per cent of children in the States of Punjab, Haryana, Jammu and Kashmir, UP, Meghalaya, Nagaland, Manipur, Goa and Kerala find going to private schools more favourable.
- Another revealing fact is the quality of teaching at these government schools. Though the enrolment rates become a matter of triumph for the government, learning skills which ought to be found in the 2nd standard are often achieved only by the 8th standard.

The District Information System of Education (DISE) has published its Analytical Report in 2005. The analysis of data reveals that many schools in the country are still not equipped with many of basic facilities. So much so that about 4 per cent primary schools and 12 per cent upper primary schools do not have a proper building. Nearly 17.5 per cent primary schools and 7.7 per cent upper primary schools have only one teacher. More than 9-10 per cent of schools do not have provision of blackboards and drinking water facilities are available to only one-fifth in these schools. Playground and boundary walls are not available in most of the schools along with any toilet facilities. Girls' toilets are not available in more than two-thirds of the upper primary schools. More than 90 per cent of schools are deprived of electricity connection and hence computer facilities. From the above it is clear that the country's top priority today has to be education focused if the goals of quality universal elementary education have to be achieved.

Thus, though the literacy rates across the country increased impressively from 52.21 per cent in 1991 to 65.38 per cent in 2001, the country still has more than 296 million illiterates of age 7 and above and male/female differential in literacy is also high at 22 percentage points. The literacy of Dalit women in Rajasthan is 1/5th of the national average.

Prima-facie, it seems that the Census data do not present the true picture of the literacy status of the population. There may be measurement errors in enumeration also, which may be because of a variety of reasons:

- First, those who are treated as literates, many of them may be illiterates. Their ability to read and write with understanding is questionable. This can be checked on sample basis. The external evaluations conducted in the past also support this argument (NLM, 1994).
- Second, many a time when children in households are reported to be in schools, the enumerator unconsciously treated them as literates, which may not always be true. In all practical purposes, a child of Grade I was treated as literate in 2001 Census so as the Child of Grade II. A child aged 9 or 10, if reported enrolled in school, may also not necessarily be literate because of the lateral entry. Many of them may still be in Grade I or II.

TABLE 2

Percentage of Rural Habitations having Primary and Upper Primary Schooling Facilities (1993-02)

Sl. No.	*Name of the State*	*Primary Within Hab.*		*Primary Up to 1 Km*		*Upper Primary Within Hab.*		*Upper Primary Up to 3 Km.*	
1.	Andhra Pradesh	69.73	78.49	88.57	93.91	13.82	24.49	65.40	74.73
2.	Karnataka	60.36	67.44	83.75	88.41	24.71	30.66	85.32	88.26
3.	Maharashtra	64.70	67.64	84.22	91.17	25.37	28.95	78.42	78.18
4.	Orissa	48.96	51.54	82.42	82.93	13.47	19.77	77.24	73.55
5.	Rajasthan	51.11	53.41	74.58	79.84	14.59	21.07	64.43	78.26
	INDIA	49.79	53.04	83.36	86.96	13.87	18.45	76.15	78.11

Source: 6th and 7th Educational Survey (2005), NCERT, Government of India, New Delhi.

CHART I

Children Attending School (1991 and 2001 Census)

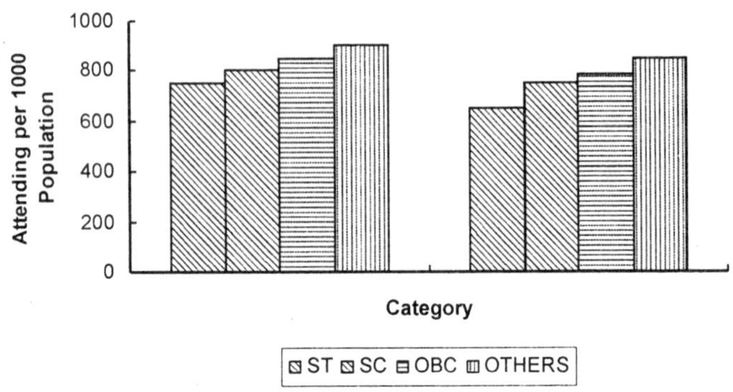

- Lastly, the majority of enumerators in Census 2001 were the local school-teachers. This may also perhaps be one of the factors that might have influenced number of literates.

From the above it is clear that Andhra Pradesh ranks highest in drop out rates in all categories of SC/ST children, with girls being greater victims in all classes. In most of the cases the axe falls on the girl child. With meager income, many parents with four or five school-going children on an average find it difficult to spend equally for the schooling needs of all children. So the variations of choices emerge, namely educate one child, withdraw the girl child, push the better performing child to another level or let the girls continue in government schools and move the boys to hostels. These are the extra costs among all the factors that deter the poorest from accessing schools even if they are in the same village.

As per 2001 Census, Muslims, Christians, Sikhs, Buddhists and Parsis declared as Minority by Government notification 1993, constitute 18.42 per cent of total population. The main factor responsible for socio-economic backwardness

TABLE 3

Dropout Rates Among SC and ST Boys and Girls (2006)

(Percentage)

Categories	*AP*	*Karna-taka*	*Maha-rashtra*	*Orissa*	*Rajasthan*
Dropout SC Boys I-V	44.09	6.12	17.02	44.99	53.07
Dropout SC Girls I-V	44.12	14.03	18.21	42.36	36.29
Dropout SC Boys VI-VIII	63.41	27.19	30.03	63.73	69.65
Dropout SC Girls VI-VIII	68.87	51.61	38.22	67.17	80.07
Dropout ST Boys I-V	63.29	4.88	34.42	59.58	52.19
Dropout ST Girls I-V	68.47	4.96	42.82	63.19	38.31
Dropout ST Boys VI-VIII	76.80	53.81	59.12	76.49	70.42
Dropout ST Girls VI-VIII	82.49	56.80	65.14	76.56	79.63

Source: Selected Education Statistics (2006), Government of India, New Delhi.

of the minority communities, particularly the Muslim community, is the lack of access to the common school system. This is particularly true in the case of Muslim girls. In 2006-07 financial year, the corpus of the Maulana Azad Education Foundation which provides financial assistance to implement educational schemes for the benefit of the educationally backward minorities has been enhanced to Rs. 200 crore from Rs. 100 crore. The High Level Sachar Committee in 2005 made some important recommendations relating to measures to be undertaken for "high quality education", good quality government schools specifically for Muslim girls. Quality Education is thus an important tool to uplift the weaker sections to enable them to join the main stream for inclusive growth.

The Indian Constitution assigns special status to the Scheduled Tribes (STs) also. Traditionally referred to as adivasis, vanbasis, tribes, or tribals, STs constitute about 8 per cent of the Indian population. There are 573 Scheduled Tribes living in different parts of the country, having their own languages, which are different from the one mostly spoken in the State where they live. There are more than 270 such languages in India. According to the 2001 census, the tribal population in India is 74.6 million. The largest number of tribes is in undivided Madhya Pradesh (16.40 million), followed by Orissa (7 million) and Jharkhand (6.6 million).

There were 16 million ST children (10.87 million of 6-11 years and 5.12 million of 11-14 years) as of March 2001, out of the total child population in India of about 193 million in the age group of 6 to 14 years (Selected Educational Statistics—2000-01, Government of India). Education of ST children is considered important, not only because of the Constitutional obligation but also as a crucial input for total development of tribal communities.

An increasing number of researchers strongly advocate the use of the mother tongue or home language as medium of instruction in early stages of education. This assumes greater significance in the context of education of tribal children because their mother tongue is often quite distinct from the prominent languages in the state or regional languages. ST children face problems wherever teachers do not speak their dialect at all. From the perspective of language, it is desirable to have a local teacher from the same tribal community.

Although research evidence has demonstrated the positive consequences of bilingual or multilingual schooling on cognitive development and social interaction processes, tribal children would require special programs to be able to cope. The Constitution of India allows the use of tribal dialect (mother tongue) as the medium of instruction if the population of the tribe is more than 100,000.

Some relevant Action-Points and Strategies to meet the Challenges to achieve Inclusive Education

(a) Dropouts and Enrolment

- Enrolment targets achieved to be closely monitored by the concerned local Committees, by recording the data once every month.
- Regular checks on number of absentees of children at lower classes and for long durations may be done. The Committees to contact the parents in case of long absentees.

- Retention is as much of importance as enrolment since the latter is one time affair and these figures are no guide to actual number of children attending classes in practice.
- Mere incentives alone are not sufficient in themselves to enhance children's access to quality education. Most of the times, scholarships and sponsorships creates negative impact on the siblings of the family. This needs to be carefully thought out with proper monitoring and guidance.
- Mid-day Meal Scheme needs to be streamlined properly, enhancing the present amount of Rs. 2 per pupil to at least Rs. 3 as is being done in Tamil Nadu. Involvement of appropriate NGOs is to be strengthened for better implementation of the scheme.

(b) Teachers' Absenteeism/Training and Awareness

- Teachers' absenteeism to be monitored and noted not only by government officials but by parents and community as a whole. Appropriate systems at school level needs to be worked out.
- The ACER 2006 revealed that only 33 per cent of schools reported all teachers present with no absenteeism. The large percentage of Absenteeism of teachers, particularly at Primary level needs to be rectified.
- Teachers' duties from government work on Surveys and all other duties not related to teaching to be reduced as far as possible and some alternative teachers/para teachers/vidya volunteers to be appointed to enable regular teaching in cases where such duties are unavoidable.
- Investment in teachers and teacher education need to be made in a systematic way that appreciates the inter-relationship among the economic, political, structural, and practice aspects of the education system.

(c) Educational Incentives and Reforms

- The 'single text book policy has to be replaced by the textbooks for multiple linguistic communities,' thereby making the curricula much easier for the rural masses.
- Further, Education reforms that promote change from content-based syllabi to a 'learning outcomes' model have significant implications for learning resources.
- The passing and implementation of the Right to Education Bill, again on priority basis will help the disadvantaged groups.
- To enable multiple exit points after class VII to enable students to take up vocational training.
- School uniforms and alternative transport system can help poorer students ease some problems of clean and variety clothes everyday. In this effort the Community can contribute small amounts and start bus services.
- Scholarships and sponsorships can help promote girls' education.
- Delays in purchase of equipments, even lapse of grant funds for a particular financial year were found to be common reasons for poor performance in schools. Timely sanction of funds by Government authorities need to expedited.
- Campaign on child labour, in particular girl child to be spread to all districts of the state. Study conducted showed 20 per cent of these children are full time workers and 60 per cent in the age group of 5-14 years have never attended any school or had any formal education.
- The Mid-day Meal Programme an incentive for children to attend school has to cater to the prescribed nutritional norms. There is need for revision. 'Single Dish Meals' with broken wheat (dalia) or rice incorporating some amount of pulse or soyabeans along with seasonal vegetables can be an alternative for achieving these norms.

- Separate Toilets for Girls and Boys should be mandatory not only to facilitate proper sanitation facilities, but also to enable retention of girl students in particular.

(d) Public-Private Participation/Private-Private Partnership Approach

- In the Private-Private Approach, there are good examples of International Clubs like Lion's, Rotary and others joining hands with other NGOs, both internationally and nationally in their endeavours in the field of Education.
- Infrastructure is one area where there is urgent need of both Private-Public Participation as well as Private-Private Participation. From ACER 2007, it is clear that only 16-20 per cent of schools both at Primary and Upper Primary levels on an average had toilet facilities and about 30 per cent had no drinking water facilities. There is hence need to re-examine the designs and school building models for different capacities of school children.

(f) Community Participation-The Inclusive Model

- The "whole school approach" creates an inclusive environment for the entire community.
- Building strong People's Movement and thinking many steps ahead laterally and not vertically. The "Inverted Pyramid" is the model to be adopted for total community participation. Closer and frequent coordination with elected representatives of PRIs.
- The Government should adopt common school system imparting same quality of education throughout the country. Recently a Survey has been conducted and recommendations submitted regarding common school system to the Bihar Government.
- Creating awareness and viable open

communication channels between education administrators/implementers and local officials, teachers, parents and children, with Right to Information.

- The community-based associations of youth groups have been playing a key role in supporting the new leadership of women, dalits and tribals in Panchayati Raj Institutions and Urban Local Bodies in India.

(g) e-learning

- New systems of distance learning and Web-enabled education can be used to reach remote and underserved regions and segments of the population.
- Students, teachers, parents and the whole community can benefit a great deal with ICT programmes on Education.

These above interventions enables engagement of citizen leaders in initiating range of collective as well as individual actions at the community level. They facilitate bottom-up local level planning and are competent to mobilize Gram Sabhas, Ward Sabhas, Line Departments and Governance Institutions for accessing services. Schools have an important role to play-diminishing all social-cultural distances by building a sense of solidarity. Community elders with their positive participation and involvement can help solve many existing problems both financial and physical. Thus what is required is a systematic, accountable and transparent approach without piecemeal inputs. This would help to meet the challenges of universal access to inclusive quality education.

References

Sen, Amartya (2007), Development as Freedom, Oxford University Press, London.

Annual Report, 2006-07, Ministry of Rural Development, Government of India.

Bangladesh Women's Health Coalition, BWHC at a Glance, Dhaka, Bangladesh.

Bihar Education Project (SITAMARHI).

Child Labour (Prohibition, Rescue and Restoration of Childhood) Act, 2007.

Common School Education System (2007), Report by Expert Committee under the Chairmanship of Professor Muchkund Dubey on schools in Bihar.

District Elementary Education Report Card (2005-06), Sarva Siksha Abhiyan, Government of India.

Economic Survey, 2005-06, Government of India.

Rao, Hanumantha V. (2006), Growth of Elementary Education: Fifty Years of Andhra Pradesh, 1956-2006.

Indira Kranthi Patham, Unleashing the Power of the Poor from the Grassroots, Department of Rural Development, Government of A.P.

Meera, Lal (2008), "Convergence of Quality Education and Delivery of Health Services to Weaker Sections in Andhra Pradesh", Report submitted to C.G.G. Government of A.P. by Indian Institute of Economics, Hyderabad.

Mehta Kapur Aasha and Shepard, Andrew (2006), Ed. Chronic Poverty and Development Policy in India, Sage Publications, Delhi.

Mehta Arun C. (2005), Elementary Education in India—Where Do We Stand? State Report Cards, NIEPA, New Delhi.

Radhakrishnan R. and Rao, K. Hanumantha and Reddy, B. Samby (2006), Extreme and Chronic Poverty and Malnutrition in India: Incidence and determinants in Edited Book Mehta and Shepard.

Vimala, Ramchandran, Mehrotra, Rishiand and Jandhyala, Kamaeshwari (2007), Incentives in Elementary Education. Do they make a difference? *Journal of Education Planning and Administration*, Vol. XXI, Number 2, April, 2007.

Successful Governance Initiatives and Best Practices, Experiences from Indian States, Planning Commission, and Government of India.

The Probe Team (PROBE, 1999), Public Report on Basic Education in India, Oxford University Press, New Delhi.

Thomas, P.V., Chronic Poverty in Rural Areas: the Role of Government Policy, in Edited Book Mehta and Shepard.

UNESCO World Education Report 1995, (1995), Paris.

Working Group Report of the Development of Education of SC/ST/ Minorities/Girls and other Disadvantaged Groups for 11th Five-Year Plan (2007-12), Government of India, Planning Commission, New Delhi.

14

Indian Education System: The Turmoil Continues

P.K. BHARGAVA

Since early sixties, with the notable contributions of T.W. Schultz, G.S. Becker, H.S. Bowman, F.H. Harbison, C.A. Meyers, N.F. Denison, and others, the importance of human capital has been realized and acknowledged in the process of growth and development of nations. Infact, with the passage of time it is now increasingly recognized that the growth of physical capital assets depends to a large extent on human capital formation which is the process of acquiring and increasing the number of people who possess necessary skills, knowledge and experience required for economic growth and development of a country. Therefore, "Human resource development has necessarily to be assigned a key role in any development strategy, particularly in a country with a large population. Trained and educated on sound lines, a large population can itself become an asset in accelerating economic growth and in ensuring social change in desired directions. Education develops basic skills and abilities and fosters a value system conducive to, and in support of, national development goals, both long-term and immediate"

(GoI, 1985-90). Human resources of a country thus need to be developed through education and training in a manner whereby changing needs and requirements of the economy for skilled and trained manpower are met to achieve the targets of growth and development. According to T.W. Schultz, formally organised education at various levels—elementary, secondary and higher—is one of the important methods of developing human capital (Schultz, 1961).

Amongst the various components needed to develop human capital, education is most important. It is education which develops basic skills in man, increases productivity of labour, brings about desired social change, and strengthens research and development for accelerated growth and helps to enlarge the wealth of the nation. It may also be pointed out that return on investment (expenditure) in education is far more rewarding than investment in physical assets. On the basis of his study for the US economy, T.W. Schultz pointed out that expenditure on education contributed 3.5 times more to the increase in gross national income as against investment in the physical capital during the period 1900 to 1956 (Schultz, 1961).

Expenditure on education—being an investment in man—should, therefore, receive the highest priority in any development strategy as it enables the nation to develop the required type of human resources to match the needs as also the objectives of growth and development of an economy. It has, therefore, been rightly emphasised that expenditure on "Education is the most crucial investment in human development. Education strongly influences improvement in health, hygiene, demographic profile, productivity and practically all that is connected with the quality of life" (GoI, 1999). The Approach Paper to the Eleventh Five Year Plan thus states that "A key element of 11th Plan strategy should be to provide essential education and health services to those large parts of our population who are still excluded from these. Education is the critical factor that empowers participation in the growth process, but our performance has been less than satisfactory, both overall and in bridging gender and other divides. Overall literacy is still less than 70 per cent and rural female literacy less than 50 per cent with corresponding rates even lower among the marginalized groups and minorities" (GoI, 2006). The Approach Paper also emphasizes that "Education in its broadest sense of development of youth is the most critical input for empowering people with skills and knowledge and for giving them access to productive employment in the future" (GoI, 2006).

In view of the extremely important role of education but a very unsatisfactory state of affairs in this regard, it is urgently required that steps must be taken to develop more facilities for quality education by increasing the quantum of expenditure. While the States are expected to play a major role to develop the educational infrastructure, the fact of the matter is that the share of expenditure devoted to education and allied activities has declined in a majority of States. The cumulative expenditure of States on educational services has declined from 20 per cent in 1995-96 to around 18 per cent in 2007-08. It is also reported that States' total budgetary expenditure has grown by an annual compound rate of 15 per cent during the last 14 years from 1990-91 to 2003-04, their expenditure on social sector (including education) increased by about 12.5 per cent during the same period. The share of social sector in States' total expenditure as a result also declined from 32.9 per cent in 1990-91 to 25.3 per cent in 2003-04 budgets (*The Economic Times*, 2003). There is also a significant deepening of inter-State differences in per capita education spending across States. This is clearly borne out by the fact that per capita fund flow to education in 2005-06, varied from Rs. 483 in U.P. and Rs. 487 in Bihar to Rs. 1,034 in Maharashtra and Kerala and Rs. 1,777 in Himachal Pradesh—a difference of more than three times between the lowest and highest expenditure. This is the situation when the States' share in the Central kitty has increased substantially over the years and the States themselves have also augmented their resources.

Prior to 1976, States were assigned the exclusive responsibility in respect of education. The Constitutional Amendment of 1976 placed education in the concurrent list. As a result, the Union Government was expected to play a significant role in the sphere of education and ensuring the

TABLE I

Government (Centre and States) Expenditure on Education

(At Current Prices)

Year	*Rs. Crore*	*Per cent of GDP*	*Per cent of total expenditure*	*Per cent of social sector expenditure*
2000-01	67,000	3.19	11.3	50.8
2001-02	68,071	2.99	10.6	49.4
2002-03	71,298	2.96	10.3	50.3
2003-04	75,607	2.74	9.6	49.3
2004-05	84,111	2.67	9.8	48.7
2005-06	96,365	2.69	10.0	47.2
2006-07 (Revised)	1,19,199	2.88	10.4	46.5
2007-08 (Revised)	1,33,284	2.84	10.2	45.3

Source: *Economic Survey*, 2007-08 and for earlier years.

standards and quality of education in the country, without their being a slowdown in the responsibility of the States. Table 1 presents combined expenditure of the Centre and the States on education. The Table shows that total expenditure on education during the period 2000-01 to 2007-08 (Revised) continued to increase and it almost doubled, from Rs. 67,000 crores to Rs. 1,33,284 crores. However as a percentage of GDP it continued to decline during the period 2000-01 (3.19%) to 2004-05 (2.67%), to slightly increase to 2.69 per cent in 2005-06 and to 2.88 per cent in 2006-07 (Revised), respectively. It stood at 2.84 per cent in 2007-08 (Revised). It may be noted that throughout the period, excepting 2000-01 (3.19%), expenditure on education constituted less than three per cent of the GDP. Further, when considered as a percentage of expenditure on social sector, the situation is no better. As against its share of 50.8 per cent in 2000-01, the share of expenditure on education in social sector expenditure declined to 45.3 per cent in 2007-08 (Revised). It is also evident from the Table that in the total expenditure of the Centre and the States, the share of expenditure on education witnessed a decline from 11.3 per cent (2000-01) to 9.6 per cent (2003-04), to rise to 10.4 per cent in 2006-07 (Revised) but to decline again to 10.2 per cent in 2007-08 (Revised). Looked at from any angle, the situation regarding expenditure on education has been far from satisfactory.

It may be emphasized here that expenditure on education as a percentage of GDP has been much lower than 6 per cent as was envisaged long back in 1966 by the Education Commission (also known as Kothari Commission). It was in this context that the National Policy on Education (1986) pointed out that "Since the actual level of investment has remained far short of that target, it is important that greater determination be shown now to find the funds for the programmes laid down in this policy ... It will be ensured that from the Eighth Five Year Plan onwards it will uniformly exceed to 6 per cent of the national income" (GoI, 1986). Even after elapse of so many years, it has remained merely a wishful thinking that expenditure on education be raised to the level of 6 per cent of GDP. The Approach Paper to the Eleventh Five Year Plan also states that "The 11th Plan should ensure that we move towards raising public spending in education to 6 per cent of GDP, which is an NCMP commitment" (GoI, 1985).

In spite of the tremendous importance of education, especially the higher education in a nation's life and the catalytic role that it plays in shaping the progress and prosperity of the country, Indian education system suffers from a variety of shortcomings and the turmoil continues. An examination of the expenditure during the various Five Year Plans reveals that its share has been relatively low. A glance at the Table 2 regarding the pattern of plan expenditure on different sectors of education shows that from the First Five Year Plan to Tenth Five Year Plan, higher education received allocations much below 25 per cent excepting the Fourth Five Year Plan (25%) and Fifth Five Year Plan (28%). It is only now that during the Eleventh Five Year Plan, allocation has been more than doubled as its share has been increased from 7.68 per cent in Tenth Plan to 19.29 per cent in the Eleventh Plan. Further, within the education sector, the share of higher and technical education has also been raised to 30 per cent.

TABLE 2

Plan Expenditure on Different Sectors of Education

(In percentage)

Sector	First Plan Expdt. 1951-56	Second Plan Expdt. 1956-61	Third Plan Expdt. 1961-66	Plan Holiday Expdt. 1966-69	Fourth Plan Expdt. 1969-74	Fifth Plan Expdt. 1974-79	Sixth Plan Expdt. 1980-85	Seventh Plan Expdt. 1985-90	1990-92 Expdt.	Eighth Plan Expdt. 1992-97	Ninth Plan Outlay (1997-2002) (Central Sector)	Ninth Plan Expdt. (1997-02) (Central Sector)	Tenth Plan Outlay (2002-07) (Central Sector)
1	2	3	4	5	6	7	8	9	10	11	12	13	14
Elementary Education	58	35	34	24	50	52	32	37	37	48	66	65.7	65.6
	(870)	(950)	(2010)	(750)	(3743)	(5913)	(8414)	(28494)	(17290)	(103940)	(163696)	(145233)	(287500)
Secondary Education	5	19	18	16	@	@	20	24	22	24	10	10.5	9.9
	(83)	(510)	(1030)	(530)			(5344)	(18315)	(10530)	(52311)	(26035)	(23227)	(43250)
Adult Education					2	2	6	6	9	5	3	2.4	2.9
					(126)	(248)	(1533)	(4696)	(4160)	(11421)	(6304)	(5204)	(12500)
Higher Education	8	18	15	24	25	28	21	16	12	10	10	10.3	9.5
	(117)	(480)	(870)	(770)	(1883)	(3188)	(5604)	(12011)	(5880)	(20944)	(25000)	(22709)	(41765)
Others	15	10	12	11	13	9	11	3	2	3	2	1.6	1.4
	(227)	(300)	(730)	(370)	(936)	(1071)	(2729)	(1980)	(1180)	(7398)	(4314)	(3492)	(6235)
Technical Education	14	18	21	25	10	9	10	14	17	10	9	9.5	10.7
	(215)	(490)	(1250)	(810)	(786)	(1015)	(2563)	(10833)	(8230)	(21987)	(23735)	(21095)	(47000)

(Contd.)

TABLE 2 (*Contd*)

1	*2*	*3*	*4*	*5*	*6*	*7*	*8*	*9*	*10*	*11*	*12*	*13*	*14*
Total	100	100	100	100	100	100	100	100	100	100	100	100	100
	(1512)	(2730)	(5890)	(3230)	(7474)	(11435)	(26187)	(76329)	(47270)	(218001)	(249084)	(220960)	(438250)

Notes: 1. Figures in parenthesis in millions of rupees.

2. Figures in col. 2 to col. 11 include the share of States/UTs.

@ Included under Elementary Education

Source: Five-Year Plan Documents, Planning Commission and Analysis of Budget Expenditure, Ministry of HRD.

An increase in expenditure on education, especially higher education, augurs well in the context of changing economic scenario as the economy urgently needs adequate stock of various types of skills and knowledge to compete globally. In the Eleventh Five Year Plan, not only the allocation for higher and technical education has been raised but there is more of every thing: 30 new Central Universities are to be set-up, seven IITs and IIMs, 10 National Institutes of Technology, five research institutes to be called Indian Institute of Science, Education and Research, 20 IIITs, two schools of architecture and 330 colleges in educationally backward districts. Infrastructure in existing Universities and institutions is also to be upgraded. This is a welcome development.

Over the years, the number of Universities, colleges and other institutions of higher education, along with the enrolment in them, has continued to increase. At the time of Independence, there were nearly 20 Universities and 500 colleges. The Annual Report (2006-07) of the HRD Ministry put the number of Universities at present at 369, including 222 State Universities and 109 deemed Universities. In addition, there are 18,064 colleges, including around 1,902 Women's colleges. At the beginning of the academic year 2006-07, the total number of students enrolled in the Universities and colleges was around a crore: 4.27 lakhs in University Departments and 96.01 lakhs in affiliated colleges.

To meet the increasing demand for higher education, the number of institutions as also the quantum of expenditure has continued to increase. This has, however, resulted into a paradoxical situation in the country: more expenditure has resulted into increasing number of institutions on the one hand and, on the other, the existing facilities are not utilised properly. It is reported that "... the facilities in the 5000 colleges vary widely and are, on the whole, far below the level of qualitative viability. Neither colleges nor even Universities are started after due consideration of need. For long years, these go on absorbing scarce resources without attaining even the minimum standards laid down by the UGC ... the internal inefficiency of the higher education system is evidenced not only by the poor quality of courses but also by the large number of dropouts and failures which together account for more than 59 per cent of the students enrolled" (GoI, 2006). The approach Paper to the Eleventh Five Year Plan also states that "... only about 10 per cent of the relevant age group go to Universities whereas in many developing countries, the figure is between 20 and 25 per cent. The system also suffers from a serious problem of quality. While some of our institutions of higher education have the potential to become comparable with the best in the world, the average standard is much lower. High quality institutions are finding it difficult to get quality faculty given the enormous increase in private sector opportunities for the skills most in demand" (GoI, 2006).

There is thus the serious difficulty that the quality of higher education in the country has not kept pace with the quantitative expansion. Infact, it is inadequate research accomplishments that have affected the global ranking of Indian Universities and institutions. It may be pointed out that as per the publication of the Academic Ranking of World Universities (ARWU) for the year 2007 (brought out by the faculty of the Institute of Higher Education, Shanghai Jiao Tong University, China), of the Universities in India, only two—IISc and IIT, Kharagpur—appear in the 301-400 ranking. Universities in the U.K. and U.S.A. have high shares in the top 20 and top 50 ranks. Close to half the places in the ranks 51-100 and 101-200 are also taken by the U.K. and the U.S.A. Given the historical contact with the U.K. and the U.S.A., our universities should have done better. Further, the large base should have made it possible, at least, for a few Universities to make it to the top ranks. In addition, an incentive-oriented scheme for research excellence, at least for positions of Professorship, would have proved to be more fruitful rather than following, more or less, a system of tenured promotion. Thus, in a number of Indian Universities, one finds that the number of Professors in various Departments/Faculties have increased rapidly during recent past.

In terms of the R & D (research and development) also, India lags far behind. It is reported that at present the number of scientists and engineers engaged in R & D is only 157 per million, as against fifty times more in Korea and thirty times more in Japan and U.S.A. Hence, if India has to develop as a knowledge economy it is extremely important that the higher education system of the country has to be developed and strengthened both quantitatively and qualitatively.

There is another important aspect in the context of higher education. India has integrated itself with the rest of the world economy as it is a signatory to the WTO's General Agreement of Trade in Services, including education services. India provides a big market and therefore, prior to the entry of foreign Universities and institutions, a number of issues need to be addressed and debated : it must be clearly spelt out as to how the entry of foreign educational institutions shall be regulated and administered; which Universities and institutions shall be permitted and which courses, both at the graduate and post-graduate levels, shall be permitted; whether foreign institutions shall be permitted to function independently or collaboration with some Indian institutions will be obligatory and if so, what will be the terms and conditions for the same; what part of earnings shall be permitted to be repatriated; what will happen to the structure of tuition fee as the foreigners may ask for a level playing field; unexposed to competition, will our Universities be able to compete globally; will the IITs and IIMs admit foreign students at the cost of Indian students; and what will be the role of the UGC and other bodies pertaining to higher education. These and similar issues should be examined and discussed in detail to arrive at a consensus in the broader national interest. The Bill (2007) seeking to regulate Foreign Educational Institutions (FEIs) should thus incorporate the ground realities of higher education scenario in India

Further, it may also be pointed out that at present there are as many as 14 regulatory bodies of higher education, such as the Medical Council of India, Indian Council of Agricultural Research, Dental Council and the All-India Council of Technical Education, etc. In the present set-up, individual regulatory agencies work independently of the U.G.C., and some of them are not even administered by the

Ministry of Human Resource Development which is the nodal administrative ministry for education. At times these regulatory bodies work at cross purposes. Hence, some kind of coordinating mechanism at the national level is necessary in the best interests of efficiency and effectiveness. This task should be performed by an independent regulatory body. The earlier it is done the better it would be, as the need for skilled, trained and educated manpower has immeasurably increased for the economy that is set to grow at 8 per cent or more and preparing itself to compete globally in various spheres of economic activity.

References

Government of India (1985-90), Planning Commission, *Seventh Five Year Plan,* Vol. II, p. 252.

Schultz, T.W. (1961), 'Investment in Human Capital', *American Economic Review*, March.

Schultz, T.W. (1960), 'Capital Formation by Education', *Journal of Political Economy*, December.

Government of India (1999), Planning Commission, *Ninth Five Year Plan, 1997-2002*, Vol. II, p. 101.

Government of India (2006), Planning Commission, An Approach to the 11th Five Year Plan (2007-12), December, pp. 6, 57

Government of India: Reported in *The Economic Times* (2003), December 1.

Government of India (1986), Ministry of Human Resource Development, National Policy on Education, p. 29.

Government of India: Approach Paper to the 11th Five Year Plan, *op. cit.*, p. 57.

Government of India (1985), Ministry of Human Resource Development, Challenge of Education—a policy perspective, August, pp. 46-47.

Approach Paper to the 11th Five Year Plan, *op. cit.*, p. 62.

15

Liberalisation, Globalisation and Higher Education: The Current Indian Scenario

Anil Kumar Jain

INTRODUCTION

Human capital formation is a process of acquiring and increasing the number of persons who possess skills, education and experience which are crucial for economic development of a country. Human capital is, thus, associated with investment in man and his development as a creative and productive resource. It is important to note here that "when an individual falls sick, only he and his family are affected. When institutions are affected, the ramifications are much more. And when those institutions are in higher education, the economic prosperity of the entire nation suffers." By inculcating right attitudes and motivation, education induces process of economic growth, through ensuring availability of manpower of right quantity and quality for all activities, including health and education. "The externalities of education, including the dynamic externalities of higher education are indeed immense and they have profound positive effect on economic growth." Tilak further goes on to argue that secondary and higher education enhances earnings of the individuals and contributes to development and makes a significant contribution to reduction in absolute as well as relative poverty.

According to T.W. Schultz, formally organised education at the elementary, secondary and higher levels is one of the important methods of developing human capital which is "the process of increasing knowledge, the skills and the capabilities of all the people of the country." T.W. Schultz has calculated that investment in education contributed 3.5 times more to the increase in gross national income than investment in physical capital. The Approach Paper to the 11th Five Year Plan in India also reiterates that "Education...is the most critical input for empowering people with Skills and knowledge and for giving them access to productive employment in the future." We think that discussion/analysis about higher education must be carried out in the backdrop of certain factors such as competition among traditional institutions, changing global economy, penetration of new technologies in imparting education, concept of distance and on line education system, privatisation of education, increasing role of corporate giants in education, etc. Globalisation is driving demand for an internationally competent work force and future global economy will largely depend on the ability to sustain excellence, innovation and leadership in higher education.

The present paper is divided into four sections. The first section gives a brief account of broad policy framework and growth in education. The second section gives a brief account of changes in the field of higher education after the adoption of the policy of liberalisation and globalisation in India since 1991. The third section puts forth the present state of affairs in respect of education in India. The fourth section provides some suggestions to the effect that universities and colleges may play a vital role in expanding opportunity and promoting social justice in the new environment.

POLICY FRAMEWORK ABOUT EDUCATION

Before 1976, States were assigned the exclusive responsibility in respect of education. The Constitutional Amendment of 1976 brought education in the concurrent list. After this amendment, the Union Government accepted a large responsibility of reinforcing the national and integrated character of education, maintaining quality and standards, although there was no change in the role and responsibility of States. National Policy on Education (NPE) was formulated in 1986 and the Programme of Action (POA) was updated in 1982. The modified policy envisages that education should play a positive and interventionist role in correcting social and regional imbalances, empowering women and securing rightful place for the disadvantaged and minorities. After 86th Constitutional amendment, there is an obligation for making available free and compulsory education for all children in the age group of 6-14 years. At the national level, NCMP has made a commitment to raise expenditure on education to a level of 6 per cent of GDP and at the international level, India is committed to the 'Millennium Development Goals' and 'Education for all'.

During the last decade or so, increased emphasis is being laid on secondary and higher education—both general and technical education. In the light of challenges thrown by globalisation, major expansion of higher education system has been planned. The government feels that with the increased demand for higher quality education, training of teachers has become even more important and out of box thinking is required to ensure adequate supply of quality teachers. Recently, the National Knowledge Commission (NKC) opined that the need for education enhancement opportunities is not simply rooted in the contingent needs of the economy. It is also a way to make growth more inclusive.

GROWTH IN EDUCATION AND OUTLAY

With the passage of time, literacy rate in India has gone up. Literacy rate (Persons) has gone up from 18.33 in 1951 to 34.45 in 1971, 52.21 in 1991 and further to 64.84 in

2001, although the literacy rate is higher for males as compared to females. As per 2001 Census, literacy rate for males stood at 75.26 as against 53.67 for females. However, one important phenomenon needs to be observed here. During the period of 50 years from 1951 to 2001, literacy rate for females has gone up from 8.86 in 1951 to 53.67 in 2001 (about 6 times) whereas in the case of males it has gone up from 27.16 in 1951 to 75.26 in 2001 (about 2.5 times).

With the passage of time, not only the number of schools has increased but the number of higher educational institutions have gone up. During 2005-06, general education (Arts, Science and Commerce) was being provided in 12,751 colleges and professional education (Engineering, Technology, Architecture, Medical and Teacher Training Colleges) was being imparted in 5179 colleges. In addition, there were 1473 other institutions (including research institutions), apart from about 350 Universities and University level institutions which include 20 Central Universities, 215 State Universities, 100 Deemed Universities, 5 institutions established under State Act and 13 institutions of national importance.

Total Plan outlay on education has increased with the passage of time. Total expenditure on education increased from Rs. 151 crores during First Plan to Rs. 1,143 crores during Fifth Plan, to Rs. 21,599 crores during Eighth Plan and more rapidly to Rs. 49,838 crores during Ninth Plan and Rs. 1,01,364 crores during the Tenth Five Year Plan (Table 1). While total expenditure on education has increased with the passage of time, it is unfortunate that expenditure on education as a percentage of total Plan outlay which was 7.7 per cent during the First Plan and 6.9 per cent during the Third Plan, dropped to as low a level as 2.7 per cent during the Sixth Plan, although it subsequently revived to 6.8 per cent during the Tenth Plan. Distribution of Plan expenditure on education reveals that expenditure on higher education constituted only 8 per cent of total expenditure on education during First Plan. This percentage reached to a high of 28 per cent during the Fifth Plan but dropped to 10 per cent during the Eighth Plan and has remained at that level in subsequent Plans.

Since the advent of 21st century, there is renewed

Table 1

Expenditure on Education as a Proportion of Plan Outlay

(Rs Crore)

Plan	*Total Expenditure on Education*	*Total Plan Outlay*	*(2) as % of (3)*
1	*2*	*3*	*4*
First Plan (1951-56)	151*	1960	7.7
Second Plan (1956-61)	273*	4672	5.8
Third Plan (1961-66)	589	8576	6.9
Annual Plans (1966-69)	307	6625	4.6
Fourth Plan (1969-74)	774	15779	4.9
Fifth Plan (1974-79)	1143	39426	2.9
Sixth Plan (1980-85)	2977	109292	2.7
Seventh Plan (1985-90)	7685	218730	3.5
Annual Plans (1990-92)	4915	123120	4.0
Eighth Plan (1992-97)	21599	485377	4.4
Ninth Plan (1997-2002)	49838	813998	6.1
Tenth Plan (2002-07) (Latest Estimates)	101364	1491646	6.8

Note: *Comprises of expenditure on Education and Scientific Research.

emphasis on education and total expenditure on education (Centre and States) has nearly doubled from Rs. 67,000 crores in 2000-01 to Rs. 1,33,284 crores in 2007-08 (BE), as is evident from Table 2. While it is true that major portion of government expenditure on education, especially non-plan, is borne by the State Government, in case of Plan expenditure, the Centre meets a good portion of it. However, a perusal of Table 2 reveals that government expenditure on education as a per cent of GDP, total expenditure and social sector expenditure was lower in 2007-08 (RE) as compared to 2000-01. This is a cause of concern.

Of late, there has been a significant increase in the Union Government's budget expenditure on education (Plan and non-Plan), as shown in Table 3. The total expenditure of the Union Government (Plan plus non-Plan) has increased

TABLE 2

Government (Centre + States) Expenditure on Education

Year	*Rs. Crore*	*Per cent of GDP*	*Per cent of total expenditure*	*Per cent of social sector expenditure*
2000-01	67,000	3.19	11.3	50.8
2001-02	68,071	2.98	10.6	49.4
2002-03	71,298	2.96	10.7	50.3
2003-04	75,607	2.74	9.6	49.3
2004-05	84,111	2.67	9.8	48.7
2005-06	96,365	2.69	10.0	47.2
2006-07 (RE)	1,19,199	2.88	10.4	46.5
2007-08 (BE)	1,33,284	2.84	10.2	45.3

Source: *Economic Survey*, 2007-08 and earlier years.

from Rs. 7,925 crores in 2001-02 to Rs. 29,589 crores in 2007-08 (RE) and more rapidly to Rs. 38,703 crores in 2008-09 (BE). As a result, Union Government's expenditure on education, as a proportion of GDP has gone up from 0.377 in 2000-01 to 0.730 in 2008-09 (BE) and as a percentage of total budget from 2.43 to 5.15 during the same period.

While non-plan expenditure on education is important as it is required for the maintenance and upkeep of the system, it is plan expenditure that assumes much significance, as it is plan expenditure that sets new directions for development. Here, we notice that plan expenditure of the Union Government has increased 3.4 times from Rs. 10,224 crores in 2004-05 to Rs. 34,394 crores in 2008-09 (Budget). Expenditure of Rs. 34,394 crores for the year 2008-09 represents 35.1 per cent increase over the revised estimates of 2007-08 and only 20 per cent increase over the budget estimates of 2007-08. What is more important is the fact that allocations to higher education in 2008-09 have been significantly hiked, as compared to the revised estimates for 2007-08. Allocation for higher education (Plan plus non-plan) of the Union Government was Rs. 6398 crores in 2007-08 (RE)

TABLE 3

Expenditure on Education Incurred by the Union Government

(Plan and Non-Plan)

Year	*Rs. Crore*	*Per cent of GDP*	*Per cent of total budget*
2000-01	7925	0.377	2.43
2001-02	8037	0.353	2.22
2002-03	9089	0.370	2.22
2003-04	10,177	0.369	2.16
2004-05	13,229	0.420	2.66
2005-06	17,810	0.497	3.52
2006-07	23,810	0.574	4.09
2007-08 (RE)	29,589	0.630	4.35
2008-09 (BE)	38,703	0.730	5.15

Source: 1. Union Budget, 2008-09 and earlier Budget Documents.
2. *Economic Survey*, 2007-08 and earlier years.

which has been increased to Rs. 10,859 crores in 2008-09 (BE). Plan allocation for the UGC has nearly been doubled. The allocation for education in the Eleventh Plan is likely to be Rs. 2,87,362 crores which would be 5 times the allocation of Rs. 58,265 crores made in the Tenth Plan and would constitute 18.2 per cent of total plan expenditure, compared to 7.8 per cent in the Tenth Plan. During the Eleventh Plan, it is planned to establish 30 new central universities, including 14 world class universities.

CHANGES IN EDUCATION SCENARIO AFTER LIBERALISATION AND GLOBALISATION

The process of liberalisation and globalisation has unleased the entrepreneurial spirit of our people, with many of them having global ambitions. Indian youth is keen to get into technical and scientific institutions—helping India gain as a knowledge-based economy. Towards this endeavour, private players have continued in their effort to tap the potential sector through allied services and alternative business models. The success of Information and Communication Technology (ICT) service providers is a case in point of the Government's acceptance of the corporate as a key partner in education. Consequently, with increasing privatisation, education is becoming more expensive and there is increasing use of ICT.

Liberalisation has increased returns on skills. According to a recent World Bank Report, the wage-differential between primary-educated workers and those beyond have risen sharply in India since 1990s. This is not a bad thing because it increases incentive to keep moving up the value chain. Further, during the last 15 years, social mobility has considerably increased. Free trade, retail credit, FDI, privatisation, etc. have helped the middle class Indians to live and dream better. Today, young Indians no longer depend on their fate. Social mobility has given them hope and aspirations and under competitive pressures in Indian society, nobody is going to take anything for granted. Moreover, due to sharp supply-demand mismatch at the top of the pyramid, the wage differential between primary and higher-level educated workers is rising rapidly. As a result, poor are stuck in low-skilled services, with little upward mobility.

Like the West, inequalities have increased in India after the adoption of free-market policies. According to a paper done by Debroy and Bhandari, as part of Team Lease Labour Report in 2007, Gini Coefficient in urban areas has increased from 0.330 in 1983 to 0.376 in 2004-05, while in rural areas it has increased from 0.298 in 1983 to 0.305 in 2004-05. Today, inequality has many shades—determined by money, power, skill, glamour, technical edge, etc.

PRESENT SCENARIO OF EDUCATION IN INDIA

Despite the fact that expenditure on education has increased and literary rate improved in India with the passage of time, India faces a crisis in education which is far deeper than any other nation in the world today. Structurally, the education sector is in a crisis. Out of every 100 Indians, 70 completed primary schools and only seven (between 15-60 years) completed graduation or beyond.

India's working age population (15-60 years) will swell in next 2 decades—in absolute terms by 300 million and in percentage terms from 58 per cent in 2001 to 64 per cent by 2025. Against this, the present scenario is that 90 per cent of the jobs being created today require vocational skills but 90 per cent of India's colleges impart mostly bookish knowledge. As a result, the general lowering of academic standards tends to lower the efficiency of the graduates employed both in private and public sector and does not promise well for the formation of a dynamic leadership for economic development.

A historical analysis reveals that in an enthusiasm to spread higher education, most underdeveloped countries, including India, have opened too many universities and colleges, without trying to improve the standards of education. "It is generally agreed and widely felt that the present dearth of high quality manpower for higher education institutions is the result of our past preoccupation with quantity and the inadequate attention to quality." Pulapre Balakrishnan, in his paper affirms, "It is widely accepted by now that the quality of higher education provided by the government of India has not kept pace with the quantitative expansion. This may be inferred from the fact that young Indians who are able to finance the move have now begun to leave the country soon after they finish the school." Problems of quality are confined not only to students but the shortage of high quality faculty are already being felt in the existing institutions. This has happened because "long periods of under funding of higher education, virtual ban on recruitment of faculty and other similar measures have resulted in accumulation of such problems." Last year on October 10, 2007, the Union Human Resource Development Minister, while addressing a Conference of Vice-Chancellors, described higher education as a sick child, either by design or default and ten days later he expressed disappointment over the quality of college and university education which has not kept pace with its quantitative growth.

Poor quality of education compounds the problems. A recent study has found that 38 per cent of the children who have completed 4 years of schooling cannot read a small paragraph with short sentences meant to be read by a student of Class II. About 55 per cent of such children cannot divide a three digit number by a one digit number. Further, according to a 2006 report by PRATHAM, an NGO focused on education, only 16.5 per cent of children (in class 1 to 8th) have ability to read a word and only 26 per cent are able to recognise numbers. The problem gets worse as one moves up. Barely 9-10 per cent of India's graduates are found employable. Over 90 per cent of India's 18,064 colleges and 68 per cent of its 378 universities fall under poorer B and C grade. Data collected by 60th Round of NSS reveals that only 3 per cent of rural youths (15-29 years) and 6 per cent of urban youth have gone through any kind of vocational training. One cause of poor quality of teaching is the shortage of teachers reflected in a large number of vacancies. In many areas, teacher absenteeism is a major problem. There is also substantial truth in the observation of Manoj Pant that the whole reservation debate has also gone wrong. "The purpose of reservations is to provide both social and income equality to the deprived. Yet, the basic building blocks of these are schools and not higher educational institutions. In fact, political commitment to reservation in higher education is likely to lead to a further diversion of funds to rapidly proliferating higher educational institutions at the expense of elementary education."

There are vast inter-State differentials in the field of education. The difference between literacy rates among best and worst State, as per 2001 Census, varied from 94.2 per cent to 59.7 per cent for males, from 87.7 per cent to 33.1 per cent for females and 90.86 per cent to 47.00 per cent for persons as a whole. Further, while the cumulative expenditure of States on educational services as a percentage of total expenditure has dropped from 20 per cent in 1995-96 to 18 per cent in 2007-08, there are also vast differences in per capita education spending across States. This is borne out by the fact that per capita fund flow to education in 2005-06, varied from Rs. 483 in U.P. and Rs. 487 in Bihar to Rs. 1,034 in Maharashtra and Kerala and Rs. 1,777 in Himachal Pradesh—a difference of four times between the lowest and highest expenditures.

THE WAY OUT

Time has now come when the educational sector needs to be given top priority so as to make India a global education hub. This would essentially hinge upon our ability to provide an effectively functioning education system. Towards this, access to quality education is crucial so that a reservoir of human resources may be created for subsequent absorption in jobs. Hence, effective resource deployment for improving output from education has become more a necessity than an option. Towards this end, some steps may be undertaken.

Firstly, there is need for increasing use of information and communication technology (ICT). However, mere introduction of ICT (which is happening at present) will not create the desired impact. Introduction of ICT must be accompanied by changes in ideas, processes and ways of viewing things. Towards these ends, teachers must be made partners in this endeavour because it is this class which has to decide what to and what not to deliver through ICT. There is no point to use an expensive computer screen as a replacement of blackboard. An average teacher must impart education not merely for reading and writing but he should relate it to broader definition of literacy and education. Further, there is need to build teacher capacity which is possible only when a teacher is encouraged to acquire capabilities in area of his/her discipline, improvement in teaching methods, etc. This would necessitate new and innovative methods to attract good faculty.

Secondly, there should be no compromise about 'quality' in education, especially higher education. The history of setting up of universities and other important institutions in India so far reveals that such decisions are taken more on political considerations rather than on educational and other relevant scientific and objective considerations. As a result, barring a very few, none of the Indian universities find a place in global ranking of universities. It is high time that we must improve quality of teaching in Indian universities. This would be possible only when universities show a commitment to breadth and excellence in all fields of human inquiry, engage themselves in cutting edge research whilst at the same time teaching the next generation students, allow their researchers freedom to experiment, succeed and sometimes fail and encourage inter-disciplinary research including international collaborations. In this context, leadership in universities plays a vital role in promoting quality and excellence. It should be ensured that Vice-Chancellors are appointed on merit taking into account proven administrative and academic capabilities.

Thirdly, the challenge for India today is to provide access to quality education to a large proportion of population across the country with focus on vulnerable sections of the population so as to make higher education inclusive. The task ahead is massive. India has emerged as one of the world's largest consumer of education services with a target population of more than 445 million (between the age group of 5.24 years) which is expected to increase to approximately 486 million by 2025. We shall be doing a great injustice for the future generation if we do not increase spending on higher education.

Fourthly, there is need to create a motivating environment for teachers. For this, it is necessary that a set of incentives be provided to encourage research at the college and university level by suitably rewarding academics to publish in reputed journals and take patents in diverse fields. This would also require that merit and merit alone should be taken into account at the time of appointments and promotions. Such a step would help in developing a dedicated and qualified faculty because a wrong/incompetent appointment spoils nearly thirty generations. Further, it is also necessary that pay scales of persons in teaching profession be substantially raised and they should be held accountable about their expected work.

Fifthly, there is need for increasing public-private partnership (PPP) in education sector. It has already been happening and will continue to grow. Of late, there is an increasing trend towards training of desired skills by private corporate sectors. This should be further encouraged. But, when private entrepreneurs set-up higher education facilities, there is also worrisome dimension of wide variation in quality. While there are a few institutions that provide top quality faculty and excellent infrastructure, there are also numerous educational enterprises which pay scant attention to quality and are only interested in earnings. Therefore, there is a strong case for effective and creative regulation that will go a long way in achieving quantitative expansion, without jeopardising the quality. Towards this end, the State has to continue to play a dominant role in higher education.

Sixthly, women from all economic backgrounds are entering the work force in big numbers. We must not forget that women empowerment is possible in the long-run only through education. Educated women play a prime role in bringing up educated future generation. Therefore, an enabling environment needs to be created for women to become economically, politically and socially empowered.

Seventhly, for inclusive growth there is need to expand vocational training to as large a number of people as possible. The Eleventh Plan Approach Paper has rightly observed (p. 60) that we need to expand vocational training from the present capacity of mere 2 to 3 million to at least 15 million new entrants. For this, the Plan proposes to achieve triple objectives of expansion, inclusion and excellence. (p. 63)

Finally, we must also keep in mind the erosion of values that has taken place in India. Commercialisation of education has resulted in setting up of educational establishments for profit and such persons have little moral authority to talk about ethics. It is also observed that the faculty and administrators even in the publicly funded institutions are involved in commercial preoccupations and are not in a position to talk about ethics in education. Much is known about teaching of ethics and ethical responsibilities in business schools which helps in inculcating ethical responsibilities along with team work. Therefore, it is also necessary that earnest efforts be made towards human transformation through the inculcation of human values.

References

Ahuja, Shobha (2008), "Falling Education Spending in States," *The Economic Times*, May 28.

Balakrishnan, Pulapre (2007), "Higher Education in India: Will 'Six Per Cent' Do It?", *Economic and Political Weekly*, September 29.

Desai, Jayesh (2008), "Private Participation in Education," *The Economic Times*, July 14.

Desai, Jayesh (2008), *op. cit.*

Government of India, Planning Commission (2006), Towards Faster and More Inclusive Growth, An Approach Paper to the 11th Five Year Plan, December, p. 57.

Government of India (2008), *Economic Survey*, 2007-08, p. 251.

Government of India, *Economic Survey, op. cit.*, p. A-121.

Government of India, Publication Division (2008), INDIA 2008, p. 248.

Government of India, Planning Commission, Towards Faster and More Inclusive Growth, An Approach Paper to the 11th Five Year Plan (2006), p. 59.

Government of India (2008), *Economic Survey*, 2007-08, p. A-122.

Goyal, Malini (2007), *op. cit.*, November 6.

Goyal, Malini (2007), "Employability Crisis Taking its Toll," *The Economic Times*, November 6.

Goyal, Malini (2007), "Rising Prosperity, Growing Inequality," *The Economic Times*, November 7.

Harbinson, F.H. and C.A. Meyers (1964), Education, Manpower and Economic Growth.

Pant, Manoj (2008), "Growth and Education Revisited," *The Economic Times*, June 13.

Rao, Bhanoji (2007), "Higher Education: The Quality Issue," *Business Line*, October 30.

Reddy, K.C. (2007), "On Reforming and Re-positioning the Higher Education Sector," *The Indian Economic Journal*, April-June, p. 8.

Reported in Approach Paper to 11th Five Year Plan (2006), p. 58.

Reported in *Business Line* (2008), January 26.

Richard, Alison (2008), "What makes a World Class University," *The Economic Times*, January 7.

Schultz, T.W. (1961), "Investment in Human Capital," *American Economic Review*, March.

Schultz, T.W. (1960), "Capital Formation by Education," *Journal of Political Economy*, December.

Tilak, J.B.G. (2005), "Higher Education in 'Trishanku': Hanging between State and Market," *The Economic and Political Weekly*, September 10, pp. 4029-37.

Tilak, J.B.G. (2008), "Education in 2008-09 Union Budget," *Economic and Political Weekly*, May 17, pp. 49-56.

Tilak, J.B.G. (2008), *op. cit.*, p. 54.

16

Education and Economic Development: A Gender Perspective

SANDHYA RANI DAS

Economists have long been aware of the importance of education in economic development of a country. Adam Smith as early as in the 18th century stressed the importance of education in his Wealth of Nations. Alfred Marshal at the end of the 19th century further emphasised the importance of education as a "national investment", and in his view "the most valuable of all capital is that invested in human beings" (Marshal, 1920). In the 1960s mounting empirical evidence stimulated the "human investment revolution in economic thought" (Bowman, 1960). The seminal works of (Schultz, 1961) and (Denison, 1962: 67) led to a series of growth accounting studies pointing to education's contribution to the unexplained residuals in the economic growth of western economies. Other studies looked at the impact of education on earnings or estimated private rate of returns (Becker, 1964, Mincer, 1974). A 1984 survey of growth accounting studies covering 29 developing countries found estimates of education's contribution to economic growth ranging from less than 1 per cent in Mexico to as high as 23 per cent in Ghana (Psacharopoulos, 1984).

The theories of economic growth in modern times emphasised on education, skill and acquisition of knowledge and the 20th century is known as the "Age of human capital". Education provides the foundation for economic development and social progress and unequal education tends to have negative impact on per capita income in most of the countries.

Education is an important determinant of the status of women in the society. But Women's educational levels are lower than men in most of the countries of the world. Gender inequality in education directly affects economic growth by lowering the average level of human capital. In addition, growth is indirectly affected through the impact of gender inequality on investment and population growth. That is why the International organisations and researchers in the field of education have emphasised the importance of women's education for the socio-economic development of the Third World countries.

Female education produces social as well as economic gains in the following manner:

Social Benefits

- Improvement of quality of life at home and outside
- Reduces fertility, infant mortality and child mortality rate
- Increases family health and nutritional level
- Development of art, culture and literature

Economic Benefits

- Growth of science and technology
- Promotes entrepreneurship
- Increases labour productivity, level of employment and wages

Realising the importance of female education in the socio-economic progress of the country, the present paper is an attempt to study the impact of education on the economic development in Indian states from gender prospective.

TABLE I

Rate of Literacy in the States, 2001

State	*Rate of Literacy*			
	Total	*Male*	*Female*	*Gap between Male-female*
Andhra Pradesh	60.40	70.3	50.4	19.9
Assam	62.95	71.3	54.6	16.7
Bihar	46.40	59.7	33.1	26.6
Gujarat	68.75	79.7	57.8	21.9
Haryana	67.10	78.5	55.7	22.8
Karnataka	66.50	76.1	56.9	19.2
Kerala	90.95	94.2	87.7	6.5
Madhya Pradesh	63.20	76.1	50.3	25.8
Maharashtra	76.50	86.0	67.0	19.0
Orissa	62.95	75.4	50.5	24.9
Punjab	69.30	75.2	63.4	11.8
Rajasthan	59.80	75.7	43.9	31.8
Tamil Nadu	73.35	82.4	64.3	18.1
Uttar Pradesh	55.40	68.6	42.2	26.4
West Bengal	68.30	77.0	59.6	17.4
India	64.50	75.3	53.7	21.6

Source: Census of India, 2001.

I. EDUCATION IN THE STATES

There are two important indicators of education. They are: (1) Literacy Rate and (2) Gross Enrolment of students from primary to tertiary level. The first *sine qua non* of any achievement of elementary education can be measured through the literacy rates.

The growth of male and female literacy rate in India during the 20th century is shown graphically in Fig. 1.

Rate of Literacy

The position of literacy in the states according to the Census of 2001 is presented in Table 2.

The state of Kerala is in the top in both male and female literacy rates being 94.2 and 87.7 per cent respectively. Bihar is lowest in the ladder of rate of literacy with 59.7 and

FIG. I

Literacy Rates of Male and Females in India: 1901-2001

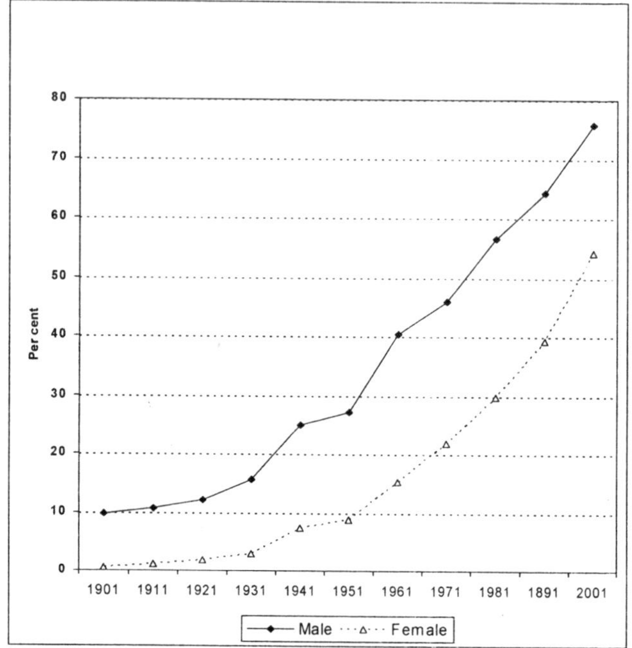

33.1 per cent for male and female respectively. But the gap of percentage difference between male and female literacy is found to be highest of 31.8 per cent in Rajasthan while Kerala enjoys lowest gap between male and female literacy with 6.6 per cent.

Women's education suffered due to limited financial resources as the government provided meagre funds for women's education. Unlike boys' education, the girls' education requires higher investment among others due to the following reasons:

1. Separate schools for girls.
2. Hostels have to be provided.
3. Escorts have to be appointed to bring the students to school and back, as the girls are not traditionally allowed outdoor for any work in those days.

4. Women teachers have to be trained and appointed, as parents did not allow their daughters in the schools with male teachers.
5. Free scholarships have to be provided as incentive to parents so that they would agree to fore go earning and labour of their daughters.

The Gross Enrolment Ratio (GER)

Primary education is regarded as the foundation for the educational system in an economy, which increases higher education and promotes human resource development. The gross enrolment ratios of boys and girls from Classes I-VIII of the 15 major states of India are presented in Table 2 (2000-01) and Table 3 (2004-05)

The total GER (I-VIII) in 2000-01 is highest in Gujarat with 103.26 and is lowest in Uttar Pradesh with 54.91. In the enrolment of boys Rajasthan commands highest position, while Karnataka tops in the enrolment of girls. The gender gap in enrolment is highest in Rajasthan. The only state where the enrolment of girls exceeds boys is Punjab.

In 2004-05 the total GER (I-VIII) is highest in Madhya Pradesh with 114.09. It ranks 30th in the Educational Development Index (EDI) among the 35 Indian states and union territories. Though the gross enrolment is highest in the state but little effort has been made to provide quality education, a key factor in student retention. (DISE's latest report)

II. EDUCATION AND INCOME

As mentioned in the beginning, education is one of the important factors of development. No country can achieve sustainable economic development without substantial investment in human capital. Education plays a crucial role in securing economic and social progress and improving income distribution. There is a positive feedback from improved education to greater income equality, which, in turn, is likely to favours higher rates of growth.

Table 4 shows the state-wise growth of per capita Net State Domestic Product (NSDP) at current prices. The table

TABLE 2

Gross Enrolment Ratio in the States (2000-01)

States	*Classes I-V 6-11 Years*			*Classes VI-VIII 11-14 Years*			*Classes I-VIII 6-14 Years*		
	Boys	*Girls*	*Total*	*Boys*	*Girls*	*Total*	*Boys*	*Girls*	*Total*
Andhra	105.22	102.88	104.07	53.46	44.26	48.95	84.28	79.40	81.87
Assam	125.44	106.81	116.94	80.02	63.27	72.00	108.35	90.44	99.54
Bihar	96.24	60.49	79.87	40.71	20.72	31.29	75.92	45.62	61.35
Gujarat	137.94	113.62	126.16	73.00	59.45	66.51	112.84	92.98	103.26
Haryana	78.10	79.78	78.88	65.80	60.16	63.18	73.58	72.61	73.13
Karnataka	116.64	110.44	113.58	78.17	70.50	74.40	101.76	94.97	98.41
Kerala	87.71	86.54	87.14	99.80	94.76	97.33	92.32	89.68	91.03
Madhya P.	120.52	101.91	111.42	70.40	46.28	58.78	101.71	81.36	91.80
Maharashtra	112.86	107.84	110.41	89.66	80.49	85.20	104.23	91.71	101.05
Orissa	129.97	94.71	112.60	66.82	43.90	55.56	105.52	75.10	90.54
Punjab	78.74	79.40	79.05	64.19	64.92	64.53	73.45	74.10	73.75
Rajasthan	138.29	83.44	111.99	103.87	47.84	77.45	125.28	70.25	99.06
Tamil Nadu	96.57	96.31	96.44	93.77	91.79	92.80	95.47	94.53	95.01
Uttar Pradesh	79.87	50.30	65.69	48.08	25.24	37.42	67.57	40.90	54.91
West Bengal	110.89	103.30	107.15	59.69	44.35	52.20	91.06	80.75	86.00
India	104.91	85.92	95.66	66.68	49.94	58.64	90.26	72.36	81.58

Source: Selected Educational Statistics, 2000-01, Ministry of Human Resources Development, Government of India.

TABLE 3

Gross Enrolment Ratio in the States (2004-2005)

States	*Classes I-V 6-11 Years*			*Classes VI-VIII 11-14 Years*			*Classes I-VIII 6-14 Years*		
	Boys	*Girls*	*Total*	*Boys*	*Girls*	*Total*	*Boys*	*Girls*	*Total*
Andhra Pradesh	96.05	97.40	96.71	73.73	69.68	71.76	87.32	86.64	86.99
Assam	105.59	104.80	105.20	72.05	67.22	69.70	92.99	90.81	91.92
Bihar	95.40	71.18	83.75	39.66	24.29	32.43	74.95	54.43	65.16
Gujarat	126.44	109.86	118.65	80.39	66.27	73.77	109.02	93.42	101.70
Haryana	80.00	84.90	82.23	77.68	74.85	76.39	79.12	81.07	80.01
Karnataka	108.40	105.73	107.10	87.64	83.19	85.47	100.38	97.07	98.76
Kerala	95.53	93.69	93.61	100.91	95.38	98.19	96.32	94.33	95.35
Madhya Padesh	135.35	128.74	132.16	89.41	76.52	83.29	118.22	108.60	114.09
Maharashtra	110.34	110.40	110.37	98.96	97.09	98.08	106.03	105.38	105.70
Orissa	131.89	127.37	129.69	78.82	69.23	74.11	111.70	105.10	108.47
Punjab	74.49	60.52	77.20	63.78	67.40	65.42	70.30	75.34	72.57
Rajasthan	125.40	116.66	121.24	84.82	54.80	70.67	110.42	94.06	102.67
Tamil Nadu	119.52	117.23	118.41	109.22	104.66	107.00	115.51	112.32	113.96
Uttar Pradesh	110.63	104.15	107.54	57.82	46.29	52.43	90.78	82.88	87.04
West Bengal	112.92	111.27	112.11	69.43	63.31	66.46	96.20	93.07	94.67
India	110.70	104.67	107.60	74.30	65.13	69.93	96.91	89.87	93.54

Source: Selected Educational Statistics, 2004-05 Ministry of Human Resources Development, Government of India.

TABLE 4

Per Capita NSDP at Current Prices

States of India	*2000-01*	*2004-05*
Andhra Pradesh	17243	23729
Assam	12797	16825
Bihar	6396	7467
Gujarat	18392	29468
Haryana	24138	35044
Karnataka	17464	24199
Kerala	19917	27864
Madhya Pradesh	11862	14534
Maharashtra	22992	32979
Orissa	10452	16306
Punjab	27863	32945
Rajasthan	12897	16800
Tamil Nadu	20927	27137
Uttar Pradesh	9541	11944
West Bengal	16521	22522
India	16648	22946

Source: Directorate of Economics and Statistics of respective State Governments (as on 25.11.2007) and for All-India-Central Statistical Organisations.

indicates that the per capita NSDP is highest in Punjab followed by Hariyana and lowest in Bihar. Six states, i.e. Assam, Bihar, Madhya Pradesh, Orissa, Rajasthan, Uttar Pradesh and West Bengal are below the Indian average of Rs.16648 per capita NSDP.

III. EDUCATION AND POPULATION GROWTH

Thomas Malthus, the great classical economist, at the end of 18th century for the first time realised the importance of growth of population for the development of the country. He linked population to food grains production. Though his thesis is not accepted today, but the fact remains that the growth of population influences the growth and the development of an economy. (Sharma, 2003)

Education is an important factor which influences economic growth through the development of human resources. There is a very close relationship between literacy improvement and birth rate. When people are educated especially the educated women gets greater opportunities for employment and income that raises the opportunity cost of their time in economic activities compared to child rearing. Such economic gains motivate families to have fewer children, build the demand for family planning services and more effective use of contraceptive methods, and lead to fertility decline. The "vicious cycle" of high birth-rates, high maternal and infant mortality and endemic poverty has been transformed into a "virtuous circle" through investment in human capital-enhancing labour productivity, reducing fertility and mortality, raising economic growth and thus securing domestic resources for further investments in people. (Birdsall and Sabot, 1993)

TABLE 5

Birth Rate (per 1000)

States	*2000-01*	*2004-05*
Andhra Pradesh	21.3	19.1
Assam	26.9	25.0
Bihar	31.9	30.4
Gujarat	25.2	23.7
Haryana	26.9	24.3
Karnataka	22.0	20.6
Kerala	17.9	15.0
Madhya Pradesh	31.4	29.4
Maharashtra	21.0	19.0
Orissa	24.3	22.3
Punjab	21.6	18.1
Rajasthan	31.4	28.6
Tamil Nadu	19.3	16.5
Uttar Pradesh	32.8	30.0
West Bengal	20.7	18.8
India	25.8	23.8

Source: Office of the Registrar General of India, Ministry of Home Affairs.

Table 5 presents the annual growth of birth rate of 15 major states in India for the year 2000-01 and 2004-05. The birth rate is lowest in Kerela followed by Tamil Nadu and West Bengal and is highest in Madhya Pradesh. The reason for lowest birth rate in Kerela is mainly due to high female literacy rate and high birth rate in Madhya Pradesh may be due to high concentration of tribal population who consider children as assets to maintain their livelihood

IV. CORRELATION ANALYSIS

In the analysis Per Capita Net State Domestic Product at current prices is taken as dependent variable. And two indicators of education, i.e. Literacy Rate and Enrolment Ratio of Students up to secondary level are taken as independent variables. Further birth rate has been taken to know the relationship between education and population growth. Correlation analysis has been made among these variables to study the impact of education on economic growth. The correlation coefficient of these variables for the year 2001 and 2005 are presented in Table 6 and Table 7 respectively.

All the correlation coefficient calculated for the year 2000-01 and 2004-05 is presented in matrix form in Table 8.

TABLE 6

Correlation of Income, Education and Birth Rate: 2000-2001

	Male	*Female*	*Total*
Income Literacy	*0.41421*	*0.48038*	*0.46498*
Income Enrolment			
Primary	-0.40654	0.02409	-0.24055
Secondary	*0.13363*	*0.40820*	*0.29235*
Birth Rate Enrolment			
Primary	0.13798	0.52320	0.17194
Secondary	-0.35613	-0.74509	-0.58554
Birth Rate Literacy	-0.65534	-0.81380	-0.76964
Income and Birth Rate	–	–	-0.31883

Source: Compiled by the author.

TABLE 7

Correlation of Income, Enrolment and Birth Rate (2005)

	Male	*Female*	*Total*
Income Enrolment			
Primary	-0.41213	-0.22758	-0.30512
Secondary	0.50368	0.67246	0.60151
Birth rate Enrolment			
Primary	0.28009	0.08963	0.17420
Secondary	-0.54435	-0.73754	-0.65360
Income Birth Rate			-0.71367

Source: Compiled by the author.

In the main diagonal the coefficient figures for the year 2001 is shown and the lower diagonal figures are for the year 2005. As the literacy figures are not available for the year 2005 the concerned cells remain empty in the lower diagonal.

FINDINGS OF CORRELATION ANALYSIS

1. Income and Literacy

There is positive correlation between the two. The correlation coefficient is 0.46498 which shows that the total literacy influences income to the extent of 21.62 per cent. The splitting figures for male and female literacy indicate a different picture, (Table-6) where the influence of female literacy on income is higher (23.07%) than the male literacy (17.15%)

2. Income and Enrolment

Here correlation is negative which indicates lower the enrolment of students higher is the income generation to the extent of 0.10 per cent. At the primary level the coefficient of correlation of males is negative with

r = -0.40654 whereas in case of females the same is slightly positive with

r = 0.02409 but surprisingly in the year 2004-05 the correlation between income and enrolment of both male and female students are negative in nature. The coefficients of

TABLE 8

Matrix of Correlation Coefficients

	Income	*Literacy*	*Enrolment*	*Birth Rate*
Income	–	0.46498	0.03197	-0.31883
Literacy		–	0.49469	-0.76964
Enrolment	0.05611		–	-0.40156
Birth Rate	0.71367		-0.17371	–

Source: Compiled by the author.

correlation are -0.41213 and -0.22758 respectively where the contributions of males are more than the females. The influence of males is 16.98 per cent while it is 5.17 per cent in case of females.

So far as the enrolment of secondary levels is concerned, both male and females have positive correlation with income. In 2000-01 the influence of enrolment on income is more in case of females with 23.10 per cent as against mere 1.78 per cent for the males. But in the year 2004-05 there is greater influence of enrolment on income in case of both male and female with 28.81 and 46.57 per cent respectively and the females still have higher influence than the males.

3. Income and Birth Rate

The correlation coefficient between income and birth rate is naturally negative with r = -0.31883 that means the birth rate has 10.16 per cent influence on income (2000-2001) but in 2004-05 the influence of birth rate on income increased by about 40 per cent with r = -0.71367 which explains 50.93 per cent.

4. Literacy and Birth Rate

Total literacy with birth rate has negative correlation with coefficient of r = 0.76964 and R^2 = 0.5923 that means there is 59.23 per cent influence between birth rate and literacy. In case of male the influence is 42.95 per cent whereas it is 66.22 per cent in case of females.

5. Enrolment and Birth Rate

Total enrolment with birth rate has negative correlation which means more the enrolment less is the birth rate but the influence is only 10.22 per cent. In case of female enrolment in primary level there is 27.38 per cent influence between the two whereas it is only 1.90 per cent in case of males in 2001, but the same is 7.84 per cent for males and 80.30 per cent for females in 2005. In secondary enrolment, it is 55.51 per cent for females and 12.68 per cent for males in 2001 but the same is 54.39 per cent for females and 29.63 per cent for males in 2004-05

CONCLUSION

Education is indispensable to economic development. Education, mainly female education affects the income considerably and plays an important role in controlling fertility, so steps should be taken to reduce the gender gap in education by appropriate policy measures by the planners.

References

Ainsworth, M.K. Beegle and A. Nyamete (1995), The Impact of Female Schooling on Fertility and Contraceptive, LSMS Working Papers 110, Washington, DC: World Bank.

Arputhamurty Savitri (1990), Women, Work and Discrimination, Asish Publishing House, New Delhi.

Census of India, 2001.

Becker, Gray S. (1964), Human Capital, New York, Columbia University Press.

Becker, Gray S. (1998), Human Capital and Poverty, Religion and Liberty Archive, Chicago, University of Chicago Press.

Behrman, Jere R. (1990), Human Resource Led Development, *Review of Issues and Development*, New Delhi, India: ARTEP/ILO.

—— and B.L. Wolfe (1987), "How does Mother's Schooling Affect the Family's Health, Nutrition, Medical Care Usage and Household, *Journal of Econometrics*, 36.

Birdsall, N. (1993), "Social Development in Economic Development", World Bank Policy Research Working Papers, WPS 1123, Washington DC.

Census of India, 2001.

Das, Sandhyarani (1999), Human Resources Development: An Analysis of Gender Dynamics in Orissa, *Vision*, Vol. XV111, Nos. 3 and 4, Bhubaneswar.

Government of India: *Economic Survey*, 2002-03, 2007-08.

Grossman, Gene M. and Elhanan Helpman, (1989), Growth and Welfare in a Small Open Economy, NBER Working Paper 2970.

Gupta, Jaipal Singh (1996), "Literacy Accelerates the Pace of Development", Creations, National Literacy Mission.

Harbison, F. and Charles, A. Myers (1968), Education, Man Power and Economic Growth, Oxford and IBH Publishing Co., New Delhi

Kate Young (1998), Gender and Development—A Relational Approach, Oxford University Press.

Kingdon Geeta Gandhi (1997), Education of Women and Socio-Economic Development, *Baha's Studies Review*, Vol. 7.

Marshall, Alfred (1920), The Principles of Economics, Macmillan, New York.

Perotti, R. (1993), "Political Equilibrium, Income Distribution, and Growth", *Review of Economic Studies*, 60.

Psacharopoulos, G. (1984), "The Contribution of Education to Economic Growth: International Comparisons", Cambridge, Ballinger Publishing Co.

Psacharopoulos, G. (1994), "Returns to Investment in Education: Aglobal Update", *World Development*, Vol. 22, p. 9.

Rehman, Kante (1995), Gender Discrimination and Development Process, *Labour and Development*, Vol. 1, No. 1.

Sarma, R.P. (2003), Population and Economic Growth in Dimensions of Population Growth, Edited by R.N. Misra, Anmol Publication Privte Limited, New Delhi.

Schultz, T.W. (1961), Investment in Human Capital", *American Economic Review*, 51(1).

Tilak, J.B. (1989), "Education and its Relation to Economic Growth, Poverty, and Income Distribution: Past Evidence and Further Analysis", World Bank Working Papers, 46.

UNDP (1996), Human Development Report, New York, Oxford University Press.

Virtuous Circles: Human Capital, Growth and Equity in East Asia (1993), by Nancy Birdsall and Richard Sabot, World Bank, April.

Vianell Mino (1990), Gender Inequality: A Comparative Study of Discrimination and Participation, Sage Publications, New Delhi.

17

Impact of Reservations on Education and Employment Development of Scheduled Castes in India: Some Issues

G. Savaraiah, M. Devarajulu and D. Subramanyam

With the advent of democracy, equality and equal treatment became the dominant feature of Indian Society. In this situation, it was realised by all that the exploitation of the weak, dominance of majority over minority, discrimination among human beings, inequality and other related issues are to be resolved in order to establish an egalitarian social order prohibition against discrimination remains a pious goal on paper unless and until conditions of life of depressed classes are improved. The constitution of India aims at the establishment of an egalitarian social democracy. The social hierarchy and social stratification came into being resulting in perpetration of injustice to the so-called lower castes (SC/STs) in India. This situation necessitated a programme for the reconstruction and transformation of a medieval hierarchical. Hindu society emphasising inequality into an egalitarian society as Ambedkar desired, based on justice, liberty, equality and fraternity the constitution created protective discrimination programme with which the causes uplift of underprivileged and disadvantaged communities particularly SC/STs under reservation policy in the country.

PROTECTIVE DISCRIMINATION PROGRAMME

Social Justice that is the protection of the rights and interests of the weak against the strong is achieved through implementation of the doctrine of protective discrimination by which various aids are given to the under privileged in all walks of life economic, education, social and political. By such measures the state does not aim at pulling down or destroying the advanced sections of society but only to up lift the down-trodden and backward people thereof, of course, by placing some reasonable restrictions on the former. Its aim is to prevent unjust enrichment of one section at the expense of the others particularly under privileged communities. In the scheme of social Justice it is spelt out in the constitution of India. Dr. Baba Saheb Ambedkar visualised that very soon a time would daun when the present down tradden people will nomore ruled but will be the rulers of this great country. In his prophetic words he exhorted his people to train themselves educate themselves, prepare themselves and to equip themselves to become fit enough to man as leaders in all walks of life and in all branches of administration. He exhorted the young educated his community to prove themselves to be second to none in whatever work is entrusted to them.

Baba Saheb's speeches and exhortations are like sermons and are sure to guide and direct not only his people but the people of the country. In one of his speeches to before independence speaking to his people, he stated, "The surest way for the salvation lies in higher education, higher employment and better ways of earning a living". On another occasion, he said, "self-elevation is not achieved by the blessings of others but only by ones own struggle and deed. In order to wipe out the fears from the eye sufferers it drawn trodden Dr. B.R. Ambedkar created a provision called reservation policy.

RESERVATION POLICY

Reservation for the scheduled castes and scheduled tribes under the constitution of India (1950) of which Dr. Ambedkar was the chief Architect is the mirror image of the Poona Pact, 1932 and the reservations introduced in public services in 1943 at the instance of Dr. Ambedkar the articals of the constitution of India that talk specifically of the reservations for the SCs/STs are 46, 330, 332 and 335, there are no time limit for the reservation in services, though the percentage changes from time to time on the basis of population. Therefore, the job reservations will continue till the constitution of India is amended. As regards the political reservations, Artical 334 put initially a time limit of ten years. But the reservations are being extended every ten years for political reasons and there have been already five extensions but little result.

IMPACT OF RESERVATION ON EDUCATION

Education is the major means by which a shift from manual to non-manual occupations can be effected with consequent enhancement of their life chances. Infact, education is one of the major tools which provides individuals in the necessary qualifications to fulfill economic roles and consequently improve their socio-ecnomic status. In the case of women education, particularly, higher education has much importance as it provides them not only requisite equipment and training for their future economic participation, but it also acts as a resolution force which is expected to liberate them from their subjugation and exploitation.

The constitution safeguards the promotion of education and economic interests of SC/STs [Arts. 15(4), 335, 46, 330, 332 and 17]. The educational reservations are being properly implemented at degree and university level in India.

Another form of assests education is also distributed on the basis of caste can also be known from the following table.

TABLE I

Percentage Distribution of Matriculation Completed People among Different Social Groups

Social group	*Persons*	*Male*	*Female*
SC's	4.9	7.3	2.3
ST's	4.9	7.3	2.3
Muslims	5.9	8.6	3.2
Hindus	8.5	12.0	4.7
All India	8.6	11.9	4.9

Source: India: Human Development Report, 1999, pp. 118-19.

It is 8.5 per cent in Hindus while the SC/STs who completed matriculation are 4.9 per cent which is lower than the national average. In the case of SC/STs female it is very low well. It can be attributable to higher to drop out rate at primary and upper primary levels during 1999. The total enrolment at primary and upper primary level shows a study increase during 1999-2000. The gross enrolment ratio at primary and upper primary level improved, perceptibly in 2001-02. The student enrolment higher education rose from 7.26 million in 1998 to 9.2 million in 2002-03. The enrolment ratio for SC/STs is low. But the percentage is still higher in upper caste Hindus because backward castes people are combined with property is high in upper caste people. Because this intellectual property, education level, profession-related training and skill is very necessary in this sector. Due to this ownership of intellectual property employment and income of all activities in industrial and service sector is entirely controlled by these people. Therefore lower caste Bahujanas could not compete with upper caste minority people in these sectors. The private service sector has provided employment opportunities of 19 per cent of the Indian population.

In the higher education, the gross enrolment for SC/STs shows lower (5.7) when compared with forward castes (8.4) most of the SC/ST children are going to the educational institutions completely based on the reservation benefits gender gaps are particularly significant in rural areas and for higher age groups. Across Social groups, enrolments are lower for SC/STs, indicating disadvantages along caste lines that are likely to perpertuate their povery. While better outcomes on the whole are associate of higher economic status of the household, the correlation is stronger in urban areas.

IMPACT OF RESERVATION ON EMPLOYMENT

The implementation of the reservations in the services centre was first started in India. The effective enforcement of reservation policy is to be practised in a democratic way in our country with a view to equal and full participation of down-trodden people in the development of the country. The following table gives the employment profile of scheduled caste in central government. Representation of SC/ST in central services in 1993-94 is as following.

TABLE 2

Employment Profile of SCs/STs in Central Services

	Total	*SC*	*Percentge*	*ST*	*Percentge*
A	64,197	6293	9.80	1967	3.06
B	107,120	13036	12.17	2513	2.35
C	23,09,003	367410	12.91	125,424	5.43
D	10,49703	217617	20.73	72,164	7.87

Source: GoI, Commission Reports on SC/STs, 1993-94.

It is observed from Table 2, as against their reservation of 22.5 per cent, the Scheduled Castes and Tribes has a share of only 12.86 per cent among a group official posts and 14.52 per cent of 'B' group posts it reveals that their representation in central government services is quite in adequate. The same trend has also found in the case of SC/STs representation in central public sector enterprises (undertakings) which is evident from Table 3.

However, the reservation for the ministerial posts (manual posts) of group D is more than adequately for SCs

TABLE 3

Representation of SCs/STs in Central Public Sector Enterprises (1993-94)

	Group	Total	SC	Percentge	ST	Percentge
A	191236	14088	7.37	3600	1.88	6
B	2162250	14794	9.12	5473	3.28	–
C	1197782	224074	18.71	100852	8.42	–
D	533646	116878	21.90	52075	9.76	–
Total		2084914	36834	17.74	162000	7.77
Group D		25362	21606	85.19	801	3.16
Grand Total		2110276	391440	18.55	162801	7.71

Source: *Ibid.*

* Excluding sweepers

GoI, Commission, Reports on SC/STs, 1993-94.

and STs (*except in central government services* Table 1). It indicates that for the scavenging and sweeping works, only the SCs/STs are suitable and easily available whereas for the official posts, the reservation was not fulfilled. The back log of vacancies for SCs/STs in central government departments and in public undertakings has been increasing since 1995.

With regard to the reservations in universities, the particulars of teaching posts in universities are shown in Table 4.

TABLE 4

SCs/STs Teachers in Universities in Percentage (1993-94)

Designation	SC	ST	SC+ST
Professors	1.0	0.4	1.4
Associate Professors	2.1	0.5	2.6
Assistant Professor	4.2	1.2	6.4
Others	7.02	1.0	8.02
At all levels	3.03	0.9	4.02

Source: *Ibid.*

The above table shows that the representation of SCs/STs in teaching posts is extremely poor. It is disheartening to note that all universities in south India have been implementing reservations for all posts but in A.P. there is not reservation for the post of professors on the ground of inefficiency and incompetence among the Dalit candidates. This has been basically due to lukewarm attitude of the authorities in the union departments education which did not take any action on the recommendations of the commissioners for SC and ST to go in for legislation to make it mandatory for the universities to follow reservation orders issued on the government of India from time to time.

The SCs/STs baglog vacancies have not been filled since 1999 in India in Andhra Pradesh alone there are more than 5000 vacancies are pending in many departments of those veterinary and animal husbandry. The government of Andhra Pradesh has been extending the time to fill to backlog vacancies every time citing the reason—suitable candidates are not available in this department. More than 3000 vacancies are SCs/STs backlog found in Indian universities including Engineering colleges and Medical colleges. Government used to advertise these posts before the elections after wards they will forget about the backlog vacancies. If these posts sincerely filled majority of the SCs/STs will occupy to the good positions, thereby improve their socio-economic status.

CONCLUSION

The reservations became a strong pole which supports the weak man to stand in the society on par with the strong man infact the reservations in educational institutions and in-services made the scheduled caste and tribes to occupy posts the secretaries and commissioners and president of India. If the government is in a good spirit to implement the rule of reservation in educational institutions, the grass enrolment of SCs in higher education touches more than 9 per cent. If the government sincerely implements the rule of reservation the scheduled caste and tribes will reach to the higher levels and dominate in all activities on the whole, we can conclude the effects of reservations are positively spreading among the weaker sections in the country.

18

Education—A Key to Economic Development

VARADA R. DESHPANDE

INTRODUCTION

In the process of economic growth, it is essential to attach more importance to the accumulation of physical Capital. The growth of tangible capital in an economy depends to a considerable extent on the rate of human capital formation. The key to development is man and that his abilities, values and attitudes must be changed in order to accelerate the process of development.

Human Capital formation plays an important role in economic development of the nation. The term human capital formation means, 'the process of acquiring and increasing the number of persons who have the skills, education and experience which are critical for economic and political development of the Country.

Human Capital can be developed in many ways—e.g. by providing health facilities and services, on job training, formally organised education at the elementary, secondary and higher level, study programme for adults, etc.

Lack of investment in human capital, is responsible for slow growth of under-developed countries. For investment in human capital education and training is essential. It has been observed that LDCs import physical capital for its development but due to the lack of critical skills, they fail to utilise it properly. The technological change is the basic determinant of economic growth. Educational development is a pre-condition of technological change. However, inadequate investment in education makes the people backward and illiterate.

Education is a key factor for development and this can take place only if we maintain quality at all levels. Education sets the right direction for development of the Country. Its quality determines the status of development in industry, technology, research and culture. The developed countries in the world, invest heavily on education as they feel that development is linked with educational activities. Education hence plays a key role in developing competence to achieve the changing economic goals. The basic aim of education should be to produce a large number of educated people for career building, eradication of poverty, miss concepts, blind beliefs and above all, to reduce gap between the rich and the poor so that we can think of establishing socialist pattern of society.

PRESENT SCENARIO OF HIGHER EDUCATION IN INDIA

An enormous quantitative expansion in Higher Education has taken place since Independence with respect to number of Institutions, Teachers as well as students' enrolment. Higher education is looked upon as the only way to ensure vertical mobility of people in the job market and in society as well. Hence, the massification of higher education. With respect to financing, Government has gradually taken over the responsibility almost in totality in accordance with social commitments. However, the economic reforms of 1991 based on a strategy of liberalisation, privatisation and globalisation alter the scenario on the education front too, especially of higher education. While earlier higher education was heavily subsidised keeping in view its role in national and social development. In the post reform period, the

Government began to promote the idea that higher education was a "non-merit" good. The Ministry of Finance in 1997 prepared a paper on "Government subsidies in India" which characterized higher education as non-merit subsidy and sought a drastic reduction in State funding of higher education. It has proposed that over a period of 5 years, subsidy be brought down from 90 per cent to 25 per cent. This proposal was further upheld by the Ambani Birla Report (2000) which also recommended reduction in subsidies. The change in Government's policy was the outcome of the World Bank's advice to developing countries which declared higher education to be a "non-merit good" in its report, "Higher Education Lessons of Experience" (1994). The World Bank, however, was forced to revise its stand and in a later report "constructing knowledge societies"; new challenges for tertiary education (2002). Higher Education again came to be classified as a public good.

With the adoption of the reform programme in India, the Government began to actively encourage the private sector to enter this field of activity with almost no restriction.

Reduced State funding has resulted in privatisation and commercialisation of higher education beyond reach and aspirations of the average students. At the same time Universities were asked to reduce their expenditure and to seek alternative sources of finance. However, all they did was to raise fees and introduce several self-financing courses.

The scenario of higher education outlined above is rather discontenting with respect to access as well as equality considerations. Only a small percentage of students can afford the higher fees of self-financing courses offered by the private Institutions or those of Foreign Universities. With Government gradually withdrawing itself from shouldering the responsibility of financing higher education and the increase in fees in most institutions, equality considerations have been placed on backburner. Government's objective of establishing a socialistic pattern of society seems to be mere theoretic so far as constitutional commitment towards higher education goes.

Another noticeable development in higher education has been the entry of foreign universities/institutions through twinning programmes and franchises with private educational institutions in India. Counties like U.S.A., U.K., New Zealand and Australia are keenly wooing the Indian students and making concentrated efforts to market their "educational wears", however, none of the top ranking foreign universities is operating in India.

POLICY TRUSTS IN HIGHER EDUCATIONS

The country today, is in the midst of major social, economic and technological change. The process will affect not only the market economy of the country but the whole system of higher education, which has to prepare its graduates for participation in the social and economical development of the country. Information Technology will have a major impact on the structure, management and the mode of delivery and the structure of education system. The national policy of education 1986 (amended in 1992) states "Higher Education provides people with an opportunity to reflect on the critical social, economic, cultural, moral and spiritual issues facing humanity. It contributes to the national development through dissimilation of specialised knowledge and skills. It is, therefore, a crucial factor for survival. Being at the apex of the education pyramid, it has also a key role introducing teachers for the education system.

FOCUS ON QUALITY HIGHER EDUCATION

In the emerging knowledge economy, building a strong human capital base to complement the natural resource endowment and available physical capital and to exploit the human resource potential is regarded Critical to India at this stage of an expanding economy.

According to recent research and fresh analysis of secondary data, secondary and higher education enhances earnings of the individuals and contributes to development and makes a significant contribution to reduction in absolute as well as relative poverty. Clearly, the challenge for India is to provide access to quality higher education to a larger proportion of population across the country with focus on

Vulnerable Sections of population with a view to make higher education inclusive.

The closing decade at the second millennium has witnessed far reaching political, economic development that have affected the people all over the world. The breakdown of geographical boundaries, spread of free market economy and growth into communication technology have transformed mother earth in a global village. This has far reaching implications on higher education, the world - over, affecting our perceptions about the role of a University the curricula, teaching methodology and research, it is also going to change the profile of our students and demand of a different quality from teachers.

HIGHER EDUCATION IN 21ST CENTURY

Today, there is a need for education that is not confined to a single faculty. The courses from faculties in a 'Cafeteria' mode are required. The present single faculty-based package model of education is unlikely to meet the demands of manpower requirement of tomorrow. Today, the need is that an engineering student has to study finance or management or history and a medical student must be familiar with all aspects of Sociology. The whole range of related issues concerning teaching, examination, students, college, research, quality, art structure of various bodies, etc. will also undergo changes proportionately to the demands of 21st century higher education. The focus of education will change from 'teaching' to 'learning' from contents to 'skills' from 'teaching organisation' to 'learning organisations'. Only the learning organisations can cater to today's dramatic demands. Not only will the global market reward learning, it will severely punish the lack of learning.

PURSUING EXCELLENCE IN INDIAN HIGHER EDUCATION

Achieving excellence in higher education should be an objective that needs to be pursued with all sincerity. For this, following actions are required—

1. To establish National Qualification Framework which specifies through description characteristics of output required (in terms of knowledge, skills and aptitudes) for qualifications at different levels. (Doctors, Masters, Degrees and Diplomas).
2. To set benchmarks for all levels of education and disciplines that leave space for innovation.
3. Strengthen the existing accreditation agencies and encourage the establishment of additional agencies especially in the professional discipline, to effectively cover the multitude of institutions.
4. Promote effects leading to internalisation of curricula, establishment of network and collaboration with Universities at an international level. Private sectors should be encouraged to set-up first class institutions.

At the University Level

- Implement national policies and programmes related to higher education such as those related to academic restructuring curricula development, examination system, etc.
- Ensure regularity in terms of academic calendar, class attendance and academic community interactions.
- Promote harmony between student and faculty and co-ordination between different stakeholders.
- Higher education should get more funding from Government.

References

Ashu Pasaricha (2005), WTO, Self-reliance and Globalization, Deep and Deep Publication Pvt. Ltd., New Delhi.

Jagannath Mohanty, Current Trends in Higher Education, Deep and Deep Publication Pvt. Ltd., New Delhi.

Jugale, V.B. (2004), Globalization, Growth and Poverty (2007), *Indian Economic Journal*, Vol. 55, No. 1, April-June.

Lekhi, R.K. (2005), The Economics of Development and Planning, Kalyani Publishers, New Delhi.

Powar, K.B. (2004), Quality in Higher Education, Ananmya Publishers, New Delhi.

Setumadhavrao (1996), Making Higher Education Effective, Devika Publishers, New Delhi.

19

Implications of Expansion in Higher Education on the Labour Market

V. Vaithianathan and A. Sugirtha Rani

SETTING THE RESEARCH PROBLEM

Youth unemployment rates have been growing annually at more than 15 per cent all over the world. According to UN Report on Youth Unemployment (2000), the problem is worse in Asia. This region accounts for 54 per cent of world's unemployed youth population. India accounts for a major chunk of Asia's unemployed. By 2001, there were 212 million young people in India, but only 23.6 per cent could be absorbed in the labour force. Simultaneously there has been a marked decrease in the number of jobs on offer from the organised sector (less than 10%). As a result, the emphasis of job creation has shifted to the informal sector.

At present, three billion people live on less than US $2 per day as poverty continues to escalate. In many countries, especially in the developing world, half of those people are under the age of 24 years. In almost all countries improvements in living standards have been minimal and reflect no substantial change in the lives of the vast majority, and in more than 20 countries are worsening considerably.

The number of young people globally is about to become the largest in history relative to the adult population. At present, more than 50 per cent of the population is under the age of 25, or just over three billion individuals are youth or children. In terms of youth alone (age 15-24 years) there are over 1.3 billion youth in the world today. This means that approximately one person in five is between the age of 15 and 24 years, or 17 per cent of the world's population is "youth" and 84 per cent of the worlds' youth lives in 89 per cent by 2025. These implications for instability represented by this overall scenario are alarming and likely to continue. As the majority of these youth live in some cases no access to basic water and sanitation services, health care facilities and schools. Some of the barriers and inhibiting factors to a vibrant and dynamic youth force are;

- More than 153 million young men and women are illiterates; of this, 96 million women are illiterates. On average, over 30 per cent of young women are illiterate in Africa and South Central Asia.
- A high percentage of youth never complete school; two out of 3 dropouts are young girls.
- In most developing countries less than 25 per cent of girls attend secondary school.
- Upto 60 per cent of all new sexually transmitted infections (STIs) including HIV/AIDS are with youth.
- Between one-third and two-thirds of rape victims world wide are age 15 or younger.
- Youth have access to poor natural resources, with limited use and quality (including water and air); and
- Majority of youth in developing countries is involved in the informal sector and have limited chances of earning a decent living and breaking out of the poverty cycle.

In terms of employment and livelihood opportunities the scenario is just as frightening as corresponding to the demographic trend. More young people are about to enter the labour between world-wide than over before in history. Between now and 2010, 700 million young people will enter the labour force in developing countries (more than the entire labour force of the developed countries in 1990). The International Labour Organisation (ILO) projects more than a billion jobs will need to be created to accommodate these new workers and reduce unemployment.

Furthermore, the majority of youth, on average 80 per cent is economically active, but is underemployed. This implies that they do not earn a sufficient amount, or work for a sufficient period of time to earn a living and for a sufficient amount, or work for a sufficient period of time to earn a living and to contribute to their community. The ILO estimates that there are approximately 70 million unemployed youth, and in general terms, they assert that the youth unemployment rate is double that of the adult population.

The problem of youth unemployment is rapidly assuming dangerous proportions in many countries as their economies and educational systems are unable to accommodate these numbers of youths. In many developing countries even low levels of economic growth are not predicted and thus limit their labour absorptive capacity. Indeed shrinkage of their economies, the related livelihood opportunities is expected. Economists advise that the current system will not meet the supply of the labour available. Thus, youth unemployment is an urgent global issue has repercussion in demographic, social, economic, health and environmental spheres. These impacts will be felt at the individual, familial, national and global levels if not addressed and this is a prescription for disaster.

But youth unemployment has other national and global impacts notably increase violence, crime, and political instability. Desperation can drive many people into living outside the law both to survive and as a means of expressing dissatisfaction at the apparent neglect of their very existence. Many of the unstable countries are also those with very high youth unemployment rates.

If provided with an enabling environment and opportunities, youth in both developed and developing countries can be key agents for social change, economic development and technological innovation. Youth bring with them boundless energy, imagination creativity, ideals and a limitless vision for their future and societies in which they live. If not utilized, they are wasted person. Thus, it is imperative that youth are harnessed as part of society. This can be achieved through providing sustainable and decent employment and livelihood opportunities for them.

The accumulation of human capital is widely perceived to be a key ingredient to bring per capita incomes. As workers become more educated and more skilled, their productivity improves, hence raising income levels. It is this time of though that has to the rapid expansion of higher education across the developing world. Since most developing countries are relatively scarce in skilled labour, their marginal product should be high, given diminishing returns of factors of production. It would be very costly to a developing country, if many of its educated workers are unemployed. However, this is exactly what we see in many developing countries, today, including Malaysia, China and India.

Whilst the Harris-Todaro Model is mostly frequently used in the context of unemployment among uneducated, it is not clear why unemployment among the educated should be subject to different economic forces. This paper is to advocate causes account for urban graduate unemployment. The most appealing alternative explanation relates to this study is that the implications of expansion in higher education on the labour market.

EDUCATION AND ECONOMIC GROWTH

Individuals are interested in taking more schooling partly because they can earn more and get better jobs; with more schooling can be a source of social mobility. Similarly, nation-states and regions are interested in raising the average level of schooling in their population because they link that doing so will improve productivity, increase economic growth, raise the quality of jobs in the economy, and reduce poverty and inequality.

Some of the earliest work in the economics of

education argued that a major effect of more education is to improve labour's capacity to produce. Because highly educated workers are more literate and numerate they should be easier to train to do more complex tasks. Further, they should have work habits, particularly a greater awareness of time and more internalized norms that would make them more dependable.

Nations with more educated labour forces are characterized by higher output per worker, but typically these nations also have more physical capital per worker. Exactly how education increases productivity, how important it is, and in what ways it is important are difficult questions, which economists have been unable to answer definitely. Controversy also surrounds the kind of education that contributes most to growth—general schooling, technical formal training, or on-the-job training—or what level of education contributes most to growth—primary, secondary, or higher education as a key factor in economic growth has grown stronger in recent years.

One of the clues that education does contribute to growth and how much may contribute is that with higher levels of economic growth have labour forces with higher levels of formal schooling. Such a macroeconomic approach to the relation between education and economic growth emphasises the correlation between the stock of human capital and the increase in economic output per capita. This may just indicate that as individuals earn more income, they purchase more schooling for their children. In that case schooling would be primarily consumption good, not an investment good. However, economists have been able to show that, on average, countries that have sustained high levels of economic growth are also those who have higher levels of literacy and have invested steadily in raising the education of their labour force.

With the shift to an information economy, globalisation and flexible organisation of production, economists have taken these arguments about human capital in the production process a step farther. Theories of development argue that developing nations have a better chance of catching up with the more advanced economies when they have a stock of labour that have the skills to develop new technologies themselves or to adopt and use foreign technology.

In this kind of model, more education in the labour force increases output in two ways:

- Education adds skills to labour to produce more output.
- Education increases the worker's capacity to innovate.

The major objective of the present study is that to study the unemployment problem among the educated youth in Tamil Nadu. For this study, the related information were collected from various issues of Tamil Nadu Economic Appraisal and Statistical Handbook of Tamil Nadu. Further, for this study, the relevant variables such as, number of higher education institutions, job-seekers at higher educational level, applicant on live register and enrolment of students in various institutions have been used for the same. Furthermore, attempt has been made about the public expenditure on education to the total budget expenditure as well as the share of social sector.

TABLE I

Employment Exchange Statistics in Tamil Nadu

Year	*Employment exchange office*	*Registration effected (lakhs)*	*Vacancies notified ('000s)*	*Placed in employment ('000s)*	*Placements in registration (%)*
1999-00	34	644.7	32.2	23.8	3.7
2000-01	34	622.5	31.6	18.2	2.9
2001-02	34	568.6	19.6	15.6	2.8
2002-03	34	401.2	7.8	8.6	2.1
2003-04	34	358.0	4.4	3.4	9.5

Source: Tamil Nadu Economic Appraisal (Various issues).

JOB SEEKERS IN TAMILNADU

The total number of applicants on the live register of all the 34 employment exchange offices spread over the state provides the size of educated unemployed persons inspite of certain limitations.

By the end of 2003-04, the number of job seekers in the state were 49.85 lakhs, against 52.31 lakhs recorded by the end of 2002-03, of which, about 35 per cent were women. It is pertinent to note that registrants on the live register should not be treated as unemployed because, it is not mandatory for those who registered their name on the live register and get absorbed elsewhere have to inform Employment Exchanges of their current real status.

The actual number of educated job seekers had attained the level of 35.33 lakhs by the end of 2003 from 33.83 by the end of 2002. The relative share of educated job seekers with less than graduation accounts 78 per cent followed by graduates (17%) and postgraduates (5%) of the total applicants.

UNEMPLOYMENT AMONG YOUTH IN SELECTED STATES

The degree of unemployment among the youth is an indicator of the under utilisation of the labour force. One disquieting feature prevailing at the state and national level is the relatively higher unemployment level among youth. It is estimated by the survey that the persons aged 15-29 years accounted for 25.29 per cent of the total population. In the labour surplus economy like India many of the youth remain unemployed and some chronically unemployed. The survey results point a higher level of unemployment among youth, as compared to that of in the overall population. The unemployment rate was higher for the urban youth than that of rural. Compared to the female youth in male youth, the rate was higher in rural India.

Between the period 1993-94 and 1994-2000, the unemployment rates of youth have increased for males in rural and urban areas and for females in rural areas. The table shows the unemployment rates among youth in the southern states and Maharashtra during 1999-2000.

TABLE 2

Educational Level of Job Seekers

Qualification	*2002-03*	*2003-04*
Less than graduate	26.74	27.43
	(79.0)	(77.6)
Graduates	5.42	6.13
	(16.0)	(17.4)
Postgraduates	33.83	1.77
	(4.9)	(5.0)
Total educated job seekers	33.83	35.33
	(100.0)	(100.0)

Note: (Figures in brackets indicate percentage share to total).
Source: Tamil Nadu Economic Appraisal: 2003-04, 2004-05.

Among the major states the unemployment rate among youth was higher in Kerala in both usual status and currently daily status categories of rural and urban areas. As for Tamil Nadu, current daily status rural unemployment obtained at 181 during 1999-2000. Against all India rates, the state had higher rates of unemployment in respect of usual status (rural) and current daily status of rural and urban areas.

UNEMPLOYMENT AMONG EDUCATED IN SOUTH INDIA

In the 55th round results of National Sample Survey (NSS), unemployment rate of educated (secondary and above level) for the year 1999-2000 report brings to light that unemployment rate among the educated was higher than those of with below secondary level of education.

Unemployment rates that prevailed in Tamil Nadu and Kerala are higher that of not only all India but also other neighbouring states (Andhra Pradesh and Karnataka) under both usual status (adjusted) and current weekly status.

Institutions, Enrolment and Public Expenditure on Education in Tamilnadu

The core content of the present study is that the implications of expansion of higher education on the labour

TABLE 3

Unemployment Rate among Youth—Southern States and Maharashtra (1999-2000)

State	*Usual status*		*Current daily status*	
	Rural	*Urban*	*Rural*	*Urban*
Andhra Pradesh	18	93	99	148
Karnataka	16	72	58	105
Kerala	217	250	363	343
Maharashtra	39	133	104	165
Tamil Nadu	51	100	181	156
All India	37	112	110	154

Source: Tamil Nadu Economic Appraisal (Various issues)

market. Hence, an attempt has been made for the study by using secondary data from the various issues on Tamil Nadu Economic Appraisal.

TABLE 4

Educated Unemployment Rate in Southern States

State	*Usual status*		*Current daily status*	
	Rural	*Urban*	*Rural*	*Urban*
Andhra Pradesh	68	69	100	77
Karnataka	45	55	56	59
Kerala	198	175	235	207
Tamil Nadu	106	66	123	75
All India	67	74	84	82

Source: NSSO 55th Round.

From the above table, there were only 545 higher educational institutions during 1999-2000 and this has increased to 742 in the year 2004-05. Similarly, the enrolment of students has also increased from 613758 to 800005 from 1999 to 2005. It is an interesting fact that the number of educational institutions and students' enrolment shows an

TABLE 5

Institutions, Enrolment and Public Expenditure on Education

Year	*Institutions**	*Enrolment**	*Expt. on education#*	*% to total budget expt.#*	*% to social sector#*
1999-2000	545	613758	434871.82	20.98	56.89
2000-2001	616	648140	439599.87	20.21	56.41
2001-2002	699	697344	429286.88	19.91	55.92
2002-2003	737	692952	414532.71	16.14	51.99
2003-2004	747	759739	417506.11	16.52	48.56
2004-2005	742	800005	455619.78	15.85	46.87

Note: *related to higher education
related to overall educational expenditure
Source: Tamil Nadu Economic Appraisal (Various issues).

increasing trend when compared to the public expenditure on education from the states' total expenditure, which explores the decreasing trend of 20.98 per cent in 1999-00 to 15.85 per cent during 2004-05. Similarly, the percentage distribution from social sector indicates that the diminishing trend of 56.89 per cent during 1999-2000 to 46.87 per cent in the year 2004-05. From this, it is found that there is a negative relationship between the growth of institutions and enrolment of students with the public expenditure pattern on education from the total expenditure of the state.

The major objective of this present study is that to analyse the problems for youth educated unemployment in India. In the previous paragraphs, the level of unemployment and the number of educated youths have registered in the employment exchange office in Tamilnadu also analysed. To support this secondary received information, the primary data collected from randomly selected 215 educated youth unemployed in Salem District for further processing of this research. To analyse this objective, the information about demographic, socio and economic details have also been gathered from the same. Beyond these general variables, the individual details such as name of the degree, type of institute the youth has studied, the expenses made to obtain the particular degree (UG/PG), in which year they have registered their degree in employment exchange office, number of interviews the respondent attended, reasons for not getting job through personal interview, and reasons for unemployment also captured. Moreover for this research, the collected primary data has been analysed with the help of simple statistical tools like mean and percentage.

DESCRIPTIVE ANALYSIS (PRIMARY SURVEY)

The descriptive analysis shows the detailed information about the demographic, socio-economic background of the respondents.

TABLE 6

Demographic and Socio-economic Details

Variables	*Minimum*	*Maximum*	*Mean*
Age (years)	20	33	26.78
Family size (No. of members in the household)	2	7	4.5
Family income (Rs. per month)	1500	50000	5059.13
No. of personal interviews attended	1	12	5.34
Years completed after registration in employment exchange office	1	18	7.52
Expenditure on higher education (Rs.)	800	1,25,000	22075
Social status (SC/ST)		65.2%	
Type of education (Degree)		47.8%	
Name of the Degree (Bachelor of Arts)		39.8%	
Type of institution (Government)		56.5%	
Interest in self-employment (No)		79.8%	
Total		215	

Source: Primary data.

From the responses of the respondents the average age of the educated unemployed youth was around 27 years, and most of them were in the productive age group but without contributing anything to the economic activity to the household as well as to the nation. Most of them belong to the marginalised (SC/ST) group, when compared to rest of the social group in the study area, which shows a positive sign of enrolment and inclusion in social sector also. Meanwhile, the average size of the family shows that around 5 members. In case of income of the household, they earn only the normal income of Rs. 5059 per month. Similarly, the household expenditure on higher education was around Rs. 2275. Beyond these descriptive data analysis, the details with respect to educated unemployment explores that around 5 times the youth has attended personal interviews by them. In addition to this, they have registered their degree in employment office that crossed around 8 years. It is quite interesting that, still they have been waiting for their job through employment office and they are also not interested to work in private sector. Most of them (48%) have obtained the degree level and they are in Bachelor of Arts (39.8%) group in their educational level.

The respondents have obtained their degree in government institutions (56.5%) alone, where the cost of education is highly economical and viable to that particular marginalised community. Moreover, in these (government) institutions only these stakeholders can able to get financial assistance for their studies in the name of scholarships and fellowships, etc. Further, they are not in a position to do some other job-oriented courses, which is highly demanded in the job market. In addition to this, these educated unemployed youth are not interested to do self-business (79.8%) because of the requirement of huge investment.

REASONS FOR FAILURE IN PERSONAL INTERVIEWS

In continuation of the above table, the researchers have captured the reasons for failure in personal interviews the respondents have attended. This is due to the fact that of poor communication skill (34.1%), inefficient in expressing their views and ideas (23.5%), irrelevant answer to the prescribed question (23.5%) and no more additional qualifications (18.8%) they have not obtained like computer knowledge or certificate courses, etc. Moreover, it is observed that, most of the educated unemployed had their bachelor degree in arts and they studied in government institutions (both school and college) through local language medium of instruction (Tamil medium) and which is relatively less quality education provider when compared to the private institutions. It is a common phenomenon that those who are in Tamil medium, they are not good in English communication. Inspite of this problem, they are unable to go through the personal interview, eventhough they are good in subject and all other things.

REASONS FOR EDUCATED YOUTH UNEMPLOYMENT

The major objective of the present study is that to analyse what are the reasons for the educated youth unemployment. In the previous paragraphs, a detailed discussion was made on the unemployment level in different categories of higher education viz., the registered unemployment youth in employment exchange office in UG or PG level. To support or to verify the received facts, reasons have captured by posing a simple question to the respondents.

TABLE 7

Reasons for Educated Youth Unemployment

Reasons for unemployment	*No. of respondents*	*Per cent*
Not interested in private sector employment	17	7.8
Expecting/interested in government job	88	40.9
No job security in private employment	35	16.5
No suitable job opportunity for their educational qualification	75	34.8
Total	215	100

Source: Primary data.

From the tabular analysis, it is inferred that around two fifth (40.9%) reasoned out that either they are expecting or interested in government job alone and interested in private employment (7.8%). In addition to this, there has been no suitable job for their educational qualification (34.8%) and also no job security in private employment (16.5%). From this, it is observed that, because of the expectation and interest in government employment, so far the respondents have been unemployed.

CONCLUSION

From the analysis of the study, the unemployment among youth remains a problem that needs to be tackled in a massive way. A conscious attempt is being made in the country to tackle the problems of unemployment and to provide youth with opportunities of increasing their employment opportunity and their capacity for self-employment. Moreover, the economists have focused mainly on the quantitative aspects of higher education and the number of graduates in the labour force in assessing whether an economy is allocating resources maximum growth and development. China is expanding its higher education system the most rapidly, and India, the least rapidly. Although many analysts believe that India has sufficient absolute number of engineers, scientists and has advantages over China in moving towards an information-based advanced service economy. Eventhough the country is enjoying sufficient level of stock of human capital; on the other hand, it is also experiencing the problem of educated youth unemployment. Hence, the solution to this problem is that, the number of graduates are important, where the issue of critical thinking and innovativeness which would be fostered by college teachers who know how to develop and nurture the skills in students and higher education institutions that provide incentives for such teaching may even more important in the future.

REFERENCES

Asoka, H. (2006), "Investing in Education in India: Inferences from and Analysis of the Rates of Return to Education Across Indian States", Unpublished Ph.D. Dissertation, Stanford University School of Education.

Asaridis, C. and Drazen, A. (1990), "Threshold Externalities in Economic Development", *Quarterly Journal of Economics*, 105(2).

Bassanini, A. and Scarpetta, S. (2001), "Does Human Capital Matter for Growth in OECD Countries? Evidence from Pooled-mean-group Estimates", OECD Economic Department Working Papers, No. 282.

Blaug, M. (1972), "Educated Unemployment in Asia: A Contrast Between India and the Philippines", *The Philippine Economic Journal*, 11.

Duraisamy, P. (2002), "Changes in Returns in Education in India, 1983-1994: By Gender, Age-Cohort and Location", *Economics of Education Review*, 21(6).

Kapur, D. and Mehta, P.B. (2004), "Indian Higher Education Reform: From Half-Baked Socialism to Half-Baked Capitalism", Hard University, Center for International Development, Working Paper, No. 108.

Nalla, Gounden A.M. (1967), "Investment in Education in India", *Journal of Human Resources*, 2(3) Summer.

Carnoy, Martin (2006), "Higher Education and Economic Development: India, China and the 21st Century", paper presented at the Pan Asia Conference: Focus on Economic Challenges, Stanford Center for International Development.

Statistical Handbook: Tamil Nadu (2006).

Tamil Nadu Economic Appraisal, 2002-03, 2003-04, 2004-05 and 2005-06.

Tilak, J.B.G. (2003), "Higher Education and Development", in the Handbook on Educational Research in the Asia and Pacific Region (eds. J.P. Kleeves and Ryp Watanabe) Dordrecht: Kluwer Academic Publishers.

20

India and the Knowledge Economy: India, China and the 21st Century

Mukti Patel and Deepak Agarwal

OVERVIEW

One of the world's largest economies, India has made tremendous strides in its economic and social development in the past two decades and is poised to realise even faster growth in the years to come. After growing at about 3.5 per cent from the 1950s to the 1970s, India's economy expanded during the 1980s to reach an annual growth rate of about 5.5 per cent at the end of the period. It increased its rate of growth to 6.7 per cent between 1992-93 and 1996-97, as a result of the far-reaching reforms embarked on in 1991 and opening up of the economy to more global competition. Its growth dropped to 5.5 per cent from 1997-98 to 2001-02 and to 4.4 per cent in 2002-03, due to the impact of poor rains on agricultural output.

India has a rich choice set in determining its future growth path. Figure 1 shows what India can achieve by the year 2020, based on different assumptions about its ability to use knowledge, even without any increase in the investment

FIGURE 1

India: Real Gross Domestic Product Per Worker, Alternative Projections, 1995-2020

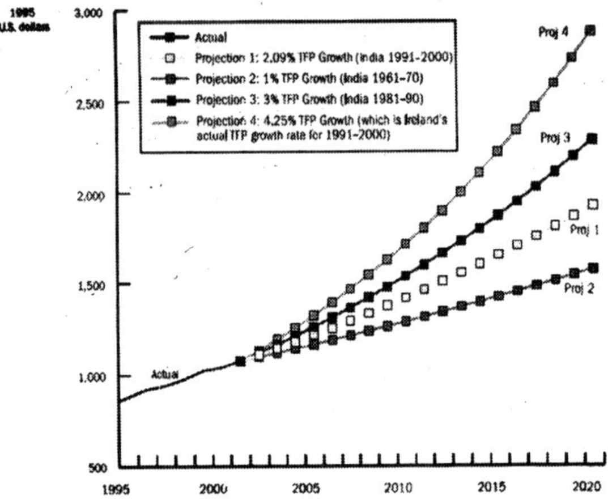

Note: For all four projections, capital, labor, and human capital are assumed to grow at their 1991-2000 average annual growth rates for India, that is. 5.41. 2.23 and 0.58 percent, respectively. For the growth TFP decomposition to be more precise, labor force figures rather than total population are used as a measure or the amount of "labor" available factor of production in the Indian economy. According to World Bank databases, in 2001 India's GDP (in 1995 U.S. dollars) was 5495 billion and its population was 1.03 billion, of which only 461 million were in the labor force. As such India's GDP per capita in 2001 was approximately 5480, whereas GDP per worker was around $1.070.

Source: Knowledge for Development Programme.

rate. Here, total factor productivity (TFP) is taken to be a proxy for a nation's learning capability. Projection 1, 2, 3 and 4 plot real gross domestic product (GDP) per worker (1995 U.S. dollars) for India assuming different TFP growth rates fro 2002 to 2020. Projection 4 is an optimistic scenario that is based on the actual TFP growth rate in Ireland in 1991-2000.

India can no doubt reap tremendous economic gains by developing policies and strategies that focus on making more effective use of knowledge to increase the overall productivity of the economy and the welfare of its

FIGURE 2

Knowledge Economy Index: India, Comparators, and the World, 1995 and Most Recent Period

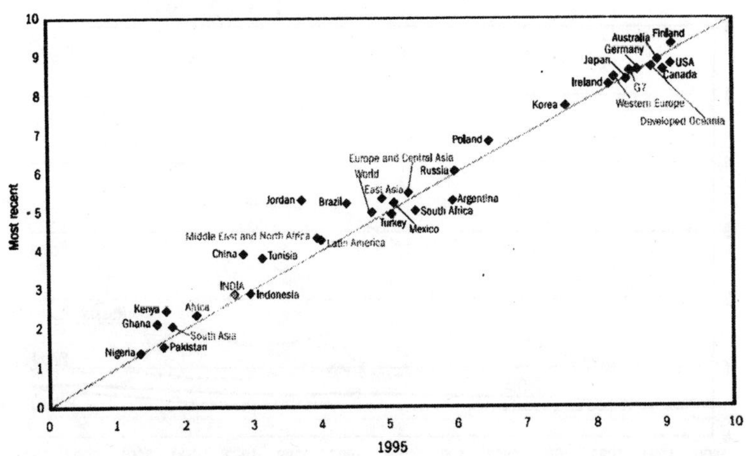

Note: Countries in the northeast section of the figure arc the global leaders. Countries above the 45-degree line have improved their position in the knowledge economy index (KEI) for the most recent period for which data are available relative to their position in 1995 (or closest available date in the mid-1990s) and *vice-versa* for countries below the line.

Source: World Batik, "Knowledge Assessment Methodology;" http://wwvv.wctrldbank.org/kam.

population. In so doing, India will be able to improve it international competitiveness and join the ranks of countries that are making a successful transition to the knowledge economy.

Embracing the Knowledge Economy

The time is very opportune for India to make its transition to the knowledge economy—an economy that creates, disseminates, and uses knowledge to enhance its growth and development. The knowledge economy is often taken to mean only high-technology industries or information and communication technologies (ICTs). It would be more appropriate, however, to use the conqept more broadly to cover how any economy harnesses and uses new and existing

FIGURE 3

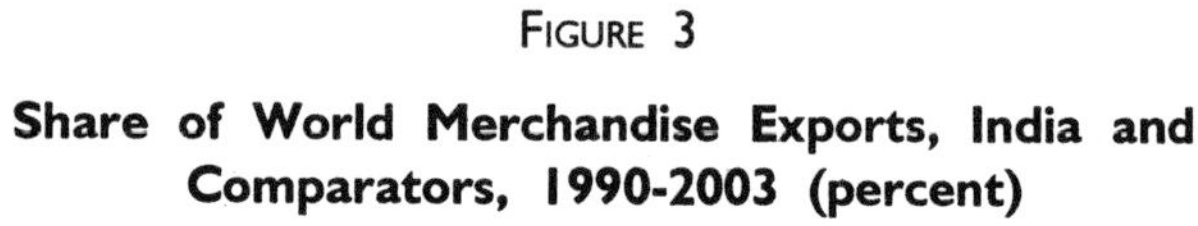

Share of World Merchandise Exports, India and Comparators, 1990-2003 (percent)

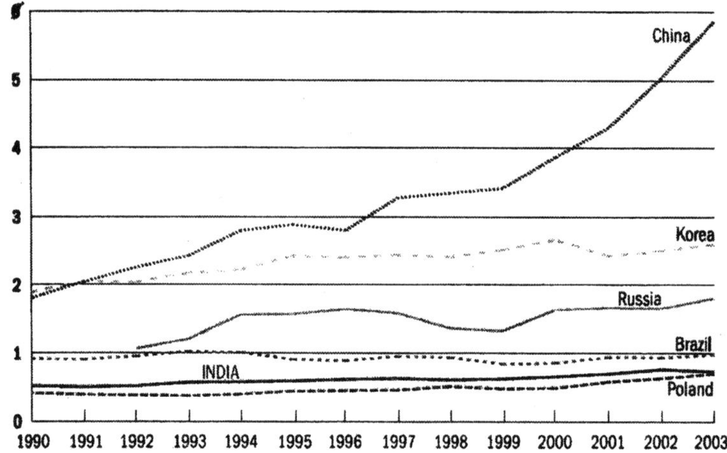

Source: World Bank staff analysis undertaken using World Bank internal database.

knowledge to improve the productivity of agriculture, industry, and services and increase overall welfare. In India, great potential exists for increasing productivity by shifting labor from low productivity and subsistence activities in agriculture, informal industry, and informal service activities to more productive modern sectors, as well as to new knowledge-based activities—and in so doing, to reduce poverty and touch every member of society. India should continue to leverage its strengths to become a leader in knowledge creation and use.

Advantage India

India has a critical mass of skilled, English-speaking knowledge workers, especially in the sciences. It has a well-functioning democracy. Its domestic market is one of the world's largest. It has a large and impressive Diaspora, creating valuable knowledge linkages and networks. The list goes on: macroeconomic stability, a dynamic private sector, institutions of a free market economy, a well-developed financial sector, and a broad and diversified science and technology (S&T) infrastructure. India has created profitable niches in information technology (IT) and is becoming a global provider of twenty-century; software services. It stresses that to be competitive in the global knowledge economy of the twenty-first century; India should continue to focus its efforts on further reforming its overall economic and institutional environment and improve its overall trade and investment climate

The following are some of the key issues that India needs to address in each of the four pillars to spur growth and innovation and, in so doing, increase economic and social welfare.

STRENGTHENING THE ECONOMIC AND INSTITUTIONAL REGIME

Taking advantage of the knowledge revolution's potential hinges on effective economic incentives and institutions that promote and facilitate the redeployment of resources from less efficient to more efficient uses. A key feature is the extent to which the legal system supports basic rules and property rights. India's economic and institutional regime has several strengths: flourishing entrepreneurship and free enterprise; a strong infrastructure for supporting private enterprise; capital markets that operate with greater efficiency and transparency than, for example, those in China; an advanced legal system; and an independent judiciary.

India has other intrinsic advantages, such as macroeconomic stability, a large domestic market, and a large and relatively low-cost and skilled workforce. It also has a critical mass of well-educated workers in engineering and science and, unlike China, abundant raw materials.

India is still a relatively closed economy compared with other Asian economies, in which exports account for a much larger share of GDP (33% in China and 38% in the Republic of Korea, compared with only 15% in India in 2003). Although this means that India is somewhat protected from global trends, the downside is that it does not benefit from stronger foreign competitive pressures to improve performance or from the ability to draw on more cost-effective foreign inputs, such as capital goods, components, products, or foreign investment, which embody more advanced knowledge. As a result, India is losing market share to its major competitors, especially China (Figure 3), where reforms have moved ahead much more rapidly; therefore, to speed up trade reform and be able to export, Indian firms need to be allowed to import the materials and technology they need.

DEVELOPING EDUCATED AND SKILLED WORKERS

Education is the fundamental enabler of the knowledge economy. The knowledge economy of the twenty-first century demands a set of new competencies, which includes not only ICT skills, but also such soft skills as problem solving, analytical skills, group learning, working in a team-based environment, and effective communication. Fostering such skills requires an education system that is flexible; basic education should provide the foundation for learning, and secondary and tertiary education should develop core skills that encourage creative and critical thinking.

A strong basic education system is a necessary precondition to underpinning India's efforts to enhance further the productivity and efficiency of its economy. China's experience in this area is instructive as its emphasis on secondary education has provided it with a firm basis for expansion of manufacturing activities on a global scale. India has made substantial progress in increasing literacy and increasing primary and secondary enrolments and overall education attainment (Table 1). But the country still accounts for one-quarter of the world's 104 million children out of school. The participation of girls in the 6- to 14-year-old age group in elementary education is low.

India also possesses a large pool of highly educated and vocationally qualified people who are making their mark, domestically and globally, in science, engineering, IT, and research and development (R&D). But they make up only a small fraction of the population. To create a sustained cadre of "knowledge workers," India will need to develop a

TABLE I

India: Educational Attainment of the Total Population Age 15 and Older, 1980-2000

				Highest level attained						
		Population over age 15 ('000s)	*No school-ing (%)*	*First level*		*Second level*		*Post secondary*		*Average years of school*
				Total	*Compl.*	*Total*	*Compl.*	*Total*	*Compl.*	
India	1980	423,306	66.6	12.6	4.7	18.5	5.4	2.4	0.7	3.27
	1990	542,391	55.8	20.5	7.6	20.5	5.6	3.3	1.7	4.10
	2000	680,072	43.9	28.2	10.5	23.8	6.5	4.1	2.2	5.06

Source: Barro and Lee (2001).

more relevant educational system and reorient classroom teaching and learning objectives, starting from primary school. The new system would focus on learning, rather than on schooling, and promote creativity. It would also improve the quality of tertiary education and provide opportunities for lifelong learning.

In India, efforts have been put into establishing a top-quality university system that includes many world-class institutions of higher learning that are competitive and meritocratic, such as Indian Institutes of Technology (IITs), Indian Institutes of Management, Indian Institute of Science, and the Regional Engineering Colleges (RECs).

In the area of scientific and technical education, even though India produces almost 200,000 scientists, engineers, and technicians a year, it has not been obtaining the full economic benefit from this skill base, because of the mismatch between education and the labor market. Many professionals also leave the country in search of better opportunities, which leads to brain drain.

The success of China in achieving higher growth reveals the importance of a workforce with a basic education that can be trained. This leads to the issue of skills development and training. India too will need to develop various job training programs to be globally competitive.

In addition, India should develop a system of lifelong learning, which encompasses learning from early childhood through retirement and includes formal learning (schools, training institutions, and universities), non-formal learning (structured on-the-job training), and informal learning (skills learned from family members or people in the community).

Some of the main issues in strengthening India's education system, therefore, include the following:

- Improving efficiency in the use of public resources in the education system, and making the education system as a whole more responsive to market needs, as well as ensuring expanded access to education that fosters critical thinking and learning skills for all, not just the elites.
- Ensuring consistency between the skills taught in

primary and secondary education and the needs of the knowledge economy; introducing materials and methods to teach students "how to learn," rather than stressing occupation-specific knowledge.

- Reforming the curriculum of tertiary education institutions to include skills and competencies for the knowledge economy (communication skills, problem-solving skills, creativity, and teamwork) that also meet the needs of the private sector.
- Raising the quality of all higher education institutions, not just a few world-class ones (such as the IITs).
- Embracing the contribution of the private sector in education and training by relaxing bureaucratic hurdles and putting in place better accreditation systems for private providers of education and training.
- Establishing partnerships between Indian and foreign universities to attract and retain high-quality staff and provide opportunities for students to receive internationally recognised credentials.
- Increasing university-industry partnerships to ensure consistency between research and the needs of the economy.
- Using ICTs to meet the double goals of expanding access to and improving the quality of education.
- Investing in flexible, cost-effective job training programs that are able to adapt quickly to new skill demands generated by changing markets and technologies, aligned with the needs of firms.
- Developing a framework for lifelong learning, including programs intended to meet the learning needs of all, both within and outside the school system.
- Making effective use of distance learning technologies to expand access to and the quality of formal education and lifelong training.

LOOKING AHEAD

India has already developed a vision and strategies to address its transition to the knowledge economy. In the main, its initiatives have, however, largely been developed around the three functional pillars of the knowledge economy (education. innovation, and ICTs). But to get the maximum benefits from investments in these areas, these initiatives must be part of a broader reform agenda, because some elements of India's current economic and institutional regime are constraining full realisation of India's potential. India will, for example, not reap the full benefits of its investments in increasing education, ramping up ICTs, or even doing more R&D unless its broader institutional and incentive regime stimulates the most effective use of resources in these areas, permits their deployment to the most productive uses, and allows entrepreneurial activity to flourish to contribute better to India's growth and overall development.

CONCLUSION

In sum, India is well positioned to take advantage of the knowledge revolution to accelerate growth and competitiveness and improve the welfare of its citizens and should continue to leverage its strengths to become a leader in knowledge creation and use. In the twenty-first century, India will be judged by the extent to which it lays down the appropriate "rules of the game" that will enable it to marshal its human resources, strengths in innovation, and global niches in IT to improve overall economic and social development and transform itself into a knowledge-driven economy. Sustained and integrated implementation of the various policy measures in these domains would help to reposition India as a significant global economic power, so that it can rightfully take its place among the ranks of countries that are harnessing knowledge and technology for their overall economic development and social well-being.

References

AIMA (All India Management Association), 2003, India's New Opportunity, 2020: Report of the High-Level Strategic Group.

Huang, Yasheng, and Tarun Khanna (2003), "Can India Overtake China?" Foreign Policy. July-August.

India, Planning Commission (2001), India as Knowledge Superpower: Strategy for Transformation. New Delhi.

Kalam, A.P.J. Abdul, and Y.S. Rajan (2002), India 2020: A Vision for the New Millennium, New Delhi: Penguin Books India.

The Tata Group (2005), "40 Hours is All it Takes to Teach an Indian to Read.

Higher Education and Economic Development: India, China, and the 21st Century, by Martin Carnoy, Stanford University.

21

Higher Education: A Critical Factor for Human Development in India in the Era of Globalisation

BIRENDRA KUMAR JHA AND SHAMBHU PRASAD SHAH

No inquiry into the poverty of nations could hope to be complete without a study of the quality of men's lives (Gunnar Myrdal, 1972) and education is one of the basic elements for improving economic and social life of a man. Qualitative aspects of population are of great importance from the point of view of the development of a nation and the welfare of the people but it has been the tendency of the planners to think primarily in terms of 'how many'—how many students enrolled, in how many courses, in how many institutions and not in terms of how well they learned, what they were taught, or how to improve the educational system they inherited from their colonial masters to speed up development. India is one of the largest reservoir of human resources in the World, next to China but unfortunately, human development received no due priority in the past. Since the early 1990s, there has been a notable shift in the focus of development planning from mere economic growth to enhancement of human well-being. Of course, the paradigm of development in the recent past has been shifted from PCGDP or PCGNP to human well-being. The Planning Commission which has prepared a document in titled Towards Faster and More Inclusive Growth' reveals the changing outlook of our planners. Of course, the process of development is no more conditioned by Harrod-Domar's technical co-efficients and the rate of growth of physical capital alone, human capital is any surging ahead to replace physical capital as the sole mover of the growth process (Chadha, 2003). And so there is a new approach stressing the importance of education as a basic ingredient of human capital base in this age of knowledge economy, which have accorded high priority to human capital formation have performed relatively better in terms of economic growth, employment, reduction in income inequalities and alleviation of poverty (Rangarajan, 1999). Many countries of the world like Germany, Australia, U.S.A., etc. have developed themselves due to proper human capital formation. The World Bank evidences indicate that as much as 64 per cent of growth is explained by human capital alone while the shares of physical and natural are much lower recording 16 per cent and 20% respectively. Dension (1967) estimated that 40 per cent growth in real national income during the period 1948-63 in The United States could be attributed to improvements in human capital. The Nobel Laureate Amartya Sen has also repeatedly pointed out that no country has developed with an illiterate and unhealthy population. Indian planners hold a clear-cut conception in this concern and they have revealed the that "Without adequate development of human resources in the widest sense, we cannot avoid set backs to the process of development itself. An effort at generating demand for labour must be accompanied by a strategy to upgrade skills of the new entrants to the labour force. There is a plus-point in favour of India in the sense that the age structure of our population is such that the proportion of our active labour force will continue to rise at a rate when most industrialised countries, and even China, face an increasing dependency ratio. This is an asset we must take full advantage of. This is a boon if we create an environment which ensures highly endowed human resources. That can be possible only through higher education. It is needless to say that a country, rich in educated and skilled work force has great potentials to produce, disseminate, adapt knowledge to enhance growth.

As reported in Human Development Report, 2005 India is ranked 127th out of 177 countries with an HDI value of 0.602. Human Development Index (HDI) for some selected countries in different groups for the year 2003 as reported in human Development Report, 2005 can be visible from the following Table 1.

TABLE I

Human Development Index, 2003 for Selected Countries

Country	*HDI value 2003*	*HDI Rank*
Norway	0.963	1
Canada	0.949	5
United Stales	0.944	10
Japan	0.943	11
Saudi Arabia	0.772	77
China	0.755	85
Sri Lanka	0.751	93
India	0.602	127
Paakistan	0.527	135
Bangladesh	0.520	139
Kenya	0.474	154
Nigeria	0.453	158
Niger	0281	177
World	0.741	–

Source: UNDP, Human Development Report, 2005.

Among 177 Countries 57 countries were in high human development range (HDI) between 0.5 to 0.8) 88 countries including India were in medium human development range (HDI value between 0.5 to 0.8) and rest 32 were in low human development range (HDI value less than 0.5).

ROLE OF HIGHER EDUCATION

"Higher education is of paramount importance for

economic and social development. Institutions for higher education have the main responsibility for equipping individuals with the advanced knowledge and skills required for positions of responsibility in government, business and the professions. Estimated social rates of return of 10 per cent or more in many developing countries also indicate that investment in higher education contribute to increase in labour productivity and to higher long-term economic growth which are essential for poverty alleviation (World Bank), Further it goes on to add, "Higher education investments are important for economic growth. They increase individual's productivity and incomes, as indicated by rate of return analysis, and they also produce significant external benefits not captured by such analysis". UNESCO in a paper entitled, "Documents of policies for the change and development of higher education maintains, state and society must perceive higher education not as a burden on federal budgets but as a long-term domestic investment, in order to increase economic competitiveness, cultural development and social cohesion. As a conclusion one could say that the public support to higher education is still essential in order to ensure its educational, social and institutional mission" (UNESCO, 1995). A well established correlation between investment in higher education and the level of social, economic and cultural development of a country has been recognized in this paper of UNESCO. Indeed, in a vast body of literature on the role of education in economic growth and numerous associated aspects, the positive effects have all along been acknowledged, in varying form and content. The best example is a set of pioneering studies under which Schultz pleaded that expenditures on education must be treated as an investment in the increased capacity of labour to produce material goods. Although the quantitative results of these early studies were highly disparate across countries, yet positive effects of education are more weighty in determining the productivity levels of individuals. The beneficial interactions between higher education and such socio-economic variables as fertility, health and gender discrimination, on the one hand, and a heightened level of human articulation, including the urge to 'question and improve itself, improve one's immediate environment,' 'develop self-propelling norms of progress' and 'play better citizenry', on the other are now much better recognized (Knight, 1996, Birdsall, 1997). Thus, it needs hardly to be emphasized that human capital, most ostensibly in the form of higher education would be an extremely important, perhaps an inescapable, input for the future of developing economy like India.

We all are aware of the fact that how important invention and innovation are for long-term economic progress and how critical higher education is for the promotion of both. Also, higher education presides over the all round social and cultural advancement of the people of our populous country. Education in general and higher education in particular, which ensures availability of man power of right quantity and quality for all activities including health and education, has to be the equalizer in an otherwise efficiency driven market economy. Tilak, (2005) clarifies that "The externalities of education, including the dynamic externalities of higher education are indeed immense and they have profound positive effect on economic growth." Of course, behind the phenomenal economic might of China is its human resource, with adequate skills and commitment to hard work. A good 21 per cent of the males and 17 per cent of the females of the relevant age group in China re-enrolled in tertiary education. The percentages in the case of India are 14 and 9 for males and females respectively (K.C. Reddy, 2006). It is needless to say that tertiary education is now considered critical from the standpoint of achieving overall economic and social development. In many developing countries earnings of workers with higher education have risen substantially unlike in the past. In Latin America and the Caribbean, labour market returns to those who compeleted primary or secondary education have declined sharply while the returns to those with tertiary education have improved (World Development Report, 2007, p. 31). Recent research suggests that the increase in the number of skilled workers may have in fact boosted the value of further education and made it more important for growth. According to World Development Report, 2007 in many countries building a workforce with higher order skills is an important part of improving the climate for investment, acquiring a competitive edge, and generally maintaining an engine of growth.

The 2007 World Development Report maintains that "The situation of young people today presents the world with an unprecedented opportunity to accelerate growth and reduce poverty. Because labour is the main asset of the poor, making it more productive is the best way to reduce poverty. This requires enhancing the opportunities to earn money and developing the human capital to take advantage of those opportunities" (World Development Report, 2007, p. 2) and so India, to reap benefits from this demographic dividend needs to formulate appropriate expansion without compromising on both equity and quality. The role of higher education in national development cannot be denied in India since the lop-sided employment structure that has steadily evolved itself over the preceding decades leaves no options but to effect a substantial switchover of workers from agriculture to non-agricultural activities, in the years to come too.

It is needless to say that in the rapidly changing globalized economy knowledge is the driving force and quantity and quality of highly specialized human resources determine their competence in the global market which has increased opportunities for those countries with good levels of education and *vice versa*.

HIGHER EDUCATION IN INDIA

Today, India is the third largest higher education system in the world after China and the U.S.A. in terms of enrolment and in terms of the number of institutions, the country is the largest higher education system in the world. India has a strong tradition of higher education since ancient times. On the guidelines given by Macaulay and Wood's Dispatch (1857) the first three universities—Culcutta, Madras and Bombay were established in 1857. To begin with, colleges set-up in India were affiliated to British Universities and the pre-independence period 1857 to 1947 remained the period of slow development of institutions of higher education in India but there has been substantial growth in higher education after Independence with respect to number of institutions, teachers as well as student enrolments. However, the percentage of students enrolled in higher education in India is only 8, which is less than percentage of enrolled students in other developing countries like Thailand, Philippines, Indonesia, Mexico and Brazil having 20.1 per cent, 27.4 per cent, 11.1 per cent, 14.8 per cent and 11.3 per cent respectively. Due to lack of facilities for effective vocational education at the school level, there has been overcrowding of higher education institutions, despite the fact that it had little relevance for the job market, which requires maily skilled labour force. Overall status of vocational and technical education is low in the country resulting in abysmally low level of human capital base in comparison to many countries (Jha, B.K., 2008).

The colonial era ended by paving the masses of people mostly untouched by any formal education. This holds true particularly for the largest countries in the region, India, Pakistan and Indonesia. They entered their time of independence with a very low rate of literacy, probably far below one fifth of the adult population (Gunnar Myrdal, 1972). At the Independence India had 20 universities and 500 colleges located in different parts of the country. It enrolled around a hundred thousand students in higher education. Participation of women was limited and those who graduated annually were no more than a couple of dozen or so (G.M. Bhatt and S.A. Padder, 2008). In the post-independence period, higher education has expanded fast, and it is mostly public in nature. On the eve of India Golden Jubilee of its Independence, that is by 1995-96 there were 228 universities of which, there are 15 central universities set-up by the Acts of Parliament, 164 state universities set-up by Acts of state legislatures, and 99 deemed to be universities set-up under the UGC Act. These 228 universities include 8 open universities and 33 agricultural universities and the remaining institutions of national importance and 4 other independent institutions. The total number of institutions of higher education including universities and colleges have increased to 17973.

TABLE 2

Growth of Higher Education Institutions and Enrolment in India

Year	*Universities*	*Colleges*	*Total HE/s*	*Enrolment (in million)*
1947-48	20	496	516	0.2
1950-51	28	578	606	0.2
1960-61	45	1819	1864	0.6
1970-71	93	3277	3370	2.0
1980-81	123	4738	4861	2.8
1990-91	184	5748	5932	4.4
2000-01	268	11146	11412	8.8
2005-06	348	17625	17973	10.5

Source: UGC.

TABLE 3

Estimated Stock of Manpower by Major Categories

	2001	*2000*	*1991*	*1981*
Graduates				
Arts	8769.0	8392.8	5501.9	3242.6
Science	4024.9	3837.7	2430.3	1434.6
Commerce	4853.1	4573.6	2468.0	1054.2
Post Graduates				
Arts	3917.3	3718.4	2185.3	1113.6
Science	805.0	767.1	482.1	292.4
Commerce	902.5	841.7	403.5	148.3

Source: Statistical Outline of India, 2003-04.

Thus, the disturbing feature has been the proliferation of universities and colleges, especially for general education, which donot prepare for a career while a majority terminate at the bachelor's degree level. Moreover, the degree-holders have little knowledge or skill, they remain unemployable thus adding to the growing mismatch between the educational system and the employment market and exacerbating the phenomenon of educated unemployment.

TABLE 4

Technical Education

	2001	*2000*	*1991*	*1981*
Engineers				
Degree-holders	1024,4	969.5	519.6	304.9
Diploma-holders	1531.0	1456.5	859.3	425.8
Graduates				
Medicine	391.9	380.5	296.11	219.5
Dentistry	24.04	22.9	13.9	8.0
Agri-Science	238.6	231.2	168.4	109.8
Veterinary	6.5	46.3	34.4	24.4

Source: Statistical Outline of India, 2003-04.

TABLE 5

Growth of Degree Diploma Institutions and Sanctioned Intake in Engineering in Post-Independence Era

Year	*Degree*	*No. of Institutions in take*	*Diploma*	*No. of Institutions in take*
1950	50	3700	48	4200
1960	110	16000	195	26500
1970	143	18200	309	43500
1980	158	28500	332	49200
1990	337	66600	879 1	122002
2000	776	185753	1215	211894
2003	1203	359721	197	24298

Source: (i) Technical Education in Independent India.
(ii) The AICTE Annual Reports.

Hereby, it is worth-mentioning that there are significant social and economic difference between developed and developing countries and many of the underlying causes of these differences are rooted in the long history of development of such nations and include social, cultural and economic variables, historical and political elements, international relations, geographical factors. These, however, do not tell the whole story. The social and economic growth of the developed countries is dependent on an essential emphasis on education, science and technology. The basic problems of developing countries like India are the weak educational and scientific infrastructure and a lack of appreciation of the importance of education in general and higher education in particular as an essential ingredient of economic and social development. An essential prerequisite to a country's technological progress is early recognition of necessity of a good educational system. This was one of the key factors that contributed to Japan's economic success.

TABLE 6

Expenditure on Higher Education in India (Center+State)

Year	*Expenditure on. Education as % of GDP*	*Expenditure on Higher Education as% of Expenditure on Education*	*Expenditure of Higher Education as % of GDP*
1989-90	3.59	15.6	0.34
1990-91	3.52	12.S	0.33
1991-92	3.44	9.78	0.41
1992-93	3.78	10.79	0.40
1993-94	3.68	10.97	0.39
1994-95	3.61	10.81	0.37
1995-96	3.60	10.14	0.35
1996-97	3.57	9.77	0.35
1997-98	3.53	10.01	0.38
1998-99	3.85	9.93	0.46
1999-2000	4.17	10.21	0.41
2000-01	4.27	10.72	0.43
2001-02	3.81	9.83	0.38
2003-04	3.79	9.75	0.39
2003-04	3.50	9.27	0.35
2004-05 (RE)	3.68	9.63	0.37
2005-06 (BE)	3.73	9.71	0.36

Source: Analysis of Budgeted Expenditure on Education, Ministry of HRD, GoI, New Delhi.

India is in the process of transforming itself into a developed nation by 2020. Yet have 350 million people who need literacy and many more who have to acquire employable skills to suit the emerging India and the globe.

Over the last 50 years, successive governments have been committed to achieving the national goal of universal education. However, 35 per cent of our adult population are yet to achieve literacy. The expenditure on education as a percentage of our gross domestic product has direct impact on our literacy. Today our expenditure on education in India is little more than 4 per cent of our GDP and if we have to achieve nearly 100 per cent literacy, it is necessary to increase its expenditure on education to about 6 to 7 per cent of the GDP. As percentage of total expenditure on education the expenditure on higher education came down from 15.69 per cent in 1989-90 to 9.71 per cent in 2005-06 (BE).

HIGHER EDUCATION IN THE ERA OF GLOBALISATION

Globalisation is a process associated with increasing economic openness, growing economic interdependence and deepening economic integration in the World economy. It is used in a normative sense to prescribe a strategy of development based on a rapid integration with the World Economy (Deepak Nayyer, 2007) Whereas in a positive sense it describes a process of integration into the World Economy. Indeed, it is a multi-dimensional phenomenon and its gathering momentum is also beginning to reshape higher education.

Globalisation which is driven by market forces whether the threat of competition or the lure of profit has let to the emergence of higher education as business. Globalisation which is driven by the technological revolution in transport and communication which has set aside geographical barriers so that distance and time matter little; has led to a dramatic transformation in distance education as a mode of delivery. It is discernible in the national context as well as in the international context with a rapid expansion of cross-border transactions in higher education.

The impact of globalisation is visible in terms of what

is taught as well as what is researched and choices of students were not longer shaped by their interest but on the contrary, the popularity and the availability of courses are being shaped by market as students and parents display strong revealed preferences to demand higher education that makes young people employable. The employability of students is, of course, a driving force behind the creation of more places for vocational courses in higher education and it is also inducing universities to introduce new courses, for which there is a demand in the market, because these translate into lucrative fees as an important source of income. The research agenda of universities is guided by markets as resources for research in life science, medicine, engineering or economics are abundant while resources for research in philosophy, linguistics, history or literature are scarce which reveals a premium on applied research and a discount on theoretical research. Globalisation is beginning to influence professional education like engineering, management, medicine or law with a view to coaxing a harmonisation of academic programmes as these professional education has become more global and less national. The world of distance education is somewhat different as market forces and technical progress have opened up a new world of opportunities in higher education for those who missed the opportunity but these opportunities and access come at a price which may not be affordable for some, particularly in developing countries or transition economies.

In India higher education has come at the cross-roads in the era of globalisation. The state played a key role in the development of higher education after Independence but the situation has changed with the adoption of LPG strategy and advocates of privatisation and commercialisation of Indian higher education system are optimistic that it will improve quality efficiency and accountability in the educational institutions. G.K. Pillai, Special secretary, in the Ministry of Commerce, GoI, is of the opinion that every year the outgo from India on education to foreign countries is more than $ 4 bn. If foreign universities are allowed to set-up shop in our country, this huge amount can be very well saved (George, 2006). Even as Prime Minister, Dr. Manmohan Singh is seeking more and more private investment in higher education but education wants privatisation and commercialisation of higher education to be restricted to the minimum desirable level majority view at a meeting on the issue organized by National Institute of Education Planning and Administration (May, 2006) attended by 64 eminent economists favoured a law banning such commercialisation and recommended unanimously.

- All commercialisation of education, which should be unambiguously defined, should be banned by a suitable Act of Parliament.
- Private investment in education may be encouraged. However, it must be made clear that this cannot be for profit-making purpose, in however disguised a form.

Indeed, education cannot be treated as an industry, opening up of the education sector for foreign players. It will lead to rampant commercialisation of education which is already suffering from commercialisation and this is reason for denying to open the education system by several countries of Third World and muslim nations as doing so might affect the local and cultural sensitivities in addition to commercialisation. It is but true that investment in higher education particularly science, technology, research, etc. both by government and private sectors is required but private sectors should not be allowed to be guided mainly profit motive. There is no denying the fact that India has no quality education and there is no scope for quality improvement in the case of privatisation and commercialisation of higher education because private institutions function on the principle of profit maximisation. While until now there is no formal private university in India, there are large number of private colleges in the general and technical education spheres. Private colleges that form about three-fourths of the total number of colleges, are of two types : privately managed but publicly funded colleges familiarly known as government aided colleges, and privately managed and funded colleges known as unaided colleges. The private aided colleges have not contributed significantly to easing the financial burden of the government, as more than 95 per cent of the recurring expenditure, and sometimes even the capital expenditure, is met by public exchequer. Pure or unaided private colleges do provide financial relief to the government in providing higher education, but at huge and long-term economic and non-economic cost to the society. In the recent period, growth of private engineering and medical colleges has been remarkable. They charge donations and capitation fees. While other colleges are, by definition, non-profit institutions, many of these institutions not merely cover their costs, but also make profits, which are not necessarily reinvested in education (G.M. Bhatt and S.A. Padder, 2008) and so is the government may encourage private initiatives in higher education but not commercialisation.

Gunner Myrdal has rightly observed that "the main reforms in education in all underdeveloped countries are of a qualitative nature (Gunnar Myrdal, 1970). In India, there exist a number of sub viable institutions and as many as almost 50 per cent of the 9703 affiliated colleges in 1997-98 are not eligible for the UGC assistance as they either do not fulfil the conditions for recognition under our Act (2F) or even if recognized do not come under our grant (12B) for want of minimum requirements. There are, approximately 9703 colleges of which 4935 are recognized for development grants as of 1997-98. Thus, the most worrisome fact has been the proliferation of the universities and colleges, mainly for general education (B.K. Jha, 2005). It is estimated that one college is established everyday, sometimes with the possible exception of Sundays, and one university is established every three or four months (A.S. Desai, 1999) providing the bachelor's degree to a majority of the student (80%) who expect to find a job, but suffer only frustration. The U.R. Rao Commission which has reviewed the performance of all technical education trans-attention to the unsustainable expansion of technical education and makes for reaching recommendation to achieve excellence in this sector. In his report he has observed, "a serious situation has arisen in recent years because of mushrooming of a large number of private technical institutions and polytechnics. Barring some exceptions, there is scant regard for maintenance of standards. "For instance there are 1208 engineering degree colleges in which 986 are in the private sector with a total sanctioned intake of over 0.36 million students. Further there are 1006 MCA and 930 Master of Business Administrations with an intake of about 53000 and 64000 students respectively. Obviously, this is occurring of the expense of quality.

In the global era we need scientists and engineers. We need bio-technologists. We need more technical hands and skilled labours. Where are they? They are not here because Macaulay is still here we are in need of job-oriented education. We need to check brain drain. Then, education may prove instrumental in economic development of our country (B.K. Jha, 2006). Of course "At any point of time, weakening of higher education sector would weaken the forces of competitiveness and efficiency in the functioning of different sectors of economy" (Panchmukhi, 2002), There is no need to be frustrated and there is need to take some positive bold steps in this direction. Our first Prime Minister has rightly observed that" Given opportunities, India can produce hundred or thousand of absolutely first class people in various branches of work and knowledge. But the people donot have those opportunities." It is but true that India ranks second in terms of availability of scientists and engineers and also in domestic software companies in international markets (Dutta Lanvin and Fina, 2004). However. India also suffers due to brain drain as its ranking is 54. Brain drain can have a debilitating effect on national governing structures, management capacities, productive sections, and tertiary institutions. For example, at least 40 per cent of the graduates of highly regarded Indian Institutes of Technology seek employment abroad for which globalisation has widened the scope. A strong steps need to be taken to attract Indian professors, researchers and Scientists working abroad into Indian world class institutions by offering a chair and lucrative conditions for leaving their foreign engagements. At the same time in terms of enhancing quality with quantitative growth in enrolment strategy, attempt must be made to improve the infrastructure and quality (i) few excellent institutions be identified to develop world class institutions, (ii) a small number of potential institutions be developed into excellent institutions, (iii) a large number of less than average institutions be developed into average institutions, and (iv) institutions that are not viable in terms of students and teachers should be merged into viable institutions or converted into some other useful institutions (S. Bhushan, 2005). An additional resource should be mobilised to develop these institutions which must offer comprehensive programme of research and teaching and should emerge as 21st century institutions of excellence. The model to be followed essentially draws inspiration from Higher Education Project 211 launched in 1995 in China or 21st century centers of Excellence plan in Japan started in summer of 2002 and the new policy of Brain Korea 21 designed to elevate the quality to world class standards in selected graduate schools and selected fields of natural sciences (S. Bhushan, 2005).

The UGC recognizes that the new global scenario poses challenges for higher education system which it has not had to face in its history and it becomes highly desirable to achieve global standards of higher education. Each university and college needs to define its mission and its vision and tailors its programmes, accordingly. Making higher and technical education systems more purposeful involves in enabling the system to respond to the emerging challenges of globalisation (B.K. Jha, 2006). It is painful that India which was well reputed for its good quality educational system, where students outside of our country came to get such education had gradually lost such prestigious status in this concern with an adoption of Macaulay's model of education designed to serve of British Raj (B.K. Jha, 2008). For revival of our lost prestige, it is desirable that education is all about creativity and creativity is all about commitment. Without commitment you cannot have good education, which has more to do with quality than with quantity which is also important (Arun Kumar, 2005)

Undoubtedly, it is a tragedy that while we need to generate more knowledge, our public university system, which was doing some good research, is in a deep crisis because of inadequate funding. So, many public universities are hardly doing any research because of financial crises and the private universities which are mushrooming all over are doing little or no research because they only wish to make high profits (Arun Kumar, 2005). In the era of globalisation such type of scenario in higher education system has emerged which has adverse repercussion on the quality of education. The culture of markets and the advent of commercialisation could erode both values and morality that are the life blood of higher education. The commercialisation of universities means business in education and the entry of private players in higher education means education as business. Thus, there are dangers inherent in such commercialisation and so the real challenge is in improving the system. Realising the importance of competition in the global era competition between universities for academic excellence is highly desirable but what we expect from our mai-baap culture. A defeated politician, not academician, is appointed as a chancellor of universities. A distinguished vice-chancellor of a presidency university is harassed by the staff of a chancellor and the most worrisome is the appointment of vice-chancellor on political basis and not on merit basis. For quality improvement at the higher educational level it is required to attract the best human resources to teaching for which teaching at the higher education level needs to be more lueratic in comparison to other services as found at one time but it has lost its attraction as a most desirable profession. On the contrary, at least Bihar remained such a state where all the measures for humiliating teachers at higher education level were taken by the government and teaching in such level lost its prestigious value. And so there is need for making higher education such attractive profession to attract talented persons in this from all the corners of the nation and abroad too.

Hereby, it is noteworthy that our government is conscious for improving quality of higher education. The HRD Ministry and the National Knowledge Commission (NKC) have recommended linking all educational and research institutions of higher pearning through a broadband network and they have agreed that internet connection needs to be provided to students and faculty. While NKC's recommendation covers all higher education institutions, the HRD Ministry has decided to provide free internet connection to faculty in central universities IIL's and IIM's. This will cost Rs. 50 crore annually. With broadband connectivity, the NKC also wants institutes to adopt e-governance for the benefit of students and teachers. NKC chairperson, Sam Pitroda in his recommendations submitted to Prime Minister Manmohan Singh said, "To optimise the potential of institutions engaged in generation and dissemination of knowledge, it is important to connect them (the institutions) through a high speed broadband network." The plan will cost Rs. 200-400 crore annually for 1000 institutions. In addition, there would be one time capital investment of about Rs. 1000 crores for upgrading the local Area Network of these institutions.

EMERGING REALITY

Long before globalisation Mahatma Gandhi expressed his opinion, "I donot want my house to be walled on all sides and my windows to be stuffed. I want the culture of all the lands to be blown about my house as freely as possible. But I refuse to be blown-off my feet by any". What is happening now ? In the era of globalisation we accept to be blown-off our feet and we are not ready to accept the stark reality that any thoughtless entry into the global educational market can end up in harming the vital interests of students for generations to come. We are not ready to decide about the nature and extent of globalisation that can be constructively introduced in our socio-economic and educational system. Moreover, we are forgetting to give due priority to the paramountcy of national interests. There needs to be alert to know warning bell of World Bank's Tasks force, 2000. "Globalisation can lead to unregulated and poor quality higher education with the world-wide marketing of fraudulent degrees or other re-called higher education credentials." (World Bank's Task Force, 2000) And now the situation has emerged in which India is likely to turn into "an increasingly attractive market for foreign universities and hence other nations are going to use GATS' provisions to their advantage." (Arun Nigvekar, 2002)

Education, as a service industry is part of globalisation process under the umbrella of General Agreement on Trade in Services (GATS) and this might "force countries with quite different academic needs and resources to conform to structures inevitably designed to service the interest of the most powerful academic systems and corporate educational providers breeding inequality and dependence." (Altbact, 2002) The crux of globalisation in education sector is that the teaching learning is no longer for building of nation but a business tor profit-making.

India will have close to 11 million students seeking higher education by 2011, and a sizeable number of them will look abroad for it (P. Singh and A.K. Singh, 2008). Recently, the European Union has announced 100 Erasmus Mundus fellowships for Indians as Europe like America and Australia wants to attract bright, young Indians for education, skilled work and perhaps citizenship. The most worrisome is the malafide intentions behind attracting Indian students for higher education. For instance, counselor, Education, Science and Training, Australian High Commission, Quentin Stevenson Parks said. "India has the required intellectual capital and we need bright students for our projects and ventures." Likewise the assistant secretary of state, consular affairs, US department of state, Maura Marty stated, "The education industry in the US is a $ 12 bn industry...... Students and business travelers became our number one priority so that we could regain the competitive advantage of attracting students to the US. It was our responsibility to make visa process as efficient a process as we could as the hard earned salaries of Indian parents are best applied in American Versities. Indian students bring a great diversity to our campus, great experience, great wisdom and they are good students. Thus, globalisation has widened the scope for brain drain.

The Indian students' need to go abroad stems from the fact that they feel that the western markets offer better job opportunities with high pay packets, they are safe from the point of law and they offer a good quality of life what is attractive to an Indian is the global recognition for a foreign degree. Until now, a UK or a US degree was more acceptable worldwide company. The Indian Institutes of technology have now got global recognition thanks to the large number of Indians who have reached position of eminence in the United States (P. Singh or A.K. Singh, 2008). And so policies for higher education need to be formulated in the pursuit of development, so as to minimize the dangers and capture the opportunities.

References

Gunnar Myrdal (1972), Asian Drama: An Inquiry into the Poverty of Nations, Vintage Book. New York.

Gunnar Myrdal (197 1), The Challenge of World Poverty, Penguin Books.

Sudhanshu Bhushan (2005), Knowledge Economy and Higher Education in *The Indian Journal of Labour Economics*, Vol. 48 and 4, Oct.-Dec.

Arun Kumar (2005), In Social Sector Development (ed.), Dolly Arora.

A.B. Desai (1999), Higher Education at the Cross Roads of the 20th and 21st Centuries (booklet).

Rangarajan (1999), Indian Economy: Essay on Money and Finance UBSPD, New Delhi.

P. Singh and A.K. Singh (2008), Emerging Trends in Education in the Global Era (ed) Meenu Agrawal Impact of Globalisation on Development, Deep and Deep Publication, New Delhi.

G.M. Bhatt and S.A. Padder (2008), Indian Higher Education in the New Millennium: Challenges and Opportunities (ed.), Meenu Agrawal. Education in Third World and India, Kanishka Publication, New Delhi.

Deepak Nayyer (2007), Gobalisation: What Does it Mean for Higher Education in *Economic and Political Weekly*, Dec. 15.

B.B. Bhattacharya (2007), Education, Skill Formation and India's Economic Development, Presidental Address in the 90th Annual Conference of IEA.

K.C. Reddy (2006), On Reforming and Re-positioning the Higher Education Sector, Presidential Address of the 89th Annual Conference of IEA.

G.K. Chadha (2003), What is Dominating the Indian Labour Market? Peacock's Feathers or Feet in the 45th Annual Conference, ISLE.

B.K. Jha (2006), Economic of Indian Education, Health and Human Development: Emerging Challenges in the Global Era. In the 89th Annual Conference, Vol. 15A.

B.K. Jha (2008), Role of Higher Education in Developing Country like India: Identifying Worry Spots (ed.), Meenu Agrawal, Education in Third World and India, Kanishka Publication, New Delhi.

Different Governmental Reports National and International.

22

Access to Higher Education: Weaker Section and Equity

BHARAT BHUSHAN AND NEERAJ KUMAR

In the first decade of 21st century inter connectivity between nations, between regions to regions and place to place has increased. The knowledge also has got no boundary line. Therefore, it is essential to examine the impact of globalisation and education. Our ancient Rishies give the slogan of "entire universe is ours". Education has already crossed the national boundary line. In the new global scenario; the restructuring of state has led to the restructing of education policy also across the globe. The emphasis on efficiency outcome and productivity in the restructuring of state has been a hallmark of restructuring of education policy also. This has led to the formulation of market-friendly education policies with greater role for private corporate sector. The obvious outcome of this process is that efficiency and outcome have become parameters of an educational policy. Efficiency refers to reduced cost and outcome refers to results of examination.

Efficiency in education system assume that education is one of the many commodity to be sold in the market.

Students are perceived as potential consumers, the teachers as factors of production and schools and colleges as factories to produce degrees and certificate at the minimum cost possible. Here education becomes a means of earning profits. Social justice, equity and ethics are sacrificed for profit. State withdraws itself and 'survival of the fittest' become the norm of educational system in market-economy.

There is constant reduction in expenditure on higher education in real terms. It has never crossed 4 per cent of GDP whereas the target is 6 per cent as fixed by New Economic Policy (NEP). Birla-Ambani Report (2000) advocates full cost recovery from students and immediate privatisation of entire higher education. The report considers education as a "profitable market". Finance Ministry (Government of India) suggested higher education as "non-merit goods" to deduct subsidy over it. There is constant and consistent attempt by the Government for reduction in the subsidy on higher education and increase institution fees. The scholarships to weaker sections is not sufficient to meet the costs involved. Loans are no remedy. The bitter truth is that changes in the educational policy in India in the name of globalisation will adversely affect the educational attainment of weaker sections in India. Mainly, the upper caste rich people will have access to technical and professional higher education.

It will mean only primary and secondary education to SCs and STs and mainly the upper caste rich people will have access to higher education. It will promote caste rigidity and inequality in the attainment of higher education.

Education has been the most powerful weapon for the upward maturity of the weaker sections via the linkages with job market. The dream of India Government and the World Bank along with the economists like Prof. Amartya Sen to empower the weaker section in India through trusted primary and secondary education may remain a pipe dream in the absence of a provision of a strong complementary higher education system for the weaker sections. Basic and secondary education alone will not make the weaker section competent enough to competent in the global market. The weaker section students will be locked into low paid domestic job markets and will remain poor. This is how globalisation will reinforce caste-based inequality in India.

The crux of the issue involved is that with liberalisation and privatisation and market section of higher education. Specially the technical education has become very costly and expensive. It is beyond the reach of SCs and STs most of whom are poor, on the other hand the objective of Union Government is to use higher education as a tool of equaliser with providing maximum opportunity to students belonging to SCs and STs. For this scholarships, bank loan and other concessions have been provided to them. Unfortunately reservation policy has not been implemented in right earnest. Banks are hesitant to grant loans to them and it becomes for the weaker section to enter into the field of higher education specially technical and managerial education is rising rapidly. As a result, poor or stuck is low-staller services with little upward mobility.

SOME IMPORTANT POINTS ARE NOW SUGGESTED

1. There is need for increasing use of information and communication technology.
2. There should be no compromise about quality in education as in high time that one must improve quality of teaching in Indian University.
3. The challenge for India today is to provide access quality education to a large proportion of population across the country with focus on vulnerable sections of the population across the country so as to make higher education inclusive.
4. There is a need to create a motivating environment for teachers and they should be held accountable about their expected work.
5. There is need for increasing public private partnership (PPP) in education sector.
6. An enabling environment needs to be created for women to become economically, politically and socially empowerment.
7. For inclusive growth, there is need to expand vocational training to a large number of people as possible.

8. It is also necessary that earnest efforts we made towards human transformation through the inculcation of human value.

References

Rao, Bhanoj, (2007), Higher Education: The Quality Issue", *Business Line*, October 30.

Tilak, J.B.G. (2005), "Higher Education in Trishanku Hanging Between State and Market, *Economic and Political Weekly*, September 10 (2005).

Schultz, T.W. (1961), "Investment in Human Capital", *American Economic Reviews*, March 30 (2007).

Schultz, T.W. (1960), "Capital Formation by Education," *Journal of Political Economy*, December, 1960.

Government of India: *Economic Survey*, 2007-08.

Reddy, K.C. (2007), "On Reforming and Re-positioning the Higher Education Sector", *The Indian Economic Journal*, April-June

Goyal, Malini (2007) "Rising Perspective, Growing Inequality", *The Economic Times*, November.

PART III

EDUCATION IN INDIA: INTER-STATE DISPARITIES

23

Dynamics of Education and Economic Development: An Experience of Indian States

R.K. RANA AND SUPARN KUMAR

I. INTRODUCTION

It has been widely recognised that human capital plays a dominant role in the growth and development of an economy. The last four decades have witnessed an intensive concern about the researches on investment in human capital which has also been inspired by the pioneering works of T.W. Shultz (1961, 1962) and Garry S. Becker (1964a, 1964b, 1964c). In today's competitive age the focus of every economy is, therefore, on the human capital formation which may be the outcome of the availability of proper health and quality education to the masses in the country. The increase in the efficiency of human capital through these factors may also increase the productivity in the economy, which is one of the important measures of growth of an economy.

However, there are some factors such as the unending increase in population, prevalence of poverty, low per capita income, uneven distribution of income, increasing trend in terrorist activities, alarming increase in corruption, existence of weak and unstable governments, etc., which inhibit the growth of human capital formation in the Indian economy. These are the factors which are negatively-related to the health and education of the individuals which further affect the human resource development at the macro-level. It therefore, becomes obligatory for the concerned governments to take care of such negative factors existing in the economy.

It is obvious that health and education are the two main components in the human capital formation; however, the focus in the present paper will remain on different dynamics and aspects of education sector only. Education is a panacea for all evils in the Indian economy and it is a fact as all the problems of the economy are somehow related to education (Dua, 2006). It is, therefore, of paramount interest to access the different dynamic role including relationship and pattern of education in the context of Indian states and this kind of study can find its applications for attaining the objective of inclusive and balanced development of the economy.

Most of the earlier studies, e.g., Mincer (1958), Houthakker (1959), Millar (1960), Keat (1960), Denison (1960), Behrman *et al.* (1985) and Galor (1989), etc. have been conducted in various countries to ascertain the contribution of human capital as a factor in improving its earning prospects. In India too, Dutta (1982) and Harbhajan Singh (1983, 1984) have identified human capital as a source of income inequality. However, the present study departs from the earlier studies in the sense that it is directly related to education and its examination through various aspects in the context of the Indian economy.

II. METHODOLOGY

The education, being a central variable for the growth and development of an economy, needs a comprehensive analysis and for this purpose the present study has been divided into three sections. In section-I, the literacy rate in India has been examined from different aspects over the last five decades.

Section-II is devoted to the State-wise analysis taking literacy ratio as their dependent variable. The search of some independent variables which may affect the literacy ratio of the states has also been made. A variety of multiple (linear as well as log-linear) regression models, to explain the behaviour of literacy ratio in the Indian states, have been attempted for two decades, i.e., 1991 and 2001. To examine the dispersion of the variables among the states, the use of co-efficient of variation has been made.

In the final section, an attempt has been made to examine whether literacy ratio in the Indian states can play the instrumental role in the growth of per capita state domestic product (SDP) by taking linear as well as log-linear regressions between them where per-capita SDP is considered as a proxy variable to measure the development of a state in India. A significant relation between the two will certainly be a hint in enhancing the per-capita SDP of a state which is lagging behind with the increase in its literacy ratio. Finally, a time-series regression (linear and log-linear) between literacy ratio (dependent) and percentage of budget expenditure on education to GDP (independent) has been considered to examine the significance of percentage budget expenditure on education.

Overall, the effectiveness of literacy in examining the growth and development of the Indian states has been elaborated. For the overall and balanced growth of the Indian economy, the present study carries an important place particularly in the present era of globalization.

III. DATA SOURCE

The key variable of the present study has been literacy rate in India from different angles, e.g., males, females, rural and urban areas, and caste during various decades. For the state-wise analysis of literacy, it has used poverty ratio (X_1), per-capita state domestic product (X_2), percentage of budget expenditure to gross domestic product (X_3), and number of institutions (X_4) at two decades, 1991 and 2001 as independent variables. The relevant data on the above variables have been procured from Censes of India 1981, 1991 and 2001, Report of the Expert Group on Estimation of Proportion and Number of Poor (1993), Government of India, *Economic Survey* (1994-95) and (2005-06), Ministry of Human Resource Development, etc.

The period of the study varies over five decades (1951 to 2001) and the data for the state-wise analysis of the literacy ratio are taken only for two decades (1991, 2001). Some requisite calculations and compilations have been made on the available data to describe the various aspects related to literacy in India and Indian States. The main findings of the study, through requisite calculations from the data, have been produced in the section of 'results and discussion' below.

IV. RESULTS AND DISCUSSION

SECTION I

In the present section an attempt has been made to examine literacy in India, in heuristic manner, with a number of related aspects. Table 1, throws light on the growth of literacy and gender inequalities in India over a period of six decades (1951 to 2001). The data reveal that literacy has improved from 18.20 per cent in 1951 to 65.38 per cent in 2001. But the literacy rate of males rose from 27.16 per cent to 75.96 per cent during this period but those of females from 8.86 per cent to 54.28 per cent only, which explicitly reveals inequality in sex education. This nature of disparity in sex education has also been highlighted in the last column of the table.

This disparity ratio between male and female literacy rate, shown by this column, is witnessing a declining trend (3.1 to 1.4) during these decades which is a positive sign for the overall development of the social sector and economy. It also implies that female literacy rate during the last 50 years has been growing at a faster rate than male literacy. During the period, female literates increased by 513 per cent, but male literates grew by 180 per cent which is a healthy trend and needs to be strengthened.

Table 2 is based on the distribution of literates and illiterates among population aged 7 years and above by sex

TABLE I

Progress of Literacy Rate in India

(in per cent)

Year	*Persons*	*Male*	*Female*	*Disparity Ratio (M/F)*
1951	18.33	27.16	8.86	3.1
1961	28.31	40.40	15.34	2.6
1971	34.45	45.95	21.97	2.1
1981	43.67	56.50	29.85	1.9
1991	52.21	64.13	39.29	1.6
2001	65.38	75.96	54.28	1.4

Note: Literacy rates for 1951, 1961 and 1971 relate to population aged 5 and above. The rates for years 1981, 1991 and 2001 relate to the population aged 7 years and above.

Source: *Census of India, 2001.*

and area during 1981 to 2001. The Table 2 reveals that male-literacy rate improved from 49.7 per cent to 58.58 per cent in rural areas during the last three decades, whereas female literacy rate increased from 21.8 per cent to 38.33 per cent. The disparity ratio declined from 2.28 to 1.53. As against this, the situation in urban areas was much better. Male literacy improved from 76.8 per cent in 1981 to 81.0 per cent during 1981 to 1991. While during 1991 to 2001, it witnessed a decline from 81 per cent to 75.04 per cent, which may be due to the shift of illiterate working class from rural areas to urban areas whereas female literacy improved from 56.4 per cent to 63.3 per cent during this period. Consequently, the disparity ratio declined from 1.36 to 1.19. This has underlined the fact that urbanization has a much greater positive effect in improving female literacy.

But in absolute terms, the number of illiterates was 302 million in 1981 but they increased to 468 million in 2001. In the urban areas the illiterates have grown from 42.5 million to 87.3 million during 1981 to 2001, while in the rural areas, they have grown from 260 million to 381 million for the same

TABLE 2

Distribution of Literates and Illiterates Among Population Aged 7 Years and Above by Sex and Area

Years/	Literates			Disparity	Illiterates		
Areas	Persons	Male	Female	Ratio (M/F)	Persons	Male	Female
			1981				
All areas	234.15	157.08	77.07		302.6	120.96	181.10
	(43.6)	(56.5)	(29.8)		(56.4)	(43.5)	(70.2)
Rural area	146.60	103.51	43.09	2.28	259.59	104.80	154.71
	(36.1)	(49.7)	(21.8)		(63.59)	(50.30)	(78.2)
Urban area	87.55	53.57	33.98	1.36	42.47	16.16	26.31
	(67.3)	(76.8)	(56.4)		(32.7)	(23.2)	(43.6)
			1991				
All areas	349.76	223.70	126.6		320.41	124.77	195.04
	(52.2)	(64.2)	(39.2)		(47.8)	(35.8)	(60.8)
Rural area	218.32	148.38	71.94	1.91	271.81	106.69	165.12
	(44.5)	(57.8)	(30.3)		(55.5)	(42.2)	(69.7)
Urban area	131.44	77.32	54.12	1.27	48.60	18.08	30.52
	(73.1)	(81.0)	(63.9)		(26.9)	09.0)	(36.1)
			2001				
All areas	560.69	336.53	224.15		467.92	195.62	272.30
	(54.51)	(63.24)	(45.15)		(45.49)	(36.76)	(54.85)

Rural area	361.87	223.55	138.32	1.53	380.62	158.05	222.57
	(48.74)	(58.58)	(38.33)		(51.26)	(41.42)	(61.67)
Urban area	198.82	112.98	85.83	1.19	8730	37.57	49.73
	(69.49)	75.04	(63.32)		(30.51)	(24.96)	(36.68)

Source: Census of India, 1981, 1991 and 2001.

period. This has highlighted the need for strengthening the efforts to increase literacy further, particularly in rural areas.

It can be easily observed from Table 3 that the highest number of persons fall in the category of primary class, which appears to be logical. Similarly, the lowest number of persons lie in the category of non technical diploma. The persons in other classes vary in between these two extreme cases. Another important feature of the table is that males out number females in all the categories of education as mentioned.

Section II

In today's scenario education is at the central place and may be taken as a panacea for curing all evils in the economy. The present section is, therefore, devoted to the study of the factors that may affect the literacy in the economy. With the objective of balanced development of the Indian economy, a state-wise analysis, for the search of independent variables affecting literacy, has been conducted at two different points of time. By presuming a linear relation between the literacy ratio (dependent variable) and poverty ratio, per capita SDP, percentage of budget expenditure on education to GDP, as independent variables, a few models with alternative permutations have been considered and their estimated results have been presented in by Table 4. It may be seen from the table that X_2 (per capita SDP) and X_3 (percentage of budget expenditure to GDP) are the two significant factors that may affect the literacy in the Indian States. Therefore, the states that are lagging behind in education may enhance it and bring it to the level of other states by increasing their per capita SDP and percentage of budget expenditure to GDP. This is the prime implication from this table and the central as well as the concerned state governments should consider it as a policy measure in improving the literacy of the states poor in education. This kind of policy measure will certainly boost the knowledge in India uniformly and help in attaining the objective of balanced development of the Indian economy.

TABLE 3

Classification of Education in India by Sex (2001)

Sex	*Below Primary*	*Primary*	*Middle*	*Matric/ Secondary*	*Inter-mediate Senior Secondary*	*Non-technical Diploma*	*Tech. Diploma*	*Graduate and above*
Persons	144831273	146740047	90226846	79229721	37816215	386146	3666680	37670147
Male	81148130	83525450	55940422	51201516	24596339	258604	2900839	25533308
Female	63683143	63215497	34286424	28028205	13219876	127542	765841	12136839

Source: Census of India, 2001.

TABLE 4

Estimated Results of the Regression Parameters (1991)

Sr. No.	*A—(Linear Relationship)* *Independent Variables*			*B—(Log-Linear Relationship)* *Independent Variables*		
	X_1	X_2	X_3	X_1	X_2	X_3
Dependent Variable(Y) (Literacy Ratio)						
1.	-0.11	0.0053*	7.74*	0.162	.92*	0.74*
	(0.50)	(5.45)	(3.67)	(1.03)	(3.99)	(3.48)
2.	—	0.0052*	6.86*	—	0.40*	0.397
	(5.59)		(6.03)		(16.07)	(2.63)
3.	—	—	12.38*	—	0.47*	—
			(12.3)		(74.69)	

Notes: (i) Figures in parentheses are t-values.

(ii) Y=Literacy Ratio, X_1=Poverty Ratio, X_2=Per-capita SDP, X_3=Percentage of budget expenditure on education to GDP.

(iii) *— The coefficients are significant at a=0.01.

Similarly, the Part-B of table, displays the behaviour of the literacy in the Indian states with the help of log-linear relationship between the dependent and independent variables. The results from the Part-B of the table reveal almost the same pattern as is shown in Part-A, and follows the similar kind of Interpretation.

Table 5 is related to the year 2001 and is very much similar to the Table 4. It can be seen from the table that the same two independent variables (X_2 and X_3) are significant in explaining the behaviour of the literacy among the Indian States. However, there is a significant shift between the estimated values of the parameters for this decade (1991 to 2001). The estimated results for the year 2001 are quite lesser than that of the year 1991, but the results are still significant, i.e. the impact of the factors has declined during the ten year period, which may be due to some external factors.

The other change is that the sign of the coefficient of poverty ratio has been reversed, i.e., has become positive in 2001 which was negative in 1991 though statistically insignificant. It seems to be illogical and it needs be further probed. The rest of the explanation of the estimated results for those two periods is almost similar and hence disposed of.

Table 6 is based upon the coefficient of variation for the variables among the Indian States for these two periods (1991, 2001). This measures the magnitude of the relative dispersion among the states and can be used to compare the level of inequality for two periods (i.e., 1991 and 2001). The table reveals that the disparity in literacy has declined from 24.83 per cent to 15.29 per cent which is a very healthy sign for the Indian economy.

Similarly, the inequality in X_3 (per cent of budget expenditure on education to GDP) has also reduced from 27.91 per cent to 17.87 per cent, i.e., the Indian states are heading towards a uniform distribution for this variable and is again a positive sign to promote the level of education among the states uniformly. However, the picture for the other two variables (poverty and per capita SDP) with regard to inequality is quite dismal.

TABLE 5

Estimated Results of the Regression Parameters (2001)

A—(Linear Relationship) B—(Log-Linear Relationship)
Dependent Variable (Y) (literacy Ratio)

S.No.	Independent Variables				Independent Variables			
	X_1	X_2	X_3	X_4	X_1	X_2	X_3	X_4
1.	0.24	0.002*	1.21*	5.28	0.09	0.36*	0.08	0.02
	(1.09)	(5.29)		(2.14)		(1.26)	(1.28)	(4.72)
	(0.45)		(1.13)					
2.	0.35	0.002*	1.00	—	0.07	0.39*	0.09	—
	(1.76)	(5.99)	(1.80)		(1.45)	(11.7)	(0.64)	
3.	—	0.002*	1.76*	7.24	—	0.36*	0.22*	0.006
		(6.14)	(6.58)	(1.89)		(10.1)	(2.13)	(0.48)
4.	—	0.002*	1.85*	—	—	0.41*	0.09*	—
		(6.81)	(6.43)			(37.7)	(2.72)	
5.	—	—	3.39*	—	—	0.44*		
			(16.4)			(156.9)		

Notes: (i) Figures in parentheses are t-values.
(ii) Y=Literacy Ratio, X_1=Poverty Ratio, X_2 =Per-capita SDP, X_3=Percentage of budget expenditure on education to GDP, X_4=No. of institutions.
(iii) *—The coefficients are significant at a=0.01.

TABLE 6

Coefficient of Variation (C.V.) of the Variables

Year	Y	X_1	X_2	X_3
1991	24.83	32.02	6.81	27.91
2001	15.29	52.13	36.93	17.87

Note: C.V.'s are calculated from the data on state variables using the formula: C.V.= s/x*100.

SECTION III

Here, in this section the effect of literacy rate has been examined on the growth and development of Indian states. The per capita state domestic product has been taken as a proxy measure for the growth and development of a state which is a simple and convenient way to represent the set of complex factors needed to measure the development of an economy. In this way, the present analysis is a simple approximation for the real and complex picture of the development of the Indian States.

The estimated results of the parameters have been shown in the Part-A of Table 7. In linear case, the regression coefficient (446.39) is statistically significant at one per cent level of significance. It implies that corresponding to one unit increase in literacy rate there is an increase of Rs. 446.40 in the per capita income of a state, which further has a policy implication in the sense that the states who are still backward must concentrate in enhancing their literacy level. In log-linear terms also the relations between per capita income of a state and its literacy rate is positive and statistically significant. The estimated regression coefficient (2.39) is statistically significant and it is the elasticity of per capita income to the literacy rate. Such type of empirical study is quite valuable for the policy formulations in an economy.

In Part-B of the table, a linear as well as log-linear regression between literacy rate(dependent) and percentage of budget expenditure on education to GDP for the Indian economy as a whole have been highlighted for the period

TABLE 7

Estimates of the Regression Models (2001)

Sr. No.	Model	A Coefficient	A t-Value	A R-Square	B Coefficient	B t-Value	B R-Square
1.	Linear	446.39*	4.76	0.80	12.51*	9.35	0.98
2.	Log-Linear	2.39*	5.38	0.84	0.64*	9.40	0.98

Notes: A—Dependent variable is per-capita SDP and independent variable is Literacy ratio.

B—Dependent variable is Literacy Ratio and independent variable is percentage of budget expenditure on education to GDP.

*—The coefficients are significant at a=0.01.

1951 to 2001. The results are again significant with the positive relationship between them. This implies that the share of expenditure on education to GDP may be taken as a significant instrument to enhance the literacy level in the economy, which is very necessary for its survival in today's competative world.

V. CONCLUSION AND SUGGESTIONS

The present study has investigated the pattern of education in India and its role in the development of Indian states and reached the following conclusions:

1. The literacy rates in India for persons, males and females during 1951 to 2001 have respectively increased from 18.33 per cent to 65.38 per cent, 27.16 per cent to 75.96 per cent and 8.86 per cent to 54.28 per cent.
2. During the last five decades female literates have increased by 513 per cent, while this increase for male literates is 180 per cent.
3. The literacy rates in India for persons, males and females during 1951 to 2001 have respectively increased from 3.1 to 1.4 (Table 1).
4. Its increase in female literacy ratio for rural areas is 4.2 times than that of males and it is 2.4 times

of male literary ratio in urban areas. The decline in male illiterates for rural areas is 1.48 times than that of females and the corresponding ratio for urban areas is 1.05 (Table 2).

5. The disparity ratio between male and female literacy (1981 to 2001) in rural and urban areas has declined from 2.28 to 1.53 and 1.36 to 1.19 respectively (Table 2).
6. The number of males is greater than female for every class made on education
7. The independent variables X_2 and X_3 are found to be statistically significant in linear and log-linear multiple regressions for the decades of 1991 and 2001, and the effect of X_2 and X_3 in 2001 is half of the effect in 1991.
8. The co-efficient of variation (CV) for the Indian states have declined for Y and X_3 and have increased for X_1 and X_2 over the two decades.
9. The literacy ratio is affecting per capita SDP significantly for both linear as well as log-linear regressions.
10. There is significant relationship between Y and X_3 for India as a whole in case of a time series regression models.

Suggestions

Out of a large number of factors affecting literacy ratio in Indian states only a few have been found significant in capturing the variation in state-wise literacy and such factors may be used as policy variables to increase literacy in those states that are lagging behind in such a crucial variable. It has been revealed that the inequality in X_1 and X_2 has increased over the decade (1991 to 2001) which is not good for the economy. The steps must be taken by the respective governments to reduce this inequality among the states to their lowest levels. In today's scenario, the growth and development of an economy is undoubtedly based on the human capital formation for which knowledge is the most crucial input. Therefore, to acquire mere literacy is not sufficient, it is the globally competitive knowledge which may place the economy in the list of the advanced economies of the world.

For the purpose, the focus must be on the quality education which in the prevailing conditions is not feasible. It is because the cost of the quality/professional education is increasing alarmingly and the poor persons may, therefore, be deprived of its attainment. The policy of reservation by the government in this is a solace for scheduled and backward castes, but it does not benefit the poor persons of other classes. Therefore, there is a need to moderate the reservation policy suitably so that every poor in the economy is covered. The reservation policy in this shape is quite deceptive and it should be based on the income of the households so that poors from all classes may be benefited. This kind of policy is very necessary to improve human capital of the economy and to make it globally competitive.

VI. LIMITATIONS OF THE STUDY

The area of the present study could be extended to many more aspects of education with more additional factors affecting it in India. However, the limitations of data availability, space, time and labour has confined us to restrict ourselves to the present study only. If these limitations would have not been there, the study would have been more fruitful.

REFERENCES

Atkinson, G.B.J (1983), Economics of Education, Hodder and Stoughton, London.

Becker, G.S. (1993), Human Capital, A Theoretical and Empirical Analysis with special references to Education, Chicago IL, University of Chicago Press.

Biswas, A. Arbinda *et al.* (1976), The New Education Pattern in India, Vikas Publication House.

Dreze, Sen (1997), Indian Development: Selected Regional Perspectives, Oxford University Press, *New Delhi.*

Dua, H.K. (2006), "Education Panacea of All Evils", *The Tribune,* August, Chandigarh, p. 1.

Government of India (1986), "NPE", Department of Education, Ministry of Human Resource Development, New Delhi.

Houthakker, H.S. (1959), "Education and Income", *Review of Economics and Statistics*, Vol. 41.

Jandhyala, Tilak, B.G (1997), "Five Decades of Under-Investment in Education", *Economic and Political Weekly*, Vol. 32:36, pp. 2239-41.

Majumdar Tapes (1997-98), "Economics of Indian Education for the Next Century" *The Indian Economic Journal*, Vo1. 45, No. 4.

Mincer, J. (1958), "Investment in Human Capital and the Personal Income Distribution", *Journal of Political Economy*, Vo1. 66, 1958.

Salim, A. Abdual (1995), "Subsidization of Higher Education in Kerala: A Socio-Economic Analysis", *The IEI*, Vol. 42, No. 4.

24

The Role of Education in Economic Development—An Inter-State Analysis

Alka Samra

Indian economy has experienced an average annual growth rate of around 6 per cent during the last two decades. Although compared to several East Asian economies, this was quite impressive. In terms of per capita income, the improvement has been noticed around 4 per cent per annum in the recent period as compared to less than 1.5 per cent in the earlier period. Further, during the recent period, there has been a steady acceleration in the growth performance.

But the problem of regional disparities within a country is increasingly becoming a matter of great concern to policy-makers in most of the developing countries. In a vast and varied country like India this is a natural phenomenon of the growth process. The Indian economy presents a very deplorable picture of inter-regional disparities reflected in income distribution, urbanization, agriculture, education, industrial production and the state of infrastructure in different states. There are many economic, historical, geographical and political reasons behind regional disparities. The important cause of growing disparities is the difference in natural and created endowments in different states. As per the poor performance in irrigation and power sectors, the green revolution in Bihar and Rajasthan has not turned as green as in Punjab, Haryana, Tamil Nadu and Uttar Pradesh.

The causes of disparities are the unequal distribution of public revenue among the states. During all the years of planning considerable investment has been concentrated at a few places like Mumbai, Ahemdabad, Delhi, Kanpur, Calcutta, Chennai and Bangalore, etc. And the flow of capital and concentration of economic power continue to be biased in favour of large cities and the location of functions and facilities continue to be urban biased due to market imperfections such as factor immobility, price rigidity, ignorance of market conditions, lack of specialisations and lack of division of labour, etc.

Education is a critical input for investment in human capital. As against the goal of 6 per cent of GDP, the total expenditure on education in India is currently 3.99 per cent of GDP (2001-02). Plan expenditure on education has also increased rapidly since the First Five Year Plan. A high priority has been accorded to this sector in the tenth five year plan, with an allocation of Rs. 43,825 crore as against Rs. 24,908.38 crore made available in the ninth plan, representing an increase of 76 per cent. During the tenth plan Rs. 28,750 crore has been allocated for elementary education. It shows education in every sense is one of the fundamental factors of development. No country can achieve sustainable economic development without substantial investment in human capital. In spite of this, great disparities in expenditure on education are found in India. So the main purpose of this study is to show the educational disparities in India and its impact on economic development.

OBJECTIVES OF THE STUDY

The main objectives of the study are:

1. To identify regional disparities in education and economic development.
2. To see the inter-relationship between education and economic development.

METHODOLOGY

To derive a composite index from a set of variables, a wide variety of multivariate statistical techniques are available. One needs to look for an alternative dimension reduction technique which will summarise the whole set of information into a manageable form without much loss of the information related to original data. Though the composite index can be built up using simple techniques like ranking and indexing methods, but these techniques have many drawbacks which have been criticised by many researchers like Dandekar Committee (1984), Kundu and Raza (1982) and Sarker (1995). Main drawbacks are arbitrariness and allocation of equal weights.

In this study Principal Component Analysis is used. In this analysis a set of original variables is transformed to a new set of uncorrelated variables called principal components. These new variables are linear functions of the original variables and derived in decreasing order of importance. The objective is to find out only a few components which account for most of the variation in the original data set. It reduces a set of variables to much smaller size without loosing the properties of the data.

The Education Development Index is a composite of these variables:

1. Adult Literacy Rate.
2. Enrolment Rate (Percentage of Enrolment in 6-14 Age Group).
3. Number of Primary Schools Per Thousand Population.
4. Percentage of Habitations having Educational Amenities.
5. Teacher-Pupil Ratio.

To see the role of education in economic development, the Composite Index of Economic Development is also computed with the help of these variables:

1. Per Capita Gross Domestic Product at Constant Price (1993-94=100).
2. Per Capita Consumption Expenditure for 30 Days.
3. Percentage of People Above Poverty Line.
4. Employment Rate.

After computing the composite index of economic development, it is correlated with education development using Karl Pearson's Correlation of Coefficient.

EMPIRICAL ANALYSIS

Five variables have been considered for education development index. The loading structure and other related statistics are depicted in the Table 1

It is observed from Table 1 that percentage of enrolment in 6-14 age group has the highest (0.70845) loading in the principal component and it explains the maximum correlation followed by primary schools per thousand population and adult literacy rate. It is also found from the table that percentage of habitations having educational amenities and teacher-pupil ratio do not play significant role in educational development. The table also depicts that the average adult literacy rate is only 63.88 per cent. It affects the enrolment ratio and seems that almost 6 per cent children are not enrolled in the schools. It is surprising to say that the average number of primary schools per thousand is only 1.179.

The regional disparity in educational development has also been examined by coefficient of variation, shown in Table 1. The table shows that highest variation (51.06%) is found in primary schools per thousand population followed by teacher-pupil ratio (37.19%) and percentage of habitations having educational amenities (17.94%).

Four variables for economic development have been considered for the construction of the economic development

TABLE 1

Principal Component Loading and Coefficient of Variation for Educational Variables

S. No.	Variables	Mean	Factor Loading	Coefficient of variation
1.	Adult literacy rate	63.88	.42807	17.78%
2.	Percentage of Enrolment in 6-14 age group	94.25	.70845	15.68%
3.	Primary schools per thousand population	1.179	.70636	51.06%
4.	Percentage of habitations having educational amenities	79.39	-.37845	17.94%
5.	Teacher-pupil ratio	34.42	-.73938	37.19%
	Variation explained		37.4%	

Source: Computed.

index. The loading structure and other related statistics are depicted in Table 2.

TABLE 2

Principal Component Loading and Coefficient of Variation for Educational Variables

S. No.	Variables	Mean	Factor Loading	Coefficient of variation
1.	Per Capita Gross Domestic Product (Rs.)	11916.28	0.83747	36.68%
2.	Per Capita Consumption Expenditure (Rs.)	622.98	0.96262	21.09%
3.	Percentage of People Above Poverty Line (%)	77.12	.87767	15.28%
4.	Employment Rate (%)	80.37	– 0.12082	18.33%
	Variation explained		60.3%	

Source: Computed.

It is observed from Table 2 that per capita consumption expenditure has the highest loading (0.96262) in the principal component followed by percentage of people above poverty line and per capita gross domestic product. The employment rate is not as significant as compared to other factors for the economic development. The table also shows that on an average one Indian national consumes only Rs. 622.98 worth of things that are absolutely necessary in a month. Low per capita income leads to the fact of lower consumption expenditure. It is observed that only 77.12 per cent of India's population lives above the poverty line. In other words, 22.88 per cent of the total population still lives below the poverty line and 19.63 per cent population is unemployed. Thus, the basic problem of India lies in the circle of poverty, hunger and economic imbalance.

The regional disparity in economic development has also been examined by coefficient of variation, shown in the Table 2. It shows that highest variation (36.68%) is found in per capita gross domestic product followed by per capita consumption expenditure (21.09%) and employment rate (18.33%).

Composite Index of Education and Economic Development

By using the above mentioned factor loadings education development index and economic development index is computed and presented in Table 3.

Table 3 depicts that the highest value of the state indicates the top position for the both education and economic development. The value of the education development index varied from -0.56 to 2.25. Himachal Pradesh is on the top position with 2.25 value followed by Jammu & Kashmir (1.33) and Madhya Pradesh with the value 1.25. On the other side, Bihar (-0.56) has the lowest value followed by Uttar Pradesh (0.07) and West Bengal (0.15).

Table 3 also shows the index value of economic development. The value of economic development varied from 3.37 to 1.51. Punjab is on the top with a value of 3.37 followed by Haryana (3.25) and Gujarat (3.10). Bihar is the poorest (1.51) of all followed by Orissa (1.61) and Madhya Pradesh (1.89).

TABLE 3

Education Development Index and Economic Development Index (2004-05)

S. No.	States	Education Development Index		Economic Development Index	
		Value	Rank	Value	Rank
1.	Andhra Pradesh	0.78	8	2.54	10
2.	Assam	1.24	4	2.07	13
3.	Bihar	-0.56	17	1.51	17
4.	Gujarat	0.45	12	3.10	3
5.	Haryana	0.26	14	3.25	2
6.	Himachal Pradesh	2.25	1	3.03	5
7.	Jammu and Kashmir	1.33	2	2.75	8
8.	Karnataka	0.69	10	2.67	9
9.	Kerala	0.55	11	3.07	4
10.	Madhya Pradesh	1.25	3	1.89	15
11.	Maharashtra	0.75	9	3.02	6
12.	Orissa	0.94	6	1.61	16
13.	Punjab	0.36	13	3.37	1
14.	Rajasthan	0.97	5	2.35	12
15.	Tamil Nadu	0.83	7	2.84	7
16.	Uttar Pradesh	0.07	16	1.90	14
17.	West Bengal	0.15	15	2.49	11

Source: Computed.

Cluster Analysis According to Education Development Index

According to education development index, states are classified into three groups, i.e. high, moderate and low developed region. The state-wise classification is shown in Table 4.

Table 4 show a clear-cut dominance of moderately developed region (58.83%) followed by low (29.41%) and high developed region (11.76%) respectively. The value of high developed region ranges between 3.37 to 2.75. It consists of only 2 states, i.e. Himachal Pradesh and Jammu and Kashmir. Bihar, Haryana, Punjab, Uttar Pradesh and West Bengal show the low level of educational development due to less enrolment ratio and adult literacy rate.

TABLE 4

Clustering of States According to Education Development Index

Group	*Value*	State		
		No.	*%*	*Name*
High developed	2.25-1.31	2	11.76	Himachal Pradesh, Jammu and Kashmir
Moderately developed	1.31-0.37	10	58.83	Andhra Pradesh, Assam, Gujarat, Karnataka, Kerala, Madhya Pradesh, Orissa, Rajasthan Tamil Nadu
Low developed	0.37-(-0.57)	5	29.41	Bihar, Haryana, Punjab, Uttar Pradesh, West Bengal
Total		17	100	

Source: Computed.

Cluster Analysis According to Economic Development Index

According to economic development index, states are classified into three clusters, i.e. high, moderately and low developed region. State-wise classification is shown in Table 5.

Table 5 show the clear-cut dominance of high developed region (47.06%) followed by low (29.41%) and moderately developed region (23.53%). Assam, Bihar, Madhya Pradesh, Orissa and Uttar Pradesh comprise the low developed region because the per capita gross domestic product of these states is low and the percentage of people above poverty line is also much less compared to other states.

Relationship between Education and Economic Development

Education enriches people's understanding of themselves and world. It improves the quality of their lives and leads to broad social benefits to individual and society. Education raises people's productivity and creativity and promotes entrepreneurship and technological advances. It plays a crucial role in securing economic and social progress

TABLE 5

Clustering of States According to Economic Development Index

Group	*Value*	*State*		
		No.	*%*	*Name*
High developed	3.37-2.75	8	47.06	Gujarat, Haryana, Himachal Pradesh, Jammu and Kashmir, Kerala, Maharashtra, Punjab, Tamil Nadu
Moderately developed	2.75-2.13	4	23.53	Andhra Pradesh, Karnataka, Rajasthan, West Bengal
Low developed	2.13-1.51	5	29.41	Assam, Bihar, Madhya Pradesh, Orissa, Uttar Pradesh
Total		17	100	

Source: Computed.

and improving income distribution. Education brings all the positive changes in variable factors of production as well as in infrastructure development. No one can deny the importance of education. It can be said that education is a pillar on which the major part of an economy stands, if the pillar is strong enough to hold the economy, the irregularities can be reduced very easily and the economy will multiply. And if the pillar of education is weak and fragile the irregularities may push the economy downward and the economy may fall down. Thus, economic development depends on the quality workforce and this quality workforce can be acquired by developing professional, social and communication skills through education.

To examine the relationship between education and economic development, Karl Pearson's correlation coefficient is computed. The correlation coefficient is:

Correlation Coefficient Between Education Development Index and Economic Development Index

r = 0.167

The result indicates that the relationship between education and economic development is significant at 5% level of significance. Although the 'r' value (0.167) is very low but education is positively correlated with economic development. It shows education is indispensable to economic development. No economic development is possible without good education. A balanced education system promotes not only economic development, but also productivity and generates relatively higher income per capita. Its influence is noticeable at the micro-level of an individual family. Although the correlation is positive but it is low, it explains that education is not the only one sector which influences the economic development but other sectors, i.e. agriculture, infrastructure, industrial development are also responsible for development.

The state-wise comparison of education and economic development is presented in Table 6.

Table 6 shows that high educational development of states leads to high economic development. There are only two states—Himachal Pradesh and Jammu and Kashmir, which comprise high educational development and economic development. On the other side Bihar and Uttar Pradesh comprises low education and low economic development. It is seen from Table 6 that although Gujarat, Kerala, Maharashtra and Tamil Nadu are economically developed states but there educational development is still moderate.

It is surprising to see that although the education development of Haryana and Punjab is low yet their economic development is high because the economy of these two states is agriculture-based and the share of agriculture is high in gross domestic product. The share of Haryana and Punjab is 29.3 per cent and 38.6 per cent respectively. And also the share of agriculture in total employment of Haryana and Punjab is 50.3 per cent and 45.6 per cent respectively. It seems that although Punjab and Haryana are educationally backward, but they proved economically forward due to agriculture-based economy. Thus, economic development not only depends on education but other sectors are also equally important for economic development.

TABLE 6

State-wise Comparison of Education and Economic Development

Level	*Economic Development*		
	High	*Moderate*	*Low*
Education Development			
High	Himachal Pradesh, Jammu and Kashmir	–	–
Moderate	Gujarat, Kerala, Maharashtra, Tamil Nadu	Andhra Pradesh, Karnataka, Rajasthan	Assam, Madhya Pradesh, Orissa
Low	Haryana, Punjab	West Bengal	Bihar, Uttar Pradesh

Source: Computed.

CONCLUSION

In general, development can be viewed as multi-dimensional phenomenon. Development generally means the improvement of people's lifestyles through improved education, income, skill development and employment. Here a composite index of education and economic development is constructed. The findings of the analysis support the general perception about the states. The states in India are marked with wide disparity in education and economic development. Some states are better in terms of economic development while states like Kerala and Tamil Nadu have recorded remarkable social progress. The role of education in promoting basic capabilities emerges as the prerequisite to economic development. Faster development requires government action to improve elementary education especially for younger generation. Kerala has set the example and has clearly established the primary benchmark for other states in India. Although expanding gross domestic product and other related variables is one of the most fundamental input to the economic development, yet the basic objective of development should focus on the expansion of human capabilities, i.e. education which has been neglected for long in India.

REFERENCES

Agarwal, A.N. (1991), Indian Economy: Problems of Development and Planning, New Delhi: Wiley Eastern Limited.

Dandekar, V.M. (1995), The Indian Economy, 1947-92, Population, Poverty and Employment, Vol. 2, Sage Publications.

Das, A. (2001), Socio-Economic Development in India, Development and Society.

Hall, P. (1983), Growth and Development, Oxford: Martin Robertso.

Kundu, A. and Raza, M. (1982), Indian Economy: The Regional Dimension, New Delhi: Spectrum Publishers and Distributors.

Sarker, P.C. (1998), Regional Disparities in India: Issues and Measurement, Bombay: Himalaya Publishing House.

Sen, A. (1997), Indian Development: Selected Regional Perspective.

Statistical Abstract of India (2004), Government of India.

25

Higher Education and Growth of the Indian Economy: The Emerging Scenario in Relation to Inter-State Disparities

MANISH DEV

India, with a meager 2.4 per cent of the world surface area and a whooping 16.7 per cent of the world population, is the fourth largest economy of the world in terms of ppp (purchasing power parity) after USA, China and Japan. Her one billion plus population is residing in 28 States and 7 Union Territories under a quasi federal structure. There are wide variations across these states/UTs in regard to physical geography, culture, manpower and other socio-economic conditions. Indian economy has crossed over the regime of 'Hindu Growth Rate' (2.5% to 3.5%) and secured a path of 'Secular Growth Rate' (5-6%). At present it is the second fastest growing economy of the world with 9 per cent growth rate after China. But, this growth scenario is uneven in the sense that some states have achieved rapid economic growth of the order of 10.00 per cent or more, while others have languished.

For an economy growing at 9 per cent plus per annum, the need for a skilled workforce increases immeasurably and enough concern has been voiced by industry and global analysts that if there is one field in which India has to do some rapid catching up, it is education in general and higher education in particular. But the need for higher eudcation enhancement opportunities is not simply rooted in the contingent needs of the economy. It is also a way to make growth more inclusive and more evenly distributed. Despite 6 decades of planning and existence of world-class institutions of higher learning, a large section of the population does not have access to basic education, what to say of higher education. As per a report of Ministry of Human Resource Development, out of a total 19.4 crore children in the 6-13 age group, 1.34 crore (6.94% of this group) were out of school in July-October 2005 (Bhagat, 2007). More shockingly, the survey estimated that of those children not in school, 68.3 per cent have never been to a school and 31.7 per cent are dropouts after one or more years of schooling. The situation more worse at higher education level, as young Indian move up the education chain, a large number of youths never make it to the college or university level. The Gross Enrolment Ratio for class 9-12 in 2004-05 was 39.91 per cent; note the drop in the ratio from 51.65 per cent for classes 9 and 10 to only 27.82 per cent for classes 11 to 12. While only 27 per cent of Indian children make it to higher secondary education (Class 11 and 12), those reaching college and universities constitute a smaller percentage (Bhagat, 2007). The access and quality of higher education in India is not up to the mark as per the requirements of rapidly growing economy. The biggest challenge of India as its GDP continues on robust growth made in the coming decade will be finding adequately skilled, educated and trained manpower. India's current GDP is $ 1.25 trillion and at an annual growth rate of 7.0 per cent, it could double to $ 2.5 trillion in 10 years. But what could derail our growth was finding skilled and trained manpower (Pai, 2008).

The goal of this paper is to try to make some sense of the differential performance of Indian higher education system in relation to economic growth in the recent part. The paper is divided into Four sections. The first section deals with the growth pattern of Indian state during the last decades of planning. The second section covers the growth of Indian Higher Education system in terms of access and equity. The third section concentrates on the quality aspects of higher education and finally the fourth section is a concluding one.

GROWTH PATTERN OF INDIAN ECONOMY DURING PLANS

Indian economy has grown steadily over all the Five Year Plans (Table 1). It is another thing that growth performances were varied in different Plans. Percentage growth rate of GDP were well short of the targeted growth rates from Second to Fourth Five Year Plan. From the Fifth Plan to Eight Plan growth rates achieved were consistently higher than those targeted. The trend has broken with a short-fall in the actual *versus* targeted growth in the Ninth and Tenth Plan. However, the economy has moved decisively to a higher growth phase, with growth rate at market prices exceeding 8 per cent in every year since 2003-04. GDP growth rate during 2005-06 and 2006-07 was 9.2 per cent and 9.2 per cent respectively that made the Indian economy, the second fastest growing economy of the world after China.

But, the growth pattern of the country is not evenly distributed as is reflected in Table 2. There are wide disparities in growth performance amongst states. Punjab, Haryana and Himachal Pradesh were the top performers during sixties and well ahead of national average, while all the BIMARU States along with Andhra Pradesh could register growth rate of 0.7-1.6 per cent.

Punjab and Haryana maintained their top slot even during seventies, but the Maharashtra reached at the top. None of the BIMARU States could improve their position and remained well below the national average. Situation changed considerably during eighties when Rajasthan, a BIMARU State, emerged as the front runner with 5.9 per growth rate and attained Third position. Haryana was at the top but Punjab slipped to Sixth Place. Poorer states like Orissa, Uttar

TABLE I

Growth Rates of Gross Domestic Product of Indian Economy

Plan/Year	*GDP Growth Rate (%)*
*2001*First Five Year Plan	3.6
Second Five Year Plan	4.3
Third Five Year Plan	2.8
Fourth Five Year Plan	3.3
Fifth Five Year Plan	4.8
Sixth Five Year Plan	5.7
Seventh Five Year Plan	6.0
Eight Five Year Plan	6.8
Ninth Five Year Plan	5.3
Tenth Five Year Plan	7.9

Source: GOI (2008); Draft Eleventh Five Year Plan, Vol. I.

Pradesh, Bihar and Madhya Pradesh improved their positions too. The era of economic reforms saw an improvement in the performance of the states having a sound manufacturing base, and as result in surge of acceleration in manufacturing activities since 1991-92, Karnataka, Gujarat, Tamil Nadu, Rajasthan and Maharashtra and West Bengal too, attained higher positions in growth ladder. During 1990-2000 to 2005-06 the exponential growth rate of NSDP at current prices is as high as 13.41 per cent for Gujarat which is at the top. Haryana again emerged as a fast moving state with second place. Notably Orissa, a poor performer so far, registered a growth rate of 11.02 per cent and reached to third place. So is the case with Andhra Pradesh that moved to higher place for the first time. BIMARU States remained well below the national average during the first half of the new millennium.

Thus, it is clear from the above discussion that discrepancies between income growths of states have widened, with richer states having grown faster than the poorer states. There are differences in incomes within the states, as well, between urban and rural areas, between genders and in individual incomes (Agarwal, 2008). Inter-Ministry Task Group on Redressing Growing Regional

Imbalances identified 170 most backward districts (including 55 extremists affected districts) in the country. These districts have poor educational status and infrastructural facilities along with a low standard living (GoI, 2007, pp. 163-64).

Even in highly developed states, there are regions and districts whose indicators are comparable to those of the poorest districts in the most backward states. Despite the efforts made, regional disparities have continued to grow and the gaps have been accentuated as the benefits of economic growth have been largely continued to concentrate to better developed area (GoI, 2007, pp. 165-66).

These disparities are reflected in the attainment of education. Data regarding literacy rate reveals that all the highly developed states, have higher literacy rates (Kerala with a moderate growth rate, is an exception to this) World Bank Development Policy Review finds high correlation between literacy rate and rank in GDP per capita. Four lowest ranked states in terms of GDP per capita also ranked lowest in HDI, with Bihar, Uttar Pradesh and Rajasthan ranking lowest in literacy rates as well (Agarwal, 2008, p. 12). Standard deviation 1.85 in relation to Growth Rate of NSDP at Current prices, 1.96 in relation to growth rate of per capita NSDP at current prices, confirms that there are disparities amongst states in the growth pattern. This disparity is more significant in literacy rate and Gross Enrolment Ratio in Higher Education, but the data regarding ratio of graduate and above to total literate people in the states shows more consistency (Tables 2 and 3).

Coefficient of correlation between growth rate of per capita NSDP at current prices and literacy rate is +0.405, which confirms that states with higher per capita income have higher literacy rate. A lower correlation coefficient between per capita income growth rate and ratio of graduate and above to total literate population shows that high growth rate of per capita income does not necessarily result in attainment of a degree. Highly literate Kerala has only 5.66 per cent graduate and above out of total literate persons in the state. On the contrary, a poorer state Bihar has 6.78 per cent graduate and more persons out of total literate population which is above the national average. It is also

TABLE 2

State-wise Growth Rates of NSDP and Per Capita NSDP at Current Prices, Literacy Rate, GER in Higher Education and Ratio of Graduate and above in Total Literate

S. No.	*State*	*NSDP growth*	*Per capita NSDP growth rate 1999-2006*	*Literacy rate 2001*	*GER (%) in higher reducation SES (2000)*	*Ratio of graduate and above (%) (2001)*
1.	Andhra Pradesh	10.07	8.87	60.5	9.66	7.08
2.	Assam	9.19	7.29	63.3	9.40	4.84
3.	Bihar	7.09	4.95	47.0	6.16	6.78
4.	Gujarat	13.41	11.43	69.1	10.01	6.29
5.	Haryana	12.25	9.90	67.9	9.99	6.60
6.	Himachal Pradesh	10.09	8.25	76.5	15.22	5.46
7.	Jammu and Kashmir	9.24	6.55	55.5	9.78	6.90
8.	Karnataka	9.82	8.40	66.6	7.96	7.32
9.	Kerala	9.53	8.40	90.9	18.08	5.66
10.	Maharashtra	10.36	8.58	76.9	14.14	7.64
11.	Madhya Pradesh	6.53	4.48	63.7	10.48	6.11
12.	Orissa	11.02	9.81	63.1	8.21	5.97
13.	Punjab	6.74	4.90	69.7	10.86	6.51
14.	Rajasthan	7.92	5.64	60.4	8.85	5.31
15.	Tamil Nadu	8.22	7.28	73.5	12.05	5.42
16.	Uttar Pradesh	8.12	5.95	56.3	9.59	6.56
17.	West Bengal	9.40	8.06	68.6	6.30	6.75
	All India	10.17	8.40	64.8	10.08	6.70

Sources: (i) For NSDP growth rate and per capita NSDP Growth Rate; *Economic Survey*, 2007-08.

(ii) For Literacy Rate; *Economic Survey*, 2007-08.

(iii) For GER; Inter-Ministry Task Group of Planning Commission.

(iv) For Ratio of Graduate and above; Census of India, 2001.

noteworthy that Bihar has lowest gross enrolment ratio in the country, but have more graduate ratio. And Kerala, with highest Gross Enrolment Ratio has a very low level of graduate and above ratio. So is the case with Himachal radesh and Tamil Nadu. Maharashtra is the only state in the

TABLE 3

Inter-state Disparities in Growth and Status of Higher Education in India

S. No	Measures	Standard deviation	Correlation between NSDP growth rate and	Correlation between per capita NSDP growth rate and ....
1.	Growth rate of NSDP at current prices	1.85	–	+ 0.967
2.	Growth rate of per capita NSDP at current prices	1.96	+ 0.967	–
3.	Literacy Rate	9.95	+ 0.291	+ 0.405
4.	Gross Enrolment Ratio in Higher Education	3.06	+ 0.112	+ 0.161
5.	Ratio of Graduate and above to literate population	0.77	+ 0.136	+ 0.105

Source: Calculated with the data of Table 2.

list with a high GER and high ratio of graduate and above population to total literate population. The above phenomenon has two explanations—

1. Younger generation in Bihar (along with Jharkhand prefer civil services and thus acquiring a degree is a pre-condition to that.
2. Younger generation in Kerala and Tamil Nadu prefer job-oriented courses after senior secondary education and for them graduation is not a necessity.
3. Younger generation of Andhra Pradesh, Karnataka and Maharashtra prefer the degree level education, especially in engineering and technology because of easy availability of engineering and technological institutions in these states.

GROWTH OF HIGHER EDUCATION IN INDIA

In its size and diversity, India has the third largest higher education system in the world, next only to China and USA. Access to higher education was very limited and elitist before independence, with enrolment of less than a million students in 500 colleges and 20 universities. The growth of higher education, at least quantitatively, appears to be very impressive since independence; the number of universities has increased from 20 in 1947-48 to 367 in 2006 (18 times) and the number of colleges from 496 in 1947-48 to 18064 in 2005-06 (35 times) and enrolment from 0.2 million in 1947-48 to 13.93 million in 2005-06 (69 times) (GoI, Annual Report, MHRD, 2006-07).

The Indian Higher Education System is now more mass based and democratised with one-third to 40 per cent of students coming from lower socio-economic status and women comprising of some 35 per cent of enrolments (Tilak, 2006). In the spheres of technical education by 2004 India had 1478 engineering and technology colleges, 629 pharmacy colleges, 118 architecture, 71 hotel management and 5190

TABLE 4

Growth of Higher Education Institutions and Enrolment in India

Year	*Universities*	*Colleges*	*Total HEIs*	*Enrolment (in million)*
1947-48	20	496	516	0.2
1950-51	30	578	608	0.2
1960-61	45	1,819	1,864	0.6
1970-71	93	3,277	3,370	2.0
1980-81	123	4,738	4,861	2.8
1990-91	184	5,748	5,932	4.4
2000-01	266	11,146	11,412	8.8
2005-06	367	18,064	21,431	13.9

Source: UGC (Universities include central, state, private and deemed-to-be universities as also institutions of national importance established both by the central and the state legislatures).

teacher education colleges making a total about 7486 institutions. In respect of post graduate educational institutions there are 1052 MBA/PGDBM and 97 MCA colleges in 2005-06.

In terms of distribution, there are some distinguishing features in the distribution of colleges in different states. There is a north-south imbalance in the number of colleges. Southern states such as Maharashtra, Andhra Pradesh and Karnataka have 2441, 2096 and 1865 colleges respectively, which is 36 per cent of the total colleges in the country. Some major northern states such as Assam, Bihar, Uttranchal, West Bengal, Jharkhand lag behind other states in the number of colleges. Even the larger northern states, such as Uttar Pradesh, Madhya Pradesh and Rajasthan have less number of colleges as compared to their southern counterpart.

GROWTH IN STUDENT ENROLMENT

Growth of higher education is best judged by analysing two key factors: (i) Gross enrolment ratio at higher education level, i.e. access, and (ii) Quality of higher education. Another factor that gives a better look of the growth of higher education is a comparison between demand and supply. In terms of supply-side what needs to ascertained is that all those who have passed senior secondary examination are eligible and willing to join higher education must have an access to the institutions of higher learning. Secondly, the growth of higher education, both in terms of number and diversification, must meet the growing manpower needs of the economy and society. In this way, the supply side of higher education has backward linkages with school education and forward linkages with economy in terms of supplying skilled manpower to the economy. Although the number of colleges in almsot every discipline have increased significantly during the Ninth and Tenth Five Year Plan, these are still not sufficient to accommodate all those students who pass their intermediate examinations. A large number of applicants for admission and high cut-off list confirms this notion.

Gross Enrolment Ratio is a good measure to assess the

access to education in the country/region/class. It is the ratio of students enrolled at each level of education, as a proposition of the population of the relevant age group. In case of higher education, relevant age group is 18-24 years.

TABLE 5

Growth in Higher Education : Enrolment, Gross Enrolment Ratio, and GNP Per capita (Selected Developed and Developing Countries)

Country	*Enrolment in million*		*Percentage increase*	*GER (%) 2001*	*GNP per capita (US $) 2004*
	1990-91	*2001-02*			
USA	13.71	15.93	16.2	81	34,280
China	3.82	12.14	217.7	13	890
India	4.95	10.58	113.6	11	460
Japan	2.90	3.97	36.8	49	35610
UK	1.26	2.24	78.1	64	25120
France	1.70	2.03	19.4	54	22730
Italy	1.45	1.85	27.7	53	19390
Brazil	1.54	3.13	103.0	18	3070
Russia	5.10	8.02	57.3	70	1750
Canada	0.84	1.19	41.7	58	21980
Indonesia	1.59	3.18	99.7	15	690
Philippines	1.71	2.47	44.3	31	1030
Australia	0.49	0.87	79.1	65	19900
Malayasia	0.12	0.56	358.9	27	3330

Source: (i) For 1990-91 (or nearest year)—Statistical year book of UNESCO.

(ii) For 2001-02 (or nearest year)—UNESCO Institute of Statistics (2005)

(iii) For GNP per capita—UNESCO, EFA Global Monitoring Reports (2004).

GER in India was only 11 per cent in 2001, which was the lowest in select countries including the top ten economics of the world. GER was as high as 81 per cent in USA, 70 per cent in Russia, 64 per cent in UK and 54 per cent in France. GER was higher in fast developing countries such as Brazil, Indonesia, Malaysia and China (Table 5).

TABLE 6

Enrolment of Levels and Major Disciplines in India

Year	Ph.D.	PG	General graduate art, science and commerce	Technical graduate (Engg., Medical, B.Ed.)	Total higher education (degree) (2+3+4+5)	Diploma	Total higher education (degree, Diploma) (6+7)
1980-81	25417	291341	1886428	239267	2442453	430126	2872579
1990-91	32468	354216	3285776	416828	4089288	796686	4885974
2000-01	45004	647338	7244915	688625	8625882	987279	9613161
2001-02	53119	647016	7139497	790050	8629682	1104594	9734276
2002-03	65357	782590	7633125	1035701	9516773	1199785	10716558
2003-04	65525	806636	8026147	1110840	10009148	1191447	11200595

Source: Selected Educational Statistics, Different Years, Ministry of Human Resource Development, New Delhi.

Total enrolment in higher education is presented in Table 8, which reveals that 11.2 million students are enrolled in different disciplines in the country in 2003-04. The total different enrolment in Ph.D. and postgraduate courses is 65525 and 806636 respectively, which shows a rather low research base in relation to total enrolment in higher education. Technical education has grown at 364.26 per cent as compared to 325.46 per cent during the period 1980-81 to 2003-04.

There are some notable changes in enrolment pattern in India during the last 25 years. The graduate enrolment as a proportion to total enrolment is increasing, the postgraduate enrolment as a proportion to total enrolment is decreasing. The proportion of doctorate to postgraduate enrolment is almost constant at 8 per cent. Science and technology graduate as a proportion to total graduate has declined from 32 per cent in 1980 to 29 per cent in 2003. Recent years have also shown a decline in the number of science graduate in relation to technical graduates. Still, the ratio of technical to total graduate is low at 8 per cent. It is important to note that the demand for teachers is high as a result enrolment in B.Ed. courses is increasing, especially in northern states such as Uttar Pradesh, Uttranchal, Madhya Pradesh, Rajasthan and Haryana. The fall in vocational enrolment to total higher education enrolment is matter of concern for higher educational planners.

ENROLMENT AT DISAGGREGATE LEVEL

NSS data for 1999-2000, population census data selected education statistics and another data set of NSS (2003-04) provide detailed information at disaggregate level and a detailed analysis is being presented here regarding the level of enrolment between (i) rural and urban, (ii) inter-state, (iii) Inter-caste, (iv) Inter-religion, (v) Gender based, (vi) Occupational group-wise, and (vii) Poor and non-poor.

TABLE 7

Gross Enrolment Ratio in Rural and Urban Areas in India

(%)

	SES data 2003-04	*NSS data 1999-2000*	*Census data 2001*
Rural Area	7.76	5.58	8.99
Urban Area	27.20	21.74	24.52

1. Rural and Urban

Significant disparities exist in GER between rural and urban areas. GER for rural and urban area was 7.76 per cent and 27.20 per cent respectively in 2003-04 GER in urban area is four times high as compared to rural areas. As per NSS data the GER for rural and urban area was 5.58 per cent and 21.74 per cent respectively. The population census came up with the GER of 8.99 per cent for rural areas and 24.52 for urban area in 200 per cent.

The Eligible Enrolment Ratio worked out to 51.1 per cent for rural area and 66 per cent for urban area—latter being higher by 15 percentage points. In simple terms it shows that only half of the rural students who pass their higher secondary examination go to higher education which is less by 15 percentage points compared with urban areas.

TABLE 8

Access to Higher Education in India

Gross Enrolment Ratio* (GER%) in Age Group 18-23 years: 1999-2000*						
States	*Total Graduates*			*Total Higher Education****		
	Male	*Female*	*Total*	*Male*	*Female*	*Total*
Andhra Pradesh	9.03	5.57	7.25	12.16	7.29	9.66
Arunachal Pradesh	3.98	0.41	2.22	4.29	0.51	2.42
Assam	9.37	7.11	8.28	10.81	7.88	9.40
Bihar	6.92	2.84	4.91	8.79	3.47	6.16
Goa	7.55	11.57	9.71	18.69	16.55	17.54
Gujarat	8.78	7.43	8.11	11.22	8.80	10.01
Haryana	8.55	6.81	7.73	11.14	8.69	9.99
Himachal Pradesh	11.78	11.41	11.58	16.85	13.84	15.22
Jammu and Kashmir	9.44	6.83	8.17	11.19	8.30	9.78
Karnataka	6.68	3.94	5.31	10.06	5.86	7.96
Kerala	12.46	15.54	14.05	15.56	20.43	18.08
Madhya Pradesh	9.28	8.94	9.12	11.00	9.91	10.48
Maharashtra	11.13	8.08	9.70	16.81	11.10	14.14
Manipur	11.00	9.06	10.05	14.59	12.53	13.58
Meghalaya	6.62	5.40	5.99	7.22	7.05	7.13
Mizoram	8.39	2.98	5.61	10.23	5.63	7.87
Nagaland	13.28	13.44	13.35	13.93	14.15	14.04
Orissa	9.20	4.29	6.71	11.55	4.94	8.21
Punjab	8.01	7.25	7.65	10.14	11.64	10.86
Rajasthan	8.93	5.62	7.36	10.99	6.48	8.85
Sikkim	4.98	1.31	3.25	7.39	2.36	5.01
Tamil Nadu	11.83	7.30	9.45	15.23	9.19	12.05
Tripura	7.16	3.08	5.24	7.85	3.84	5.97
Uttar Pradesh	9.83	5.10	7.58	12.60	6.29	9.59
West Bengal	6.45	2.97	4.68	8.69	3.98	6.30
A & N Island	4.28	10.43	7.56	4.33	11.04	7.91
Chandigarh	17.96	23.90	20.18	23.26	31.23	26.24
Delhi	13.74	20.27	16.38	19.73	23.26	21.16
Lakshadweep	0.00	0.57	0.34	0.00	0.57	0.34
Pondicherry	15.67	7.90	11.81	18.81	11.90	15.37
India	9.22	6.30	7.79	12.13	7.94	10.08

Note: * GER = Total grade and diploma enrolled/population in 18-23 age group.

**These include only those enrolled who have attained higher secondary and above education.

***Degree+Diploma

Source: NSS, 1999-2000.

2. Inter-state Disparities in GER in Higher Education

There are considerable inter-state disparities in the level of higher education. As per NSS data GER at aggregate level is about 10.08 per cent in 2000, it is more than national average in states/UTs like Chandigarh (26.24%), Delhi (21.16%), Kerala (18.08%), Goa (17.56%), Punduchery (15.37%), Himachal Pradesh (15.22%) and Maharashtra (14.15%). GER is as low as 0.34 per cent in Lakshadweep, 2.23 per cent in Dadra and Nagar Haveli, 2.42 per cent in Arunachal Pradesh. GER in Bihar is 6.16 per cent which is no surprise to anybody, but 7.96 per GER in Karnataka, a developed state, is a matter of concern for the policy-makers of the state, so is the case with West Bengal which has GER as low as 6.30 per cent. The real tragedy is that of West Bengal which produces only graduate 14000 engineers a year. Mr. T.R. Mohandas Pai, Director HR, Infosys Comments, "I was shocked to tears because Kolkata was the place where the earlier generation went for higher education.... but now they have no capacity.

3. Gender Disparities

The access to higher education is also low for girls as compared with boys. The GER for male is 12.12 per cent and 8 per cent for female. In case of SC female it is only 3.48 per cent as compared to 14.11 per cent for general female. For rural SC female the GER in higher education is only 1.70 per cent. Urban SC female are somewhat in better position in this regard.

4. Occupational Variations in GER in Higher Education

Significant variations can be seen from the Table 10 in GER in higher education among various occupational classes. In rural area GER for Agricultural labourers is only 1.41 per cent as compared to 18.55 per cent for others. In urban areas casual labourers have GER only 3.26 per cent as compared to 50.15 per cent for others.

5. Inter-Caste Variations

In 2003-04, the GER was about 13.22 per cent at over all level. However, there are significant disparities across

TABLE 9

Access to Higher Education by Caste Group—2000

Socio-Religious Group	*Gross Enrolment Ratio (GER%) in Age Group 18-23 years (1999-2000)*		
	Total Higher Education		
	Male	*Female*	*Total*
ST	7.19	5.71	6.43
SC	6.63	3.48	5.09
OBC	8.99	4.91	7.00
General	19.20	14.11	16.74
Total	12.12	8.00	10.10
	Rural		
ST	5.74	4.53	5.1
SC	5.07	1.70	3.40
OBC	5.88	2.27	4.10
General	11.79	6.19	9.01
Total	7.53	3.61	5.58
	Urban		
ST	17.08	14.56	15.83
SC	12.19	10.75	11.53
OBC	17.82	12.96	15.51
General	30.50	27.87	29.28
Total	23.28	19.99	21.74

Source: NSS: 1999-2000, Position with 10.75 per cent GER.

social groups. The GER for STs, SCs, OBCs and others (non SC/ST/OBC) was 5 per cent, 7.51 per cent, 11.34 per cent and 24.8 per cent respectively (Thorat, 2006). As per the NSS data these figures came out to be 6.43 per cent, 5.08 per cent, 7.00 per cent and 16.74 per cent respectively in 1999-2000. Thus the GER for others is 5 times higher than ST, 3 times higher than SC and about 2 times higher than OBC in 2003-04.

TABLE 10

GER in Higher Education in India (1999-2000) per Occupational Structures of Household

HH Type	*ST*	*SC*	*OBC*	*OTH*	*All*
		Rural			
Self-Employment Non-Agriculture	2.53	3.77	3.97	7.73	5.17
Agricultural Labour	0.67	1.63	1.16	1.93	1.41
Other Labour	0.91	1.52	4.26	4.02	2.99
Self-Employed in Agriculture	3.04	3.95	4.21	8.33	5.64
Others	35.39	14.15	11.54	22.08	18.55
All	5.12	3.38	4.10	9.00	5.58
		Urban			
Self Employed	6.15	7.37	10.05	22.09	15.74
Regular Wage and Salary	27.33	18.04	22.19	33.72	28.10
Casual Labour	1.53	2.61	3.34	4.30	3.26
Others	40.38	29.52	41.57	59.60	50.15
All	15.87	11.55	15.53	29.28	21.75

Source: NSS 1999-2000.

TABLE 11

Inter-Social Groups Disparities in GER in India

Year	*Source*	*Gross Enrolment Ratio in Higher Education*				
		ST	*SC*	*OBC*	*Others*	*Total*
1999-2000	NSS	6.43	5.08	7.00	16.74	10.10
2001	Popn. Census	7.46	8.39	9.29	15.57	13.80
2003-04	NSS	5.00	7.51	11.34	24.89	13.22

6. Inter-religion Disparities

It is evident from the Table 12 that SC/ST/OBC persons belonging to Hindu religion lag far behind to their higher caste Hindu population in terms of GER in higher education.

TABLE 12

GER on Religion Basis in India (Per cent)

Religion	*NSS 2003*	*NSS 2000*				
		SC	*ST*	*OBC*	*Others*	*All*
Hindu	13.47	4.88	6.16	7.06	19.71	10.00
Muslim	8.19	1.83	4.41	3.94	5.91	5.30
Others	30.87	NA	NA	NA	NA	NA
Jain	57.43	NA	NA	NA	NA	NA
Christians	27.29	9.97	NA	NA	NA	NA
Sikhs/Buddhists	15.00	1.81	NA	NA	18.94	11.00
Total	13.22	6.43	5.08	7.00	16.74	10.10

It is worth to mention here that the SC from all religion suffered from a lower access to higher education as compared with their higher caste counterpart. However, between various religious groups, SC from some religious groups suffer more in access to higher education than other for instance the GER of SC Buddhist is relativity high (14%) followed by SC Christian (9.97%), SC Hindu (4.88%) and SC Sikh (2.33%) (Throat, 2006).

7. Access to Higher Education for Poor

It is clear from Table 13 that wide variations exist in access to higher education between poor and non-poor as per NSS data for 1999-2000.

GER for the poor was 2.43 per cent which was almost Six time lower compared with 12.81 per cent for non-poor. In rural and urban area the GER for poor was 1.30 per cent and 5.51 per cent respectively as compared with 7.12 per cent and 27.15 per cent for non-poor respectively.

Concludingly, the growth of higher education has been uneven with full of disparities in relation to its access to

TABLE 13

Gross Enrolment Ratio for Poor and Non-poor in India 1999-2000

Social Group	*Gross Enrolment Ratio*		
	Poor		
	Rural	*Urban*	*Total*
ST	1.11	4.78	1.55
SC	1.35	3.86	1.89
OBC	1.13	5.16	2.30
Others	1.66	7.00	3.58
All	1.30	5.51	2.43
	Non-Poor		
ST	7.81	23.19	9.7
SC	4.38	15.71	6.68
OBC	5.10	19.98	8.69
Others	10.74	34.01	19.73
All	7.12	27.15	12.81
	Entire Population		
ST	5.12	15.87	6.43
SC	3.38	11.55	5.08
OBC	4.10	15.53	7.00
Others	9.00	29.28	16.74
All	5.58	21.75	10.10

various sections of the society. The present status is not only inadequate, but also inefficient in the sense it does not fulfil the aspirations of the weaker sections of the society. There are wide range of disparities which are prevalent on rural-urban, inter-state, inter-caste, inter-religion and gender basis. On regional basis, state like Bihar, Jharkhand, Chhattisgarh, Orissa, West Bengal, Madhya Pradesh and whole lot of North-East states lag far behind with their counterpart States of south. Socially, SCs; STs and other backward castes and particularly females of these groups are worst placed in the field of higher education.

QUALITY AND EXCELLENCE IN HIGHER EDUCATION

Several recent studies have revealed that Indian Higher Education system is facing a deepening crisis with declining standards and poor governance (Naik, 2006; Chauhan, 2006; Tilak, 2006; Thorat, 2006; Bharadwaj and Dev, 2007). Despite the existence of mechanism to maintain the quality; the overall standard of higher education has continued to deteriorate, thus reducing the value of an academic degree from most institutions of higher learning. According to sources in industry, only about a fourth of the graduates are employable. There is a growing shortage of skills along side a high prevalence of unemployment among graduates (Naik, 2006). Dr. Manmohan Singh, the Prime Minister of India commented recently about the poor quality of higher education in the country. Almost two-third of universities and 90 per cent of the colleges are rated below average on quality parameters.

University Grant Commission has came up with a starting admission; over half of the students who pass, higher secondary don't even enter the higher education stream, 90 per cent of colleges and 68 per cent of universities across the country are of middling or poor quality. On almost indicators of quality, from faculty standards to library facilities, from computer availability, teacher-student ratio, higher education is in crying need for an upgrade.

The 'quality gap' in both universities and colleges is alarming (NAAC, 2007).

- A quarter of faculty positions in universities remain vacant.
- 57 per cent teachers in colleges do not have either a M. Phil or Ph.D. degree.
- There is only one computer for 229 students, on an average, in colleges.

The above status of quality of gap is eye, opening. According to Mr. Sukhdeo Thorat, there are mainly two reasons for this quality gap: (i) availability and quality of facilities, and (ii) quality of faculty. Thorat further says that

TABLE 14

Quality Gap in Indian Higher Education System

	Degree of Benchmarks		*Quality Gap*
	All Universities/ Colleges	*(As 'A' Grade) Universities/ Colleges*	
Universities			
Departments (per University)	29	34	5
Sanctioned Faculty (per University)	287	432	145
Filled up Faculty Position (per University)	220	329	109
Faculty members with Ph.D.	158	432	274
Number of Teachers (per department per university)	8	10	2
Number of books in Library	2,88,913	3,52,886	63,937
Colleges			
Student-Teachers Ratio	27	20	7
STR (for permanent Teachers)	33	30	3
Teachers (per college)	47	78	31
Permanent teachers (per college)	39	54	15
Ad-hoc Teachers (%)	9	25	16
Books (per college)	11,966	15,215	3,249
Journals (per college)	13	22	9
Students (per computer)	229	145	84

Source: NAAC Report, *Indian Express*, June 9, 2007.

one key factor behind the quality gap is the under investment in higher education since 1980s.

Several colleges and institutions have been established as self-financing institutions during the last two decades. No doubt these institutions have created large number of additional seats in various disciplines in higher education. But, majority of these institution are in short of quality faculty. They are running on 'Surrogate' faculty (Chauhan, 2007).

CONCLUSION

Indian higher education system suffers from wide

disparities on regional (i.e. inter-state disparity), social (i.e. general, SCs and STs), economic (poor and non-poor) basis. It also suffers from yawing gap in funds, as well as from archaic regulatory mechanism, poor quality, and low efficiency. One of the biggest problems of social equity in India arises from the poor access of higher education to the common man. It is reflected in Gross Enrolment Ratio, which is amongst the lowest in the World. This is perhaps due to the mistaken notion that Universal literacy is adequate for the masses and the higher education is only meant for the elite. However, a much higher GER—to around 40-50 per cent is a need of hour to make the Indian masses a knowledge society, which is a fundamental requirement of a rapidly growing economy like India. If this is not done properly on priority basis, the large number of young people entering the working age group will not be able to convert them into Human Capital, enriching themselves and the country. And, thus India will not be able to reap the fruits of so-called 'demographic dividends'.

The government has a sole responsibility to provide basic education to all its citizen and also make them efficient and skilled worker, so that they are able, with full of their capabilities, to contribute in nation-building. Because of rising costs of higher education and increasing needs of it, it appears that public funding is not suffice to meet the growing demands of higher education in view of the pressure on fiscal deficit. Public private partnership is the only viable solution in this regard. A tactic shift in the higher education system in India has become extremely urgent. A strong and coherent framework for regulation must replace the current system of multi-regulatory bodies which have created confusion and plethora of constrictive rules.

There is a need for consolidation and upgradation of universities and colleges, keeping in mind the requirements of the industry and other sectors of the economy, competitive practices must be allowed to make the system market-oriented. Non-marketing education streams must be protected. Regulatory framework should ensure that new monopolies and cartelization mechanism are not created. In view of existing regional-social economic disparities in the higher education, target-oriented efforts are required for the expansion of higher education institutions in the areas, neglected so far. Higher education should be accessible to the whole of the society. Hence to make it affordable is a must. Quantitative growth along with high quality of higher education will make the higher growth of the Indian Economy more sustainable in long-run.

References

Agarwal, Pawan (2008), "Towards Excellence : Higher Education in India", Working Paper No. 178, Indian Council for Research in International Economic Relations.

Bhagat, Rashida (2007), "Out of School—An Elementary, Unaddressed Problem", *The Hindu Business Line,* New Delhi, June 1.

Bhagat, Rashida (2007), "India's Dismal Record on Many Fronts", *The Hindu Business Line,* New Delhi, Dec. 12, p. 8.

Bharadwaj, Sanjeev and Manish Dev (2007), "Commercialization and Privatization in Indian Higher Education System in Relation to Quality", In Meenu Agarwal (ed.)—Education in Third World and India, Kavishka Publishers, New Delhi, pp. 346-55.

Chauhan, Shyam Sunder Singh and Sangita Gupta (2007), "Access and Equity in Indian Higher Education System : Problems and Prospects", In Meenu Agarwal (ed.)—Education in Third World and India, Kavishka Publishers, New Delhi, pp. 329-45.

GoI (2006-07), Annual Report, 2006-07, Ministry of Human Resource Development, New Delhi.

GoI (2002), Tenth Five Year Plan (2002-07), Planning Commission, Vol. III, New Delhi.

GoI (2008), Eleventh Five Year Plan (2007-12), Planning Commission, New Delhi, Vol. I, pp. 165-66.

NAAC (2007), "Assessment of the Higher Education", National Assessment and Accreditation Council, UGC, Ministry of HRD, New Delhi.

Pai, T.V. Mohandas (2008), "Key Note Address on Creating India's Tomorrow—The HR Challenge", Chennai, *The Hindu Business Line,* April 12, New Delhi.

Throat Sukhdeo (2006), Higher Education in India: Emerging Issues Related to Access, Inclusiveness and Quality", Nehru Memorial Lecture, University of Mumbai, November 24.

Tilak, B.G. (2006), Quoted in Higher Education : Must Not be in Perpetuity", *The Hindu Business Line,* New Delhi.

26

Distribution of Benefits of Government Expenditure on Education—An Empirical Analysis of Coimbatore District in Tamil Nadu

K. GOVINDARAJALU

I. INTRODUCTION

The generalisation that investment in human capital promotes economic growth dates back to the time of Adam Smith. Kiker (1968) emphasised the importance of investing in human skills. Schultz (1961) and Denison (1962) proved that education contributes directly to the growth of national income by improving the skills and productive capacities of the labour force. The early attempts to measure the contribution of education to economic growth were based either on the growth accounting approach, used by Denison and others or on the rate of return to human capital, an approach adopted by Schultz and others. These works led them to find that a considerable proportion of the rate of growth of output in the United States was due to investment in education. This was also very well established by Psacharopoulos (1985).

II. NEED FOR STATE INTERVENTION IN EDUCATION

The role of state in education has been recognised from the earliest times. There had always been state patronage for education in ancient India. State aid was given to the educational institutions. It has now been recognised that every child up to a certain age has a right to receive education and it is the duty of the state to make adequate provision for it. Even Adam Smith, the apostle of national liberty and *laissez-faire*, was in favour of state-controlled elementary education. John Stuart Mill, belonging to the classical tradition, also advocated that the state should provide for both elementary and higher education and that the elementary education should be made compulsory.

There is an increasing realisation that there are certain goods and services such as defence, law and justice that have some characteristics which make it altogether impossible to provide them through the market (Musgrave, 1959). These types of goods and services, often referred to as 'social goods', are consumed in equal amounts by all and it is not possible to exclude anybody from enjoying them. There is another set of goods and services called 'merit wants' which are "subject to the exclusion principle and are satisfied by the market within the limits of effective demand". But price mechanism cannot fully measure their true social values and costs, and private decisions based on the market prices will not provide optimal results. Hence, to ensure optimal allocation of resources, both these 'social' and 'merit' goods have to be provided through state intervention.

Though public expenditure on education is advocated on the grounds of its favourable distributive effects, doubts are also expressed regarding its effectiveness in achieving the desired objectives. The expansion of education in the last six decades has relatively achieved few of the objectives. However, the distribution of access to education, despite the growth of public expenditure, is found to be favouring relatively high socio-economic groups. It is also evident that public expenditure on education has also been used to subsidise the education of middle and upper income groups at the cost of the poor. And the expansion of education as a result of public support is associated with the rise in the educated unemployment and income inequalities. All these problems associated with public expenditure on education need a careful examination.

III. OBJECTIVES AND METHODOLOGY

The present study on the distribution of benefits of government expenditure on education in Coimbatore District, Tamilnadu was undertaken with such a perspective. In our empirical study, the distribution of education among different income and social groups is undertaken. It is examined by using per capita government expenditure, on education at all levels of education.

I. Design of the Sample

As the present study needed information on socio-economic background and educational details of the households, a primary survey was conducted. The study considered the households who sent their wards to government and aided institutions only as it was aimed to identify the beneficiaries of government expenditure on education. In order to conduct the survey, the sample households were selected in stages. In the first stage, Coimbatore district was selected purposively as it is the district where the researcher has been working for the last about twenty years. In the second stage, out of the nine taluks three taluks were selected viz. Coimbatore North, Coimbatore South and Palladam. Though there is little homogeneity between these taluks in terms of the development of agriculture, industry and education, all these nine taluks have almost similar socio-economic characteristics. These taluks represented the characteristics of the rest of the other taluks except more urban characters in Coimbatore North. In the third stage, revenue blocks were selected. In order to have equal representation, households were selected from all the 8 blocks (3 from Coimbatore South, 2 from Coimbatore North and 3 from Palladam).

2. Data Collection

The pilot survey was conducted to test and finalise the questionnaire which was used in the present study. Thereafter, the primary data were collected for the specific purpose of this study during 2006 using the questionnaire. In this study information related to household income, expenditure, asset, demographic characteristics, working hours of parents, employment details, number of children receiving education, dropouts, household expenditure on education, government assistance on education received by each child in the family, etc. were collected. The study included all levels of education which is commonly classified as primary (1-5 standards), middle (6-8 standards), high/ higher secondary (9-12 standards) and higher education (above 12 including technical education) while studying the distribution of benefits of government expenditure on education, the analysis was made according to these four levels of education. Details about the nearby schools and colleges, fees structure in government and aided institution, concessions provided to students according to their social status, free uniforms and books were also collected. Apart from these the researcher established good rapport with the people of each village and explained the nature and purpose of the study to get reliable data. They co-operated and helped in all possible ways for getting the reliable data.

IV. DISTRIBUTION OF BENEFITS OF EDUCATION AND EDUCATIONAL EXPENDITURE

This analysis was undertaken by using informations generated through a sample survey in the study area. The sample households were identified through the multi-stage random sampling technique. At the first stage taluks were identified. At the second stage blocks were identified and then villages. At the final stage households were enumerated in the selected sample villages. To get informations regarding enrolment of students and school dropouts in the households, schools were also consulted. In order to know the exact value of government assistance provided, directly and indirectly, to the students, a primary survey was conducted in the schools in the district. The study covers all levels of education, i.e. primary, middle, high/higher secondary and higher education. To assess the value of services received by households, the households having students at different levels of education, information relating to private cost, public assistance, type of institution, etc. was collected from all the students of the family. The study considered those families having wards studying in Government/Government aided institutions as a beneficiary of government expenditure on education.

Access to and utilisation of public services have been a long standing issue in many developing countries. Hence, we are interested to measure these indicators among different income and social groups in the study area. By estimating these indicators one could establish that which group or section of the population is benefited by government expenditure on education or not.

In this section of the study, an analysis is made to understand the pattern of distribution of public expenditure on education among different income and social groups. For this purpose a simple method is adopted as outlined below. The analysis was based on the computed mean enrolment rates for each level of education by income quintiles and social groups. It was multiplied with the per capita government expenditure on education for different levels of education. This was computed using secondary data collected from government records. The per capita expenditure on education worked out on an average as Rs. 430.30 for primary level, Rs. 204.20 for middle school level, Rs. 947.20 for high/higher secondary level and Rs. 2454.4 for higher education. From this information it was possible to find out the pattern of educational expenditure with the help of a simple model which is briefly outlined here. (Das Gupta and Tilak)

The average share of each household received in the public expenditure on education by quintiles or social groups, say Z_i, (i = 1 ...... 5 quintiles) can therefore be expressed as:

$Z_i = (E_{ij}\ C_j)$
$i = 1..... 5$ quintiles

j = Four levels of education (primary, middle, high/ higher secondary school level and higher education).

Where E_{ij} represents the mean enrolment rate of the ith quintile and jth educational level, and C_j represents the public expenditure per pupil for the jth level. The direction and magnitude of the variation of Z_i as i increase gives us an indication of how equitable the distribution of public expenditure on education is.

he values of Z_i for different quintiles are given in Table 1. The quintiles being computed on the basis of household per capita income. The corresponding values of K_i have also been given in the table where K_i denotes that:

$$K_i = Z_i - Z$$

where,

Z is the mean of the Z_i (i = 1 .... 5)

If there is equitable distribution of public expenditure, then Z_i as well as K_i would be decreasing function of income quintiles.

The pattern of distribution of government expenditure on education by income quintiles is presented in Table 1. The calculated Z_i values and K_i shows (and hence K_i) an increasing function of income quintiles. The Z_i increases as

TABLE I

Pattern of Distribution of Government Expenditure by Income Quintiles and Levels

Income Quintile	*Level of Education*					
	Primary	*Middle*	*High/Hr. Sec.*	*Higher*	Z_i	K_i
(1)	(2)	(3)	(4)	(5)	(6)	(7)
Lowest 20%	327.02	154.90	64.54	4.30	550.78	242.34
2nd quintile	223.75	89.84	303.10	269.98	886.69	-93.56
3rd quintile	176.42	89.84	388.35	294.52	949.15	-156.01
4th quintile	150.60	51.05	549.37	539.96	1290.99	-497.86
Top 20%	73.15	18.37	454.65	859.04	1405.22	-612.09

the income increases. This shows that the government expenditure on education was more favourably distributed for the higher income groups. But the K_i shows decreasing function of income which means that the difference between the share of public expenditure per household and its mean was decreasing as income was increasing. Hence, from this analysis we understand that more share of public expenditure on primary and middle education goes to the lowest quintile and higher share from higher education expenditure goes to top quintile groups.

V. PATTERN OF DISTRIBUTION OF GOVERNMENT EXPENDITURE BY SOCIAL GROUPS AND LEVELS

In this section, analysis on the pattern of distribution of government expenditure by social groups is presented by using the same method as used for income quintiles. The mean enrolment rate by levels of education for the different social groups had already been calculated and per pupil cost on different levels of education was also calculated.

The method has been reworked as under:

$$Z_i = - (E_{ij}\ C_j)$$

where,

i = Four different social groups viz., OC, BC, MBC and SC/ST, and

j = Four levels of education.

E_{ij} represent the mean enrolment rate of the ith social group and j^{th} level of education and C_j represents the per pupil expenditure on education for the jth level of education. The direction and magnitude of Z_i as i decreases gives us an indication of how equitable the distribution of public expenditure on education among social groups is.

The values of Z_i for the different social groups and the corresponding values of K_i have also been presented in the Table 2. The K_i in the table denotes—

$$K_i = Z_i - Z$$

where,

Z is the mean of the Z_i

If the distribution of public expenditure on education is equitable among social groups, then the values of Z_i as well as K_i should be an increasing function of social groups..

It is observed from Table 2 that the value of Z_i for Other Communities was 29.69, the value for backward communities was 1007.018, for most backward community it was 712.43 and 306.2026 for scheduled caste/scheduled tribe groups. It is clear from the analysis that the pattern of distribution was in favour of backward and most backward community and then scheduled caste/scheduled tribe. K_i also denotes the same result. The negative function was observed for backward community and the lowest value for most backward community. Scheduled caste and other communities were the third and fourth beneficiary group of government expenditure.

TABLE 2

Pattern of Distribution of Government Expenditure By Social Groups and Levels

Social Group	*Level of Education*					
	Primary	*Middle*	*High/Hr. Sec.*	*Higher*	Z_i	K_i
(1)	*(2)*	*(3)*	*(4)*	*(5)*	*(6)*	*(7)*
OC	10.75	1.63	10.41	6.87	29.68	763.44
BC	275.39	149.06	312.57	269.98	1007.01	-213.88
MBC	206.54	87.80	246.27	171.80	712.43	80.70
SC/ST	73.15	75.55	123.13	34.36	306.20	486.92

VI. INFLUENCE OF THE GOVERNMENT ASSISTANCE ON ENROLMENT OF STUDENTS

In order to estimate the influence of the government assistance on the enrolment, the multiple linear regression model is used in this section of this study. In this study the level of enrolment is the dependent variable and the socio-economic factors including government assistance are the independent variable.

Enrolment = f (b0+b1 HINCPM + b2 M3OCC + b3 M6OCC + b4 PRICOST + b5 M2OCC + b6 M1OCC + b7 GATOT + b8 M4OCC + b9 F4OCC + b10 BC + b11 MHOURSOF + b12 SCST + b13 FHOURSOF + b14 M2AGE + b15 F3OCC + b16 F6OCC b17 M2SCH + b18 OC + b19 RURAL + b20 M5OCC + b21F2OCC + b22 FAMSIZE + b23 M1SCH + b24 F1OCC + b25 M1AGE + b26 F5OCC + b27 MBC + b28 CHILDREN + b29 M1 INC)

It may be written in the equation form as,

$$Y = a + b_1X_1 + b_2X_2 \ldots\ldots + b_nX_n + U$$

where,

FAMSIZE = Family size
HINCPM = Average Household income per month
CHILDREN = Number of children
PRICOST = Private Cost of education
FHOURS OF = Father's hours of work per day
MHOURS OF = Mother's hours of work per day
M1AGE = Father's age
M1SCH = Father's schooling in years
M1INC = Father's income
M2AGE = Mother's age
M2SCH = Mother's schooling in years
GATOT = Total Government Assistance
F1OCC = Father's occupation is farming (owning land)
F2OCC = Father's occupation is self-employment
F3OCC = Father's occupation is government employee
F4OCC = Father's occupation is private employee
F5OCC = Father's occupation is daily wage labour
F6OCC = Father's occupation is unemployed
M1OCC = Mother's occupation is farming (owning land)
M2OCC = Mother's occupation is self-employment
M3OCC = Mother's occupation is government employee
M4OCC = Mother's occupation is private employee
M5OCC = Mother's occupation is daily wage labour
M6OCC = Mother's occupation is unemployed
RURAL = Location of residence (rural = 0, urban = 1)

BC	=	Backward Community
MBC	=	Most Backward Community
SCST	=	Scheduled Caste/Scheduled Tribe
OC	=	Other Community

It is observed from Table 3 that the government assistance provided to the students had positively and significantly influenced the enrolment of students in government and government aided institutions. The influence of government assistance was at one per cent level. Likewise

TABLE 3

Influence of Government Assistance on Enrolment

Variable	β	t
HINCPM	-1.03107E-05	-0.550
M3OCC	0.193261	0.876
M6OCC	1.231400	1.543
PRICOST	7.818402E-04	2.502*
M2OCC	-0.165914	-0.945
M1OCC	-0.254869	-0.558
GATOT	0.413542	6.700**
F4OCC	0.202945	1.760
MHOURSOF	-0.020085	-1.243
FHOURSOF	0.017742	1.164
M2AGE	-0.004900	-0.742
F3OCC	0.229828	1.423
F6OCC	-0.185240	-0.654
M2SCH	0.023307	1.802
OC	-0.277544	-2.487*
RURAL	0.029273	0.263
M5OCC	0.071595	0.557
FAMSIZE	0.040292	0.806
M1SCH	0.030088	2.130*
F1OCC	0.499479	1.003
M1AGE	-0.015380	-2.304*
(Constant)	0.966522	3.057**
R^2 = 0.44154	N = 563	

Note: *significant at five per cent level
**significant at one per cent level

father's schooling has also significantly influenced the enrolment of their wards. It means that the rate of enrolment was high if he was educated. The case of private cost was different. It denotes that higher the private cost, higher was the enrolment. Another significant inference from this analysis is that the other community (forward community) households had lesser enrolment in government and government aided institutions. The age of the father also had played a vital role in the enrolment of the children. It means that the aged father did not prefer to send their children to school. It may be understood that the households having aged father might have preferred to send their children to work than sending them to school and to look after the family.

VII. CONCLUSION

In this study, it has been attempted to find out the distribution of benefits of education and educational expenditure using the mean enrolment rate. It reveals that the lower levels of education were availed of more by the lower income groups and higher levels of education benefited the higher income groups. It denotes that higher income groups preferred private institution than government institution as far as lower levels of education was concerned. More or less it was established both in rural and urban areas. The analysis on the distribution of government expenditure also reveals that the primary and middle levels of education was availed of more by the lower income groups and higher education was availed of more by the higher income groups. The above analysis proves the hypothesis that the lower levels of education are pro-poor and higher levels of education pro-rich.

Another analysis to measure the influence of government assistance on enrolment reveals that the government assistance had positive influence on enrolment at one per cent level. It means that the government assistance provided in the form of fee concession, books, bus fare concession, uniform, scholarship and mid-day meal scheme had positively influenced the enrolment of students. The study very well established that the financial assistance provided by the government to the students had positive significance on the enrolment of the students. In a nutshell, it is underlined that the distribution of education and educational expenditure was in favour of poor as far as lower levels of education were concerned and it was in favour of higher income households as far as higher education was concerned. Another significant inference from this study was that the income criteria have played a significant role rather than the social group criteria.

References

Aaron, M. and Mcguire, M. (1970), "Public Goods and Income Distribution", *Econometrica*, Vol. 38, pp. 113-132.

Ahuja, S.P. (1978), "Distribution of Benefits from Government Expenditure", The Institute of Economic and Market Research, New Delhi.

Arrow, J. Kenneth (1971), "An Utilisation Approach to the Concept of equality in Public Expenditure", *Quarterly Journal of Economics*, Vol. LXXXV, No. 3, August, pp. 341-355.

Arumugam, P. (1983), "Cost and Demand for Secondary Education in Tamil Nadu", an unpublished Ph.D. Thesis, University of Madras.

Ayesha Yaqub Vawda, (2003), "Who Benefits from Public Expenditure on Education", Institute of Economic Afairs, Blackwell Publisher, Oxford.

Dasgupta, A.K. and Tilak, J.B.G. (1983), "Distribution of Education among Income Groups—An Empirical Analysis", *Economic and Political Weekly*, August, 14, Vol. XVIII, No. 33. pp. 1442-1447.

Duraisamy, P. (1988), "An Econometric Analysis of Fertility, Child Schooling and Labour Force Participation of Women in Rural Indian Households", *Journal of Quantitative Economics*, Vol. 4, Nos. 2, pp. 293-316.

Gupta, A.P. (1980), "Who Benefits from Government Expenditure in India", [Mimeographed], Indian Institute of Management, Ahmedabad.

Jan Vant Eind Gerrit *et al.* (1986), "Evaluating the Distribution of Public Expenditure", *The Review of Income and Wealth*, Vol. 32, No. 3, Sep, pp. 77-85.

Jimmenez Emmanual (1986), "The Public Subsidisation of Education and Health in Developing Countries"—A Review of Equity and Efficiency", *Research Observer*, No. 1, January.

Majumdar, Manabi and Vaidyanathan, A. (1994), "Access to Education in India: Retrospect and Prospect", *Journal of Educational Planning and Administration*, Vol. III, No. 4, October, pp. 353-403.

Meerman Jacob (1979), "Public Expenditure in Malaysia", Who Benefits and Why? Oxford University Press, Oxford.

Mehrotra. S. (2004), "Reforming Public Spending on Education and Mobilising Resources", *Economic and Political Weekly*, Feb. 2008.

Moonis Raza (1991), "Higher Education in India", Association of Indian University, New Delhi.

Panchamukhi, P.R. (1981), "Inequality in Education", Centre for Multi-Disciplinary Research, Dharwad.

Psacharopoulos, G. and Woodhall, M. (1985), "Education for Development– An Analysis of Investment Choices", World Bank, Oxford University Press, New York.

Reddy, B. Shiva (1991), "Public Expenditure on Education: A Case Study of Andhra Pradesh", *JNU News*, XII(8), August.

Selowsky Marcelo (1979), "Who Benefits from Government Expenditure? A case study of Colombia", Oxford University Press, New York.

Tamil Nadu—An Economic Appraisal, Government of Tamil Nadu.

Tilak, J.B.G. (1989), "The Political Economy of Education in India", Department of Education Studies, Universities of Virginia, USA.

Tilak, J.B.G. (1990), "Education and Earnings: Gender Difference in India", *International Journal of Development Planning Literature*, Vol. 5, No. 4, pp. 131-139.

Tilak, J.B.G. (2004), "Publish Subsidies in Education in India", *Economic and Political Weekly*, Jan-2004.

Van De Walle Dominique (1992), "The Distribution of the Benefits from Social Services in Indonesia 1978-87", World Bank Conference on Public Expenditure and the Poor: Incidence and Targeting, Washington, DC, June 17-19.

27

Human Capital Investment on Education: A Study on Rural Households in Tamil Nadu

E. Nanda Kumar

INTRODUCTION

The term Human Capital refers to the process of acquiring and increasing the number of persons who have the skills, education and experience which are critical for the economic and the political development of a country. Human capital is thus associated with investment in man and his development as creative and productive persons. The concept of human capital refers to the fact that human being invest in themselves, by means of education, training, or other activities, which raises their future income by increasing their lifetime earnings. Economists use the term "Investment" to refer to expenditure on assets which will produce income in the future. Investments in Human Capital produces benefit both for the individual and the society. The concept of human capital can be applied not only to education and training, but to any activity which increases the quality and productivity of the labour force and thus helps raise future income levels (George Psacharopoulous, 1987).

Human Capital also defined as the stock of skills and productive knowledge embodied in people (Rosen, 1987). In terms of economics, capital is that which is a factor of production and which helps to enlarge productive potential of the society. Human being is a capital asset, which yields a stream of economic benefits over his working life. Human capital is a part of man (Schultz, 1971). It is "Human" because it is embodied in man and it is "Capital" because it is a source of future satisfaction or earning or both. Human capital, unlike other physical assets, cannot be sold but can be acquired by means of investing in oneself. Investment in human capital includes all activities that increase human resources (Nickell *et al.,* 1976). Expenditure on human resource and development has come to be regarded as an investment. (Dhingra, 1988). It seems to be perceived as a process of contributing to and developing the quality embodied in human beings (Mathur, 1981).

INVESTMENT IN EDUCATION AND ECONOMIC GROWTH

Education represents both consumption and investment, on one hand, it is valued for its immediate benefits, but on the other, it helps to create income in the future by providing educated workers with skills and knowledge that enable them to increase their productive capacities and thus receive higher earnings. Expenditure on Education is a valuable investment. Education matters, economically—for economic growth, reduction in poverty and inequalities, improvement in income distribution, besides contributing to other social, political and cultural dimensions of development and human development. From a narrow point of view of economic returns also, there is sufficient justification for public funding of education, in comparison with other economic sectors.

Investment in Human Capital is widely viewed as the expenditure on education, health, training, career related knowledge and skills which improve the productive capacity of the person, increase his adaptability to the changing requirements of the economy, improves the quality of human being and increase the future monetary income potential of a person, family and the nation at large. Does investment in education necessarily enhance economic growth? There are compelling reasons that it should, but the empirical evidence does not always support this conclusion. Individuals are willing to take more years of schooling partly because they can earn more and get better jobs, on average, with more schooling. For many, more schooling can also be a source of social mobility. Similarly, nation-states and regions are interested in raising the average level of schooling in their population, in part, because they think that doing so will improve productivity, raise the quality of jobs in the economy, and increase economic growth.

The link between education and economic growth in some of the early work on the economics of education was based on the argument that a major effect of more education is that an improved labor force has an increased capacity to produce. Because better-educated workers are more literate, they should be easier to train. It should be easier for them to learn more complex tasks. In addition, they should have better work habits, particularly awareness of time and dependability. But exactly how education increases productivity, how important it is, and in what ways it is important are questions that have no definite answers. A shortage of educated people may limit growth, but it is unclear that a more educated labor force will increase economic growth.

NEED FOR THE STUDY

Human Capital is by all counts the most crucial factor in the process of economic development. Investment in Human Capital includes investment in education, health and nutrition. For an accelerated economic development it is necessary that not only the physical but also the human capital is accumulated at a high rate. In the present state of technological advancement it is absolutely essential to regard education and training as the most potential ingredients of capital. Actually, education is now being regarded as the first investment in existing human capital.

The evidence in economics strengthens the view that promoting Human Welfare need; among the other things, investment in people in the form of education. It is necessary for individual as well as national development and welfare such forms investment in children or people are taking place. So even though education is available at much subsidized rate, children's are not availing of it to the extent it should. When one attempts to understand the reason behind this state of affairs, it revels the fact that the individual household which plays crucial role in such investment. So to understand the factors which are influencing the investment in children it becomes necessary to understand the family/household decision-making process and more especially the allocation for resources of children's education providing by them.

OBJECTIVES OF THE STUDY

- To study the Socio-economic Conditions of the Rural Households.
- To analyse the Pattern of Investment in Education of Rural Children.
- To analyse the presence or absence of gender discrimination among sample respondents of rural households.

DATA SOURCES AND METHODOLOGY

To achieve the above objectives primary data was collected from the rural households of Kinathukadavu Block in Coimbatore District, Tamil Nadu. Based on the different income groups, 142 rural households were selected at random and the pattern of investment and gender discrimination on human capital investment on children's were analysed with the help of mean, standard deviation and stepwise regression.

Analysis of the Data

The collected data has been analysed by using Ordinary Least Squares (OLS) and Stepwise Regression

Method. To analyse the empirical work we use regression analysis. It is used in this analysis because it would explain Parental role in developing human capital of children. In other words it would explain the determinants of volume of expenditure incurred by the parent on the education of children. In this study dependent variable is a continuous variable. Independent variables, such as occupation of father or mother and education of father and mother are dichotomous or categorical variables in the regression and are treated as 'dummies'. Therefore, our basic model is Ordinary Least S(OLS) regression with continuous and dummy regressors.

$$E.EDU = a_1 + \sum_{i=1}^{n} b_1 Xij + U_1$$

where,

E.EDU are the dependent variables,
E.EDU stands for Education expenditure on children,
i : stands for independent variable,
j : stands for individual child,
Xij : (I = 1.........n) are the independent variables continuous or dummy variables, and
U_1 and U_2 are unobserved random variables.

Specifically the model hypothesised that the parental role of investment in human capital (i.e.) expenditure on education/health is a function of total monthly income of the family, age of father, age of mother, education of father and mother, size of the family, occupation of head of the family.

RESULTS AND DISCUSSION

The first equation of table shows that the total monthly income, Age of father (in years), Education of father and Education of mother have emerged significant on Investment of Education for their Children. The model shows that the income is the important determinant for investment in education, with one per cent level of significance. Higher the

TABLE I

Regression Results of Expenditure on Education of Children

Variables	*Equation 1*	*Equation 2*	*Equation 3*
Constant	3.432	3.248	2.725
	(51.375)	(37.408)	(12.566)
Total Monthly Income	0.530	0.406	0.354
	(7.207)*	(5.014)*	(4.333)*
Age of Father in years	0.160	0.188	–
	(2.157)**	(2.621)***	
Age of Mother in years	0.138	0.169	0.038
	(1.840)	(2.333)	(0.294)
Education of the Father in years	0.258	–	0.281
	(3.181)**		(3.520)*
Education of the Mother in years	0.169	0.024	0.076
	(2.097)***	(.235)	(0.758)
Total size of the family	0.011	0.044	0.037
	(0.155)	(0.613)	(0.525)
Occupation of the family head	0.003	-0.046	-0.035
	(0.033)	(-0.602)	(-0.461)
R-Square	0.281	0.332	0.365
F	51.940	32.812	25.137

Notes: *1% Level of Significance; **5% Level of Significance; ***10% Level of Significance.

income more the investment on education. Age of father shows five percent level of significance; it shows that with increasing age father allocates more funds on education for his children. Education of father is also important for investing in education, if the father is well educated he invests more on his children's education. Likewise, mother's education also influences the investment in education with 10 per cent level of significance. This model shows only 28 percent of variations in household expenditure on education.

The second equation of table reveals that total monthly income and age of the father in years are statistical significant. Total monthly income shows one per cent level of significance where it indicates higher income in the family brings increase in the household investment in education of children. Similarly, age of father shows 10 per cent level of significance because the age of father is considered to be important in the context of investing in education for their children. After certain stage in one's life, productivity declines and during this stage of father, the services of children may be required more than the earlier period and hence the role of father declines. This model explaines variation by about 33 per cent.

The equation 3 shows, Total monthly income and Education of father in years are statistically significant at 1 per cent level of significance. All the three models show that income is significant to the investment on education of children. Education of father influences the investment on education of their children. Higher levels of education of father reflects both the greater and efficiency in the production of human capital and a better perception of the returns to schooling for the children; educated father tends to provide better schooling for their children than a less educated fathers.

GENDER DISCRIMINATION

The differential treatment of children at household level on the basis of their gender is much talked about subject in Economics and Sociology. Since we have ventured to study the household resource allocation in education it is in order to look into the discrimination if any in the expenditure on education of boys and girls.

Based on the mean we have attempted to analyze the gender discrimination between the boy and girl in the rural households. Based on the expenditures made by the parents for both of their children we have calculated mean and standard deviation and Co-efficient of variation for Education.

Table 2 shows that the extent mean expenditures spent on both boy and girl child for their education and we can infer the gender discrimination was there in the rural area. The mean education expenditure spend on the male child is Rs. 615.42 whereas in case of female child they spend on an average less amount on the education that is Rs. 587.50. Educational expenditure on male child is more than on

TABLE 2

Mean and Standard Deviation for the Amount Spent on Education between Male and Female Children

Expenditure	*Mean*	*STD. Dev*	*CV. (in Rs.)*
Male	615.42	633.098	97.21
Female	587.50	970.640	60.53

female child. This implies that there is more awareness now for treating equally girl and boy child without discrimination. This has led to more enrolment of girl children in schools and colleges.

CONCLUDING OBSERVATIONS

Education serves to develop individuals to become competent and responsible citizens by giving men and women an opportunity to acquire an understanding of the values and philosophy of their life (Swanson, 1981). Children included several aspects such as provision of various facilities, providing motivation, guidance, supervision and participation of the parents in educational activities. The standard economic literature has shown that the schooling is an important engine of growth, but schooling is at best a weak proxy of all human capital.

In this analysis, an attempt has been made to collect information regarding the parental role in developing human capital of children—a case study at Kinathukadavu, Coimbatore District, Tamil Nadu. The results show that most of the families are sending their wards to private schools as compared to government schools. As for the reasons for selecting of schools, most of the parents prefer to give good education to their wards through private schools; one-fourth of household prefer government schools because of low income and not investing more on education of their children. Educational expenditure for male child was more than the female child. This implies that there is need of awareness among the parents to invest more on education for female child and treating equally girls and boys. This will help avoid discrimination among the children. This will help ensure more enrolment of girl children in schools and colleges in the present knowledge society.

REFERENCES

Becker, G.S. (1964), "Human Capital: A Theoretical and Empirical Analysis, with Special Reference to Education", Columbia University Press, New York.

Benson, C.S. (1982), "Household Production of Human Capital: Time Use of Parents and Children as Inputs", McMahon, W.W., Geske, T.

Bouchard, P. (1998), "Training and Work: Myths about Human Capital", Thompson Educational Publishing, Toronto.

Blaugh, M. (1976), "The Empirical Status of Human Capital Theory: A Slightly Jaundiced Survey, *Journal of Economics*, Lit. 14.

Duncan Thomas (1991), "Gender Differences in Household Resource Allocation". Living Standards Measurement Study, Working Paper No. 79, World Bank, Washington.

George Psacharopoulos (1987), "Education Research and Studies", Pergamon Press.

Kiker, B.F. (1967), "The Concept of Human Capital in the History of Economic Thought", *The Indian Economic Journal*, Vol. XIV.

Mark Schonewille (2001), "Does Training make a Difference? Institutional Environment and Returns to Human Capital", Paper for the International Labour Market Conference at Aberdeen, University of Nijmegan.

Martin Husz (1998), "Human Capital, Endogeneous Growth and Government Policy", Peter Lang Gmbh.

Meeneesha Shukul (2007), "Investment In Human Capital by Families", *Journal of Social Sciences*, 14(2).

Nagapal, C.S., Mittal, A.C. (1963), "Education for Economic and Social Development" Economics of Education (perspectives in modern economics), Anmol Publication Pvt. Ltd.

Paul, T. Schultz (1992), "The Role of Education and Human Capital in Economic Development: An Empirical Assessment", Paper presented at the Conference on Economic Growth in the World Economy.

Philip, H. Brown (2006), "Parental Education and Investment in Children's Human Capital in Rural China", Economic Development and Cultural Change, the University of Chicago. Vol. 54.

Rubenson, K. (1992), "Human Resoruce Development: A Historical Perspective", In L.E. Burton, In Developing Resourceful Humans: Adult Education within the Economic Context, New York, Routledge.

Schultz, T.W. (1961), "Investment in Human Capital". *The American Economic Review*, 1(2), 1-17.

28

Tibetans Higher Education: A Socio-Economic Outlook

A Case Study in Chennai

V. Renuka Devi, Shweta V. and Sindhu T.S.

Education is one of the most crucial empowering tools for an individual. Education lays the foundation for a better life and throws open doors to employability. Compulsory primary education is instilled by the constitution to all citizens but for immigrants especially refugees, though survival is the priority, for young children, education is pre-condition for a comfortable life in the ever changing world.

India is a country that is a place of asylum for many people leaving their homeland, especially those from neighbouring countries including Bangladesh, Srilanka, and Tibet. Tibetan people are the focus when it comes to education, as the population of Tibetans in India is large. According to the Tibetan demographic survey conducted in 1998, hundred and eleven thousand Tibetans are in exile of which 85,000 are in India. In a first periodic report brought out by the HRD ministry in 2001 on rights of child, the Tibetan refugees are figured at 93,100. However, the UNHRC report gives a provisional estimate of about 77,500 Tibetans in India. In 2005, 2445 refugees came into exile in Dharamsala.

Though most Tibetans came to India as there is a fear of persecution in Tibet, the trend has since changed. Since 1960, a lot of young children have come to India, crossing the giant Himalayas, treacherous mountain stretches that are snow capped, and surviving the months long ordeal of walking through cold winds and storms. The escape from Tibet to India in itself is a dream; however, a larger dream is to survive in a new country with a completely different Diaspora.

The Indian Government gave the Tibetans land in different parts of the country to settle themselves. The Tibetans have used it most effectively to develop a model community and make them self-reliant. Recognising the need to build stronger minds and healthier children, who are Tibet's future. Tibetans, under the guidance of his Holiness Dalai Lama, set-up nursery that later developed into children's village and schools.

THE ROLE OF GOVERNMENT OF INDIA

The Indian Government provided shelter to the religious leader Dalai Lama and 85000 Tibetans who fled their country in 1959. The Tibetans were given lands for settlement in different parts of India. The largest Tibetan settlement in India is at Bylakuppe, Karnataka. The Tibetans on reaching Indian border are given an identity certificate, with which they are free to travel within the country. The Indian government later since 1979 also gave citizenship to second generation Tibetans. It is seen that India is the only country that accepts all refugees and has not signed the 1959 convention and 1967 protocol on refugees. Although there is pressure from China, India remains firm on safeguarding the rights of Tibetans and does not deport them. India has also worked towards the cause of education by establishing central schools for Tibetans.

THE TIBETAN COMMUNITY

Tibetan Community is seen as a model community of people who are self-sufficient and self-reliant. They have pulled themselves together and made the most efficient use of resources at their disposal. Not only have they been successful in safeguarding their religion and culture but also display a very impressive and inspiring example of building community, working together and ameliorating the masses.

The Tibetans are mainly engaged in farming and handicrafts. This community is progressive and well balanced. The various Tibetan settlements have been so developed and prosperous which today house a number of schools and medical centres. The schools have a sufficient boarding system and homes to accommodate the increasing number of children moving into India.

EDUCATION IN TIBET AT A GLANCE

Tibet referred as Tibetan Autonomous Region (TAR) now, has seen a grim educational scenario since the Chinese occupation. With more young refugees seeking opportunities outside Tibet only a smaller percentage of Tibetans remain to study in Tibet especially for higher education.

The United Nations Development Programme ranks Tibet the last among its provinces in the human development for year 2002. Xinhua, the Chinese national news agency, cites the illiteracy rate of young people to be 34.27 per cent, though the White Paper on Modernisation in Tibet in 2001 declared that the illiteracy rate among youth was 32.5 per cent. The Human Development Report, 2006, shows that the regions in which Tibetans are located fall in the lowest eight ranks in the overall Human Development Index (HDI), with the TAR being the 31st, which is the lowest rank, and Qinghai being the 27th. As for school attendance rate, the percentage for TAR is 77.9 while the overall percentage for China is 98.7 per cent.

By the end of 2005, there were 890 elementary schools, 1,568 teaching centers, with a total student number of 328,000 and an attendance rate of 95.9 per cent for the children of

TABLE I

Number of Schools by Level and Type: Tibetan Autonomous Region (TAR)

Year	*Regular institution of higher learning*	*Secondary schools*	*Secondary special schools*	*Regular Secondary schools*	*Primary schools*	*Kindergarten*
1980	4	98	24	74	6206	256
1985	3	70	14	56	2315	21
1990	3	78	15	63	2474	37
1995	4	102	16	86	3943	29
2000	4	110	12	98	842	21
2005	4	128	10	118	896	42

school age; there were 93 junior middle schools, with 121,000 students and an attendance rate of 75.4 per cent.

Tibet has senior middle schools, with 33,000 enrolled students, as well as 10 secondary vocational schools. The total number of students in the senior-middle-school phase has reached 46,000 and the attendance rate has risen to 30 per cent. The average number of years of study for 15-year-old youngsters has reached five.

The movement of Tibetans into other countries for purpose of education follows the following important causes:

(a) *No minority status*: At the end of 2005, the population of the Tibet Autonomous Region reached 2.77 million, a net increase of 33,200 over 2004. The average population density stood at 2.26 people per square km, equaling one-60th of the national average. They do not however follow the minority regulations. China has in fact made Chinese the medium of instruction in schools which is against the minorities. This came into effect in 1998.

(b) *Politicising education*: As part of its preferential policies toward local ethnic groups, a flexible method of enrolment is applied in all schools by lowering the passing marks of local ethnic groups and then taking into account their test results. While it is true that admission to the University of Tibet in Lhasa does not require high grades, Tibetans must pass an entrance exam in Chinese to enrol in the university.

(c) "TAR" Board of Education (TARBOE) issued a new directive in 2003 to inhibit the educational progress of Tibetan youth by instituting new testing procedures for government-funded college education. The TARBOE now mandates that every student applying for standard government educational funding undergo ideological testing prior to the standard written exam for entrance to college or vocational training programs.

(d) In the TAR, very few graduated become employed as there are only scanty vacancies in the Government service.

EDUCATION FOR TIBETAN REFUGEES—THE BEGINNING

With the Chinese invasion of Tibet in 1950, Dalai Lama and thousands of Tibetans moved out of Tibet and took refuge in India. The very first establishment being their settlement at Dharamsala. The immediate concern was the care taking of malnourished and destitute children. There are heart-warming stories of the children leaving their homeland, leaving behind their family and friends for a brighter future. The main reason being "EDUCATION" which is at its grass roots in Tibet.

Initially, with the help of Government of India a nursery for Tibetan refugee children was established. In sometime as more children arrived the pressure of overcrowding and the need to empower the children was realized as they were the future of Tibet. The nursery, therefore, gradually expanded and took a shape of a small village. In 1971, Tibetan Children's Village (TCV) took over a small nursery in Patlikulh in Dharamsala and expanded it into a residential school. In 1972, it was formally registered under the societies act as Tibetan children's village. Since then to address the problem of education of Tibetan children many TCVs have been established, not only in north India but also in the south. Tibetan Homes Foundation (THF) is a registered charitable institute dedicated in working for the care of orphan, semi-orphan and destitute Tibetan refugee children. Almost four decades have gone by since its small beginning in November 1962 at Mussoorie by His Holiness Tenzin Gyatso the XIVth Dalai Lama.

At the request of Dalai Lama, the Government of India in 1961 established the Tibetan schools society now known as Central Tibetan Schools Administration (CTSA), an autonomous body regulated by the Indian Ministry of Human Resource Development, to manage and assist schools in India for the education of the children of Tibetan refugees.

GROWTH OF TCV AND CTSA SCHOOLS

There are 28 CTSA schools whose enrolment is currently 9,991 students. The schools run under CTSA are Central School for Tibetans (CST). Six of these schools (CST Mussoorie; CST Shimla; CST Dalhousie; CST Darjeeling, CST Mundgod and CST Kalimpong) that in addition to day scholars provide hostel and boarding facilities to a total of about 1,700 students are known as residential schools. The remaining 22 schools that do not have such facilities are known as day schools.

There are 8 senior secondary schools, 5 secondary schools, 8 middle schools and 7 primary schools established by CSTA.

The following are some of the salient features of the Central Schools for Tibetans:

- Central Schools for Tibetans are located at places that have a sizeable population of Tibetans. Most of these schools are located in hilly and far-flung areas.
- The medium of instruction in these schools from Pre-primary to Class V is Tibetan and English from Class VI to XII. However, Hindi is taught as

a compulsory subject from Class VI to VIII and as optional from Class IX onwards.

- The schools follow 10+2 system of Education.
- Central Schools for Tibetans prepare students for All India Secondary School Examination (X) and All India Senior School Certificate Examination (XII) conducted by Central Board of Secondary Education, Delhi.
- CTSA has six Residential schools up to +2 stage at Mussoorie, Dalhousie, Shimla, Darjeeling, Kalimpong and Mundgod with hostel facility for both boys and girls.

During 2001-02, there were 70 schools spread all over India, including Senior Secondary, Secondary, Middle, Primary and Pre-Primary schools and grant-in-aid schools. In the year 2004, 9132 students received education in schools run by CTSA.

The TCV schools also expanded with a greater inflow of refugees. TCV Ladakh was established in 1975 to help the children in remote areas. Today there are 8 TCV schools which are:

1. *Upper TCV Dharamsala*—Established in 1970, as a product of a massive re- organization of nursery for children arriving at road construction camps. It has 1794 children.
2. *TCV Patlikuhl (now Chauntra)*—Established in 1971, as TCV took over a nursery and later converted it into a residential school. By 1979 there were 300 children. There are over 900 children now. This TCV had educational facilities till class eight has eight dormitories and two hostels.
3. *TCV Ladakh*—Established in 1975, with seed money from his holiness and land donated by the Indian government. Today TCV Ladakh is a SOS village with its own school and facilities. At present it accommodates 1921 children.
4. *TCV Bylakuppe*—Established in 1981, at the largest concentration of Tibetans in south India. Currently

the village has 30 homes, two hostels and complete facilities for education through class 12. It has 1317 children.

5. *Lower TCV Dharamsala*—Established in 1984 to solve the problem of over crowding in upper Dharamsala. This school is now developed up to class 10. Over the years the school has developed into one of the best residential schools in exile solely financed by Tibetan parents
6. *TCV Bir*—Founded in 1990, TCV took over the new Tibetan school housing 68 students who lived and studied in rental houses there. Presently the village has 12 children's homes each housing 30-40 children.
7. *TCV Gopalpur*—The latest addition TCV established in 1997, spread over 31 acres and a senior secondary school. It accommodates 1441 children. It is a self-contained, children's community with 32 homes, a medical centre and hostels for boys and girls. The attached school complex has complete facilities for education from Kindergarten to Senior Secondary.
8. *TCV Selakui*—started in 2001. It now has 272 students.

FUNDING FOR THE SCHOOLS

An average of 950 Tibetan students graduate from different Tibetan schools in India every year. The Department of Education (Dharamsala) offers scholarship to about 200 students for further education. The CST schools provide for free boarding to students from poor families and others are considered paid boarders. Since 1975 the governing body has approved the special case of Indian born Tibetans who wish to join residential schools provided their parents pay for boarding and lodging. Free education is imparted to students from primary to Class XII.

The TCV schools are funded by the Tibetan Government in exile as well as donations from willing hearts.

PROBLEM OF HIGHER EDUCATION

Tibetan students receive good education from CST or TCV schools in India at concessional rates. However the core problem that stands tall is the problem of higher education. Though there are a number of Tibetan schools, collegiate education seems a far dream for most Tibetans. The system of school education however, imparts vocational training to girl students to enable them to fetch jobs. Infact, vocational training is compulsory in CST schools. Those interested can take up further vocational training at VTC, Selakui established in 2000, which can accommodate over 204 youths. The centre imparts technical skills to youth in various trades enabling them not only to be absorbed in industries but also equip them to go for self-employment.

However, when it comes to regular courses in colleges, the students will have to move out of their regions into cities. Those students having guardians or parents who can sponsor their education will not have much problem; however, the students who are desirous of higher education in a good college but coming from poor families or those who are destitute have no financial support. Collegiate education is not only expensive but the cost of mobility seems too burdensome.

To identify the problems of Tibetan students when it comes to collegiate education, a survey was conducted among 100 Tibetan students out of 180 who are studying in Chennai. The following were the outcome of the survey:

The respondents included 42 males and 52 females.

The respondents were of the age group 19-24.

79 of them from TCV school, 12 from CST, 5 from THF and 4 from private schools.

• The students moving to Chennai for higher studies find it difficult to get admission into colleges as they do not have relatives or friends here to guide them. According to the survey, the students mostly stay in groups and a few opt for hostel. Their guardianship becomes an issue as they do not have relatives in Chennai. If their siblings live in Chennai then it is not an issue. Some students have their friends as guardian, 23 per cent have their seniors as guardians and 19 per cent are under the care of *Ms.Asha Reddy,* a social worker.

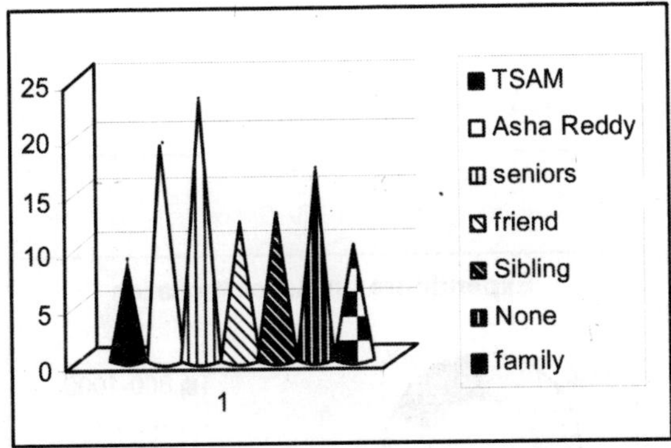

TABLE 2

Guardian in Chennai

TSAM	9
Asha Reddy	19
Seniors	23
Friend	12
Sibling	13
None	17
Family	10

Some willing seniors who faced problems during their admission help the freshers seeking admission.

- **Accommodation**

It is also seen that most students stay as groups. However, the financial constraint on them makes them avail cheap houses in the suburbs.

The major problem with accommodation and lodging is their expense on gas. Since, they are only refugees and do not hold the citizenship here and they are unable to get cylinders and have to go for commercial purchase of fuel.

TABLE 3

Expenditure on Accommodation

In Rupees	*Number*
800-1000	19
1000-1500	23
1500-2000	23
2000-5000	35

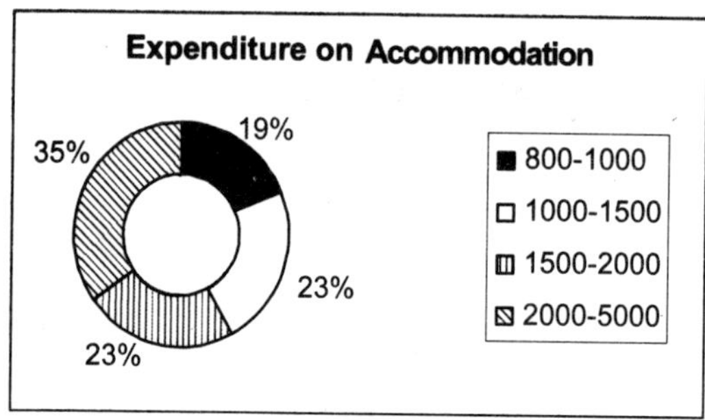

- **Lack of funds to pay for their education**

The Tibetan students get sponsorship from their schools. However these funds are insufficient for them to relocate to Chennai. According to the survey about 35 per cent of the students spend about Rs. 2000 to Rs. 5000 per month on accommodation. For a year they have to spend more than 100,000 rupees, for which their school sponsorship is not enough. The student's are forced to work to earn some money.

TABLE 4

Expenditure for Higher Education

4000-6000	10
6000-8000	14
8000-10000	20
above 10000	56

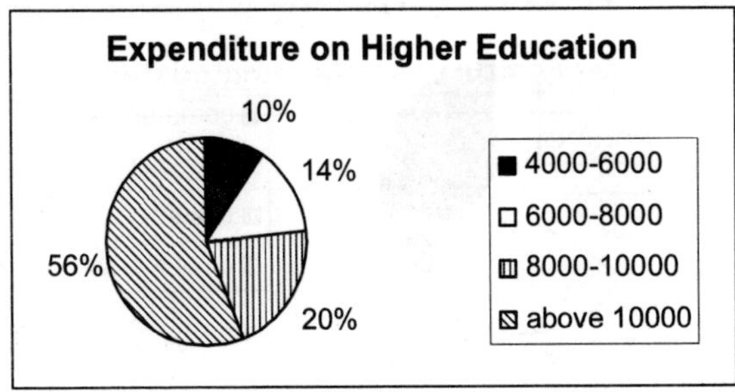

Other Problems

Apart from accommodation and funding the Tibetan students face problem of communication, financial burden and security problems. The survey showed that 40 per cent of the students suffer a language barrier. Their everyday movement through public transport is difficult. The auto-drivers are not too conversant in English. 26 per cent of the respondents have financial strain, take care of everyday expenses. 9 per cent face security problems. There is a fear of being harassed and ill-treated. 25 per cent of the respondents face all three problems which highlights the plight of students. The problem of communication develops as these students come to India when they are too young, around age of five to ten years, where they have studied only Tibetan or Chinese. They are given training once they reach any Tibetan settlement. Therefore, initially communicating in English seems difficult. Secondly, the students come to Chennai from the north or other state. Tamil is a completely alien language to them and it is difficult to communicate to the locals, for people, who are not that conversant in English.

TABLE 5

Problems Faced by Tibetan Students

Communication	40
Financial	26
Security	9
all of the above	25

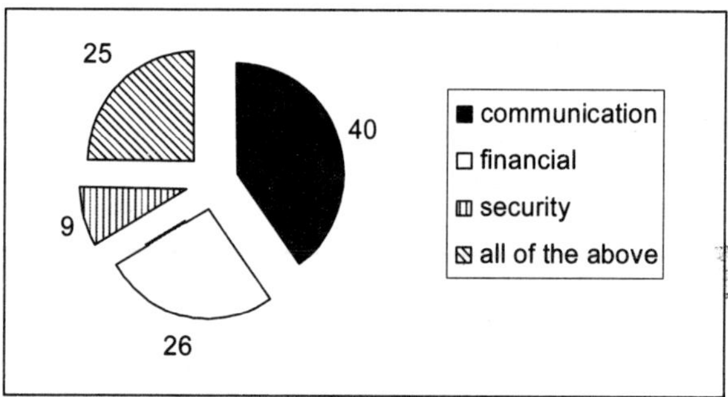

he students also face problems during admission to colleges. Apart from the lack of proper guidance to the students because of being new to the city, the Tibetans fall under the OC category which is very competitive. These students come from a CBSE background which makes it even tougher.

A startling fact is that only a few Tibetans are able to go for professional education such as engineering or management or visual communication. This is because of the lack of necessary financial strength to invest in these courses. The students get a sum of Rs. 10000 to 20000 from their schools on successful completion of the course. This is given to them as a yearly allowance to invest in collegiate education. However, Most students only manage to get admission into arts and science courses given that they compete in the general category and have a financial constraint. The survey reveals that only 3 per cent are studying professional courses at Masters' level.

TABLE 6

Category of Students

UG Sciences	7
UG Arts	74
PG Sciences	1
PG Arts	15
Professional	2
M.Phil	1

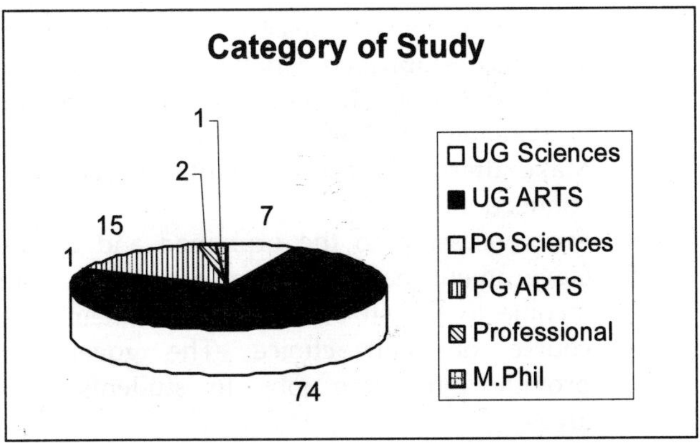

To address the problems of Tibetan students and act as a forum to bring together and help each other Tibetan Students Association of Madras (TSAM) was formed. However, the real help has to come from the Government of India to take forward the children community.

Every year about 2000 children move to India from Tibet. To help them in bringing up in the right path much need to be done. The schooling has been taken care of by THF and SOS villages. However, collegiate education is available outside Tibetan settlements only.

WHAT THE GOVERNMENT OF INDIA CAN DO?

1. Although the scholarships are awarded to students by their schools they are insufficient. The schools only provide limited scholarships. Taking into account that the expenditure on education not only includes the college fees but the payment for examination, for books and taking special courses such as computer applications becomes too high. As seen from the survey, if a student wants to opt for professional courses or skill oriented courses then it is unattainable given the lack of funds. Award of more scholarships to Tibetan students and enable them to take up professional courses.
2. Like in Tibetan settlements Government of India has to provide a decent accommodation for the

Tibetan students, at least in the metropolitan cities. TCV has established Tibetan Youth Hostel in Delhi and Bangalore. However no such accommodation is available in Chennai.

3. Make alternative arrangements for acquiring a gas connection.
4. Fee concession to the orphaned and destitute.
5. Government has to ensure alternative sources of income to the students to enable them to study a course of their choice. The government can provide part time jobs to students in specific areas.
6. The admission into colleges should be made easy. A quota for refugees can be set in colleges or a relaxation in cut-off marks should be given.
7. The age limit for Tibetan students should be intimated to the colleges.
8. Most Tibetan students live away from family and often take their seniors to be guardians. There is a lack of a elderly person to guide and motivate them and to share their views and problem in everyday life. The solution to this problem can be the development of compulsory teacher-ward set-up especially for Tibetan students. There can also be a Tibetan students counsellor preferably a Tibetan to take care of their welfare.

References

Catriona Bass (1998), Education in Tibet Policy and Practice Since 1950, Zed Books.

Ellen Bangsbo (2004), Teaching and Learning in Tibet—a Review of Research and Policy Publications, Nordic Institute of Asian Studies (NIAS).

Bhuchung K. Tsering (2006), A Look at Quality of Life in Tibet, *Tibetan Review*, 09 February.

Human Development Report, 2001.

Human Development Report, 2006.

http://www.tcv.org.in/schools.shtml.

wcd.nic.in/crcpdf/CRC-8.PDF

China-Tibet facts, http://en.tibet.cn/newfeature/xzt_2006ssysj/xzt_2006ssysj_xzjj/t20061228_194107.htm

Tibet Centre for Human Rights and Democracy, Annual Report, 2003, www.tchrd.org/publications/topical_reports/education_in_tibet, 2003.

Tibetan Department of Education, http://www.sherig.org/publications/csr/c1.html

Tibet Demographic Survey, 1998, http://www.tibet.com/exileglance.html

Level of Education and Employment in Punjab

HARVINDER KAUR

I. INTRODUCTION

Punjab, once the most prosperous state of the country, has been lagging far behind in terms of per capita income since 1993-94. Being primarily an agro-based economy, the state has also lagged in economic growth on account of slow down in agriculture sector. At the same time, the growth of secondary sector, especially of manufacturing sector has not been of satisfactory level. Service sector, however, is emerging as fast growing sector of the economy of Punjab and constituting over 40 per cent of Net State Domestic Product (NSDP). Though this sector has bypassed industrial sector, yet industrialisation remains a pre-requisite for growth. For the sake of sustainable growth, industrialisation must not have been bypassed (Asian Development Outlook, 2007). As a result, a shift in workforce from agriculture to non-agriculture sector is taking place. Agriculture sector accounted for 62.66 per cent and non-agriculture sector 37.34 per cent of the total workforce in 1971. As of now, the proportion has almost reversed. As per 2001 Census, about 39 per cent of the working population of the state is employed in agriculture sector and 61 per cent in the non-agriculture sector.

Sectoral shifts towards non-agricultural sector, thus, require more educated and skilled workers. No doubt, the number of recognised educational institutions (like schools, colleges specifically engineering colleges, and universities) and the number of students have been increasing. These institutions ironically remain under-staffed affecting the quality of learning. As a consequence, pupil-teacher ratio has been increasing. This ratio was 43.1 at the primary stage, 28:1 at middle level and 26:1 at high/senior stage during 2006. There is an urgent need to employ more teachers in these institutions.

No doubt, literacy rate has been improving, but what irks the economists is the 16th rank that the state holds amongst 28 States and 7 UTs. Further the picture regarding level of education of people in Punjab as per 2001 Census is very disappointing. Among the literates, a little less than half (44%) are those who have below-primary or primary level of education, and a little more than one-fifth (22%) are matriculates. The proportion of those holding graduation degree or higher is a mere 6.6 per cent. Interestingly, this proportion too, is higher among females (6.7%) than the males (6.4). This fact reflects the low level of education in Punjab leading to a lack in high and middle level manpower development. Four decades back economists from industrialised countries cautioned about the occurrence of major bottlenecks in economic growth in non-industrial counties, because of lack of high and middle level manpower (Martin Carnoy, 1977).

Educated and trained manpower is one of the major inputs for economic and social development. Thus, the co-ordination between educational planning and manpower planning is seen as one of the solutions to the problem of sustainable economic growth. The important question which arises is—Is the economic condition of the state deteriorating due to a lack of vision of central and state governments? Why no serious attention is being paid towards the development of human capital in accordance with the changing needs? In the present paper, the author has made an effort to analyse the educational level of workers; pattern of employment; and expenditure on education during Annual Plans of Punjab.

II. LITERARY RATE, WORK PARTICIPATION RATE AND EDUCATIONAL LEVEL OF WORKERS IN PUNJAB

Establishment of close relations between educational and world of work has remained among the top priorities of the developed countries. Very few efforts have been made to establish such relationships by the developing countries. In India, a mention has been made of this link between education and employment in the. Eleventh Five Year Plan (2007-12). The role of education—in facilitating social and economic progress is well recognised in the plan. It mentions, "Education is the most crucial input for empowering people with skills and knowledge and giving them access to productive employment in future". The need for the adaptation of education to employment however still remains neglected.

Punjab is well known for its energetic people. Efforts to equip this energetic community with education are giving applaudable results. Table 1 reveals that the literary rate in Punjab has doubled during the last three decades from 33.67 per cent to 69.7 per cent. According to Census 2001, Punjab has 147.56 lakh literates. Among them 84.42 lakh are males, and 63.14 lakh are females. The state also has 94.35 lakh illiterates. Female literary rate in the state, has shown higher increase from 24.65 per cent in 1971 to 63.35 per cent in 2001 as compared to the male literacy rate which increased from 42.23 per cent to 75.2 per cent during 1971 to 2001. Female literary rate in the state is higher by 10 percentage points as compared to national female literacy rate.

The state has also shown a marked improvement in the work participation rate, which has increased from 28.87 per cent in 1971 to 37.58 per cent in 2001, though as per Census 2001, it still remains marginally lower than that of the country (39.26%). Female work participation rate has

TABLE I

Literacy Rate and Work Participation Rate in Punjab and India

	1971	*1981*	*1991*	*2001*	*Increase 1971-2001*
		Punjab			
Literacy Rate					
Person	34.12	43.37	58.51	69.95	35.83
Male	42.23.	51.23	65.66	75.63	34.40
Female	24.65	34.35	50.41	63.55	38.90
Work Participation Rate					
Person	28.87	31.50	30.88	37.58	8.71
Male	52.82	53.76	54.22	54.10	1.28
Female	1.18	6.16	6.78	18.68	17.50
		India			
Literacy Rate					
Person	34.45	43.56	52.21	64.84	30.39
Male	45.95	56.37	64.13	75.26	29.31
Female	21.97	29.75	39.29	53.67	32.30
WPF					
Person	33.08	36.70	37.50	39.26	6.18
Male	52.61	52.62	51.61	51.93	-0.68
Female	12.11	19.67	22.27	25.68	13.57

witnessed huge spurt, jumping from 1.18 per cent in 1971 to 18.68 per cent in 2001. But it is also lower than national female work participation rate by 7 percentage points. Gender gap in literary rate has reduced from 17.58 percentage points in 1971 to 12.08 percentage points in 2001 and in work participation rate has also fallen from 51.64 percentage points to 35.42 percentage points in 2001. This is an evidence that the gap in the literacy rate between the two sexes is not wide, but a higher gap in the work participation rate is. It clearly reflects from the data that the higher the literacy rate the higher is the work participation. The issue which needs to be addressed is the enhancement of female work participation in Punjab.

TABLE 2

Percentage of Main Workers and Marginal Workers by Sex and Educational Level in Punjab

	1981				1991			
	Main Workers		*Marginal Workers*		*Main Workers*		*Marginal Workers*	
	M	*F*	*M*	*F*	*M*	*F*	*M*	*F*
Illiterate	52.6	50.9	52.6	84.7	41.4	44.2	50.1	73.9
Literate without education	4.8	1.8	5.96	2.45	3.96	2.2	5.8	2.5
Primary	13.6	5.2	15.1	1.1	14.5	7.1	15.8	12.6
Middle	10.7	2.8	9.9	2.0	12.6	4.0	10.97	4.8
Matriculation/Secondary	11.8	11.2	10.9	1.5	18.98	13.6	12.4	5.3
Undergraduation	2.6	4.3	2.3	0.2	3.8	4.1	2.5	0.4
Graduation	2.5	6.04	2.3	0.16	5.1	18.3	1.7	0.4
Postgraduate	0.4	2.3	0.07	0.01				
Technical/Certificate/degree/ diploma postgraduate	1.0	15.3	0.95	0.1	0.6	6.6	0.8	0.17
Total	100 (4749646)	100 (178113)	100 (54698)	100 (305454)	5832852	265522	10491	153124

Sources: Computed from data available in:

(i) Census of India, 1981, Series 17, Punjab, Part-IIIA and B, Vol. I (General Economic Tables)

(ii) Census of India 1991, Series 20, Punjab, Part-III, B, Economic Tables.

TABLE 3

Employment in the Organised Sector in Punjab (Public Sector and Private Sector)

	1981	1991	2001	2002	2003	2004	2005	2006	2007
I. Public Sector									
(i) Central Government	67460	72308	79198	75000	70000	71238	70150	68036	67037
(ii) State Government	255505	293577	302124	302000	296000	289718	266854	291076	257949
(iii) Quasi Government	116606	171618	173548	174000	161000	170517	153138	166599	87140
(iv) Local Government	28224	32556	31276	30000	29000	33132	29834	29722	26916
Total I	467795	570059	586164	581000	56000	564605	519976	422460	439073
II. Private Sector	167340	221230	261083	255000	244000	261339	253104	276290	300679
Grand Total I and II	635135	791289	847247	836000	800000	825944	773116	768750	739752

Source: Economic Survey of Punjab: Various Issues

As the educational level of workers affects their efficiency and productivity, it is important to analyse the same with respect to the state. Table 2 presents the picture of percentage of main workers and marginal workers according to their sex and educational level in Punjab. A large number of main as well as marginal workers (both male and female) are illiterate, however, the percentage has witnessed a significant downward trend. The percentage of illiterate male main workers declined from 52.6 per cent to 41.4 per cent during 1981 and 1991 and that of illiterate male marginal workers came down from 52.6 per cent to 50.1 per cent. Similarly, the percentages of illiterate female main workers and marginal workers have declined from 50.9 to 44.2 and 84.7 to 73.9 respectively during 1981 and 1991. Comparatively, a higher percentage of female workers (both main as well as marginal) is illiterate. The percentage of female workers having primary, middle and matriculation level of education is lower than that of male workers having the same level of education. The situation gets reversed in subsequently higher levels of education. The percentage of female main workers having post-secondary, graduation, postgraduation and certificate/degree/diploma and postgraduate level, technical education is higher than that of male main workers. Now, we can well imagine that how a state, where only 10 per cent of male main workers, and only 30 per cent female main workers, have a level of education above matriculation (in 1991) can make desired progress. Thus, there is a dire need to upgrade the education and skill level of the existing as well as potential workers.

III. NATURE OF EMPLOYMENT IN PUNJAB

An overwhelming majority, i.e. more than 90 per cent of the workers are employed in unorganised sector in Punjab. In 1981 and 1991, the percentage of workers in organised sector was 12.0 and 12.9 respectively, which further reduced to 9.2 in 2001. Table 3 reveals the position of employment in the organised sector in Punjab. Employment in the organised sector (public and private) has been continuously declining since 2004. Of the total organised employment 439073

(59.35%) employees work in public sector, and the remaining 300679 (40.65%) work in private sector as on 31st March, 2007.

Punjab's labour force is growing at a rate higher than the rate of growth of employment. The population of the state has increased from 13551060 in 1971 to 24358999 in 2001. In percentage terms, the state has been registering a decadal growth rate of more than 20 per cent since 1971. Work participation rate on the other hand, has grown from 28.87 per cent in 1971 to 37.58 per cent in 2001, i.e. by 8.71 percentage points only. The magnitude of unemployment continues to be a cause of serious concern in Punjab (*Economic Survey*, Punjab, 2007-08). There is an acute shortage of 1.32 lakh personnel in various government departments. (*The Tribune*, Sept. 5, 2008). On one hand, government is reluctant to fill the vacancies and create new jobs, and on the other, new employment opportunities in the unorganised sector have not been able to keep pace with the growth in the labour force. Number of work seekers on the live register of employment exchange as on 31st March 2007, was 442225. Among them, 75494 were technical personnel and 232953 were non-technical freshers educated.

After the agriculture and IT revolution, an industrial revolution in Punjab is overdue. Industrial sector contributes a very low share in GSDP. It contributed less than 15 per cent of the Gross State Domestic Product for State during 2006-07. Tertiary sector has been contributing more than 40 per cent, while secondary sector has been contributing 20 to 25 per cent in GSDP since 2001. It shows that growth in service sector has bypassed the growth in the industrial sector. Development of industry, mainly through development of agro-based and manufacturing units, can revive and speed up the growth of the economy. Large and medium units have more potential to absorb technically trained and skilled manpower. The solution to optimum utilisation of human resources and rapid economic growth of Punjab economy lies in the balanced growth of three sectors, the increase in the formation of physical capital, industrialisation, and investment in education. More capital and industries would create jobs and more education and improved skill would make the population efficient, productive and more employable. All this, in turn, would increase income, standard of living, and economic growth.

IV. PUBLIC EXPENDITURE ON EDUCATION IN PUNJAB

As the issue of human resource development has been gaining momentum, the centre and the state governments are increasing expenditure on social sector, particularly on education and training. So far as Punjab is concerned, it has been behaving miserly on this front. Actual expenditure on education in various Annual Plans of Punjab is shown in Table 4.

The figures reveal that actual expenditure on general education as a percentage of total expenditure continuously increased from 2.09 per cent in 1980-81 to reach 10.2 per cent in 2001-02, but thereafter, it has been varying between 2 to 6 per cent. Similarly, actual expenditure on technical education as a percentage of total expenditure reached to the level of 2.5 per cent in 1999-2000 from 0.05 per cent in 1980-81. But thereafter, instead of increase in percentage of expenditure on technical education, which is in high demand and directly related to employment, has declined to the level of less than one per cent of total expenditure. It is thus clear that there is a lack of co-ordination between education planning and manpower planning and there is need to link education planning to the emerging needs of the labour market in Punjab.

V. SUMMARY

The name of Punjab can, no doubt, ےe included in the economically advanced regions of India, but it has lost the galory of once being the topper in terms of per capita income. It has lagged behind in terms of economic growth. Slow down of agriculture sector and unsatisfactory growth of manufacturing sector, but fast growth of tertiary sector has changed the entire structure of the economy. This has resulted in sectoral shifts. Workforce is shifting from agriculture to non-agricultural sector. To increase the

TABLE 4

Expenditure on Education in Annual Plans of Punjab

(Lakh Rupees)

Year	*General Education*		*Technical Education*		*Social Services*	
	Actual Exp.	*% to total Exp.*	*Actual Exp.*	*% to total Exp.*	*Actual Exp.*	*% to total Exp.*
1980-81*	626.60	2.09	15.01	0.05	5858.36	19.56
1989-90*	2115.27	2.43	505.17	0.58	16461.26	18.94
1992-93	1761.90	1.99	2556.88	2.88	20942.10	23.62
1993-94	3886.75	3.40	2833.98	2.48	30560	26.74
1994-95	5312.97	3.86	3873.10	2.82	37479.73	27.26
1995-96	5130.23	3.23	4141.50	2.61	32587.17	20.54
1997-98	9879.21	4.91	3073.16	1.53	41419.57	20.59
1998-99	15582.50	7.7	2677.70	1.34	45399.17	22.65
1999-2000	18224.86	10.40	4363.04	2.49	63003.35	35.94
2001-02	20414.92	10.22	1085.72	0.54	69390.29	34.29
2002-03	4805.19	2.42	463.83	0.23	50439.43	25.44
2003-04	6237.66	3.92	203.48	0.12	38484.69	24.19
2004-05	10227.07	5.2	216.67	0.11	33911.18	17.32
2005-06	15549.30	4.14	278.80	0.07	101813.77	27.12
2006-07	24095.95	5.82	457.33	0.11	109374.72	26.41
2007-08	37334.39	7.30	2655.00	0.52	158747.66	31.06

Source: Statiscal Abstract of Punjab : Various Issues.
*Social and Community Services, Approved outlay.

productivity in agriculture sector, and to meet the needs of secondary and tertiary sector, more educated and skilled workers are required. No doubt, literacy rate has been continuously improving, but level of education is very low in Punjab. Only less than one-third of the literate people are with educational level of matric and above. How a region can thus grow with such a lack of high and middle level manpower! Work participation rate has been improving, but a very low educational level of workers is a cause to worry. Punjab is a state, where 40 to 50 per cent of workforce is illiterate (census 1981 and 1991).

Besides it, more than 90 per cent of those who are working are in unorganised sector where most of them are paid very low wages. Organised sector is shrinking and new employment opportunities in the unorganised sector are not growing at a rate compatible with the growth rate of the labour force. As a result, unemployment has become a serious problem causing social and personal unrest. The above discussion leads us to the conclusion that neither human resources are fully developed, nor fully utilised in the state. Education and manpower planning is not the top agenda of the state government. Expenditure on general education as per cent to total expenditure, after reaching at 10.2 per cent in 2001-02, has plummeted to vary between 2 to 6 per cent. Similarly, actual expenditure on technical education has declined to less than one per cent of total expenditure. Apathetic approach of the government towards co-ordination between education planning and manpower planning will push the economy towards further deceleration.

References

Asian Development Outlook (2007), Education and Structural Change in four Asian Countries.

Carnoy, Martin (1977), Education and Employment: A Critical Appraisal, UNESCO, International Institute for Educational Planning.

Economic Survey of Punjab, 2007-08, Economic Adviser to Government of Punjab.

Eleventh Five Year Plan, 2007-12, Planning Commission, Government of India, Vol. II, Social Sector.

Human Development Report of Punjab, 2004, Government of Punjab.

Index